FOOD IN RUSSIAN HISTORY AND CULTURE

FOOD IN
RUSSIAN
HISTORY
AND
CULTURE

Edited by Musya Glants and Joyce Toomre

INDIANA UNIVERSITY PRESS BLOOMINGTON & INDIANAPOLIS

© 1997 by Indiana University Press

The paper used in this publication meets the minimum requirements of American National Standard for Information Sciences—Permanence of Paper for Printed Library Materials, ANSI Z39.48-1984.

Manufactured in the United States of America

Library of Congress Cataloging-in-Publication Data

Food in Russian history and culture / edited by Musya Glants and Joyce Toomre
   p.   cm. — (Indiana-Michigan series in Russian and East European studies)
   Includes bibliographical references and index.
ISBN 0-253-33252-4 (cl : alk. paper). — ISBN 0-253-21106-9 (pa : alk. paper)
   1. Food habits—Russia (Federation)—History. 2. Cookery, Russian—History.
   3. Russia (Federation—Social life and customs).   I. Glants, Musya, date.
      II. Toomre, Joyce Stetson.   III. Series.
        GT2853.R8F66   1997
   394.1′2′0947—dc20   96-41786

1 2 3 4 5 02 01 00 99 98 97

To our friends and colleagues at the Davis Center for Russian Studies, in appreciation for all they have shared with us over the years.

CONTENTS

Acknowledgments

This book is the result of a conference held in 1993 and sponsored by the Russian Research Center, now the Kathryn W. and Shelby Cullom Davis Center for Russian Studies at Harvard University. From the beginning, the Director, Timothy J. Colton, and the Associate Director, Lisbeth Tarlow Berstein, enthusiastically supported our efforts. The staff members went out of their way to help us and we could not have put on the conference without their generous assistance which went way beyond the call of duty.

The chapters included in this volume convey only in part the rich and rewarding contributions and discussions that animated the conference. The editors wish to express deepest appreciation to all our colleagues who attended and whose comments and criticisms helped shape the present book. We particularly want to note the contributions of the following scholars to the occasion: Milka Bliznakov, Svetlana Boym, Lori Citti, Elizabeth English, Patricia Herlihy, Edward L. Keenan, Sonia Ketchian, Alexander Strakhov, William Mills Todd III, and Lynn Visson.

The editors wish to thank the museums and artists who so generously gave us permission to publish their treasures, some of which have never before been reproduced in the West. These include the staff of the Historical Museum of Moscow; the State Tretiakov Gallery and its General Director, Jan V. Bruk; the State Russian Museum and its General Director, Vladimir Gusev; Deputy Director for Science Evgenia Petrova; the Director of the museum's "Mikhailovsky Castle" branch, Elena Kalnitskaya; and the Omsk Regional Fine Arts Museum and its General Director, Boris Konnikov. We are grateful to the artists Natalia Nesterova and Tatiana Nazarenko and the photographer Sam Sweezy for their kind permission to use their works as illustrations in the book. For other permissions, we thank John Stewart, the members of the Kagan family, and Regeen Najar from the Philosophical Library. Maria S. Blumina, Pamela Kachurin, Lev Nesterov, Larisa Shmagina, Mary Towle, and Florence Trefethen all were especially helpful, and we acknowledge with thanks their support and assistance.

ACKNOWLEDGMENTS

We are very grateful to the two anonymous readers who read the manuscript for Indiana University Press. No one could ask for more careful and thoughtful criticism. Their comments helped enormously in shaping the book and clarifying the arguments presented. The staff at Indiana University Press has been consistently helpful. Janet Rabinowitch, our editor, has supported this project from the very beginning and encouraged us all along the way. Her strength and patience not only improved the quality of the final text but also won our admiration and friendship.

Both editors want to thank all the authors for their contributions; their spirited cooperation made it a pleasure to work with them. We also thank our respective families, who bore with us so patiently during the long process of producing this book. We close these remarks as we opened them by acknowledging our deep debt of gratitude to the Davis Center for Russian Studies at Harvard. It has been our intellectual home for many years. The resources and opportunities it offers to scholars in our field are invaluable and we thank our friends and colleagues at the Center for all the informative seminars, lively discussions, and quiet conversations that we have shared with them.

Introduction

MUSYA GLANTS AND JOYCE TOOMRE

*The chronicle of everyday life brings the past closer to us
with a social sharpness and vividness. In order to understand Leo Tolstoy or Chekhov more clearly, for instance, we
need to know the daily life of their epoch. Even the poetry
of Pushkin achieves its full luster only for those who know
the everyday life of his era.*

—KONSTANTIN PAUSTOVSKII[1]

Scholars today widely echo these sentiments as they concentrate on simple
moments in ordinary life to help illuminate the present while enriching our
understanding of the past. In this new view of history, ordinary people sleep,
take showers, change clothes, and clean their houses. They buy things and
argue, make love and raise their children. But whatever else they do, they
must eat. Eating in this sense seems banal but, despite its repetitiveness,
subtle changes tie this common act to specific circumstances limited by time
and place.

Just as the portrait of someone who lived long ago brings us the aroma of
the epoch and gives us a chance almost to "touch" the past, so the vital thread
of food habits gives us a better understanding of human psychology, inter-
twining the material and spiritual. Bread, for instance, is a material object
with a distinct weight and shape that when eaten becomes an integral part
of the human body. But in a religious context, when a wafer (= bread) is
consumed as part of the Christian Eucharist, the wafer's symbolism transcends
its caloric value.[2]

As part of daily life, food easily becomes a metaphor for national customs, whereby the same food can trigger a different reaction depending on its national tradition. The lowly pancake illustrates this point. In pagan times, the pancake symbolized the sun; later it became associated with Christian rituals in the week before Lent, the Great Fast. These rituals, however, have a national flavor. When Russians and English bite into a pancake, they bite into different national traditions. Whereas the English may remember annual pancake races across the village green at Shrovetide, the Russians associate *bliny* with Butter Week, an annual orgy of eating remarked upon by many and satirized by Chekhov in his short story "The Foolish Frenchman."

There has been an explosion of interest in culinary history during the last two decades. Works have proliferated as scholars from a variety of disciplines have realized that examining a people's eating habits helps explain the diversity of human life no less than the study of the great historical events and the deeds of famous people.[3] This volume, the first to study the role of food in Russian culture, stems from a conference sponsored by the Russian Research Center at Harvard in 1993. Piecing together the cultural and culinary history of a people is like trying to fit together a three-dimensional puzzle where each piece is made from a different material. Food historians begin by questioning what foods were available, how they were served, and how they functioned in the society.

The chapters in this collection provide fresh insights by looking at the availability and consumption of foods at different periods in Russian history and by analyzing Russian attitudes toward food and its attendant symbolism. Each factor in the cultural food equation—production, preparation, consumption, attitude, and symbolism—operates within a well-defined context of time, social class, ethnicity, and political and religious beliefs. Taken together, these factors make up a complex of attitudes and traditions that may be called Russian foodways. Foodways are far from static; they constantly change and evolve, and urbanization and industrialization obviously cannot be ignored. In the Russian case, some centuries-old food customs survive even today in post-Soviet Russia while others terminated with the 1917 Russian Revolution.

To construct their arguments, the authors of these chapters have used chronicles, diaries, letters, police records, poems, novels, folk sayings, paintings, and cookbooks. Although the sources provide a wealth of new data for interpreting Russian culture from the perspective of its foodways, it is important to note that all of these materials were created for purposes other than culinary history. The emerging picture lacks crucial details and has many blank spots. Partly this is due to the newness of the discipline; but also, data from different fields are not necessarily commensurable. For instance, material artifacts and oral sources provide valuable evidence not otherwise obtainable, but they are categorically different from the description of a family picnic written in a personal diary or of a royal banquet inscribed in court records.

Some of the chapters in this volume focus on historical topics, while others emphasize images of food in literature and art. In fact, impervious boundaries between the actual and the symbolic roles of food do not exist. Food functions in both roles simultaneously, just as a word's multiple meanings enrich any single context. In addressing these issues, considerable attention is paid to the moral and spiritual role of food in Russian culture. Additional topics easily could have been included, most notably the role of vodka and alcoholism in Russian culture.[4] These chapters are intended to initiate a dialogue and promote further research; they are but a first step toward opening a new vista on Russian history and culture.

According to Mikhail Bakhtin, the process of eating, like the process of labor, is a collective social action whereby life vanquishes death. "In the act of eating . . . the confines between the body and the world are overstepped by the body; it triumphs over the world, over its enemy, celebrates its victory, grows at the world's expense."[5] However, not only the food itself but everything related to it, including the process of eating, enjoyed the same power. The images of food, reflecting their significance in peoples' lives, came to symbolize the relation between life and death, struggle and victory. Thanks to their importance and versatility, these images were applied widely in folklore, national traditions, customs, and beliefs, where they took on the force of real things.

Snejana Tempest illuminates these ideas in her chapter, "Stovelore in Russian Folklife," through her discussion of the multiple roles of the Russian stove in the life of the Slavs. The stoves were mammoth installations, designed primarily for heating and secondarily for cooking. Their bulk dominated peasant homes and determined the basic characteristic of traditional Russian cuisine, with its predominance of baked goods and slowly cooked soups and stews, such as the old Russian dish *niania* (nanny).[6] Tempest emphasizes the stove's symbolic role through its ability to fuse nature and culture while transforming the raw to the cooked. In this way the stove acquired its religious and ritual significance along with its traditional roles of heating and cooking. In the mind of the people, not only the stove itself but everything which was cooked there became powerful and acted as a sacred mediator between the "living" and the "other" worlds. For instance, by the ritual baking of a *karavai* (round loaf) to the accompaniment of special songs, people were asking for a bountiful harvest, a happy marriage, and myriad other favors.[7] Tempest shows how these beliefs in the special power of the stove were reflected in everyday language and in various Russian fairytales, songs, and festive occasions. Even today, these ideas and this imagery still retain a strong hold over the modern imagination, especially in the aesthetic sphere.

From the mythic we turn to written accounts of food in the Slavic world. Horace G. Lunt's chapter, "Food in the *Rus' Primary Chronicle*" deals with the earliest written segment of this story by discussing foods that were known in the East Slavic lands during the 250 years from the mid-ninth century to the beginning of the twelfth century. He analyzes the food terms used in the *Primary Chronicle*, the oldest source of written information about the ancestors of today's Ukrainians, Belorussians, and Russians. Lunt's careful interpretation of archaic terms in this early text and his explanation of their probable derivation is invaluable, because linguistic borrowings indicate the likely path of entry into a given culture.[8] A millennium later, we find that certain foods mentioned in the *Primary Chronicle* have become staples of the Russian diet.

Lunt's account of the marauding Pechengegs raises the important theme of food and power. Herodotus pointed out long ago that control of the food supply is a primary source of power for any governing group, and the chapters in this volume show the nature of this recurring problem in the Russian and Soviet context. The distribution of food is rarely a neutral act, whether it is government rationing of scarce foodstuffs or charitable handouts in a soup kitchen. Even the division of a family's Sunday chicken has its physical and symbolic ramifications.

George E. Munro's "Food in Catherinian St. Petersburg" shows how food functions as an instrument of power, not only in governmental and military situations but also in the warfare between classes. He compares the Russian capital with Imperial Rome, noting that both cities were voracious consumers of foodstuffs and that the elite in both capitals combined eating with elements of theatricality. Conspicuous consumption was the order of the day when the wealthy nobles ate off Meissen and Sèvres porcelain and Catherine the Great could order wine-spouting fountains in front of the Winter Palace to celebrate victory over the Turks. The writer Dmitrii Blagovo describes the meals in his well-to-do grandmother's household in the eighteenth century:

> Even casual dinners usually had two hot dishes, *shchi* [cabbage soup] and soup or *ukha* [fish soup], two cold dishes, four sauces, two stews, and two savory pastries . . . not to mention formal dinners which began with two hot dishes, ukha and soup. . . . [These were followed by] four cold dishes, four sauces, two stews, several kinds of savory pastries, and then dessert and candies, because it was a rare household which did not have its own confectioner and there were fresh candies every day. She [my grandmother] loved to eat.[9]

Rather than emphasizing the food habits of the wealthy, however, Munro focuses on the poor, who had to manage with much less. Since the police monitored the capital's market and commerce, Munro uses the records of these officials to deduce the availability of rations, which were supplemented by the produce from urban kitchen gardens, where many city dwellers kept their livestock. Munro enlarges his theme of food as class marker through his discussion of public eating houses in eighteenth-century Russia. Although eating out was not as common then as it is now, the history of Russian public dining developed along class lines, since different types of establishments evolved to serve a particular clientele.[10]

Food as a marker of class divisions is continued in Cathy A. Frierson's chapter, "Forced Hunger and Rational Restraint in the Russian Peasant Diet: One Populist's Vision." Frierson discusses the extreme dietary deprivations of the peasants in Smolensk Province in the 1870s as related in the letters of the well-known chemical agronomist Aleksandr Engelgardt. In these influential eyewitness accounts of rural Russia, Engelgardt used food metaphors extensively to convey his binary vision of Russian society. Engelhardt contrasted the plain healthy diet of the peasants with the rich foods of his gentry neighbors and friends. He carefully describes the dishes served in the upper-class homes at the period but makes it clear that he regarded the prodigal overindulgence of his peers as both physically revolting and morally reprehensible. Moral issues are the main concern of his comparisons and inferences. In addition, Engelgardt supplements our meager knowledge of peasant diet and, more important, indicates peasant attitudes toward their diet. The peasants ranked foods hierarchically, holding that dense black bread provided more sustenance than potatoes when strength and endurance were required for arduous labor in the fields. Given the scarcity of food and grain, peasants not only were reluctant to squander meager foodstuffs by eating more than the task required, but they held it was morally wrong as well. Through Engelgardt's letters, we understand that food and eating served as a pastime for the rich, but the poor regarded food more profoundly—as the foundation of life itself. Working hard for their bread, they showed their appreciation and respect for food through their rational eating habits.

The Russian understanding of food as a moral issue was nurtured through doctrines in the Orthodox Church. When Christianity replaced paganism in Russia, the Orthodox Church adopted and transformed many old customs, some of which incorporated a mystical essence and food symbolism. Leonid Heretz, in "The Practice and Significance of Fasting in Russian Peasant Culture at the Turn of the Century," concentrates on just one aspect of this phenomenon, the concept of fasting, which he projects against the background of popular life of that era. He shows that since early times the main goal of fasting was more spiritual than physical. In some sense fasting may be seen as a continuation of the fight between the body and the soul. Abstinence was always a way to sustain the purification of the soul. According to the Church, the periodic abstention from certain types of food should be used for contemplation of higher things. Heretz's historical survey of the symbolism of food during fasting suggests how past issues have re-emerged in Russia's contemporary struggle to revive religious and moral virtues. To quote the poet Joseph Brodsky,

> Privykai, synok, k pustyne,
> kak shchepot' k vetru,
> chuvstvuia, chto ty ne tol'ko plot'.

> Get used, my son, to the desert,
> the same as your hand gets used to the touch of the wind.
> It will give you the feeling that you are not flesh alone.[11]

Moral issues increasingly preoccupied Russian intellectuals in the late nineteenth century. All aspects of life, even eating habits, were discussed in moral and philosophical terms. Thanks to these ideas, and reinforced in large part by Lev Tolstoy's writings, vegetarianism gained many new followers at this period. Tolstoy himself was such a moral force in the society that his support gave credence to the moral issues underpinning the movement. Tolstoy became interested in vegetarianism in the 1850s, initially attracted by the notions of health, nonviolence and animal rights associated with the movement. Not until the 1880s did he develop serious philosophical ideas about vegetarianism. Tolstoy's innovation, as Ronald D. LeBlanc writes in "Tolstoy's Way of No Flesh: Abstinence, Vegetarianism, and Christian Physiology," was his Christian approach to this subject, the understanding of it as a "quest for ascetic discipline and moral self-perfection" through abstinence from meat and sex.

For Tolstoy, vegetarianism was not reducible to a plea for animal rights; nor was it simply a matter of theoretical philosophizing. To use the words of the writer and philosopher Vasilii Rozanov, who visited Tolstoy in 1903 in Yasnaya Polyana, "for Tolstoy, vegetarianism was a 'method of life,' a way of living." Observing Tolstoy surrounded by his family and guests, Rozanov noticed that although he was sitting at the same table, he was effectively isolated from everyone else. This impression was accentuated by Tolstoy's special menu. While the others were eating meat and scrambled eggs, Tolstoy ate *kisel'* and *kasha*. More than just a different menu, this peasant food evoked connotations associated with an entirely different way of life. As Rozanov concluded, "food in general either divides or unifies people."[12]

According to LeBlanc, Tolstoy advocated vegetarianism as a way of surmounting any tendency to overindulge in food and sex. This attitude helps clarify Tolstoy's otherwise cryptic remark that "virtue is incompatible with a beef-steak." Tolstoy developed his ideas of abstinence further in his novel *Resurrection* in which the phenomenon of *nekhludovshchina*, named after the protagonist Nekhludov, came to signify the embodiment of self-indulgence, which leads to licentiousness.

The story of vegetarianism in Russia is picked up and developed further in Darra Goldstein's chapter, "Is Hay Only for Horses? Highlights of Russian Vegetarianism at the Turn of the Century," in which she emphasizes the movement's social significance. One of the most colorful leaders of the movement was the writer Natalia Borisovna Nordman-Severova, who was also the wife of the Russian painter Ilya Repin. The Repins' vegetarian dinners, which featured hay as one of the main ingredients, achieved a certain notoriety among the many members of the Russian intelligentsia who frequented *Penaty*, the artist's estate, where the couple lived for years. Although Repin was already a pillar of Russian art at that time, Nordman-Severova attracted almost as much attention through her eccentricity and sensational vegetarian ideas. Some people knew one or the other spouse only by hearsay. The writer Korneii Chukovskii, for instance, recalled overhearing a woman telling her friend about Repin's death: "You know whom I mean, [the husband of] the one who was eating hay."

Goldstein highlights the role this unusual woman played in intellectual society. She wanted to transform the world by changing people's diet and liberating women from the drudgery of kitchen chores. Nordman's hay diet may have seemed foolish, but not her advocacy of women's liberation through vegetarianism. Despite some of her bizarre notions, Nordman seems to echo Engelgardt (see Frierson's chapter) when she claims that "vegetarianism is necessary for the very rich and the very poor. The poor need it because it is cheap and nourishing. The rich, in order to cleanse all the poisons from the corpses that have accumulated in their overfed organism."[13]

If both Tolstoy and Nordman-Severova in their moral aspirations represent food as a vehicle for achieving immediate spiritual purification, Fyodor Dostoevsky applied metaphors of food and eating to emphasize the *immorality* of the human urge for power and the unrelenting struggle to attain it. In "An Appetite for Power: Predators, Carnivores, and Cannibals in Dostoevsky's Fiction," Ronald D. LeBlanc analyzes how Dostoevsky expresses the human appetite for dominance through predatory images and how the dynamics of power relationships—sociological, sexual, and psychological—operate in his works.

Dostoevsky's fiction is filled with words that characterize the quality and process of eating; but unlike Tolstoy, Chekhov, and Gogol, Dostoevsky uses food imagery not as a figure of delight but as a paradigm of power. LeBlanc shows that Dostoevsky's characters do not merely eat but seek to devour, digest, and destroy. Rather than expressing taste, enjoyment, and nourishment, his food metaphors point to violence and aggression, the struggle of wolves to quash sheep. According to LeBlanc, Dostoevsky uses these distinctive metaphors to oppose good and evil and to express his ideas and hopes for a morally better world based on Christian ideals. In *The Brothers Karamazov*, for instance, when Dostoevsky gives Smerdiakov the occupation of chef while naming him so noxiously (*smerdet'* means to stink), he effectively unites the idea of food with the odor.[14] But the word *smerdet'* suggests not a random malodor but the specific stench of a corpse. In this case, Dostoevsky, by joining the smell of a corpse to the idea of food for the living, creates a metaphor for an eternal transition between life and death.

Dostoevsky's concern with the commingling of life and death is picked up again in the twentieth century in the poetry of Marina Tsvetaeva. Pamela Chester, in her chapter, "Strawberries and Chocolate: Tsvetaeva, Mandelstam, and the Plight of the Hungry Poet," shows that for Tsvetaeva life continued beyond death, whether physically through an eternal cycle of decay, nourishment, and new fruition or symbolically through poetry. She associates poetry with the juicy colorful strawberries that flourish in the nearby gardens and cemeteries. The berries growing on her grave, like her poems, link her to the hereafter. The future consumers, whether they eat the berries or read the poems, complete the cycle and join the dead with the living. Tsvetaeva compares her desire to write poetry to her desire for strawberries, both of which are equally strong. These metaphors distinguish Tsvetaeva's poetry from that of other poets, such as Mandelstam. Chester explores the tropes of strawberries and chocolate and the longings for these natural or artificial sweets to highlight the poets' contrasting views of life and death.

Just as the reforms of Peter the Great transformed Russia in the eighteenth century, the 1917 victory of the Bolsheviks revolutionized the twentieth. In both cases, all aspects of political, economic, and social life were overturned, even the ordinary details of everyday life. Whereas Peter the Great cut off the boyars' beards and ordered what and how they should eat and drink, the Bolshevik government tried to regulate people's lifestyles and transform their traditions, habits, and tastes with the goal of subordinating them fully to Bolshevik ideals. In this struggle to stamp out prerevolutionary influence, the

Soviet leaders wanted to create a new type of Soviet citizen—*sovetskii chelovek* (Soviet man)—modeled on their philosophy. With this goal in mind, they believed that every aspect of life, from the sublime to the mundane, had an ideological meaning.[15] Not even the preparation and consumption of comestibles was immune from this all-embracing doctrine. Dishes like *kulich, paskha,* and *matsa* with religious associations were particularly reviled as part of the Soviet antireligious stance.[16] In this atmosphere, in which certain dishes acquired an ideological character, it became prudent to avoid "bourgeois" foods in order not to arouse unwarranted political suspicions. The poet Vladimir Mayakovsky captured this spirit with his jingle "Esh ananasy, riabchikov zhui. / Den' tvoi poslednii prishel, burzhui. (Eat your pineapple, chew your hazel grouse. Your final day has arrived, bourgeois)."[17]

A perennial scarcity of food marked the entire Soviet period. Against this background, which ranged in severity from recurrent famines to periodic, unpredictable shortages of staples, the Soviet propaganda machine extolled the virtues of the utopian state and the arrival of a prosperity that was entirely groundless. Living conditions quickly deteriorated soon after the Bolsheviks came to power, and provisions that previously had been available started to disappear. As the writer Lidia Ivanova indicated,

> Hunger descended gradually but inevitably. . . . One summer catfish appeared on the market, but later there was nothing but dried Caspian roach [*vobla*]. Butter quickly disappeared, then any kind of vegetable oil. After they had gone, cocoa-butter appeared for a week or two; this was replaced in turn by cod-liver oil and then castor oil which we used to fry potatoes. In 1919 every morning on my way to work I bought a cup of milk from a woman on the street. For lunch I ate a few boiled potatoes that I brought from home. The bread ration was then one-quarter pound for two days. Bread and potatoes were only available on the black market, from peddlers [*meshochniki*] who sold them from sacks. Risking their lives and sometimes even hiding on the roofs of the trains, these profiteers managed to smuggle bags of flour, potatoes, and other foodstuffs into Moscow.[18]

Starvation threatened to engulf the citizenry, particularly in Moscow and Petrograd. "Piter [St. Petersburg] is dying. . . . The people are passive and do not complain . . . they stand in lines at the communal kitchens for a bowl of soup."[19] The new government responded by setting up numerous communal kitchens and relied on them for the next few years as an efficient means for feeding the hungry population.

Mauricio Borrero, in "Communal Dining and State Cafeterias in Moscow and Petrograd, 1917-1921" analyzes the establishment and function of state cafeterias in the capital cites, where hunger verged on starvation. Not all state-run cafeterias were equal, and people with clout managed to secure access to better facilities—or even bypass them altogether. Borrero emphasizes that along with the aim of alleviating the general hunger of the population, these cafeterias took on an ideological function, so that food became an instrument of power. Although the new Soviet society was theoretically classless, privileges associated with status and prestige did not disappear but only metamorphosed. Access to sufficient food became a perquisite of the elite in the new society. Precisely because of the constant shortages, the government quickly evolved a "carrot and stick" policy whereby granting or withholding food rations became a potent tool for imposing its will and manipulating the population.

Early on, the Bolsheviks initiated an effective system of special rations for different groups.[20] The authorities arbitrarily decided whom to support and whom to teach a good lesson. Food rations became an easy tool for encouraging the compliant and punishing the recalcitrant. By these means, members of the intelligentsia were quickly brought to heel. Many well-known Russian writers begged for aid from Anatolii Ivanovich Puchkov, the vice-commissar of provisions, citing as a reason their service to the regime. Korneii Chukovskii wrote, "All my talents are devoted to the service of the enlightenment of the masses and I am sure that I have the right to ask the authorities to do me a friendly favor and support my famished . . . children. I have added a doctor's certificate, in the hope of receiving the greatest possible amount of candies, bread, and, if possible, butter." Maksim Gorki interceded with the authorities for the writer Andreii Belyi, who, it is reported, received as a result "10 kg of flour, 5 kg of groats, 2 of sausages, 5 of fish, 1 of butter, 1 of candy, and 3 of sugar."[21]

Living conditions remained difficult for the next two decades. The 1920s were a period of turmoil due mainly to the New Economic Policy (NEP) and introduction of the first Five-Year Plan with its accompanying devastation of the peasantry. Famines and food shortages were rife and continued throughout the 1930s. Government policy exacerbated conditions and steadily eroded the quality of domestic life. Whereas in the 1920s the government acknowledged the shortages, by the 1930s it denied the very existence of such problems; even mentioning them became treasonable. As the bread lines grew longer, the secret police monitored those queuing up, alert for any word of discontent.[22] To support the fiction of abundance, Stalin ordered that ration cards be abolished and grain exports increased.[23]

Halina and Robert A. Rothstein's analysis of contemporary cookbooks in their chapter "The Beginnings of Soviet Culinary Arts" shows a range of responses for coping with the pervasive food shortages and dislocations of the 1920s and 1930s. Some authors, like ostriches with their heads in the sand, continued to produce old-style recipes as if the tsar had never been deposed, while others urged the consumption of soybeans and seaweed for their nutritional value and advised raising rabbits as a cheap source of protein. Taken as a whole, these books provide a glimpse of daily life during that long period when the authorities were determined to create "a socialist way of life." They reflect the tangled web of forces trying to reform people's eating habits—covering everything from how food was prepared to where it was consumed—against an opposing array of forces that resisted change. In the 1920s, when women first entered the work force in large numbers, the virtues of state cafeterias were extolled. The narrator of Yuri Olesha's 1927 novel *Envy*, for instance, dreams of establishing a state kitchen, the Quarter, which

> is going to be a gigantic establishment: the largest dining room, the largest kitchen in existence. A two-course dinner will cost a quarter. War has been declared on ordinary kitchens. . . . Women! . . . we shall restore to you all those hours that the kitchen has stolen from you— you'll get half your life back. You, young wife, you make soup for your husband. And half your day goes into that miserable puddle of soup! We are going to transform those miserable puddles of soup of yours into glistening seas, *borscht* into oceans of *borscht*, heap up *kasha* in mounds, unleash glaciers of fruit jelly.[24]

The state cafeterias did not live up to their promises. Not only were the filthy premises and poor quality of food off-putting, but people resisted having to eat at work or at other assigned locations. Despite the hardships and dual burden of working and caring for their families, women reclaimed their kitchens. Food preparation entails more drudgery than glamor, but they understood, perhaps only intuitively, what was at stake and refused to give up the modicum of power (and pleasure) that came from planning and preparing meals for their family and friends.

The vast majority of people endured a hand-to-mouth existence while a select few ate well and flourished thanks to an entrenched system of perquisites and privileges that divided this nominally classless society into haves and have-nots. For instance, the menu at a Crimean sanatorium for "higherups" "abounded in tasty dishes, with everything in which Russia is rich. Breakfast at eight, with eggs, ham, cheese, cocoa, tea, and milk. At eleven, yogurt. Then a four-course midday meal: soup, fish, meat, dessert, and fruit. During the afternoon, tea and pastries. In the evening, a two-course supper."[25]

By contrast, the artist Pavel Filonov, who was out of favor, wrote in his diary: "August 30, 1935. Ever since the beginning of June I have lived by drinking tea with sugar and eating only one kilogram of bread daily. On the morning of June 29th I made the last pancake from the flour I had saved. Then I began to prepare myself, as I have done many times previously, to live without food for who knows how long."[26]

Against a background of expanding political terror and shortage of food-stuffs the authorities mandated an atmosphere of prosperity and optimism throughout the country; all publications, including cookbooks, had to support the official position, which reached its zenith in the midthirties. In 1935 Stalin declared that "life has become more joyous, comrades; life has become gayer" and directed everyone to be merry. The "Song of the Motherland," with the lines "I do not know of any other country / Where a man can breathe a freer air!" sounded everywhere.[27] On this canvas of absolute happiness food became a symbol of power and social achievement. Hosts could emphasize their importance and confirm their status in the hierarchy simply by serving Stalin's favorite wine, Khvanchkara, or other prestigious foods like caviar and expensive sausage.

As conditions in real life worsened, abundance became the hallmark of life in films, music, literature, and painting. In the food world this dichotomy reached its apex with the publication of the *Kniga o vkusnoi i zdorovoi pishche* [The book about tasty and healthy food] in 1950. This was the height of "victorious Stalinism," the post–World War II period when the state returned "bourgeois" concepts to official and private life. Bowing to Stalin's demands, a charade began whereby life took on a false grandeur embellished with rituals from the turn of the century. This process started before the war and gathered in intensity after its conclusion. Even Christmas trees were rehabilitated, the first being lit at the Kremlin on New Year's Eve in 1935. During the war, schools were separated by sex as the society became even more regimented thanks to the militaristic uniforms introduced for schoolchildren and many civil servants. In 1944 a new family law was enacted that returned to the prerevolutionary concept of the family as the basic unit of society because that would allow easier control of the people by the state.[28]

The *Kniga* appeared in the midst of these changes to lend prominent support to the "big lie" of the leaders. It begins by quoting "the leader of all times and peoples" (*vozhd' vsekh vremen i narodov*): "The characteristic feature of our revolution is that it gives our people not only freedom, but also material wealth and the possibility of a prosperous and cultured life." The book's recipes were not intended as mundane instructions for cooking actual dishes such as *borshch, shchi,* and *kotlety* but as a striking demonstration of the benefits of living in Stalin's "paradise." According to the émigré critic Aleksandr Genis, the *Kniga* "is an encyclopedia of the Soviet way of life, where the process of preparing food became the symbol of a world transformed according to a recipe-plan. Each dish described in the book is a metaphor of the plenitude and variety of socialist life, expressed in a tightly considered menu."[29] If reality did not coincide with the book's illustrations—if the tables in the overcrowded communal apartments and dingy communal kitchens lacked the starched tablecloths and elegant dishes shown in the *Kniga*—the message was that the people should struggle harder to improve themselves and realize the socialist ideals of the party.

The *Kniga* also clearly reflects the chauvinism of Soviet national politics in the postwar years, when the Russians were declared "elder brothers" in the Soviet Union or, somewhat jokingly, "the best among the equals." In a speech shortly after the war, Stalin said, "I drink the health of the Russian people because Russia is the most outstanding nation among all nations of the Soviet Union."[30]

Food as a symbol of the relation between the Russian center and the national provinces is addressed by Joyce Toomre in "Food and National Identity in Soviet Armenia." Toomre presents an overview of traditional Armenian foodways as a prelude to questioning the subsequent Soviet influence on their development. The focus of this chapter is on the small Caucasian republic of Armenia SSR, although it could just as well be Uzbekistan, Ukraine, Estonia, or Moldova. How to ensure the survival of food habits of smaller units within a larger political entity is an issue for any regional cuisine.[31] The phenomenon is general and worldwide but has particular political relevance in the case of the Soviet Union. Although each of the former republics has its own characteristics and developed somewhat differently, each was also affected by its subordinate position, politically if not culturally. Toomre examines the feasibility of cultural autonomy under the centrally controlled government of the Soviets and questions the actual government attitude toward the national cuisines. Officially, of course, support for the national cuisines was enveloped in the propagandistic slogan "national in form and socialist in content." Although national dishes were featured at all the republic's pavilions at the successive Exhibitions of the Achievements of the National Economies (VDNKH), the question remains whether Armenian foodways—and those of the other republics—developed naturally according to indigenous customs or whether there is evidence of undue Soviet interference. Toomre finds that definitive answers are elusive, partly because the time frame is too short. Also, food traditions are unusually strong among the Armenians, who have only recently undergone intense industrialization, and any changes they have noticed in their foodways are not considered threatening.

Art critic Penelope Rowlands drew on French gastronome Anthèlme Brillat-Savarin's saying "Animals feed themselves; men eat, but only wise men know the art of eating" to quip that "while the wise may know it, only the artist can show it."[32] F. T. Marinetti and the Russian avant-gardists were capitalizing on the universal power of food tropes when they used them as building blocks in their art. Name your ingredients: spinach, tomatoes, egg whites, and prunes. The artists put them together with color and shape and ideas in mind, not taste.[33] Musya Glants, in her chapter, "Food as Art: Painting in Late Soviet Russia," shows how powerful and expressive these symbols can be. Through food metaphors, artists reveal to the viewer a vital and sensual impression of life, including its delicate spiritual nuances. Glants examines the period from the fall of Stalinism to the fall of the USSR. In these circumstances food tropes, along with other metaphors, serve either to emphasize or to shield definite ideas or feelings because, as James Yood has written, "food in a painting . . . [is] a tremendously versatile subject, a playing field of surprisingly comprehensible equity."[34] The meaning assigned to food imagery varies according to the period and artist, but in harsh totalitarian times as well as in the turbulent post-Soviet era food is an effective device for discussing human life. Glants shows that art in Russia became an expressive mouthpiece of the social issues, frustrations, and disappointments of those totalitarian years and a tool to convey the horror, cruelty, and fear of the present transitional era.

This book offers a new view of Russian civilization which emerges from reexamining its history and culture through the lens of food symbolism. The necessity of food in human life creates its universality. Yood writes:

> First we cry, then we eat. And eat and eat and eat; from birth until death, this fundamental activity continues. . . . Just as architecture makes a cultural construct out of our need for shelter, the communal meal provides social as well as physical nourishment. Eating is inter- twined with almost every aspect of our existence."[35]

The chapters in this book show how these universal themes play out in a distinctly Russian Soviet setting. What we eat and how we do it is, willingly or not, a social act defined by the time, the place, the foods presented, and the manner of serving. In these richly nuanced circumstances, each detail contributes to the whole, whether the occasion is a grand banquet or a solitary meal in the kitchen. The absence or presence of food, as well as its preparation and elaboration, helps us define ourselves and our relation to those around us and the world that we inhabit. These features inevitably turn food into a tool of power in its different manifestations—during times of war and peace, great changes, and turbulent experiences. The giving or withholding of food is perhaps the ultimate weapon of control.

The study of foodways brings together the past and present by shedding new light on former beliefs and customs. Food images in this sense convey meanings beyond their physical representation. For example, reading about the "smart *kolobok*" (small roll) described in Russian fairy tales illuminates the *Weltanschauung* of the past through the form of a bit of bread. Then later, it is not surprising that we find a newly baked roll tastier for being seasoned with its history and folklore. Writers and artists have long exploited the complexity of food metaphors in their struggle to express psychological issues and to reach their audiences emotionally.

Food has also served as a repository of national traditions, binding one generation to another. A favorite recipe passed from a grandmother to her granddaughter may carry as much emotional value as the proverbial gold ring. As Dmitrii Blagovo wrote about his grandmother's memoirs,

> All the trivial details of everyday life which we disregard at present, considering them unnecessary and tiresome, become precious after a century because they depict vividly the customs and habits of generations long gone and the life which had an absolutely different quality from our own.[36]

NOTES

1. K. Paustovskii, Introduction, in V. A. Giliarovskii, *Moskva i moskvichi* [Moscow and Moscovians] (Minsk: Vysheishaia shkola, 1980), 7.

2. Iurii M. Lotman, *Besedy o russkoi kul'ture: byt i traditsii russkogo dvorianstva: XVIII-nachalo XIX veka* [Conversations about Russian culture: everyday life and traditions of the Russian gentry from the eighteenth to the beginning of the nineteenth century] (St. Petersburg: Iskusstvo-SPB, 1994), 6.

3. R. E. F. Smith and David Christian, *Bread and Salt: A Social and Economic History of Food and Drink in Russia* (Cambridge: Cambridge University Press, 1984); Svetlana Boym, *Common Places: Mythologies of Everyday Life in Russia* (Cambridge, Mass.: Harvard University Press, 1994); and *Culture and Entertainment in Wartime Russia*, ed. Richard Stites (Bloomington: Indiana University Press, 1995).

4. English readers interested in these issues should begin with Smith and Christian, *Bread and Salt*, 74-108 and 288-326, or Patricia Herlihy, "'Joy of the Rus': Rites and Rituals of Russian Drinking," *Russian Review*, vol. 50 (April 1991), 131-147. Much less reliable but still useful is William Pokhlebkin, *A History of Vodka*, trans. Renfrey Clarke (London: Verso, 1991).

5. Mikhail Bakhtin, *Rabelais and His World*, trans. Hélène Iswolsky (Cambridge, Mass.: MIT Press, 1968), 282-283. For more on the role of food as a symbolic link between life and death, see James George Frazer, *The Golden Bough* (London: Macmillan, 1923), esp. chaps. 45, 46, 48, and V. Y. Propp, *Istoricheskie korni volshebnoi skazki* [Historical roots of fairy tales] (Leningrad: Izd. Leningradskogo universiteta, 1986), 63-69.

6. Fiodor Vasilievich Rostopchin (1763-1826), governor-general of Moscow in 1812, described this old-fashioned dish in loving terms: "*Niania* combines a calf's head, buckwheat, and fresh butter. Everything is put in a pot, which is sealed with dough. Then the pot is placed in the Russian stove for twenty-four hours. When the dish is ready, it is hard to say which is more tasty, the buckwheat *kasha* or the meat." F. V. Rostopchin, *Okh, Frantsuzy!* [Oh, the French!] (Moscow, "Russkaya kniga," 1992), 99.

7. In olden times, the Slavs imbued the *karavai* with special powers associated with God. See V. V. Ivanov and V. N. Toporov, *Issledovania v oblasti slavianskikh drevnosteii* [Research in the field of Slavic antiquity] (Moscow: Nauka, 1974), 243-259.

8. In the same way, students of French and English medieval culinary history have benefited from the work of linguists who have analyzed "The Treatise of Alexander Neckam," a culinary text written at the end of the twelfth century chiefly in an Anglo-Norman dialect of French. See *A Volume of Vocabularies*, ed. Richard Wright (N.p.: privately printed, 1857; 2d ed., 1882).

9. Dmitrii Blagovo, *Rasskazy babushki, Iz vospominanii piati pokolenii, Zapisannye i sobrannye ee vnukom D. Blagovo* [Grandmother's stories: Reminiscences of five generations, gathered and written by her grandson, D. Blagovo], ed. T. I. Ornatskaia (Leningrad: Nauka, Leningr. otdelenie, 1989), 10.

10. Restaurants in the modern sense did not then exist. Even in France they did not really function until after the French Revolution. See Barbara Wheaton, *Savoring the Past: The French Kitchen and Table from 1300 to 1789* (Philadelphia: University of Pennsylvania Press, 1983), 73-75.

11. Joseph Brodsky, "Lullaby," *Russkaia misl'*, no. 4055 (1–7 December 1994), 12.

12. E. G. Babaev, "Nravstvennaya tishina: V. V. Rozanov v Yasnoi Poliane" [Moral quiet: V. V. Rozanov at Yasnaya Polyana], *Druz'ia i gosti Yasnoi Poliany* [Friends and guests at Yasnaya Polyana], no. 1 (June 1993), 7.

13. Quoted by Darra Goldstein, chap. 7.

14. L. V. Karasev, "O Simvolakh Dostoevskogo" [Dostoevsky's symbols], *Voprosy philosophii*, no. 10 (1994), 95, 106.

15. See René Fueloep-Miller, *The Mind and Face of Bolshevism* (New York: Harper, 1965), 185.

16. After the Bolsheviks came to power, all religious observances were banned in the Soviet Union and aetheism was promoted. *Kulich*, a yeast bread, and *paskha*, a dessert made of cheese, eggs, and sugar, were an invariable component of the Russian Easter table. After the deprivations of the long Lenten fast, the richness of these traditional desserts was particularly savored. *Matsa* was associated with Jewish Passover and, for many years, its production was outlawed in the Soviet Union.

17. Untitled fragment, 1917. See *Vladimir Vladimorovich Maiakovskii (1893-1930): Stikhotvoreniia. Stikhi* [Vladimir Vladimorovich Maiakovski, 1893-1930: Poems, Verses] (Moscow: Moskovskii rabochii, 1973), 72.

18. Lidia Ivanova, *Vospominania* [Memoirs] (Moscow: PIK Kul'tura, 1992), 77-78. According to Mikhail Heller and Aleksandr Nekrich, "only 'speculations by bag traders,' who

smuggled footstuffs past the road-blocks, saved the urban population of the Soviet Republic from death." See Heller and Nekrich, *Utopia in Power: The History of the Soviet Union from 1917 to the Present*, trans. Phyllis B. Carlos (New York: Summit Books, 1986), 61.

19. S. V. Shumikhin, *Iz pis'ma S. A. Margolina k S. D. Mstislavskomu, 12 sentiabria 1920 g* [From the letters of S. A. Margolin to S. D. Mstisilavskii, 12 September 1920], cited in *Literaturnoe novoe obozrenie* [New literary review], no. 5 (Moscow, 1993), 162. See also Richard Stites, *Revolutionary Dreams* (New York: Oxford University Press, 1991), 140-144.

20. According to Lidia Ivanova, "For us, starvation stopped with the implementation of the special 'academic ration' in 1920." See Ivanova, 77.

21. A. A. Keda, "It is harmful for me to starve . . . ," *Literaturnoye novoe obozrenie*, no. 5, (Moscow, 1993), 160-161.

22. Archival reports of OGPU officials note that lines of 150 persons waiting for bread were common in December 1930 (TsA MBR. F.2. Op. 8. D. 106. L.122, 126; L. 23-50). Cited in "Ischez chelovek i net ego . . . Iz konfiskovannogo dnevnika E. N. Nikolayeva" [A man has disappeared and no longer exists. . . . From the confiscated diary of E. N. Nikolayev], *Istochnik,* no. 4, 1993, 59.

23. Ibid., 51, 60-61; Heller and Nekrich, 238-262.

24. Yuri Olesha, *Envy,* trans. Clarence Brown, in *The Portable Twentieth-Century Reader,* ed. Clarence Brown (New York: Penguin). The authors are grateful to Edythe Haber for drawing this passage to their attention.

25. Heller and Nekrich, 238.

26. Cited in Vladimir Gusev, "Gde fal'sh i gde istina" [What is false and what is true], in *Agitatsia za shchastie, Sovetskoe iskusstvo stalinskoii epokhi* [Struggle for happiness: Soviet art in Stalin's epoch] (Dusseldorf-Bremen: Interarteks–Editsion Temmen, 1994), 16.

27. Vasily Lebedev-Kumach and Isaac Dunaevsky, "Song of the Motherland," 1935; quoted in James von Geldern and Richard Stites, *Mass Culture in Soviet Russia* (Blooming-ton: Indiana University Press, 1995), 271.

28. Heller and Nekrich, 467-468.

29. Aleksandr Genis, "Krasnyi khleb: kulinarnaia istoriia sovetskoi vlasti" [Red bread: The culinary story of Soviet power], *Panorama,* no. 706 (October 1994).

30. I. Stalin, "Vystuplenie na prieme v Kremle v chest' komandujushchikh voiskami Krasnoi Armii" [Speech at a reception in honor of the wartime commanders of the Red Army, May 24, 1945], in *I. V. Stalin. Works*, vol. 2 [XV], ed. Robert H. McNeal (Stanford, Calif.: Hoover Institution on War, Revolution, and Peace, 1967), 203.

31. See Arjun Appadurai, "How to Make a National Cuisine: Cookbooks in Contem-porary India," *Comparative Studies in Society and History*, vol. 30, no. 1 (January 1988), 3-24.

32. Penelope Rowlands, "A Sense of Taste," ARTnews, 1995, no. 2, 27.

33. Lesley Chamberlain, Introduction, in F. T. Marinetti, *The Futurist Cookbook*, trans. Suzanne Brill, ed. Chamberlain (San Francisco: Bedford Arts, 1989), 7-8.

34. James Yood, *Feasting: A Celebration of Food in Art* (New York: Universe, 1992), 16.

35. Ibid., 7-8.

36. Blagovo, 8.

FOOD IN RUSSIAN HISTORY AND CULTURE

ONE

SNEJANA TEMPEST

Stovelore in Russian Folklife

In the East Slavic peasant household, the stove amounted to a multifunctional home appliance which remained an unmatched cooking unit until this century. Its secret lay in the fact that it spread the heat evenly, maintained a stable temperature for a long time, and precluded direct contact between food and fire. The cooking was achieved through dry hot air. Russian cooks, cookery book writers, and foreign travelers alike proclaimed the culinary merits and the efficiency of the Russian stove.

This appliance owed its great reputation also to the fact that it fulfilled additional functions beyond cooking and heating. For example, in the central regions of Russia,[1] the stove was large enough to act as a bathhouse. It also served as a drier for all kinds of fresh produce—herbs, mushrooms, fruit, and berries—and for clothes. When it was equipped with a chimney, the stove could be used to ventilate the house. During the day it kept the food warm and provided the requisite temperature to speed up the fermentation of *kvas* (a lightly fermented malt drink) and other drinks.

The stove's prominent location in the Russian peasant home points to its importance. The stove occupied one-fifth to one-fourth of the living space of a peasant hut. It was always built in one corner and surrounded by sleeping lofts for the younger and elderly members of the family.[2] Active adults slept on benches near the stove. Furthermore, because it took up a lot of living space, the stove played an important decorative role in the house. The size, color, and ornaments of the stove reflected the owners' prosperity. A poor household had a white stove with simple drawings, while a rich family was

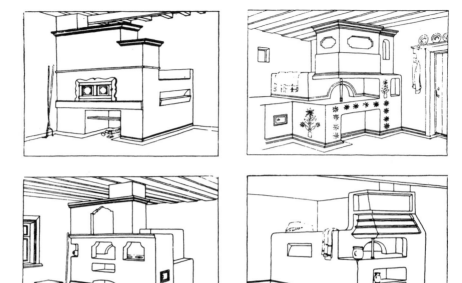

Drawings of traditional stoves from Ukraine. From V. P. Samojlovich, Narodnoe tvorchestvo v arkhitekture sel'skogo zhilishcha *(Kiev, 1961).*

able to afford tiles with inscriptions or scenes from village life. Russian craftsmen often made use of folk narratives and commonly recognized motifs to create a sort of tiled encyclopedia of peasant folk life.[3]

In short, the traditional stove governed almost all aspects of everyday life in a peasant family. There is evidence to show that in some remote and not so remote areas of Russia, the culture of the stove—its symbolic and ritualistic meaning—has endured to this day, for electricity was introduced to the peasant household inconsistently. This chapter investigates the culinary, ritualistic, and symbolic functions of the stove in East Slavic culture. Sources include riddles, magic tales, ritual incantations, and ritual celebrations, as recorded mostly during the nineteenth century in peasant villages.

To properly understand how essential the stove was in the existence of East Slavs, it is necessary to describe in some detail their living conditions. The East Slavs are a branch of the Slavic people who settled to till the land in what is currently Ukraine, Belarus, and the European part of Russia. In the Middle Ages their language grew distinct from common Slavic. It eventually ramified and crystallized into three related languages: Russian, Ukrainian, and Belorussian. A vast expanse of lowlands swept by arctic winds, the territory of the East Slavs has a continental climate with harsh, long-lasting winters and hot summers. Its northern half is covered with dense forests and does not lend itself easily to agriculture. Its southern half is known as the steppe, a largely treeless zone blessed with a rich black soil but exposed to occasional droughts. This area is known as the breadbasket of Russia.

The food of the peasants was first of all determined by the natural resources that were available locally. In the north of Russia, where the main grain was rye, the peasants generally ate dark rye bread, known as black bread. In the south of the country and in Ukraine, where wheat dominated the crops, white bread was more common. Bread was the main staple, and at every meal it was present on the tables of the people. Grains were also cooked with water into different kinds of *kasha,* a mixture reminiscent of porridge but with varying consistency. In addition to the grains, an important part of the diet came from the woods: gathering mushrooms, wild berries, and nuts was the favorite pastime of children and their grandparents, who were no longer able to toil the land. Fish and meat were highly appreciated but scarce and reserved for special occasions.

The Orthodox Church exerted a profound influence on the eating habits of the people. Orthodox believers were required to fast between 178 and 200 days per year. As a result, Russian peasant cuisine developed into a diet of opposites, with frequent alternations between fasting and feasting. Since meat and meat fat were prohibited during all fasting days (and were very expensive), Russians took to mushrooms as a meat substitute. During Lent itself, various fish pies and salted herring belonged to the diet of wealthier peasants.

The most ancient Russian beverage, *beriozovitsa,* was made from the sap of birch trees, which was kept in large tubs to achieve natural fermentation. A similar drink, *medovukha,* was made of honey, hops, and yeast fermented together. These beverages were later replaced by *kvas,* a mildly acid, sweet, dark-colored drink produced by fermenting wheat with water and sugar. Tea became widely affordable in the mid–nineteenth century, and ever since it has rivaled *kvas* in popularity.

The stove played a prominent part in the preparation of all these foodstuffs. Bread, *kasha,* mushrooms, meat and fish, the different beverages, all required processing in the stove. Generally speaking, uncooked food was not a regular part of the diet, with the possible exception of fruit and vegetables at the time of ripening. But even then, the tendency was to process them in some way, mainly to be eaten during winter.[4]

The position of the stove at the center of the material and symbolic culture of East Slavs derived primarily from its culinary function as a medium through which the raw was transformed into the cooked. As the technological appliance that enabled such a humanly engineered processing, the stove governed the conversion of nature into culture. No surprise, then, that it becomes the focus of numerous symbols, which in one way or another ultimately celebrate the creation of a cultural order.[5] The transformation of foodstuffs via the stove divided into three parts. First came the preparation of the primordial elements, especially fire and water, then the exposure of the raw food to these elements in the crucible, and finally the removal of the final product, baked or cooked food. The different elements of this culinary process were all endowed with particular symbolic values that are documented in folklore. To a large extent the symbolism of these elements overlaps.

Water and fire commanded particular respect among the East Slavs because they were perceived to act and intervene in everyday life in different ways. Distinct rituals were performed to invoke and possibly direct the power of these elements. In the Kupala rites, for example, jumping over bonfires achieved a cleansing result that paralleled bathing in the water of a river. Water and fire shared the same medicinal and purifying qualities, and both were used in magic practices. Both also received generous thanksgiving offerings.[6] In Ukraine, it was a common practice to place a pot of water in the burning stove during the night so that "the fire would not feel too hot."[7] The Soviet scholar S. A. Tokarev interpreted this custom as a kind of sacrificial offering to the fire element. The practice of lighting candles and bonfires at water sources represented a parallel offering to the water element.

The handling of water and fire in everyday life provides related evidence of the respect they inspired. Indeed, both elements were connected with a host of prohibitions. Spitting, urinating, and swearing were not permitted in their proximity; neither was quarreling or fighting, and lighting a fire or fetching water was forbidden without praying.[8] The prohibition against staining the purity of the family hearth may be explained by the belief that fire separated the land of the living from the land of the deceased ancestors. By spitting into fire one was thought to have desecrated the ancestors' domain.[9]

The stove itself, the crucible of culinary transformation, was perceived as sacred, and it acted as a mediator between the "living" world and the other world. When a family member was dying, for instance, the door of the stove was kept open so that the soul of the deceased could easily escape through the stove and the chimney.[10] According to a widespread saying, *"Pech' v domu—to zhe, chto altar' v tserkvi: v nei pechetsia xleb"* (The stove in the home is like an altar in a church: bread is baked in it).[11] In this example from the Viatka region east of European Russia, bread was evoked for its ritual rather than nutritional functions. The use of a special broom *(pomelo)* to sweep the inside of the stove was obligatory as a way of signifying the latter's extraordinary nature.[12] It was generally considered a bad omen to share the fire from the family stove with neighbors or other people, although during village epidemics all fires in stoves were extinguished and, after a communal prayer, a new, "clean" fire was lit, which was then distributed among the village households.[13]

The sacredness of the end product of culinary preparation can be best exemplified by a consideration of the symbolic value of bread. Bread was not only the most essential staple of the East Slavic diet. It figured also at the center of their cultural representations of a meal. The saying "poor is a dinner lacking bread" indicates that a meal was not considered complete without bread. And to this day the word for bread can denote or refer to a broad range of everyday activities. Not only does it symbolize the whole meal, but also, in idiomatic expressions, it stands for earnings or for work, for hospitality, and, on a more metaphorical level, for friendship. Bread signifies wealth and health. Touching on so many areas of everyday life, bread is deeply embedded in Russian culture.

The deep respect for bread can be seen in the prohibitions that regulated its preparation.[14] For instance, while bread was baking it was forbidden to sit on the stove (which usually also served as a bed for the family). It was also forbidden to sweep the floor of the house or to cut a slice of bread while other breads were being baked.

The entire process of preparing food, especially the baking of a ritual bread, imitated the sequence of conception, growth, and birth. From grinding the seeds to letting the dough swell and rise to delivering the baked goods, the cycle mirrored creation, both human and cosmic. For example, during a spring greeting ritual celebrating the rebirth of nature, East Slavs baked special breads shaped like birds. In doing so, they conjured migrating birds back to their territories. Thus the baking of ritual bread was thought to stimulate or hasten the cyclical course of nature. As part of the wedding ritual, a young, healthy, unmarried man was called to place the wedding breads on the bread board and insert it into the stove. This phallic gesture performed by the *korovainik* (named after *korovai*, the wedding bread) was meant to ensure fertility for the newly wed,[15] and was one of the rare instances of male participation in the bread baking process, or in any food preparation.

The entire winter festive period of the Russian agricultural calendar was devoted to preparations for next year's harvest.[16] Breads occupied a prominent place in most of these peasant festivities. The values associated with bread turned around notions of fertility, abundance, and prosperity. For example, during the Yuletide celebrations, the peasants walked from house to house singing carols and wishing the household members prosperity and happiness. The function of these songs was originally magical—to promote good crops, happy marriages, and wealth. Some of the New Year laudatory songs contain a demand for a ritualistic handout. In response to the songs, the hosts were supposed to offer special breads or buns baked in the shape of goats, cows, or other domestic animals, sometimes called *koliadki* (from Latin *calendae*, "the calends"), as the carols themselves were called. The offerings ensured an excellent harvest and an increase in the livestock of the household. A riddle illustrates the value of bread as a symbol of abundance: What is sifted, twisted, covered with gold? Answer: Wheat bread.[17] Here the connection between bread and gold goes beyond a simple matter of color, resting on the fact that both bread and gold symbolized abundance.

In certain rituals, bread played very graphically the role of mediating between the two worlds. For example, an East Slavic burial practice consisted of placing small ladders baked of dough beside the corpse to assist the soul to leave the body in its ascent from this world to the other world—a clear survival from heathen times and a rather conspicuous indication for scholars.[18] The image of the bread ladder is based on a metonymy: here the means stand for the goal. Indeed, bread usually was directly associated with paradise, as in a frequent incantation which a child would chant outdoors upon finding a ladybug. The child was supposed to place the insect on its palm and sing:

> Ladybug, ladybug,
> Fly to the sky,
> Bring us some bread: wheat or rye,
> But only not burnt.[19]

If the ladybug flew away, the weather was predicted to be beneficial to the harvest. The function of bread as an element establishing the connection between two worlds also prompted the custom of placing bread into the grave of a deceased person. The Russian folklorist Vladimir Propp concluded the analysis of this motive by saying that bread, together with a staff and a pair of shoes, was given to the deceased in order to facilitate "the travel along the way to the other world."[20] Characteristically, the Slavs gave a ritual loaf of bread to travelers embarking on all kinds of journeys. In Bulgaria, for example, a bread called *p"tnina* was given to mourners on their way to the cemetery. It was thought that the journey of the deceased would thereby be facilitated.[21]

In light of this intricate connection between bread and paradise, the expression *Bozhii dar* (gift of God), in referring to bread, becomes quite literal. Bread is indeed the food of the other world which is given to humanity in anticipation of its future happiness. The existence of strong prohibitions against wasting bread may derive from such belief in its sacredness. A widespread peasant custom required people to pick up all the bread crumbs scattered on the table or the floor after a meal and feed them to poultry or birds. Alexander Afanas'ev, one of the first scholars of Russian folklore, cited the belief that evil spirits would collect bread crumbs people had dropped and that if, after their death, these bread crumbs weighed more than their bodies, their souls would go to the devil.[22]

If bread is a symbol of abundance and if it establishes links, it may not be surprising that it appears also in connection with sexual intercourse and pregnancy. Indeed, the following riddles from Sadovnikov's collection are quite suggestive:

> Behind a wall, a wall
> Is a bony loaf of bread.
> Answer: Baby in belly.

> A loaf of bread lies at the corner of the hut,
> And in the bread sits a rat.
> Answer: Pregnant woman.[23]

Whether the second riddle depicts a fetus in the womb, as Sadovnikov presumes, or whether it alludes to sexual intercourse is irrelevant. In the mindset of East Slavic peasants, cause and consequence could oftentimes substitute for each other. In any event the idea of fertility is expressed eloquently enough.

Building clay-based stoves was a communal effort that took on aspects of a ritual. In the north, it carried a name of its own, *pechebit'e*—from the root *pek-* (to bake), which also appears in many objects that come into contact with the stove, and the root *bit-* (to beat). In the process of constructing the stove, unmarried young men and women were invited from all over the village to help carry the clay, crumple it, work it up into the correct smoothness, mold it and so forth. To prevent the stove from smoking excessively, the builders hid coins and incense in the clay walls.[24] During construction, the young people supported their spirits with songs, and once the stove was erected, they celebrated with dance and drink. The men were generously treated to vodka, the young women to honey-breads *(prianiki),* these offerings being called *pechnoe.*[25] Knowing the importance of a well-constructed stove that retained heat and operated economically—such a stove was honored with the special title of *pech'-pekarka* (baker-stove) or *varista pech'* (boiler-stove)[26]—the house owners made a special effort to please all participants. Thus *pechebit'e* combined hard work and the festive liminal mood of a party, a ritual which was repeated at the construction of every new village house.[27]

The most strenuous activity the stove-builders had to face was the occasional tussle with a moody house spirit. As family members moved into the new home, they were compelled to perform a housewarming ritual, which consisted of transporting coals and ashes in a clay pot from the old house into the new stove, thereby ensuring that the house spirit, *domovoi,* who lived either under the stove or behind it, had moved with the family.[28] In the same way they would move the family icons from the old house to the new home's "beautiful" corner.[29] In order to remain on friendly terms with the house spirit, the house master also placed a pot of hot porridge *(kasha)* into the stove on a special day after the family's evening meal. According to the Russian scholar I. P. Sakharov, it was believed that the *domovoi* would eat his share, known as *kudesa,* at midnight.[30]

The location of the stove determined the traditional organization of space in the *izba* (peasant house): it divided the living space into the women's part (*babii ugol,* women's corner), where all the daily female activities took place, and the men's section (*krasnyi ugol,* "beautiful" corner), where the icons hung over the large table.[31] During the matchmaking ceremony, the reluctant bride-to-be would emerge from the stove corner, the *babii kut,* onto the "beautiful" corner to indicate her approval of the groom.[32] The motion away from the family stove toward the realm of the husband was one of the significant symbols of the marriage itself.[33]

In Russia, the stove was perceived as feminine, perhaps because the baking of bread remained entirely in the domain of women. Oral folk tradition—especially proverbs, riddles, and songs—provide rich evidence. For example, a riddle from the Sadovnikov collection presented the stove and its smoke in the following terms:

> *Stoit devitsa v izbe*
> *A kosa – na dvore.*
>
> A maiden stands in the house
> And her braid is outside.[34]

Here is a riddle from the Pskov region in which the stove was compared to a woman.

Stovelore in Russian Folklife

Stoit baba v uglu,
A rot v boku.

A woman stands in a corner
With a mouth in her side.[35]

In Russian folk tales the stove frequently appears as a female character endowed with a specific, if varying, name. In this hypostasis, her main role is to reward respectful attention on the part of children by extending them protection in her bosom in case of danger. At the same time she feeds them with her breads.[36]

The motherly behavior of the stove in these folk tales is especially noteworthy in light of a rather interesting family ritual, the so-called baking of children, which confirms its feminine nature. The ceremony normally was organized by the young mothers in the village, who used the stove as a method of curing through fire. To purge an illness, they would place a sick infant or even a premature baby on the bread board and then hold it three times in the hot stove.[37] In doing so, they addressed various rhymes, chants, or sayings to the illness, "dog's old age"—a generic term for rickets, infant atrophy, hernia, etc.—which was supposedly burning away in the stove. This ritual, known as the rebaking of a child *(perepekanie rebenka)* or in some cases the rebaking of dog's old age *(perepekanie sobachei starosti),* was performed over infants in the Volga region, in the central and southern regions of Russia, in Siberia, and in certain areas of Belarus.[38] The symbolism of the ritual was based upon assimilating the child to bread dough. The East Slavs saw placing the sick child into the stove for transformation into a healthy child as parallel to the baking of the bread, i.e., to the transformation of a soft, formless substance into a perfect crisp loaf. In some areas, including the Volga regions (Kazan' and Kostroma), the bread simile was reinforced by smearing the infant's face or body with dough.[39] In Lévi-Strauss' terms, the raw was transformed into the cooked, and the stove was the place where this transformation took place.[40] The symbolic baking of the child was seen as a ritual death followed by a rebirth. The child was temporarily returned into the mother's womb—the stove—in order to be reborn healthy.[41] Thus the stove acquired yet another dimension—it functioned as the nurturing womb of a mother. A peasant saying quoted by Vladimir Dal', "The stove is our dear own mother,"[42] clearly illustrates the maternal aspect of the stove.[43]

The East Slavic folktale "The Boy and the Witch" offered a distorted, inverted form of the ritual rebaking of children.[44] In this tale, the Russian witch Baba Iaga ordered her daughter to roast a kidnapped little boy for dinner. The clever boy asked the daughter to show him the correct way of placing oneself on the bread board. After the girl dutifully sat on the board, the boy shoved her into the hot stove to be roasted. The magic tale deflected the practice of healing through fire into a bare act of murder through cooking. Commenting upon this motif, Propp raised the larger question of how and why rituals occasionally became reversed in corresponding mythological tales.[45]

The connection between the stove and temporary death underlines the notion that the stove functioned as a threshold to the other world. East Slavs believed that a baby received its soul through the stove and that the soul of a deceased person left the body through the same channel and flew out of the chimney to join the realm of ancestors.[46] Several rituals rested on the idea that the stove was a channel of communication with ancestors. A newborn baby and a dying person were brought into direct contact with the stove in order to seek their help and protection. Upon returning home from a funeral, all members of a household touched the stove and looked into its opened mouth in order to protect themselves from another death.[47] When a child was born, the midwife held it near the mouth of the stove and sprinkled it with ashes in expectation that the ancestors would grant their protection to the newly born.[48] Hence the forebears, whose favorite food was the steam rising from the chimney, participated in the everyday life of the family, receiving their share of sustenance and providing the needed guardianship for the whole family. This link between the ancestors and the living explains the numerous fortune-telling practices associated with cooking and baking. For example, if the top of the bread had tilted inward in the stove, good fortune was to follow; if it had tilted toward the stove door, misfortune was predicted.[49] Similarly, the stove itself was an important prop in fortune-telling.[50]

Different hypostases of the Russian dragon slayer—a brave protagonist of fairy tales and legends who rescues his bride-to-be from the clutches of the dragon—bore names which pointed to their connection with the stove: Ivan Popialov, Matiusha Pepel'noi, Zapechnyi Iskr, Ivan Zapechnik (from the Russian words for ashes and stove).[51] All of them received their supernatural powers through their miraculous births and were indebted in some way to the hearth. Witches also had a privileged relationship with the stove: they used the chimney to penetrate into the house. As a result people would recite ritual incantations in order to exorcise the passageway.[52]

The curative or restorative power of the stove was extended to those who lay on it or sat in its proximity. Sometimes its power was translated into a simple feeling of well-being or happiness. A common way of describing a blissful state, "as if warmed by the stove," stressed the coziness ensured by the stove.[53] A well-known Ukrainian saying described happy people as "those born in a stove."[54] Having spent some time in the proximity of the stove, a visitor, once a mere stranger, was transformed into a lifelong friend: "He who sat on the stove is no longer a guest, but a friend." In the Pskov region lying on the stove, the traditionally preferred way of idling time away, was assigned a special verb, *pechushnichat'*; a lazy person was referred to as *pechushnik* or *pechegnet*.

Thus in contrast to the Christian *krasnyi ugol,* or "beautiful" corner, the stove was the site of pagan worship. The coexistence of two competing sets of beliefs within one enclosed space does not come as a surprise. Unlike Western Europe, the East Slavic lands were marked by the existence of dual faith, *dvoeverie,* which left a deep imprint on the mindset of the people.[55] Pagan worship existed alongside Christian beliefs, and its endurance accounts for the prominence of the natural elements in the East Slavic religious mind. Just as the stove and the "beautiful" corner occupied opposite ends of the Russian *izba,* the line dividing the two demarcated pagan fire worship and Christian faith. The pre-Christian and Christian elements in the spiritual lives of the peasants coexisted for several centuries and continued to interact in the twentieth century.

In *The Raw and the Cooked* Lévi-Strauss identifies two distinct, usually concurring, uses of the symbolic language of rituals and mythology: it provides people with "the means either of modifying a practical situation or of characterizing and describing it."[56] While the two functions commonly overlap, the first one disappears in cultures where "the power of magical thought is tending to weaken, and when the rites take on a vestigial character."[57] With regard to East Slavic culture, the resilience of magical representations is remarkable, all the more so that for centuries it has coexisted with Christian faith. The stove is perceived to exert powers and to affect everyday life in ways that far exceed its mere culinary and heating functions. As a channel to the other world and hence as a means to conjure up the protection of forebears, the stove features prominently in rites that clearly aim more at effecting changes than describing a state of affairs. Its power, in turn, extends to the products it generates, chief among them bread, which is thought to promote fertility, abundance, and health as much as it symbolizes them. This homology between functions of bread and stove is striking, if not totally surprising, as essentially both belong to the imaginary language about power—to mythic representations of cosmic agency—which the East Slavs have invented in order to understand the world.

NOTES

1. A. K. Baiburin, *Zhilishche v obriadakh i predstavleniiakh vostochnykh slavian* [Dwelling in the rituals and the mindset of the East Slavs] (Leningrad: Nauka, 1983), 160.

2. Ibid.

3. Iu. M. Ovsiannikov, ed., *Russkie izraztsy* [Russian tiles] (Leningrad: Russkii khudozhnik, 1968).

4. For a more detailed description of traditional Russian food, see E. M. Velichko, N. I. Kovalev, and V. V. Usov, *Russkaia narodnaia kukhnia* [Russian traditional cooking] (Moscow: Kolos, 1992), and Joyce Toomre, Introduction, in *Classic Russian Cooking: Elena Molokhovets' 'A Gift to Young Housewives'* (Bloomington: Indiana University Press, 1992), 3–89.

5. The opposition between the raw and the cooked is one of the empirical categories that Claude Lévi-Strauss identifies as an organizational principle of mythologies. In his magisterial if complex elaboration of a "science of mythology," the French anthropologist investigates a universal "logic" of physical qualities that informs the production of mythological representations. Along with a host of other binary oppositions, all more or less equivalent to one another, the contrast between the raw and the cooked articulates the difference between nature and culture, which, according to Lévi-Strauss, goes back to an opposition between continuous and discrete quantities. See Lévi-Strauss, *The Raw and the Cooked: Introduction to a Science of Mythology,* trans. John and Doreen Weightman, vol. 1 (Chicago: University of Chicago Press, 1969).

6. S. A. Tokarev, *Religioznye verovaniia vostochnoslavianskikh narodov XIX-nachala XX v.* [Religious beliefs of East Slavic peoples in the nineteenth and early twentieth centuries] (Moscow and Leningrad: Izdatel'stvo Akademii Nauk SSSR, 1970), 65–74.

7. Ibid., 68.

8. Ibid. See also B. A. Uspenskii, *Filologicheskie razyskaniia v oblasti slavianskikh drevnostei. Relikty iazychestva v vostochnoslavianskom kul'te Nikolaia Mirlikiiskogo* [Philological inquiries into the field of Slavic antiquity: Pagan relics in the East Slavic cult of Nikolai Mirlikiiskii] (Moscow: Izdatel'stvo Moskovskogo Universiteta, 1982), 56.

9. Uspenskii, *Filologicheskie razyskaniia,* 56.

10. A. K. Baiburin, "Iz testa - polianitsu, iz devki - moloditsu," in *Mifologicheskie predstavleniia v narodnom tvorchestve* [Mythological beliefs in folk art] (Moscow: Rossiiskii Institut Iskusstvoznaniia, 1993), 95.

11. Baiburin, *Zhilishche,* 162.

12. Tokarev, *Religioznye verovaniia,* 68.

13. Ibid., 66.

14. The respect for bread may also be seen in the fact that in old legal documents bakers were referred to by their full names, while other "simple" folk were often addressed by nick-names or first names.

15. Baiburin, "Iz testa - polianitsu," 96.

16. V. I. Chicherov, *Zimnii period russkogo zemledel'cheskogo kalendaria XVI-XIX vekov* [The winter season of the Russian agrarian calendar in the sixteenth to nineteenth centuries] (Moscow: Nauka, 1957), 123.

17. D. Sadovnikov, *Riddles of the Russian People* (Ann Arbor: Ardis, 1986), 418.

18. For a discussion of this burial practice, see particularly A. B. Strakhov, *Kul't Khleba u Vostochnykh Slavian* [The cult of bread among the East Slavs] (Munich: Verlag Otto Sagner, 1991), 144.

19. From my personal memory.

20. V. Ia. Propp, *Istoricheskie korni volshebnoi skazki,* 2d ed. [The historical roots of the wonder tale] (Leningrad: Izdatel'stvo Leningradskogo universiteta, 1986), 49.

21. Strakhov, *Kul't Khleba,* 25.

22. A. N. Afanas'ev, *Poeticheskie vozzreniia slavian na prirodu* [The poetic views of the Slavs upon nature] (Moscow: Izdanie Soldatenkova, 1869), vol. 3, 763.

23. Sadovnikov, *Riddles of the Russian People,* 418.

24. Baiburin, *Zhilishche,* 160.

25. M. M. Gromyko, *Traditsionnye normy povedeniia i formy obshcheniia russkikh krestian XIX v.* [Traditional norms of behavior and communication among Russian peasants in the nineteenth century] (Moscow: Nauka, 1986), 56.

26. Velichko, Kovalev, and Usov, *Russkaia narodnaia kukhnia,* 35.

27. M. M. Gromyko, *Mir russkoi derevni* [The world of the Russian village] (Moscow: Molodaia gvardiia, 1991), 81.

28. Tokarev, *Religioznye verovania,* 70.

29. Uspenskii, *Filologicheskie razyskaniia,* 184.

30. I. P. Sakharov, *Skazaniia russkogo naroda, sobrannye I. P. Sakharovym* [The sayings of the Russian people, collected by I. P. Sakharov] (1885; reprint, Moscow: Khudozhest-vennaia literatura, 1989), 236.

31. Baiburin, *Zhilishche,* 160.

32. V. I. Zekulina and A. N. Rozov, eds., *Obriadovaia poeziia* [Ritual poetry] (Moscow: Sovremennik, 1989), 323.

33. Baiburin, *Zhilishche,* 168.

34. Sadovnikov, *Riddles of the Russian People,* 43.

35. Ibid., 41.

36. For a classical example, see the favorite children's folk tale "The Magic Geese" in A. N. Afanas'ev, *Narodnye russkie skazki A. N. Afanas'eva* [Russian folktales, collected by A. N. Afanas'ev] (Moscow: Nauka, 1984), vol. 1, 147.

37. Baiburin, *Zhilishche,* 125. For descriptions of this ritual, see A. L. Toporkov, "Ritual 'perepekaniia' rebenka u vostochnykh slavian," in *Fol'klor: Problemy sokhraneniia, izucheniia i populiarizatsii* [Folklore: Problems of conservation, study, and popularization] (Moscow, 1988), 128–130. See also Sakharov, *Skazaniia russkogo naroda,* 104 and 114.

38. Toporkov, "Ritual 'perepekaniia,'" 128–130.

39. Ibid., 129.

40. Lévi-Strauss, *The Raw and the Cooked,* 142. See also Baiburin, *Zhilishche,* 162. Lévi-Strauss notes (336) the ubiquity of the practice of symbolic roasting, which, according to him, was imposed upon people "deeply involved in a physiological process," such as "the newborn child, the woman who has just given birth, or the pubescent girl." The point of this practice was to integrate or reintegrate into culture people briefly enveloped by nature. This process was realized through the mediation of cooking fire, "whose normal function is to mediatize the conjunction of the raw product and the human consumer, and whose operation thus has the effect of making sure that a natural creature is at one and the same time cooked and socialized."

41. Baiburin, *Zhilishche,* 129.

42. Cited in Baiburin, *Zhilishche,* 179.

43. Mircea Eliade discusses the maternal aspect of the furnace in *The Forge and the Crucible,* trans. Stephen Corrin (London: Rider, 1962).

44. "The Boy and the Witch" (AT 327C). AT is the widely accepted abbreviation for Aarne-Thompson's index of folktale types. Magic tales are classified under numbers 300–749 in the index. Aarne ordered the corpus of European wondertales with the help of "logic" categories that are somewhat eclectic and unsystematic.

45. Propp, *Istoricheskie korni volshebnoi skazki,* 98.

46. Baiburin, "Iz testa - polianitsu," 95.

47. Zekulina and Rozov, *Obriadovaia poeziia,* 602. See also, Baiburin, *Zhilishche,* 165.

48. Baiburin, *Zhilishche,* 165.

49. Baiburin,"Iz testa - polianitsu," 95.

50. N. Kolpakova, *Kniga o russkom fol'klore* [A book on Russian folklore] (Leningrad, 1948), 19-20. See also Tokarev, *Religioznye verovania,* 72. For additional information, see E. V. Anichkov, *Iazychestvo i drevniaia Rus'* [Paganism and old Russia] (St. Petersburg, 1914), 280.

51. B. A. Rybakov, *Iazychestvo drevnikh slavian* [Paganism of the ancient Slavs] (Moscow: Nauka, 1981), 585.

52. Sakharov, *Skazaniia russkogo naroda,* 235.

53. Baiburin, "Iz testa - polianitsu," 94.

54. Baiburin, *Zhilishche,* 163.

55. Iu. M. Lotman and B. A. Uspenski, "Binary Models in the Dynamics of Russian Culture (to the End of the Eighteenth Century)," in Alexander D. Nakhimovsky and Alice Stone Nakhimovsky, eds., *The Semiotics of Russian Cultural History* (Ithaca: Cornell University Press, 1985), 30-66.

56. Lévi-Strauss, *The Raw and the Cooked,* 337.

57. Ibid., 338.

TWO

HORACE G. LUNT

Food in the Rus'
Primary Chronicle

Since food is a fundamental human requirement, we may confidently assume that the Rus' of the ninth to twelfth centuries—the ancestors of today's Ukrainians, Belorussians, and Russians—were constantly concerned how to produce or otherwise obtain sustenance. Yet precisely because food is such an everyday complex of problems, it is mentioned in writing only in exceptional cases: famine or feast, survival or luxury, socially proscribed or favored. Not surprisingly, then, the written record provides a spotty picture of unusual details, without the rich background of ordinary items and relationships that must have been present in each community.

The *Primary Chronicle*, or the *Story of Seasons and Years*, is the history of Rus'—the East Slavic lands and people—from the Flood to about A.D. 1117.[1] It is the major, often the only, source for information about the early East Slavs, starting with folkloric traditions reaching back to about 850, picking up with some more substantial reminiscences from about 1000, and based on written records and eyewitness accounts after 1050. The introductory paragraphs (about 5 percent of the whole text) establish that the twelfth-century Rus' are Slavs descended from Noah's son Japheth. These paragraphs also enumerate neighboring peoples. Starting with A.D. 852 (or 6,360 years from the creation of the world by Byzantine reckoning), items are assigned to particular years, although the topics sometimes have little to do with this annalistic framework.[2]

Readers should not expect the *Primary Chronicle* to be a modern sociology-oriented history book, concerned with the daily life of ordinary people and the details of their social and economic interactions. It is a diffuse and uneven selection of data about people, places, and events that will explain where "we, the Rus'," came from and how it is that we are a significant Christian nation. The overarching theme is the legitimacy of the ruler, Volodimer Vsevolodich Monomakh, Grand Prince of Kiev 1113–1125, and his lineage, going back through Volodimer Sviatoslavich (the Great, 978–1015) to Rjurik, a Norseman supposedly invited to come and rule the Slavs and Finnic peoples of the Novgorod region in 862. The work was surely compiled and transmitted by monks, and Byzantine Orthodox Christianity is an ever-present backdrop.[3] This history recounts what the chroniclers wish us to believe happened—how changes came about because of choices made by men in a chain of events punctuated by intervention of the hand of God or, occasionally, the Devil.

The account is parceled out in some 340 items, the shortest being the entry for 1029, *mirno byst'* "It became peaceful" (i.e., the fighting stopped). The longest is a 3,900-word précis of Christian history and doctrine known as the Philosopher's Speech; it constitutes over 7 percent of the total text of the *Chronicle*.[4] The disparity between the number of items on a topic and the size of individual items, that is, between the portion of the inventory and the portion of total text, points out the importance items and topics had for the editors. The most significant event was obviously the conversion of Volodimer Sviatoslavich (also known as St. Vladimir) in 988: five major items under 986, 987, and 988 make up over 12 percent of the *Chronicle,* and six shorter related items about religion and the baptism of Rus' furnish another 3.4 percent.[5] Seven items dealing with the Kiev Monastery of the Caves, its sainted abbot Feodosii, and some prominent monks make up another 11.5 percent. Altogether, some forty items about Christianity and clerics furnish well over 30 percent of the text but only 12 percent of the 340 items that make up the inventory.[6] Seven items about pagan shamans and magicians bring the total discussion of religion to a third of the text.

Sketching the lives of the favored rulers is largely accomplished with laconic brevity, but accounts of some campaigns and the deeds of a few individuals are more discursive. Some 125 items (37 percent of the inventory) deal with war and its immediate participants, 36 percent of the text, while negotiations and peace treaties are dealt with in fifteen items, only 7 percent of the text. Births, marriages, deaths, civil appointments, along with the construction of towns and public buildings are noted (25 percent of the inventory, under 10 percent of the text). General information (geography, peoples, customs, weather), brief notes on individuals, events, and topics may be lumped together as miscellaneous (20 percent of the inventory, 13 percent of the text).[7]

The chroniclers were writing for people who knew the background and the normal codes of behavior. They take for granted that the prince is chiefly a military leader with special rights and obligations to his soldiers and officers. Yet the world view of the monks determines what they record and how they interpret events. "Everyone knows" what may be eaten and what must be avoided—under normal conditions as well as on special occasions—and only exceptions need be noted. Food and drink as sources of pleasure are to be shunned; fasting is praiseworthy. Volodimer's examination of religions (see note 5) contains references to food precisely because dietary rules are presented as the chief basis for his choice of faith. On the whole, eating and drinking are set forth as either positive or negative. When they are good, they are benefits granted by a ruler to demonstrate his power and his Christian piety. Banquets for military leaders serve to reward past service and ensure continued loyalty; providing food and drink for the poor and sick is the duty of a good Christian. Abbot Feodosii of the Monastery of the Caves warns his monks (sub 1074) that much eating and excessive drinking foster evil thoughts, which lead to sin.

The story of Prince Volodimer concerns his use of the power he inherited from his father, Sviatoslav, and his grandparents Igor and Olga (whose baptism is recorded as a major event in the *Chronicle*). As ruler of Kiev, he sought to extend his domains while defending his heritage against almost continual attack from all sides. In particular, he had to be alert to repel sudden attacks by the fierce nomad Pechenegs, who for years had appeared without warning from the steppe to ravage and plunder. Again and again he fends them off, but they always come back. It is in this military context that food becomes a major topic, the subject of the entry for 997.[8]

In 991 the newly Christian Prince Volodimer established a new fortified town, Belgorod, to defend the immediate western approach to Kiev, chiefly from the endemic menace of the Pechenegs. The 997 entry begins with the abrupt statement that Volodimer has gone to Novgorod to recruit more soldiers:[9]

> At this same time, the Pechenegs found out that the prince was absent. They came and camped around Belgorod, and they would not let anyone out of the town. And there was great hunger in the town. And it was impossible for Volodimer to help, and it was impossible for him to move, for the soldiers had not yet assembled around him, and there was a great multitude of Pechenegs. And the siege of the town

went on and on, and there was great hunger. And they held a public meeting in the town and said, "Look, we are about to die of hunger, and there is no help from the prince. Is it better for us to die? Let us surrender to the Pechenegs; let them permit some to live and put some to death; we are already dying of hunger." And thus they agreed.

And there was one old man who had not been at the meeting and he asked, "What was the meeting for?" And the people told him that they were going to surrender the next day to the Pechenegs. Hearing this, he sent for the town elders and said to them, "I have heard that you are about to surrender to the Pechenegs." And they said, "The people can't bear the hunger." And he said to them, "Listen to me; don't surrender for three days, and do as I say." And they gladly promised to obey. And he said to them, "Collect at least a handful each of oats or wheat or bran from everyone." And they gladly went out and got it. And he told the women to make the mixture from which one cooks *kisel'*. And he ordered a well to be dug, and a barrel to be put in it and that the barrel be filled with the mixture. And he ordered a second well to be dug and a barrel to be put in it. And he told them to find honey. And they went and took a cask of honey—for it was buried in the prince's honey-storage chamber—and he told them to dilute it with a lot of water and pour it into the barrel in the second well. And the next morning he told them to send for the Pechenegs.

And the townspeople said, when they came to the Pechenegs, "Hold hostages from our people, and about ten of you come into the town to see what is happening in our town." And the Pechenegs were glad, thinking that they were about to surrender, and they took their hostages and themselves chose the leading men from their clans. And they sent them into the town to look around in the town at what was happening. And they came into the town and the people said to them, "Why are you killing yourselves? Can you outlast us? If you stay for ten years, what can you do to us? For we have nourishment from the earth. If you don't believe it, look with your own eyes." And they took them to the well where the flour-starch mixture was and they brought some up in a bucket and poured it into pans. And when they had cooked up the *kisel'*, they took it and went with them to the other well, and they drew up the honey-water. And they began to eat, first the townspeople and afterward the Pechenegs. And they were astonished and said, "Our princes will not believe it unless they eat it themselves." And the people filled up a wine vessel with the flour-starch mixture and honey-water from the well and gave it to the Pechenegs. And they went and told about everything that had happened. And they cooked it and the Pecheneg princes took some and they were astonished. And taking back their own hostages and releasing the others, they retreated from the town and went back home.

Food in the Rus' Primary Chronicle

Illustration of the Belgorod kisel' *episode in the* Primary Chronicle. *Photographic reproduction from the Radzivil or Kenigsberg manuscript, circa 1500 (St. Petersburg: Tovarishchestvo R. Golike and A. Vil'borg, 1902).*

This account is almost a recipe; its specifity of terms for ingredients and the completed dish here is unique not only in the *Primary Chronicle* but, with one exception we will discuss immediately, in all the pre-1550 literature of the East Slavs. My translation here cautiously retains the term *kisel'*, because the meaning seems not to be that of modern Russian or Belorussian *kisel'* (Ukrainian *kysil'*, Polish *kisiel*), a kind of starch pudding now usually made with fruit and potato flour.[10] The people of Belgorod seem to have produced a kind of gruel or porridge generically related to our oatmeal or cream of wheat.[11] Besides *kisel'*, two other technical terms are found only here. One is *tsiezh'*, a mixture that has been put through a sieve, here presumably the parboiled grain (I have rendered it "flour-starch mixture"). The other is *syta*, honey diluted with water, which is still served with *kisel'* on festive occasions in rural areas. What is vital is that the basic ingredient is grain, and here two kinds of grain are mentioned—oats and wheat (*ov's'* and *p'shenitsa*)—along with bran (*otrubi*), which could be the husks of either or both. Honey is also assumed to be available, in a specially named storage chamber.

In a much later passage, where the context does not hint at food, another word, *kut'ia*, probably refers to a second dish whose ingredients include cereals. We need information from outside the *Chronicle* to determine the basic sense. On the eve of a major battle (1103), the Rus' princes seek divine aid by vowing pledges, "one [prince promised] *kut'ia*, another alms for the poor, and others [promised to provide] the needs of monasteries." *Kut'ia* is clearly valuable: is it the same as modern Russian *kut'ia*, a ritual dish offered in memory of the dead at funerals and certain church holidays? In terms of function, very probably; but the exact meaning is elusive. Even in twelfth-century Rus', there was controversy about the way *kut'ia* was prepared and the propriety of its use in church (on the altar or elsewhere). A request for clarification of the rules was among the 101 questions about vexing problems of procedure and doctrinal interpretation put to Bishop Nifon of Novgorod (died 1156) by the monk-priest Kirik. Nifon's answer provides one interpretation, but the fact that Kirik asked the question indicates that there was disagreement.[12] The text may be somewhat corrupt, and unfortunately the vocabulary is not clear. First *sochivo* is mentioned, then *gorokh", bob", sochevitsa, rivif"*. All are definitely legumes; however, in many languages designations for individual types (such as pea, haricot, fava bean, broad bean, pulse, lentil, chickpea) have imprecise boundaries. *Sochivo* and *sochevitsa* both mean "lentil," the first being South Slavic, the second East Slavic; yet in some older texts both may possibly mean "chickpea."[13] *Rivif'* reflects Greek *revithia* "chickpeas."[14] The other two are familiar words for "peas" and "beans." To these, Nifon says, are to be added *pshenitsa* "wheat" and *konopli* "hemp, cannabis" and whatever fruit (*ovoshch'*) is available. Legumes were the traditional staple for monks in Egypt and the Holy Land, and toasted hemp seed could be eaten with them. The fruit makes the dish somewhat special. Now, *kut'ia* among modern East Slavs is the label for an enormous variety of recipes and a series of differences as to when and just how it is to be presented. In Greek it is called *koliva* (whence Slavonic *kolivo*), and there are equivalents in Armenian and Georgian. The modern recipes are usually quite elaborate, requiring spices as well as fruit and nuts:[15] it is the absence of honey that makes Nifon's recipe unique.[16] Another extended reference, this time in an explicit monastery setting, is at the same time more and less informative. The rule of the Studios Monastery in Constantinople was adopted by Abbot Feodosii of the Caves Monastery, but the Slavonic translation is surely Bulgarian, though the oldest known copy (about 1200) has some distinctive Rus' features, possibly including certain words.[17] It tells us that on St. Theodore's eve, *kut'ia*, "about three *puds*," apparently a fairly large measure, is put on dishes "with kernels [almonds?] and with dried grapes [= raisins] and with nut-kernels (*oriekhovy iadr'ci*) and other sorts of these kinds."[18] This does not tell us the basic makeup of the *kut'ia*, but the nuts and raisins and redundantly vague mention of other items ensures that it was indeed a special dish. Above all, it does not allow us to assume that such delicacies were prepared in this way in the Caves Monastery of Kiev or elsewhere in Rus'.[19]

Food in the *kisel'* episode is an immediate matter of life and death, and therefore special enough to merit the attention of the chroniclers. The Belgorod siege belongs to a type of war stratagem that goes back to Herodotus: tricking the enemy into the belief that unlimited food is available and therefore a siege would amount to wasted effort. The entry seems to be mere entertainment, for the unnamed heroes have no direct connection with Volodimer's military successes. Yet it does illustrate the banal fact that control of food supplies can be a source of power.

This chapter is not a survey of all that is known—or has been inferred or assumed—about food and drink in twelfth-century Rus'. My purpose is to register the words referring to food and drink that are actually attested in the *Primary Chronicle* and to assess the information they provide, presumably for the early twelfth century. The *Chronicle* does not use certain well-known words simply because they are not needed; no episode involves milk or soup or pepper, for example. Though many food terms can be supplied from other sources for this early period, the records are incomplete and often difficult to interpret.[20] Space allows me to mention only a few.[21]

The individual words denoting food and drink in the *Primary Chronicle* are stylistically neutral, although some can be identified as originating in the books inherited from Bulgaria. Many situations involving food and eating are in religious contexts. Some of the specific references to food are in biblical citations—many of them embedded in the comparison of religions sub 986— or in the sketches of the lives of exemplary monks. It is not surprising that of the six general words for food, two are clear borrowings from South Slavic. The broadest term is *k"rmlia*, which occurs only in the *kisel'* passage, where it was translated as "nourishment." It is associated with *k"rmiti*, which means "feed, give food to, nourish" and "bring up, nurture."

Three words for food are obviously associated with the root **ied-* "eat": *iad'*, *s"nied'*, and *iaden'e*; they were viewed by scribes as interchangeable. From the Philosopher's Speech a Russian reader could learn that Eve saw that the tree was good to eat, *dobro v" iad'* (variant *v" s"nied'*). In episodes from the lives of notable monks of the Kiev Caves Monastery, chiefly sub 1074, we find the two markedly South Slavic borrowings, *pishcha* and *brash'no*, used in very similar contexts.[22] A certain monk, Isakii, chose an extreme type of ascetisim, having as his only food (*iad'*, var. *iaden'e*) a single communion wafer (*proskura*) every other day, and he receives this food (*pishcha*) through a small opening in his cave cell. Later, having been led astray by demons and lain helpless for three years without tasting of any food (*ni ot kakogo brashna*), Isakii finally recovers. *Pishcha* usually is abstract or metaphorical. Thus in the 1037 encomium to Iaroslav, the patron of books, those who are able to eat "abundant food" (*pishchiu beskudnu* or *neoskudnu*) only because someone earlier had plowed the land and sown the seeds are compared to those who read books that have been prepared by the labor of others. The other three examples of *pishcha* are all explicitly "food of paradise." *Brash'no* is more concrete. In 907 the Greeks bring poisoned food and wine (*brashno i vino*) to Oleg and consider him a seer because he refuses to eat and drink. Oleg's treaties of 907 and 945 with the Greeks specify that the Rus' are to receive *brash'no*.

Bread, *khlieb"*, is the single most frequent food term in the *Chronicle*, occurring sixteen times.[23] It is specified as part of the rations in the 907 treaty and appears in an allusion to a psalm in a 980 editorial aside on deceit ("he who has eaten my bread has magnified deceit against me," Psalms 40:10). As in other languages, bread may be used broadly for sustenance in general, as sub 1096, when Oleg complains to Iziaslav that he has been driven from his own town: "Can it be that you don't want to give me here the bread that is mine?" *Khlieb"* is also the symbol of eastern orthodoxy, the true bread of the Eucharist, as opposed to the unleavened wafers, *opresnoki rekshe oplatki*, used by the Romans.[24]

On the whole, specific reference to kinds of food is unusual. Thus, *oats* and *bran* occur only in the episode of the Belgorod *kisel'*, and *wheat* recurs only in exotic contexts: sub 1068 in a citation from the prophet Joel (2:24) and sub 1114 in a borrowing from the Byzantine chronicle of Malalas, where miraculously rain mixed with wheat falls from the sky. To continue with grain, the term *zhito* most probably refers to grain in general; in 1024 *zhito* is imported into a region suffering from famine, while in 1071 shamans in the Rostov region accuse prominent women of hoarding *zhito*, and in 1086 a short encomium to Iaropolk Vsevolodich praises gifts *"ot" zhity""* to the church.[25] Finally, disaster strikes in 1094 when locusts eat *"mnoga zhita"*—presumably many kinds of grain (as well as every sort of grass, *vsiaku travu*).[26] In 1095 the locusts descend once more, eating grass and *prosa*—millet, for some reason in the plural.

Some sort of bread product was surely the nourishment that Abbot Feodosii of the Caves Monastery took when he literally walled himself into a cell in the caves for the forty days of the Lenten fast, but even the name is uncertain. He would take *malo kovrizhek"* or *kovrizhets'*, "a few *kovrizheks* (or *kovrizhkas*, or *kovrizhtsi*, or *kovrizhtsas*)"—with diminutive forms emphasizing the pious minimality of the supply. We may translate "a few little loaves," opining that some sort of hardtack is meant, but we must insist that the precise meaning is unknown. The nondiminutives *kovrig* and *kovriga* appear in fairly early sources, and the feminine *kovriga* is still known in Russian in the sense "round loaf."[27] However, Russian dialects have this form (with many derivatives) denoting a broad range of bread products, from ceremonial loaves to crude items used for animals. The 1230 entry in the Laurentian chronicle describes the sun as becoming "three-cornered like a *kovriga*" in the first stage of a total eclipse; this surely implies a crescent shape.

"Fruit," *ovoshche*, is mentioned as part of the provisions due the Rus' under the 907 treaty with the Greeks and as part of the booty the triumphant Prince Oleg took back to Kiev. His son Sviatoslav in 969 prefers Pereiaslavets on the Danube to Kiev because it is the center of good things, including, from Greece, "gold, brocades, wine, and various fruits (*ovoshcheve roznolichny*)." Isakii in his three-year illness refrained from fruit as well as bread and water and all other food, so we may assume that fruit was part of a normal monastic diet. No specific fruit is mentioned in the *Primary Chronicle*.[28] Nor is any vegetable named; there is only the information that some abstemious monks restricted their diet to *zel'e vareno* "boiled greens," about whose exact character we have no information.[29] The onion appears in the Philosopher's Speech: the Jews in the desert are murmuring against Moses and Aaron; they complain they had been better off in Egypt, for they "ate to the full of meat and onions (*luk*") and bread."[30]

Volodimer, as a benevolent Christian prince, makes *pit'e i iaden'e*, drink and food, available for everyone at his court (996). Moreover, to reach the sick and poor he orders wagons to circulate, loaded with *khlieby, miasa, ryby, ovoshch' raznolichnyi, med' v bochkakh i v drugykh kvas*", that is, bread, meat, fish, various fruits, mead in barrels, and in other barrels *kvas*.[31] Further, he has a Sunday banquet (*pir*") for his officers, offering *mnozhstvo ot mias" i ot skota i ot zveriny* "a great deal of meat," from domestic cattle and wild animals.[32] Note that the plural *miasa* is used regularly.[33]

The word *med'* means both "honey" and "mead," an intoxicating beverage made by fermenting honey boiled with water. It may be that in the citation about food for the public it was honey rather than mead in the barrels. On another holiday, however, mead is undeniably involved, for Volodimer, "brewing three hundred batches of mead" (*varia 300 provar" medu*) summoned his boyars and other notables. Mead is the ritual drink at the funeral feast for Olga's husband (sub 945). The availability of honey is fundamental to the Belgorod strategem, and the existence of a special princely honey chamber (*medusha*) fits with other evidence that honey was a vital economic asset. Honey as a means of paying tribute is mentioned (sub 946), and the ease of obtaining honey imported from Rus' (along with furs, wax, and slaves) is one of Sviatoslav's reasons for wishing to remain on the Danube. Monastic disapproval of Volodimer's many wives and concubines before he was baptized (sub 980) is buttressed by Solomon's warning that honey drips from the lips of an evil woman, Proverbs 5:3.

References to wine have already been cited, and it is notable that the verb *piti* "to drink" is associated with water in only two passages but with wine expressly in three episodes and with wine or mead implicitly in seven more. On being told of the Muslim prohibition against drink, Volodimer exclaims (sub 986), "For the Rus', drink is joy; we cannot be without it!" (*Rusi est' vesel'e pit'e, ne mozhem" bes togo byti*). On the other hand, the *Chronicle*'s arch-villain, Sviatopolk Volodimerich, who murdered two of his brothers, Boris and Gleb, and waged war against others, is lumped with wicked princes in general as "loving to drink wine with stringed instruments."[34] This phrase comes from a tirade against drinkers in Isaiah (5:12), following a denunciation (5:11) of those who rise early to "follow strong drink"—*kvas" goniashchim"*—through the day. In inherited texts *kvas"* usually means "leaven" (e.g., Luke 13:21, 1 Corinthians 5:6-7), but *kvas'nik"* in 1 Timothy 3:3 means "drunkard" and thereby implies a connection with intoxicating drink.[35] The *kvas* distributed by Volodimer to the public was probably a fermented drink, but it is unwise to try to specify its ingredients, for the word clearly was used for a considerable range of beverages. Nifon of Novgorod's definition of Lenten fare, in response to another of Kirik's questions, includes *kvas" zhitnyi*, "kvas of grain (or rye)," implying that other kinds existed.[36] Volodimer's *kvas* might well be beer. The word *pivo*, which since about 1500 has meant "beer" in all Slavic languages (but Bulgarian *bira*), does occur in old texts, but it is rare and means either unspecified "beverage, drink" or "drinking party, banquet." Yet the *Chronicle* does attest "hops" (*khmel'*) in a metaphorical phrase; the Volga Bulgars (ancestors of today's Chuvash) promise Volodimer peace "until stone floats and hops sink" (985). Since hops are grown exclusively for use in brewing, it seems safe to hypothesize that the authors and first readers of the *Chronicle* were familiar with beer or ale.

Offerings of food and wine as ritual welcome were surely part of the cultures of the peoples mentioned in the *Chronicle,* but the exact customs and their symbolic significance can only be guessed at. The poisoned food and wine offered by the Greeks to Oleg (907, see above) was presumably presented according to Greek custom. The Greek envoy to Rostislav (1047) proposes a toast; after drinking half of the cup, he secretly poisons the remaining wine and thus kills his host.[37] Sub 1111, the inhabitants of an eastern town, presumably Polovcians, greet the invading Rus' princes with fish and wine, very likely symbolic of obeisance. Whose ritual is involved remains obscure. The word "salt" does not occur in the *Chronicle;* the ritual presentation of bread and salt that is familiar from more modern sources is not mentioned.

Volodimer's largess demonstrates that he possesses the power to provide or withhold food, and the special feasts for his own officers show food used as an instrument for retaining power. Not only food but also utensils can be important: when his retainers complain that they must eat with wooden spoons, Volodimer commands silver spoons (*l"zhitsie*) be made for them. A very different symbolism is manifested when the skull of Volodimer's father, Sviatoslav Igorevich, is made into a cup (*chasha*) by the Pecheneg prince who killed him, "and they used to drink from it" (972).

Earlier, sub 946, the hardy Sviatoslav went on campaigns "without wagons or kettles," and he did not boil meat (*ni mias" varia*, again plural), but "slicing thinly horsemeat, game, or beef and cooking it on the coals, they would eat."[38] The terms *konina, zvierina,* and *goviadina* have a suffix that specifically designates the meat of the animal named by the stem. In this passage, horsemeat seems to be regarded as normal food. In a context of starvation (sub 971), when Sviatoslav is blocked by Pechenegs from passing the Dnepr rapids, things were so bad that a horse's head (*koniacha golova*) was very expensive ("a half grivna").[39]

Eating habits and food are used in many cultures as symbolic signals for identifying outsiders, i.e., "others," who are potentially threatening to one's community. The monks who wrote the *Primary Chronicle* are particularly alert to the improper—indeed revolting—foods believed to be permitted by non-Orthodox Christians as well as infidels. The account of Volodimer's inquiry into the religions of his neighbors emphasizes dietary rules as salient clues to the practical consequences of religious laws—more abstract theological beliefs are barely mentioned. Most prominent is pork, *svyinina* or *svina miasa*, which the Muslim and the Jewish spokesmen tell Volodimer is not to be eaten. The Khazars also forbid *zaiachina*, the meat of the hare. The *Chronicle* says that Volodimer objected to the prohibition against pork, thus implying that pork was included in the kinds of meat that he did eat.[40] Other remarks about aliens allude to the food allegedly eaten by pagans, near and remote. In the introduction to the *Chronicle*, in a passage borrowed from the Byzantine chronicle of George the Monk (Hamartolos), it says that the Hindus eat humans, and what's more they eat "like dogs."[41] Closer to home the Polovcians, a steppe tribe of nomads, are described as eating "carrion and all sorts of impure things, hamsters and gophers (*mertvechinu i vsiu nechistotu, khomieki i susoly*)." Much later, sub 1096, in a passage taken from the Revelations of Methodius of Patara, reference is made to Sun City (*S"ln'che miesto*), where there were unclean men of the tribe of Japheth who "ate all sorts of repulsive things, mosquitoes, flies, cats, and snakes, and their own dead, and miscarried fetuses and all kinds of impure animals" (*iadiakhu skvernu vsiaku, komary, mukhy, kotky, zmiie. mertvets' ne pogriebakhu no iadiakhu i zhen'skyia izvorogy iadiaxu, i skoty vsia nechistyia*).

And finally, it must not go unnoticed that the Philosopher's Speech records that the Lord gave the sons of Israel, yearning for the onions of Egypt, manna to eat.

NOTES

1. Samuel Cross's 1930 translation called it *The Tale of Bygone Years*, but in fact the words *poviest' vremennykh" liet"* in the opening line make little sense, "the tale (or story) of temporary (or temporal) years." Russian scholars long ago decreed that here, and only here, this adjective meant "past, bygone." Now, the phrase *vremena i lieta* "seasons (or occasions, or special times) and years" recurs in biblical and liturgical contexts, and equivalent Greek phrases are found in reference to histories. It is plausible that an original sequence of noun (in genitive plural) plus connective "and" (*vremen" i*) could be miscopied as a genitive plural adjective (*vremennyx*). To posit that the original text had *poviest' vremen" i liet"* is well within the bounds of justifiable emendation.

2. The *Primary Chronicle* text has come down to us only as the shared introductory portion of chronicles that continue the narration to 1292 or later but whose texts diverge after 1110. The oldest manuscript, the Laurentian copy of 1377, with two closely related copies (the Radziwill and Academy copies of about 1500) continue with events in Suzdal' and Rostov in the northeast, while the second-oldest witness, the Hypatian manuscript of about 1425, with a related copy (the Khlebnikov of about 1575), focuses on Kiev and the southwest. Despite frequent disparities among the copies, a plausible "original" version can be established. The Laurentian text is most reliably available in vol. 1 of *Polnoe sobranie russkikh letopisei* [Full collection of Russian chronicles] (PSRL), with variants from R and A; the Hypatian text, with variants from Kh, is in vol. 2.

3. Kievan culture of the eleventh and twelfth centuries was concerned with assimilating the literary heritage the Rus' had received from Bulgaria, the voluminous translations made between 863 and about 1020 from Greek into the new written language based on the Old Church Slavonic devised by Cyril and Methodius (863–885), with modifications introduced by later translators and editors. In Rus', the books were copied into a local variant of this traditional standard, starting probably in the 1030s, and by 1100 a new standard, which may be called Russian Slavonic, had emerged. The written culture of the Bulgarian Empire was dominated by monks; they selected for translation the works required in church services and those recommended for monastic use—secular writings were not on the list. The Rus' thus inherited only a narrow and specialized segment of Byzantine literature. The Church in Rus' remained largely in the hands of Greek clerics, but there is no evidence that Rus' bookmen learned Greek, much less made new translations. The PC represents some of the earliest native efforts at self-expression.

4. The whole text contains some 58,000 words, or 160–190 pages in the varying formats of modern editions. Any subdivisions other than those based on the yearly entries (which may have no text at all or may deal briefly with as many as eight topics) are subjective; my classifications here are intended only to provide a general picture of the chaotic and heterogeneous makeup of the PC.

5. The PC's longest entry is 986, which I have classed as two items. The first consists of brief statements about the Muslim, Jewish, and Roman Catholic faiths and a scathing critique of these three religions by a scholar (termed a philosopher) sent by the Greeks.

This section is particularly important for words referring to food. The second is the Philosopher's Speech.

6. For this inventory, the 2,000-word section under 1074 on monks of the Monastery of the Caves is reckoned as a single item. Other monasteries, in Kiev and elsewhere, are mentioned in many entries, but only in the briefest of phrases.

7. The great majority of items touching on the lives and deeds of several generations of rulers and their many subjects, along with the background data vital to interpreting the remarks, are extremely short. Of every three items, one will have fewer than 15 words, and one will have more than 75. No more than forty of the items are longer than 300 words, and only twenty have more than about 575 words.

8. This entry is one of the few items in the PC long enough to depict an episode in some detail.

9. This excerpt is from my translation of the PC, now being prepared for publication. It is based on a critical edition of the five witnesses (see note 2). The translation is as literal as possible.

10. As far as I could check, *kisel'* is otherwise unattested until more extensive books about everyday matters begin to appear in about 1550. A record of dishes served to the patriarch and his guests in 1699 mentions cold *kisel'* with juice, hot *kisel'* with *patoka* (the purest honey that flows by itself from the comb), cranberry *kisel'*. This last is probably like modern *kisel'*, where pectin from the fruit and starch from potato or maize flour produce a jelly.

11. This kind of preparation was widely known to Slavs as *kasha*. Modern Slavic dialects apply the term to a remarkable range of dishes, mostly made with grain (whether whole, cracked, or ground).

12. The text, with detailed analysis, is provided by Leopold K. Goetz, *Kirchenrechtliche und kulturgeschichtliche Denkmäler Altrusslands nebst Geschichte des russischen Kirchenrechts*, [Monuments of the church law and cultural history of Old Russia with a history of Russian church law], (Stuttgart, 1905), 249-51. Goetz's materials and discussion of Kirik's questions and similar Rus' ecclesiastical regulations demonstrate great variation during the early centuries; it is dangerous to extrapolate from Greek or later Slavic prescriptions, deliberations, and decisions. The chroniclers assume that their own way is known and correct; it is only rarely that the PC offers a hint that rules might differ regionally.

13. Etymologically, the root is **sok-* "juice"; lentils must be soaked before they are eaten, and typically they are served as purée, porridge, or soup.

14. Chickpeas were alien to non-Mediterranean Europe, and in any case are rarely mentioned in texts translated by Slavs. Like lentils, they must be soaked and are usually eaten in soft or liquid form, e.g., the *hummus* or *hommos* of Middle Eastern restaurants.

15. What is important is that the dish is special, with as exotic ingredients as are available. The pledges of 1103, we may surmise, were based on expectations of costly imported ingredients.

16. Etymologically, *kut'ia* is surely an adaptation of Greek *kukkia* "beans."

17. The Slavonic text is considerably more detailed than the available Greek redaction, so that the original Greek of many terms is not available. Some excerpts from the *Rule (Typicon)* were published in 1869. See A. Gorskii and K. Nevostruev, *Opisanie slavianskikh rukopisei Moskovskoi Sinodal'noi Biblioteki* [Description of the Slavic manuscripts of the Moscow Synod Library], section 3, part 1, esp. 258-262 on diet. Further samples were published in 1976 by D. S. Ishchenko, "*Ustav Studiiskii* po spisku XII v. Fragmenty" [*The Studios Rule* according to a twelfth-century copy: Fragments], in *Istochniki po istorii russkogo iazyka* [Sources for the history of the Russian language], ed. S. I. Kotykov, Moscow, 109-130.

18. The term *oriekh"* can be used for walnuts, hazelnuts, or others. For almond, we may assume that South Slavic *kliapysh'* (Ecclesiastes 12:5) might have been known to Rus' bookmen, but the normal term was adapted from medieval Greek as *migdal"*, attested in the *Studios Rule*; mod. R *mindal'* developed by about 1480.

19. The PC, remarks by Abbot Feodosii, and the answers to questions from Kirik and others (see note 12), are native Rus' sources. Translated works like the *Studios Rule*, even though clearly copied—and possibly edited—by Rus' scribes, must be viewed primarily as reflecting the Byzantine world of their origin; only with great caution can we venture to guess when their content had immediate significance to Rus' readers.

20. For example, the fig is common enough in the Bible, and some South Slavs had a word for it, *smoky*; this word was well known in Rus', but did it have a concrete meaning in Kiev or Novgorod for any but the very rich who might afford imported dried figs?

21. *Milk* (*moloko*, SSl *mlieko*) and *cheese* (*syr"*), *soup* (*ukha*, SSl *iukha*) and *bouillion, broth* (*varivo*) are well attested, but *sour cream* and *cottage cheese* and the words *borshch* and *shchi* seem to appear only after 1500.

22. Historically, the first is **pi-t-j-a*, with the root **pi-* as in *pit'e* "drinking; drink, beverage." The second originally meant "flour"; cf. Russian *boroshno* "rye flour."

23. The general *brashno* appears 9 times, *pishcha* 5, the verb "eat" 37. In contrast, *golod"*/*glad"* "hunger, famine" occurs 18 times, in eleven different passages, along with *post"* "fast" 19 times (and *poshchen'e* "fasting" 8), and *v"zd"rzhan'e* "abstinence" 15. (Compare "god" 333 times, "demon" 46, "town, fort" 303, "prince" 165, "church" 96, "soldier" and "monastery" 92, "abbot" 62, "weapon, weapons" 39, "sword" 16, "arrow" 12, "sabre" 4, "cross" 61, "sin" 53, "prayer" 43, "baptize" 49, "baptism" 23.)

24. Common Slavic *khlieb"* is surely a borrowing from some Germanic dialect, probably before 600, and is cognate to English *loaf*. The East Slavic *opriesnoki* (based on the root *priesk-* "fresh") is glossed with a West Slavic term, *oplatki*, adapted from Latin.

25. The general meaning "grain, yield, fruits, crops" fits with the etymology: Slavic *zhi-* "live" comes from ancient **gwei-*, which yields Greek *bi-os* and Latin *vi-t-a* "life."

26. *Zhito* in some regions is "rye," and this may be the sense in some of these contexts. The specific term *r"zh'* (unknown in South Slavic) is found in twelfth-century sources. *Khleb* has acquired the meaning "wheat" only in East Slavic, but exactly when is hard to determine. *Iachmen'* "barley," *p'sheno* "millet," and the generic *muka* "flour" are well known from inherited biblical texts. *P'sheno* and *p'shenitsa* are based on the passive participle of the verb *p'xati* "pound (in a mortar)." *Rice* was surely exotic; modern *ris* is borrowed from Low German.

27. Other types of bread surely were known. Old Testament passages attest *mlin"* as a sort of pan-fried bread; by about 1500 the form had become *blin*. Another biblical pancake is *skovrad'nik"* (Hosea 3:1), connected with SSl *skovrada* (Esl *skovoroda*) "frying pan." A ritual loaf, *korovai*, used particularly in weddings, is probably old; also *kolach'*, a round loaf (cf. *kolo* "wheel"), now usually a sweet cake or cookie. *Pirog* in the *Studios Rule* apparently meant "bread made from sifted flour"; it is probably a borrowing from a Turkic form parallel to modern Turkish *börek* "a small pastry with stuffing (of meat, rice)."

28. Other sources assure us that the Rus' had apples, plums, and a large variety of berries. It is probable that Oleg's booty included such durable items as dried dates and figs, while the monks were more used to berries. Note that older *ovowe*, a neuter collective (beside masc. *ovoshche'* in other early texts) means "fruit"; *frukty* does not appear before 1700.

29. The cabbage (*kapusta*) appears in a broad range of texts, starting with a note in the

second-oldest dated Slavic manuscript (1073). The *Studios Rule* mentions "salt cabbage," *kapusta solona*.

30. An early scribe misread *lukæ* and wrote *tukæ* "fat" instead; neither word recurs in the PC. The modified text still makes sense, and the error went undetected into the Hypatian and Khlebnikov copies.

31. Though *ryba* occurs nine times, no specific kind of fish is mentioned. The *Studios Rule* mentions "salted fish," *ryby prosoleny*. Nifon of Novgorod says (Goetz, 246) *ikra* "roe, caviar" can be eaten by laymen during Lent.

32. *Pyræ* is based on the root **pi-* "drink"; a proper banquet probably included ritual drinking.

33. Eggs and poultry go unmentioned, although other sources, in particular codes governing fines for stealing birds and specifying payment in kind for certain services, guarantee that chickens, ducks, geese, doves, pheasants (*teterev'*), swans (*lebed'*), cranes (*zheravl'*), and possibly partridge (*riab', oriab', eriab'*) were eaten. Copies of a traditional sermon on the rich man and Lazarus the beggar (cf. Luke 16:20–26) have interpolated varying lists of the luxurious foods on the uncharitable rich man's table, including hares (*zaiatsi*), deer (*eleni*), and boar (*vepreve*).

34. Distilled beverages were unknown; they came from the west after 1500, along with the names. The word *vodka* is adapted from Polish *wódka*, Ukr. *horilka,* and Belorussian *harelka* from P. *gorzalka*.

35. This verse is cited by the Greek Metropolitan Ioan of Kiev (died 1089) in denouncing priests who drink; the word here is the usual *p'ianitsa* "drunkard" (Goetz, 169). The noun *kvas* refers to a beverage only in East Slavic; "leaven" is the meaning elsewhere, and it is used in a series of derivatives for processes and products of leavening and fermentation and also pickling.

36. Text and discussion in Goetz (see note 12), 246.

37. Recall that the Belgorodians ate some *kisel'* before offering it to the Polovcians; this reassuring gesture is routine in situations of contact between hostile or possibly hostile representatives.

38. This passage implies that wheeled vehicles and cooking equipment were to be expected; no details of logistic planning for warfare in Rus' have come down to us. The episode also illustrates the two verbs for cooking, *var-i-* "boil, stew, brew" and *pek-* "bake, grill." The nouns *povar'* "cook" and *povar'nitsa* "kitchen" occur only in a monastery setting, except that Gleb's murderer is his own cook.

39. Eating wild horses is condemned by Feodosii of the Caves in about 1070; see note 40 below. There is no further evidence until 1169, when the Suzdal' Chronicle (PSRL 1 361.27; see note 2 above) reports that Novogorodians, under siege, ate horsemeat during Lent; this implies a desperate measure in a wartime crisis. (Novgorodian chronicles report the dire situation without mentioning horsemeat.) Centuries later in Muscovy, eating horsemeat is forbidden by church decrees.

40. He does not comment on hare, but hares are part of the rich food in the sermon about Lazarus (see note 33). Bishop Nifon says (Goetz, 294–295) it is licit to eat *vieverichina* "squirrel meat" unless it is *davlenina* "meat of a strangled creature." This stricture is based on Acts 15:29, essentially a reduction of all the old Jewish dietary laws to the abstention from "food offered to idols, and blood, and from things strangled"—a definition that was subject to constant discussion among different Christian sects. The Sixth Ecumenical Council's comment notes that some people prepare the blood of an animal artfully as food (but eating it is prohibited); a Novgorod copy (ca. 1292) of the

traditional text interpolates the definition "which they call *kolbasy*." This is the first mention of sausage among the Slavs.

41. Abbot Feodosii of the Caves Monastery, in an advisory of about 1070 to Prince Iziaslav Iaroslavich, warns against consorting with "Latins"—probably Polish Catholics—because they have improper beliefs and eat "impurely." "They eat with dogs and cats, they drink their own urine, and they eat turtles *(zhelvy)* and wild horses, and asses and strangled creatures *(udavlenina)* and carrion and bear meat *(medviedina)* and beaver meat *(bobrovina)* and beaver tail *(khvost" bobrov")*." The oldest copy is late 1300s; see I. P. Eremin, "Literaturnoe nasledie Feodosiia Pecherskogo" [The literary heritage of Feodosii of the Caves], *Trudy Otdela drevne-russkoi literatury* [Works of the Division of Old Russian Literature], no. 5 (1947) 159–184, esp. 170–71.

THREE

GEORGE E. MUNRO

Food in Catherinian St. Petersburg

In his monumental overview of urban history, Lewis Mumford characterized the imperial city of classical Rome as both a giant maw swallowing everything in its reach and a marvelously engineered cloaca spewing out its effluence.[1] However repellent both images may be, it is no accident that they have to do with food. The imperial city was a voracious consumer of foodstuffs. The excesses attributed by Petronius to the fictitious feast of Trimalchio described in the *Satyricon* gives some indication of the variety of exotic foods available to wealthy Romans.[2] Mumford's point was that the capital cities of empires consumed far more than they produced. There was also a theatricality to food consumption. Food was not simply eaten: it had to be the most costly food, the most exotic morsels, the most expansive (and expensive) quantities, the most out-of-season dishes, the most ostentatiously staged presentation at table to merit the approval of jaded and overstuffed courtiers.

Mumford's characterization applied in a quite different way to the vast majority of inhabitants of imperial capitals. They enjoyed cornucopic munificence only on those rare celebratory occasions when public feasts were held for them. On a more regular basis, however, they ate from the vast public storehouses—a simpler diet far blander but all the same a product of the imperial command to provision its capital city.

Imperial Rome was far larger in the second century than was imperial St. Petersburg in the eighteenth, but Mumford's characterization applies to Russia's imperial capital to a great degree as well. Toward the end of the reign of Catherine II, St. Petersburg annually required tens of thousands of bushels of wheat, barley, oats, rye, semolina, fresh and dried fruits and vegetables, and nuts; large quantities of beef, mutton, and pork; over three and a half million pounds of butter; and from five to fourteen million eggs.[3] In a single year the court alone consumed many tons of beef, poultry, and game animals and over half a million fish and eggs.[4] Agricultural resources over a wide area of the Russian Empire—and not just the northwest—were diverted or created to supply the capital's appetite. A canal system eventually named for Empress Mariia Fedorovna upon its completion in 1803 was begun as early as the reign of Peter I to enable St. Petersburg to be supplied with its necessities.[5] The Soviet historian Iu. R. Klokman estimated that as many as seventy or eighty thousand people traveled to St. Petersburg annually in the 1770s as workers on the river and canal craft supplying the capital.[6] The capital served as a stimulus to the growing of foodstuffs for the market. Peasants in Ingermanland, the historic province west and south of St. Petersburg, expanded kitchen gardens to grow cabbages, turnips, carrots, onions, and garlic, among other vegetables, for the new urban market.[7] Cereal production was increased in the middle Volga valley to provide the hundreds of tons of grain to be consumed in the city. In reshaping Russia's economy in order to feed a population that approached a quarter of a million souls by the end of Catherine's reign, St. Petersburg provided as unequally for its citizens as had Rome.

Banquets in St. Petersburg may not have been as dissolute as Trimalchio's feast; but surely, in terms of the varieties of food and the cost of entertainment, the banquet and ball given at the Tauride Palace on April 28, 1791, by Prince Grigorii Potemkin for Catherine the Great and other guests to celebrate a victorious war over Turkey would seem to rival it.[8] St. Petersburg occasionally saw as well the festive distribution of food to the common people. A case in point was another event celebrating the same victory over the Turks, when two veritable mountains of food with two fountains, one spouting red wine and the other white, were erected on Palace Square before the Winter Palace. Upon a signal from the empress, who stood on a balcony on the palace's second floor, the common people, held in check until that moment by a cordon of soldiers, converged on the center of the square and swarmed over both cornucopias, seizing what they could for their own consumption and that of their friends or families.[9] Like Rome, St. Petersburg also had a system of public granaries from which the common people might draw food at reasonable prices during times of shortage.[10]

We know of course that in St. Petersburg the rich and powerful ate well. To satisfy their palates, wines and brandies were imported from France and sweet wines from Hungary; fresh apples, pears, lemons, and watermelons were carried to the city by land and sea, as were Dutch cheeses, Prussian butter, and bacon from Hamburg; ices, sorbets, and other delicacies were prepared by chefs brought specially for their expertise from France and Italy. Nothing that could be prepared in the finest kitchens of western Europe could not be prepared as well by the chefs of St. Petersburg. Winter gardens and orangeries permitted herbs and garnishes to be grown year round. Testimony to the wealth and variety of cuisine can be found in the wide assortment of porcelain serving dishes and place settings either made at the imperial porcelain factory just outside St. Petersburg or ordered abroad from Meissen, Sèvres, and other producers of fine china. Formal dining rooms in the palaces of the aristocratic elite were furnished with tables easily capable of seating up to thirty people and more. Such great magnates as Ivan Betskoi, whose palace stood on the Neva's embankment immediately downstream from the Summer Garden, kept open tables for respectable company and could expect as many as fifty people to show up daily for dinner. The number that actually did attend table was dependent in part no doubt upon the reputation of the house chef. The official daily court journal records that Empress Catherine ate a formal dinner on most days with twenty to thirty courtiers, usually but not always an all-male company, listing them by name in order of precedence but rarely citing the menu.[11]

For the elite of St. Petersburg, as of Classical Rome, eating was combined with elements of theatricality. Eighteenth-century aristocratic culture, however, was not primarily a food-oriented culture. Sumptuous dishes had always been part of the elite's way in Russia (as in other countries) of distinguishing themselves from ordinary folk. To be able to eat delicacies out of season, to place on the table an array of dishes far more extensive and in much greater quantity than could possibly be consumed at one sitting was a symbol not only of hospitality and generosity but also of power. Even while providing a rich and varied cuisine, elite culture in the era of Catherine paid more attention to the container than to the contents. In this regard as in almost all others, the imperial capital's elite took their cue from the ruler. By reputation one of the worst tables in St. Petersburg in terms of the quality of preparation was that of Empress Catherine II. By her own admission she had little taste for fine food—she literally could not taste it—and as a consequence her table was one to be avoided. The food was poorly seasoned and tasteless, and little care was taken to serve it properly. This is not to say that the formalities of service were not maintined. For Catherine the food served at a formal social occasion was secondary. Far more important to her were the other activities that took place around eating. Catherine's preferred form of entertainment was the masquerade, the ball, or the theater. Iu. M.

Lotman has described the tone set by the crown and disseminated among the Russian nobility during the eighteenth century.[12] It seems to have been largely indifferent to food, placing its emphasis on other trappings of distinction: dress, manners, style, bearing. Satiating one's hunger impulse, the goal of feasts in seventeenth-century Muscovy, gave way to a concern for proper presentation of dishes. The coarseness of manners that drew the attention of foreign visitors to Russia in earlier decades yielded to a more delicate sensibility expressive of the enlightened values of court and aristocracy.[13] Hosts preferred to make their impression more by the dazzling array and decoration of serving dishes than by the taste or exotic origins of the food and drink contained therein.

But what about people for whom the cost of food was an important consideration? What exactly did average persons in St. Petersburg eat, and how was it presented? Did their diet consist simply of soup and bread, supplemented perhaps by vodka and *solenye ogurtsy* (pickles)? Or were people able to eat more balanced and variegated diets? Under what social circumstances, in what setting, did they eat?

It is not easy to reconstruct the diet of the common people of eighteenth-century St. Petersburg. From official price lists maintained by the city police we know something of the varieties of food bought and sold in St. Petersburg's markets at the time, but this may not tell us accurately what people were eating and drinking, much less how the various foods were being prepared. The police were responsible for maintaining lawful weights and measures and for ensuring that purveyors of foodstuffs in markets not demand more than the generally accepted profit margin of 10 percent. The weekly reports covered the city's well-established food markets. There was at least one market in each administrative district of the city. Markets were located in four-sided, arcaded buildings as well as in open squares or courtyards in which booths and stands were set up in leased allotted spaces.

But not everyone ate "on the market." That is to say, up to half of the people residing in St. Petersburg were not dependent upon the city's markets for their food. Many of the great aristocratic houses supplied their need for staples with produce exacted from the enserfed peasants whom they owned; the army had its own food supply system for soldiers who were increasingly assigned to live in barracks rather than being quartered with the civilian population; and other state agencies often provided food for their employees, whether hired or obligated, from state stores. A large number of residents kept kitchen gardens for their own use, sometimes selling the surplus, and a majority of homeowners kept livestock. The city's common pastureland was jealously protected from the infringement of urban sprawl by the planning commission in its projects for urban improvements. Officials estimated by the 1760s that as many as 20,000 head of cattle were kept by city residents.[14] Many of them were stabled or penned right in the middle of town in outbuildings or small sheds in inner courtyards. This remained the case well into the nineteenth century. When the disastrous fire of 1837 broke out in the attic of the Winter Palace, it was fed primarily by straw and the accumulation of dried manure from the animals kept in the attic by palace servants—a menagerie including goats, sheep, pigs, rabbits, ducks, and chickens.

Another indication that police lists of prices in food markets do not give a total picture of what was eaten in St. Petersburg is the evidence suggesting that certain types of food and drink were not even sold in the formal markets in each administrative district of the city but by street hawkers *(raznoshchiki)*. Milk, for example, is not found in the lists of food items sold in markets. Milk was sold door to door by young women from the city's suburbs, particularly Galley Haven *(Galernaia gavan')* at the western end of Vasil'evskii Island and Large and Small Okhta just upstream from the city on the right bank of the Neva River.[15]

Still, the food markets were the most important single source of supply for St. Petersburg's tables. From lists of ingredients it is not all that difficult to guess at the contents of prepared dishes. The weekly price lists compiled by police followed a formulaic organization.[16] Listed first were grains and cereals, sold by grade. We can perhaps infer the order of importance from the order in which they were listed. We find first rye, then wheat, buckwheat, barley, oats, millet, semolina, pease, and finally various malted grains. During the two weeks immediately before Easter in the Orthodox calendar, the finest sorts of flour, used in making special Easter cakes *(kulichi)* appeared on price lists. After grains came various oils (nut, poppy seed, hemp) and butter, followed by honey (subdivided into buckwheat honey and honey made from the flower of the lime or linden tree).

A surprisingly limited selection of fish was priced in the markets. Among them were various categories and qualities of sturgeon *(beluga* and *osetrina)*, caviar (both salted and pressed), smelt, and anchovies. Fish played an unexpectedly small role in the market, but the reason is not hard to find. They were ordinarily sold at river and canal landings directly from the boats of fishermen. What appeared in the markets were not locally caught fish but those that had to be transported to the city packed in barrels and jars.

Meat, on the other hand, seems to have been available at the market in a variety of cuts of various animals. Twice a year, in early winter and again at Shrovetide *(Maslianitsa)*, two or three open areas were traditionally set aside as special markets for selling whole frozen animals. One such market was

GEORGE E. MUNRO

A. O. Orlovskii, Coachmen's Market, *St. Petersburg 1820s.*
State Russian Museum, St. Petersburg.

located on Nevskii Prospekt (Avenue of the Neva) near the entrance to the Alexander Nevskii monastery. Frozen carcasses of various animals, including both large and small horned cattle, deer, pigs, sheep, hares, geese, ducks, chickens, and various wild fowl, were stood up in the snow—sometimes in comical anthropomorphic imitation—in order to entice buyers.[17] Beef was priced according to both cut and quality, with virtually every part of the animal sold. Those who could not afford the higher prices of brisket, round, ribs, or shank could perhaps purchase the head, lips, and feet (all three generally priced and sold together), the organs (liver, kidneys, rennet bag, and entrails), or suet. Mutton was priced whole, not in cuts, as was pork, with the exception of specially cured hams, both smoked and hang-dried. Veal, lamb, and suckling pig were all sold by the pair. Curiously, price lists were not maintained for domestic fowl. Was this because they were sold in venues other than the markets, perhaps by street hawkers? Later evidence from the nineteenth century suggests that this may have been the case earlier as well. Or did people keep their own fowl, from which they might also derive eggs, not to mention feathers from down to quill, each with its own use? It does seem that poultry were valued more for their eggs than their meat.

Cheeses (Parmesan, English, and Dutch) were also sold in markets, but not the local soft cheeses *(tvorog)* most commonly eaten. Like milk, cheese was sold on the streets. Other items used in food preparation that were sold in markets included vinegar from the Rhineland and of local production, horse-radish, raisins from Constantinople and Kaffa, berries, prunes, almonds, various sorts of nuts, several forms of sugar, including cane sugar from the Canary Islands. Coffee and expensive Ceylonese tea as well as cheaper black tea (Bakhcheva) were also sold. Prices were similarly maintained for exotic spices and seasonings: cloves, cinnamon, saffron, muscatel flower and nuts, cardamom, and mustard. Among the garnishes were fresh and pickled lemons, olives, capers, parsnip, and parsley. Apparently the Russian palate had not yet discovered pepper.

Finally there were the basic vegetables—cabbage, beets, and onions—together with garlic. Potatoes, so universally associated with Russia today, were virtually unknown to most Russians even in the capital city in the eighteenth century.[18] Only a few innovative souls, almost surely limited to those who read the enthusiastic recommendation of a new crop called "patetes" in an article in the *Trudy* (Works) of the Imperial Free Economic Society, were familiar with them.[19] Curiously, carrots, radishes, and turnips were likewise absent from the price lists maintained by the police.

Was it really possible that this variety of food was eaten even by the poor? How much did these foods cost, particularly the meats, in relation to the wages earned by common working people? Were they totally out of the price range of average citizens of St. Petersburg?

The police price lists were based on large units of measure. Grains, for example, were priced by the *pud* (36.11 pounds) or multiples thereof, as were meats, nuts, oils, cheeses, dried fruits, coffee, tea, and horseradish. The prices for spices were quoted by the Russian pound *(funt,* 0.9 pound avoirdupois) and those for vegetables by the hundred. Table 1 reduces the cost to smaller, retail units of measure and converts *puds* to pounds avoirdupois for selected food items.

The cost of food must of course be pegged to wages. Fortunately a good bit is known about what workers earned in eighteenth-century St. Petersburg. The following examples give some indication of the range of wages in various types of employment. In 1748 the servants Osip Leontovich Voitiakhov and Agafiia Andreevna Via, in the employ of English merchant Francis Gardner, earned 18 and 15 rubles annually plus clothing, respectively.[20] In the period from 1762 to 1768 unskilled laborers at the imperial Nevskii brick and tile factories working on a monthly basis earned three rubles a month.[21] In 1772 unskilled laborers working on the project to line canal and river embankments

GEORGE E. MUNRO

Table 1

Market Cost of Foodstuffs in St. Petersburg in 1764
Converted to English Measures
Prices in rubles and kopecks (one-hundredth of a ruble)

10 pounds of					
rye flour	.071	round	.019	almonds	.155
wheat flour	.088	ribs	.017	sugar, Canary Islands	.305
cracked wheat	.024	suet	.028	sugar, plain	.256
semolina	.305	*beef (whole pieces-large)*		coffee	.312
1 bushel of good		shank	.070	tea, Ceylonese	1.462
		cutlet	.030	tea, regular	.749
buckwheat	.534	calf pluck and liver	.250	*herbs and spices (pound)*	
ground barley	.572	kidneys	.080	cloves	2.300
oatmeal	.572	paunch (double tripe)	.100	cinnamon	3.000
millet groats	1.105	rennet bag, intestines	.040	saffron	6.500
peas	.762	head, lips, feet	.450	muscatel flower	3.300
oats	.243	*other meat (pound)*		muscatel nut	2.200
1 pound				cardamom	2.400
butter	.067	mutton	.039	English mustard	.500
nut oil	.244	smoked ham	.066		
poppy seed oil	.122	hang-dried ham	.055	*vegetables*	
hemp oil	.038	fresh pork	.050	cabbages (100 best)	.770
buckwheat honey	.058	large calves, pair	10.000	cabbages (100 worst)	.550
linden-flower honey	.055	lambs, pair	3.300	beets (100)	.660
fish (pound)		piglets, pair	1.100	onions (bushel)	.199
fresh salted osetrina	.067	*by the pound*		garlics (100)	.150
fresh salted beluga	.054	Parmesan cheese	.366	*other items*	
salted caviar	.061	English cheese	.152	fresh lemons (box)	10.000
pressed caviar	.091	Dutch cheese	.152	salted lemons (jar)	20.000
fish (bushel)		horseradish	.030	olives (jar)	.450
dried Pskov smelt	.133	raisins, Kaffa	.076	capers (jar)	.450
jar of anchovies	.490	raisins, Constantinople	.085	Rhenish vinegar (jar)	.366
beef (pound)		wine berries	.085	local vinegar (bucket)	.220
leg and brisket	.022	prunes, French	.137	parsley (100 sprigs)	.300
		prunes, plain	.050	walnuts (1,000)	1.320

with granite received a daily wage of 15 kopecks and unskilled carpenters' assistants received 25 kopecks a day. Blacksmiths on the same project received 5 rubles a month, carpenters 4 rubles, and stone chiselers 7 rubles monthly.[22] Vasilii Antipov, a worker in Christian Lehman's cotton textile plant at Shlissel'burg, was paid 4 rubles monthly in the first year of his contract and 5 rubles the second year, with the possibility of higher wages in the remaining three years of his five-year contract.[23] In 1765 muleteers (*izvoshchiki*) in the construction battalions of the Office for Constructing Her Imperial Majesty's

Houses and Gardens received 9 rubles 88 kopecks annually with another 3 rubles 88 kopecks for provisions.[24] City-hired lamplighters earned 18 rubles annually in 1770, firemen received 36 rubles annually in 1784 plus a small supplement for each fire fought, and in 1782 oarsmen on boats owned by the city warehouses took home 40 rubles annually.[25] Skilled craftsmen earned much more. Johann Jakob Tietzius, a master mason from Potsdam, found employment in 1764 with the Main Police Chancery at a salary of 250 rubles per annum.[26] It can safely be concluded, therefore, that many of the food items found in the city's markets were affordable for the common people in St. Petersburg and undoubtedly were included in their diets.

Fish and meat in particular were less expensive than one might think. Cattle were driven to St. Petersburg in large number over great distances. The Arkhangel'sk district in the north and the area around Astrakhan in the south represented the outer limits from which livestock were driven to the capital city.[27] Slaughterhouses located earlier in the century within the central city were removed early in the reign of Catherine II to the city's edge. This made it easier and more hygienic for abattoirs to dispose of unusable body parts and fluids and also eased congestion on the city's streets. From all reports the police in earlier years dreaded having to supervise the movement of large numbers of horned cattle through town. Pound for pound, cereals cost approximately one-third to one-half of the better cuts of meat. If caviar was actually available, the evidence suggests that workmen could afford it. After all, pressed caviar was traditionally part of the fare of peasants during the Orthodox Church's longer fasts. The contention has been made that Russian peasants ate healthily if monotonously in the second half of the eighteenth century.[28] With a much greater variety of foods available in St. Petersburg at affordable prices, it is not unlikely that eating habits may have begun to shift along with the move from village to city. In particular, the consumption of meat and meat products may have increased. This is not to suggest that meat was the main portion of the meal. Soups generally had a meat stock. Meat jellies *(kholodets)* or even an open-faced slice of suet on bread could have provided an important percentage of the caloric intake essential for living in the hardy northern climate.

Such exotica as lemons, coffee, tea, and imported herbs and spices were beyond the means of the simple people. Honey, on the other hand, a traditionally Russian product, may have been expensive for them but was not totally out of the question. The basic vegetables—cabbages, beets, onions, and garlic in particular—were by far the cheapest foods offered in markets. A good head of cabbage cost less than one kopeck, the hundredth part of a ruble. All four vegetables were traditional staples of the Russian peasant diet. Working people in St. Petersburg could fill their bellies with familiar fare.

The foodstuffs sold in markets were affordable for the general population only to the extent that they were sold in retail amounts. The price lists maintained by the police quoted prices in wholesale quantities: rye, for example, by the 9-*pud* (324-pound) sack and beef by the *pud* (36.11 pounds). Were foodstuffs actually marketed in such units, or were wholesale amounts the basis of pricing because products were shipped that way and it provided a simple basis for accounting? Before attempting an answer, it is useful first to examine the demographic profile of the average consumer. The majority of residents of St. Petersburg were men living there without families. As many as fifty thousand peasants migrated to the city each year during the summer season to work on construction projects. Their living arrangements were frequently crude and simple. Construction workers often slept in the buildings they were erecting. Those who were hired by the contractors in charge of the ongoing project to improve and embellish the embankments of the Neva River and the city's major canals by lining them with dressed granite stone lived together in hastily constructed shanties as work teams organized into artels. Thousands of others steered and sailed the raft and barge flotillas bringing wares downriver to the city for export or consumption. They stayed several months, often living along the riverbanks in the city's eastern (upriver) end in their overturned craft before finally chopping them up and selling them for firewood. Unlike soldiers, sailors, domestic servants, and many employees of governmental offices and bureaus, all of these men had to eat off the market. How did they manage it?

Many of the workmen in St. Petersburg came to the city already organized into artels. This uniquely Russian creation usually united men from the same town or district. Men from the same village or even the same region generally specialized in the same skill.[29] They elected a foreman from among their number, and it was he who negotiated the terms of labor with contractors, especially on construction projects. The number of men in an artel could be as few as five or as great as twenty or more. The larger artels found that it saved time and money to have their own cook. One member of the artel was designated to work more or less full time preparing food for the entire group. He visited the markets and purchased food items—and he was prepared to buy in wholesale lots, grain and meal in 324-pound sacks and meat by the *pud*. A proportionate contribution to the food budget was subtracted from each member's share of the artel's contracted wage.

But evidence from the project to rebuild the city's Morskoi rynok (Sailor's Market) following a fire indicates that food was sold in retail amounts as well.

A list was compiled in 1780 of all those renting space in Sailor's Market.[30] The space that each leased was not described as a "shop" but rather as a chest, table, or bench *(lar', shkaf, skam')*. These were not large establishments. A total of 296 people sold produce in the market. They included 60 who identified themselves as merchants *(kuptsy)*, 80 simply as townsmen *(meshchane)*, 133 as peasants, including 59 as serfs *(krepostnye)*, 54 as state peasants *(gosudarstvennye)*, and 20 as formerly under church and now state administration *(ekonomicheskie)*. Nine were women. Furthermore, the vast majority of traders in the market were legally registered not in St. Petersburg but in other towns or districts *(uezdy)*. Some were located nearby, such as Sofiia (the formal name for Tsarskoe Selo) and Kamennyi Nos, but others, such as Vologda, Sol' Vychegda, Iaroslavl', Kostroma, and Kaluga, were several hundred miles away. Curiously, none of the group was from Moscow. In all, thirty towns and districts besides St. Petersburg itself were represented by traders in foodstuffs. The majority of them seem to have been small operators, retail dealers rather than wholesale.

Cereals, whether eaten in soups and pottages or as bread, had been a staple of the Russian diet for centuries. There were more shops selling cereals in St. Petersburg than any other product. Figures from 1781 identify 498 shops specializing in grain, meal, flour, and bread. Their annual turnover amounted to at least 113,000 bags, or well over eighteen thousand tons.[31] Most of this amount was likely sold as whole grain, meal, or flour, not as bread. In 1763 there were only eleven master bakers registered in St. Petersburg.[32] More than two decades later, in 1786, when craft guilds were set up under the provisions of the previous year's Charter to the Towns, there were 205 butchers and 162 candlestick makers but only 97 bakers—all of them foreigners.[33] Moreover, there are few contemporary references to large-scale milling facilities in St. Petersburg. To the extent that citizens of St. Petersburg ate bread, it was overwhelmingly baked at home or in the institution responsible for feeding them.[34]

For other working men there were commercial eating establishments. The restaurant was barely making its appearance in St. Petersburg at this time. In fact, the word *restoran* did not gain widespread currency in Russian until the early nineteenth century, although one such establishment in St. Petersburg proudly advertised itself in 1900 as having been in business since 1786. Nobles and merchant travelers could take their meals in the hotels or inns where they stayed, although it was more common for travelers to stay with relatives or, lacking connections, make use of a letter of introduction to some significant personage or other and stay in private lodgings while in the city.[35] The common people took their meals in undistinguished eateries known as

GEORGE E. MUNRO

Table 2

Kharchevye in St. Petersburg, 1789-90

First Admiralty		29
Ward 1	8	
Ward 2	21	
Second Admiralty		1
Ward 1	1	
Ward 2	0	
Third Admiralty		12
Vasil'evskii Island		93
Ward 1	24	
Ward 2	22	
Ward 3	24	
Ward 4	3	
St. Petersburg Side		24
Vyborg Side		15
Moscow Quarter		0
Foundry Quarter		0
Rozhestvenskaia Quarter		0
Iamskaia karetnaia Quarter		0
Total		174

kharchevye (also as *kharchevni,* singular *kharchevnia*), from the word *kharch,* which can be translated into English roughly as "grub."

The *kharchevnia* differed considerably from its better-known cousin, the *traktir* (tavern). The latter was primarily a drinking establishment in which eating was of secondary importance. *Kharchevye* have been largely ignored by historical scholarship because their scale of operation was small and presumably not of long duration.[36] Relatively informal establishments, they often escaped the notice of the authorities and therefore of historians. We do have one interesting list, however, of commercial enterprises operating on ground floors and in the basements of residential buildings. The list was made in response to a request by the city government interested in regulating and taxing these eateries. According to this list—which surely identifies no more than a portion of the *kharchevye* operating in St. Petersburg—they were distributed unevenly in several parts of town, not necessarily in those where working men would be expected to predominate. Table 2 identifies the location of such establishments district by district.[37]

Vasil'evskii Island had the largest number. Vasil'evskii was associated in the late eighteenth century with the city's merchant port facilities—thus employing workers as stevedores, carters, and such like—and with tanneries, among other establishments. The three Admiralty districts made up the most central part of the city. This was where the imperial palaces (including the rambling wooden Summer Palace and masonry Winter Palace) were located, as well as the palatial residences of the aristocracy, many of the chanceries and bureaus of the imperial government, barracks for elite guards regiments, and the residences of diplomats and eminent foreign residents of the city. Still, nearly a fourth of the cheap eating establishments catering to working people were to be found there as well. The four districts lacking *kharchevye* entirely were characterized by their small detached cottages. All of them were located south of the Neva River. Together they made up the southeastern-most quadrant of the city. To judge from contemporary visual evidence, the buildings there had more in common with village *izby* (peasant cottages) than with urban structures. They were home to petty artisans, the coachmen who were responsible for staffing the imperial post service, and other migrants to the city who had managed to acquire a small plot of land and build some sort of house on it.

To understand the phenomenon of the *kharchevnia* more completely, it may be instructive to look in detail at some of the establishments located on Vyborg Side, the northeastern-most district of the city lying north and east of the Neva and its delta. The following chart lists the names of building owners and of the proprietors of the *kharchevye* located in the buildings.

Building owner	Kharchevnia owner
Andrei Ivanov, purveyor of coffee to court	Petr Ivanov Beliakov, peasant
Ivan Boroshnev, local merchant	Danil Ivanov, peasant
Aleksei Ovchinnikov, local merchant	Ovchinnikov himself
Fedor Bragin, sergeant	Lavrentii Larionov, local townsman
Pelageia Petrovna, soldier's widow	Fedor Timofeev Cheburakhin, peasant
Ivan Fedorov, junior officer	Ivan Andreev Sychev, peasant
Tikhanova, sergeant's widow	Gerasim Fedorov, peasant
Stepanida Matveeva, sergeant's wife	Arkhip Vasileev, peasant
Mikhail Skorniakov, local townsman	Petr Kuznetsov, Romanov townsman

Avdokia Cheroslova, local merchant widow	Kozma Gerasimov, peasant
Mikhail Pastukhov, Nerekhotsk merchant	Ivan Alekseev Sigarev, peasant
Dmitrii Alekseev, major	Martyn Samarin, local townsman
Baroness Anna Ivanovna, widow	Petr Alekseev Sivarov, peasant
Matvei Vasil'ev Zinov'ev, major	Grigorii Romanov Tarasin, peasant
Petr Maksimovich Kulebiakin, major	Aleksei Nazarov, peasant

In eleven of the fifteen cases the owners of the *kharchevye* were peasants. In only one case was the building owner also the owner of the eatery. In two of the remaining three cases a merchant registered in St. Petersburg rented the space for the eating establishment from a building owner who served in the army, and in the other the shop owner was a merchant from another town and the building owner a St. Petersburg merchant. Fully a third of the building owners were women, and in four of these five cases the woman was identified as a widow. Renting out space for an eatery provided a source of income for women in a culture where there were few respectable ways for them to earn a living. On Vyborg Side as in other parts of the city, peasants ran the *kharchevye* as places where other peasants could take their meals commercially.

Because the *kharchevnia* served only food and not drink, it was not regulated as closely as the *traktir*. The *traktir* was continually under suspicion as a place where stolen goods might be fenced, where other crimes against person or property might be plotted, and where prostitutes made contact with their clients. Fights and other minor disturbances of the peace were far more common in the *traktir* than in the *kharchevnia*. The *traktir* may also have brought together a larger range of people from across social lines. A man would drink with someone with whom he might not eat. The tendency for behavior in the *traktir* to cross over the line of what was socially and legally tolerated was made a matter for humor in the following light-hearted list of rules for a *traktir* catering to people of the better sort:

1. Leave all ranks outside the doors and likewise all hats and especially swords.
2. Precedence and snobbishness or any such like thing, when they exist, are to be left at the door.
3. Be merry, yet nothing damage or break, and don't gnaw on the furniture.

4. Sit, stand, and walk about as seems fitting, but do not sponge from anyone.

5. Speak moderately and not so loud as to cause headaches or earaches to those nearby.

6. Argue without becoming overly passionate and overheated.

7. Do not fly off at the handle and shout, but at the same time do not become boring and morose.

8. When innocuous diversions are concocted by someone, others are not to join in.

9. Eat for sweetness and for taste, but pour moderately, so that everyone might always be able to find his legs as he goes out the door.

10. Do not carry quarrels outside the house; and what goes in one ear had better go out the other before exiting the doors.

   If any one is found derelict in any of the foregoing by the testimony of two witnesses, then for every wrongdoing he must down a glass of cold water, not excluding even the ladies, and read a page of *Telemachus* aloud. And anyone who violates three articles in one evening must recite six lines from *Telemachus* by heart. And if anyone violates the tenth article, he is not to be permitted to enter anymore.[38]

Eating in St. Petersburg's *kharchevye* may have been devoid of theatrical aspects, but theatricality was clearly present in the city's *traktirs*.

Imperial St. Petersburg may not have rivaled the excesses of imperial Rome in its eating and drinking, but it did exert the same sort of power over the empire to satisfy its own wants. In the course of the eighteenth century, especially in its second half, food production in Russia's interior was increasingly harnessed to meet the demand. The resultant system of food supply made it possible for not only the elite but also the city's general population to eat well enough, even in years of high prices and shortage. While caution is necessary in arguing from the lack of evidence, it is nonetheless significant that there is no record in either official sources or diaries, correspondence, and memoirs of public disturbances in St. Petersburg during Catherine's reign because of high prices or shortages of food.

If St. Petersburg could be compared to Imperial Rome in its ability to consume, it fell short of Rome's capacity in the other point made by Lewis Mumford and cited at the beginning of this chapter, that of the marvelously engineered sewer. While the better avenues of St. Petersburg were supplied with sewers in the eighteenth century, the city was not identified in anyone's mind with gastronomic excesses on a Roman scale. To be sure, it was associated with a decline of morality in Russia. Both M. M. Shcherbatov and A. N. Radishchev made this point in their respective critiques of Catherinian Russia.[39] But criticism of St. Petersburg drew less on images related to food than on those related to the water that surrounded and the swamps that undermined the city. The curse placed on St. Petersburg, allegedly first voiced by Peter the Great's abandoned wife Eudoxia Lopukhina, was that it disappear beneath the waves, that it drown—an act of ingestion to be sure, but into the lungs not the stomach.

NOTES

The author would like to thank the International Research Exchanges Board and Virginia Commonwealth University for grant support that made the research for this chapter possible. He would also like to thank the staffs of the Russian State Archive of Old Charters, the Russian State Historical Archive, and the State Historical Archive of Leningrad District for their assistance.

1. Lewis Mumford, *The City in History: Its Origins, Its Transformations, and Its Prospects* (New York: Harcourt, Brace & World, 1961), esp. chap. 8.

2. Petronius Arbiter, *The Satyricon,* and Seneca, *The Apocolocyntosis;* both trans. with intro. and notes by J. P. Sullivan (New York: Penguin, 1986), 51-91.

3. Johann Gottlieb Georgi, *Opisanie rossiisko-imperatorskago stolichnago goroda Sanktpeterburga i dostopamiatnostei v okrestnostiakh onago* [A description of the imperial Russian capital of St. Petersburg and its environs]. (St. Petersburg, 1794), 588-593.

4. Petr Nikolaevich Stolpianskii, *Vverkh po Neve ot Sankt-Piter-Burkha do Shliushina*: *Putevoditel'* [Up the Neva from St. Petersburg to Shliushina: A guidebook] (Petrograd, 1922), vol. 1, 47.

5. See Robert E. Jones, "Getting the Goods to St. Petersburg: Water Transport from the Interior 1703-1811," *Slavic Review,* vol. 43, no. 3 (Fall 1984), 413-433.

6. Iurii Robertovich Klokman, *Ocherki sotsial'no-ekonomicheskoi istorii gorodov severo-zapada Rossii v seredine XVIII v.* [Essays on the social-economic history of the cities of northwestern Russia in the middle of the eighteenth century] (Moscow, 1960), 105-106.

7. See L. V. Milov and L. N. Vdovina, "Kul'tura sel'skokhoziaistvennogo proizvodstva" [The culture of agricultural production], in V. A. Aleksandrov et al., *Ocherki russkoi kul'tury,* chast' I [Outlines of Russian culture of the eighteenth century, part I] (Moscow, 1985), 117, 120.

8. L. I. D'iachenko, *Tavricheskii Dvorets* [The Tauride Palace] (Leningrad, 1988), 2-3.

9. Rossiiskii gosudarstvennyi istoricheskii arkhiv (RGIA) [Russian State Historical Archive], *fond* [fund] 470, *opis'* [index] 124/558, *delo* [item] 4.

10. A brief summary of the history of public granaries in St. Petersburg throughout the eighteeenth century may be found in George E. Munro, "Feeding the Multitudes: Grain Supply to St. Petersburg in the Era of Catherine the Great," *Jahrbücher für Geschichte Osteuropas* [Annuals for East European History], vol. 35 (1987), no. 4, 503-506.

11. Ministerstvo imperatorskago dvora [Ministry of the Imperial Court], Kamerfur'erskii tseremonial'nyi zhurnal, 1762-1796 [Ceremonial Daily Log] (St. Petersburg, 1853-1896).

12. Iu. M. Lotman, *Besedy o russkoi kul'ture. Byt I traditsii russkogo dvorianstva, XVIII–nachalo XIX veka* [Conversations on Russian Culture. Way of Life and Traditions of the Russian Nobility, Eighteenth and Early Nineteenth Centuries] (St. Petersburg: "Iskusstvo-SPB," 1994).

13. R. E. F. Smith and David Christian, *Bread and Salt: A Social and Economic History of Food and Drink in Russia* (Cambridge: Cambridge University Press, 1984), 112–116.

14. *Polnoe sobranie zakonov Rossiiskoi imperii s 1649 goda,* Sobr. 1 [Complete collection of laws of the Russian Empire since 1649, first series] (St. Petersburg, 1830), vol. 18, no. 13.125 (May 27, 1768), 679.

15. Georgi, *Opisanie,* 672; A. L. Shapiro, "'Zapiski o peterburgskoi gubernii' A. N. Radishcheva" [A. N. Radishchev's "Notes on Petersburg Province"], *Istoricheskii arkhiv* [Historical Archive], vol. 5 (1950), 258.

16. This particular example is drawn from Russkii gosudarstvennyi arkhiv drevnikh aktov (RGADA) [Russian State Archive of Old Charters], *fond* 16, *delo* 481, *chast'* 1, *listy* [sheets] 5–7 *ob.* [reverso]. The ensuing discussion of food prices is based on it.

17. Georgi, *Opisanie,* 126–127.

18. In 1765 the Ruling Senate issued instructions on growing potatoes, noting that "although this vegetable has been grown for some time in Russia, notably in St. Petersburg and in the palace and manorial gardens in that vicinity, and also in market gardens, still to this day it is little used by the common people. . . ." Quoted in George Vernadsky et al., eds., *A Source Book for Russian History from Early Times to 1917.* (New Haven: Yale University Press, 1972), vol. 2, 453. See also the discussion in Smith and Christian, *Bread and Salt,* 199–200.

19. The Imperial Free Economic Society was founded in 1765 with the support of Catherine II. Its purpose was to discuss and disseminate new methods and technologies in agriculture and industry. It was "free" in that it was not subordinated to any higher governmental agency. By the time the society ceased publishing its *Works* in 1915, some 280 volumes had appeared.

20. RGADA, *fond* 294, *opis'* 2, *delo* 561, *listy* 170a–186.

21. RGADA, *fond* 16, *delo* 434, *chast'* 1, *list* 245 *ob.*

22. RGADA, *fond* 16, *delo* 447, *chast'* 1, *listy* 70–73.

23. S. N. Valk et al., eds., *Istoriia rabochikh Leningrada, 1703–1965* [A history of Leningrad's workers]. (Leningrad, 1972), vol. 1, 56.

24. RGIA, *fond* 467, *opis'* 73/187, No. 103, *list* 28 *ob.*

25. RGADA, *fond* 16, *delo* 521, *chast'* 1, *list* 39; *fond* 248, *delo* 5693, *listy* 289–290; "Polozhenie o anbarakh" [The Regulation on Warehouses] (1799).

26. Roger P. Bartlett, *Human Capital: The Settlement of Foreigners in Russia, 1762–1804* (Cambridge: Cambridge University Press, 1979), 167–168.

27. The traveler Jonas Hanway referred as early as the 1750s to the bringing of "fresh provisions a thousand English miles by land, as those can witness who have often eat in St. Petersburg the beef of Archangel." Jonas Hanway, *An Historical Account of the British Trade over the Caspian Sea, with a Journal of His Travels.* (London, 1753), vol. 2, 139. See also Milov and Vdovina, "Kul'tura sel'skokhoziaistvennogo proizvodstva," 116.

28. Isabel de Madariaga, *Russia in the Age of Catherine the Great* (New Haven: Yale University Press, 1981), 460, 552; note 9 on 640 draws attention to the far better living conditions for peasants on the Kurakin estate in Penza in 1774 than in 1916.

29. Aleksandr Pavlovich Bashutskii, *Panorama Sanktpeterburga.* (St. Petersburg, 1834), vol. 2, 112–113.

30. RGADA, *fond* 16, *delo* 504, *chast'* 1, *listy* 79–90.

31. RGADA, *fond* 16, *delo* 511, *list* 3.

32. RGADA, *fond* 291, *delo* 12005.

33. Gosudarstvennyi istoricheskii arkhiv leningradskoi oblasti (GIA LO) [State Historical Archive of Leningrad District], *fond* 221, *opis'* 1, *delo* 115, *listy* 1-4.

34. For further discussion and elaboration on these points see Munro, "Feeding the Multitudes," 489-491.

35. M. I. Pyliaev, *Staryi Peterburg: Razskazy iz byloi zhizni stolitsy* [Old Petersburg: Tales of the capital's past life], 2d ed. (St. Petersburg, 1889), 443-444.

36. The term is not mentioned in the best brief history of Russian food culture, Smith and Christian's *Bread and Salt*. But see their excellent distinction among various types of drinking houses on 89-90, 215-216.

37. The source for the table and the ensuing discussion is found in GIA LO, *fond* 781, *opis'* 2, *delo* 680, *listy* 9-39.

38. These rules are printed on a framed broadside now hanging in the State Hermitage Museum, room 171. *Telemachus* refers to *Les Aventures de Télémaque* [The adventures of Telemachus] by the French educator François de Fénelon, whose ideas about education and upbringing appealed strongly to Catherine the Great.

39. Mikhail Mikhailovich Shcherbatov, *On the Corruption of Morals in Russia,* ed. and trans. A. Lentin (Cambridge: Cambridge University Press, 1969); Alexander Nikolaevich Radishchev, *A Journey from St. Petersburg to Moscow,* trans. Leo Weiner, ed. Roderick Page Thaler (Cambridge: Harvard University Press, 1958).

FOUR

Cathy A. Frierson

Forced Hunger and Rational Restraint in the Russian Peasant Diet: One Populist's Vision

In May 1872, subscribers to Imperial Russia's leading progressive journal, *Notes of the Fatherland,* opened its pages to find this passage:

> Someone begging for crusts is ashamed to beg and, coming into an *izba* [hut], having crossed himself, stands silently at the threshold, having said, usually to himself, in a whisper, "for the love of Christ, give." No one pays any attention to him; everyone is busy with something or talking and laughing, as if no one had entered. Only the woman of the house goes up to the table, takes a small piece of bread, from two to five *vershoks* [around six by six inches] in size, and gives it to him. He crosses himself and leaves.[1]

With these lines, Aleksandr Nikolaevich Engelgardt, scion of an old noble family, prominent St. Petersburg chemist, and recent exile to one of his family's estates in the Dorogobuzh district of Smolensk Province, drew his educated and urban readers into the world of the "hungry village."[2] He was writing from Batishchevo, where he had taken up residence following his arrest and loss of position at the St. Petersburg Agricultural Institute in 1870 as a result of radical student gatherings during his tenure as rector there. Subject to internal political exile,[3] Engelgardt turned immediately in 1871 to two endeavors that would occupy him during his years in Batishchevo: applying his knowledge in agricultural chemistry to farming on his estate and writing a series of letters to *Notes of the Fatherland* describing the world surrounding Batishchevo. His letters "From the Country" would become, by their conclusion in 1887, the most important and influential eyewitness account of rural Russia in the late nineteenth century.

Engelgardt used the practice of begging for crusts of bread *(kusochki)* in his first letter "From the Country" to illustrate his new understanding of the realities of rural existence, which confounded the images of rural life he had taken with him as he departed from St. Petersburg for his exile in 1871. The most important of these realities, he argued, was the specter of hunger, which was constant, pressing, and all important in defining the daily lives of peasants in his area. Engelgardt identified food as a subject that would enable him both to entertain and to inform as he drew his readers into the subsistence economy of the Russian village. Throughout the letters, activities surrounding the cultivation, processing, distribution, and consumption of food products found a place in Engelgardt's reconstruction of his world. The question of consumption would ultimately become the most important, for it drew him beyond description of the peasant milieu into a moral indictment of his own gentry culture.

There are several reasons why food and eating were so central to Engelgardt's experience and portrait of rural life. First, his own regimen shifted from one of eating in St. Petersburg restaurants and privileged hostesses' homes, where he enjoyed oysters, foreign cheeses, and French wines, to a diet constrained by the produce of the gardens and fields of Batishchevo and the culinary repertoire of his peasant housekeeper, Avdotia. Engelgardt had a modest income which permitted virtually no luxuries beyond his nightly indulgence in vodka, so he had to adapt quickly to rural eating habits. Second, Engelgardt was a chemical agronomist whose very decision to take his exile in the form of residence on an abandoned family estate stemmed from his desire to apply his knowledge to agriculture. In Smolensk Province, this meant that he was dealing primarily with cereal crops as the staple of local farming. Third, his relations with local peasants often revolved around their need for grain, which they borrowed from him in exchange for labor in his fields. This alerted him to the marginality of their existence. Engelgardt was also much impressed by Darwin's *Origin of Species* and tended to perceive Batishchevo and its environs as a tableau of the struggle for existence tempered by systems of mutual aid. Just as for the species described by Darwin, so for the peasants of Engelgardt's neighborhood, survival or extinction was often a matter of maintaining access to enough food to subsist from one season to the next. Finally, Engelgardt judged that such phenomena as *kusochki* could indeed become emblems of rural life in the perception and consciousness of his urban audience, as they had been from the earliest writings by Russian intellectuals on the peasantry.[4]

By turning to food as both subject of inquiry and metaphor in his commentary, Engelgardt joined his peers Tolstoy and Dostoevsky in identifying it as a cultural marker in a binary vision of Russian society.[5] Indeed, Engelgardt explored the question of cuisine in Russia through a series of binary oppositions which served to underscore the sense of division in Russian culture.[6] At the same time, he strove to produce an analysis of peasants' food habits that was embedded in a rich, what we would call "thick," description of their culture. Engelgardt's text thus lends itself to at least two purposes for the study of food in Russian history and culture. First, it offers information on diet and cuisine in Russian culture as a precursor to both anthropological and culinary history approaches to the society.[7] Second, it serves as an example of the uses to which food was put in the debates about Russian culture that dominated political-literary journals in the post-Emancipation era.

Engelgardt's eyewitness account of life in and around Batishchevo in the Dorogobuzh district of Smolensk Province was the centerpiece of two debates that dominated public discussion in the first thirty years following the Emancipation: the peasant question and the agrarian question. The former consisted of a broad debate about the nature of the Russian peasant and the future role of the emancipated peasantry in developing Russia. The latter tended to focus more narrowly on problems of Russian agriculture. As a prominent chemist, Engelgardt enjoyed tremendous authority as he held forth from his family estate on almost every aspect of peasant culture and agricultural reform. For anyone who hoped to be a legitimate voice in the public discussion of the peasantry and farming in Russia, Engelgardt was required reading.[8] Readers received his letters as a source of empirical information on the subjects literary authors were addressing through their fiction or journalists were addressing in their essays. Engelgardt's letters from the country, then, constituted one of the major commentaries of his time and, as such, provide us with the opportunity to examine how food had made its way into the sensibilities of intellectuals confronting the various layers within their national culture.

Food as an Element of Subsistence

Engelgardt used food to construct two broad paradigms in his letters. The first was the paradigm of the subsistence economy of the Russian village. The second was the paradigm of the rational nature of peasant society and the irrational nature of educated Russian society. His first two letters carefully

CATHY A. FRIERSON

V. G. Perov, Reapers Returning from the Field in Riazan Province, *1874.*
State Tretyakov Gallery, Moscow.

displayed the web of a subsistence economy in rural culture. It was in this context that he discussed the practice of begging for crusts of bread and stressed the power of hunger to shape rural relations. In his third letter "From the Country," Engelgardt declared,

> If I knew how to paint, I would paint a "reaper," but not the kind they usually paint. There would be the most narrow field, scraggly rye, the sun would burn, a *baba* [peasant woman] in only a shift, wet with sweat, with a groggy face gone dark from hunger, with dried-up blood on her lips, mowing, beginning to reap the first sheaf—but she will not even have any grain tomorrow, because she won't have time to grind it. She will already be satisfied with *kasha* made from steamed rye.[9]

This image of a starving peasant woman struggling to bring in enough rye at the earliest possible moment of the harvest to prepare a green mash departed dramatically from idealized notions of the countryside as the seedbed of Russian culture and the home place of a bountiful or nurturing Mother Russia. Engelgardt offered instead a calendar of hunger, providing a description of the progressive worsening of the peasant diet in the months between one harvest and the next: "In our province, even in years of a good harvest, rare is the peasant who has enough of his own grain to last until the next harvest; almost everyone has to buy grain, and those who have nothing with which to buy grain send their children, old men and old women to beg for 'crusts' in the commune."[10]

Because of this inability to make it from one harvest to the next, Engelgardt explained, peasants almost inevitably experienced a steady deterioration of their diet.

> Beginning in the autumn, when there is still a supply of rye, they eat
> pure bread in abundance, and if the head of the household has been very
> frugal, they will even have adulterated bread through the autumn—I
> have seen peasants like this. Beggars come, they give out crusts. But
> then the head of the household notices that the grain is running short.
> They eat a little less, not three times a day, but two, and then one. They
> add chaff to the bread. . . . When a *muzhik* [male peasant] has used up
> all of his grain and there is nothing else to eat, the children, old women,
> old men put on sacks and go to beg for crusts in neighboring villages.
> . . . When the crusts begin to run out, they hitch up the horse again
> and go begging. Some feed themselves this way the whole winter and
> even gather a reserve for the spring. . . . When it becomes warmer, the
> mushrooms come up, but one works badly on mushrooms alone.[11]

This was one of many passages in which Engelgardt turned to this theme,
adding scene upon scene of the peasants' efforts to make it through the hungry
months of late autumn through the summer without starving to death.
Women who were unable to come by flour during the hungry months or
green rye at the beginning of the harvest, he suggested in an ellipsis ("While
the women . . ."), exchanged their bodies for the bread to fill them. His
housekeeper found this perfectly understandable, "'And what on earth are you
going to do,' Avdotia says, 'and . . . not starve to death!'"[12]

The progression—from pure bread to "chaff," or adulterated, bread to raw
mash or prostitution—clearly shocked Engelgardt. He wanted to make the
peasants' hunger and their want as palpable as possible. For this reason, he
offered a graphic description of chaff bread, which, he explained in his second
letter,

> is prepared out of unwinnowed rye, that is, a mixture of rye with chaff,
> ground directly into the flour, out of which bread is made in the usual
> way. This bread is a doughy mass, permeated with thin needles of chaff;
> it has no special taste, it's like ordinary bread, its nutritive value is, of
> course, less, but its most important disadvantage is that it is hard to
> swallow, and someone who is not accustomed to it cannot swallow it at
> all. If he does swallow, then he'll begin to cough and cough and feel
> some kind of uncomfortable sensation in his mouth.[13]

Crusts of bread and loaves of prickly chaff bread were the staples of the peasant
diet for most of the winter and spring months, Engelgardt explained. In his
letters, they constituted not only genuine elements in the peasant's material
existence but also symbols of their exploitation at the hands of privileged
members of Russian society. It was against the backdrop of the hungry village

that Engelgardt went on to articulate his binary vision of Russian food cultures.

✿ Diet as Evidence of the Rational Peasant

Coming from the world of the privileged intelligentsia, the upper echelons of the bureaucracy, and the leading coterie of Russian scientists, Engelgardt experienced a complex of mental, physical, and emotional shocks as he settled into his chosen site of isolation. As an inveterate rationalist and scientist, however, he was determined to figure out how the peasants had adapted and were continuing to adapt to the conditions which so unsettled him. Out of his determination to sort out the strands of the web of the peasants' culture came the second major piece of Engelgardt's legacy for Russian culture and peasant studies: the model of the rational peasant. In the simplest formulation, Engelgardt believed that there was a reason for every aspect of village culture, and he took up the challenge of identifying and displaying those reasons to his urban readers. One of the most concentrated examples of this effort focused on the peasant diet, which Engelgardt described as a revelation to him, and which he offered as a model of intelligent, rational adaptation to the needs of labor and economy. This rational adaptation, in turn, would come to serve as a moral contrast to the irrational food habits of the gentry and privileged urban residents of Russia in Engelgardt's construction. His focus in this exploration of food cultures was on consumption.

Engelgardt's description of the rationale of the peasant diet came in his seventh letter from Batishchevo, which marked the apex of his populist tendencies during his exile. Delighted with the logic that he had discovered in the peasants' attitudes toward food and eating, Engelgardt exploited the opportunity this topic presented to contrast the reasoned pragmatism of the Russian peasant with the irrational patterns of educated Russians' excessive consumption. Out of a disquisition on the eating habits of one group of peasants, he was able to develop a metaphor for cultural division in Russia that began with the subject of potatoes.

Strolling around his estate one autumn day, Engelgardt came across a group of diggers whom he had hired to clear his meadows. He was surprised to note that they were eating a lunch that consisted solely of boiled potatoes. He had expected the diggers, who were prosperous and known for their good diet among the peasants, to dine on more elaborate fare. Puzzled, he asked the foreman of the group to explain. The peasant responded by offering Engelgardt a description of the calculated food habits of his men and of peasants in general. It all depended, he explained, on the kind of work and the kind of pay. "Everybody knows that you'll work as well as you eat. If you eat potatoes, then you'll make potatoes. If you eat *kasha,* you'll make *kasha.*"[14] He went on to say that he and his men were eating only potatoes that day because Engelgardt was paying them a daily wage, which they would receive regardless of the amount of work they finished. Thus it wasn't worth it to consume heartier, more costly fare. Because they didn't intend to exert themselves excessively, they could economize on their food. For the first time in his life, Engelgardt encountered people who ate less than they could, who decreased their consumption to meet their absolute needs in terms of energy.

Engelgardt was frankly fascinated by the level of calculation in the diggers' diet.

> People know *precisely how much they can work on what kind of food, and what kind of food is appropriate for which kind of work.* If you can haul away, say, one cubic meter of dirt in a certain amount of time on food that consists of cabbage soup with salted beef and buckwheat *kasha* with lard, then by substituting barley for the buckwheat *kasha,* you will haul less . . . ; on potatoes, even less. . . . The digger, the man who chops firewood, the wood-cutter, each knows this with complete precision, so that, knowing the price of food and labor, he can calculate with utter precision which food is more profitable for him and he *does* calculate it.[15]

Here we have a St. Petersburg scientist infatuated with the untutored yet precise scientific reasoning of peasants. He was moved to proclaim that "German scholars have already studied feeding livestock to the point that they know how much and what kind of fodder one needs to fatten up a bull or to receive the greatest quantity of milk from a cow, but the diggers, I think, when it comes to feeding a working man, can outsmart scholarly agronomists."[16]

Not only the peasants' calculation of their dietary needs, but also their food preferences challenged Engelgardt's concepts of nutrition. He found that virtually every opinion about diet held by educated Russians was turned on its head in the peasant milieu. Whereas educated Russians placed greatest emphasis on meat as the key to a good diet, peasants measured a diet by the amount of fat it contained: "The more fat there is in food, the better. . . ."[17] A peasant hostess's way of honoring a guest was to load up the meal with fat. Thus "a village *baba* offering a fried potato or fried mushrooms, will pour raw hempseed oil over them without fail." [18] Not meat but fat was the food for a day of hard labor in the field. The best possible breakfast was "simply a piece of pork lard. . . ."[19]

Meat was also less important than acid, and specifically lactic acid, as a component of the peasants' diet. Engelgardt found that peasants in his area believed that "without something acidic, lunch for a worker is no lunch."[20] For this reason, cabbage soup made with sauerkraut was the staple of the peasant diet. *Borshch* made from pickled beets satisfied the same requirement. If these staples had run out in the summer, sour whey or sour cream in fresh vegetable soup provided the lactic acid. If even these were unavailable, peasants would turn to a sour *kvas,* a sour-mash, fermented drink made from husks of sour black bread. Engelgardt found this aspect of the peasant diet perfectly logical. "It is clear that given the traditional composition of popular Russian foods, this acid, and in all probability the salt that accompanies it, are absolutely necessary for the diet."[21]

Engelgardt was also struck by the way the peasant diet provided a balance of digestible foods and foods that were difficult to digest. Whereas the diet of educated Russians was designed to eliminate all foods that were difficult to digest, peasants insisted on the need to incorporate them, especially for fieldwork during harvest. An American child might be urged to eat her oatmeal because it will "stick to her ribs"; the Russian peasant called for solid food that would "hold you to the earth," so that during mowing, for example, your feet would "be, so to speak, driven into the earth every minute when you make a stroke with the scythe."[22] Good, solid food for heavy labor "stays in the belly for a long time" and makes it possible to work long and hard in the field, "because as soon as the intestine is empty, it is impossible to work at hard jobs and it is essential to eat again."[23]

Dense, coarse, heavy, sour black bread satisfied these requirements and thus was a major part of the diet. The ideal worker's lunch consisted of heavy, sourdough black bread; cabbage soup with fatty, salted beef or pork; and buckwheat *kasha* with butter or lard. With a glass of vodka to wash this all down, Engelgardt concluded, this meal would be "the most solid, the kind that makes it possible to do the maximum of work: to haul the greatest quantity of dirt, to cut the greatest quantity of firewood, to saw the greatest quantity of boards."[24]

Fatty, salted beef or pork was preferable to fresh beef or pork because it was more difficult to digest and thus kept the belly full longer. On the 180 days when the Orthodox Church prescribed some kind of fast, salted meat would be replaced by salted fish, probably smelts, and butter by hempseed oil.

A good meal was one which not only held peasants to the earth, but also made them thirsty. The denser the meal, the more the peasant would want to drink at the end of it. Thus Engelgardt reported this kind of appraisal of a prosperous peasant: "The food is good at his place: everything they eat is dense, you won't break the bread into pieces, the *kasha* is like wood, you can cut the pudding *{kisel'}* with a knife."[25] A truly satisfied peasant would seize a bucket of *kvas* at the end of the meal and drink half of it down in one gulp.

While that image might suggest a gluttonous appetite, Engelgardt's vision of the peasants' diet was the very antithesis of gluttony. In his construction of their world, peasants ate not for pleasure but primarily and consistently for fuel. Their subsistence economy granted them no room to consume beyond their basic energy needs. Their consumption patterns displayed an essential equilibrium that was tied to their life of labor. In this way the peasants' food culture was a manifestation of the rational, subsistence economy that shaped their existence in Engelgardt's representation.

He went beyond this rather straightforward articulation of the rational peasant, however. In his world view, anyone who ate more than he or she needed had crossed over from subsistence to excess, from being caught in the struggle for existence and being its potential victim to overconsumption and exploitation. In this representation, he moved from simply recounting the components of the peasant diet as distinct from that of educated Russians to a moral evaluation of the eating habits of these two groups within the same culture.

Food as a Metaphor for Cultural Division and Exploitation

The revelation for Engelgardt about the peasant diet was not so much its content as its logic. That privileged Russians and Russian peasants had different diets was news to no one, including Engelgardt himself.[26] That peasants had an articulated comprehension of the uses of food that varied with their energy needs was news and, furthermore, news that buttressed the binary vision of Russia as a world of haves and have-nots, of those who profited from the labor of others and those who provided the labor.

During his first encounter with the diggers on his estate, Engelgardt asked the foreman if his men would work harder if he, Engelgardt, paid them higher wages and ordered them to eat well while they were on his job. The foreman replied, "Food doesn't make you work when you don't push yourself. Food, you know yourself, only makes you be more lazy, not work. . . . If we did it that way, our food would turn to fat, then we would stuff ourselves on your place so much that the boys wouldn't let a single *baba* get past us!"[27] This reply suggests that at least this particular peasant considered eating beyond one's basic needs to be a step down the slippery path toward sloth and sexual license. Eating would then be more than a necessity; indeed, it would be a seductive pleasure. In Engelgardt's description, peasants rarely viewed eating primarily as pleasure. The calculation that lay behind their rational diet exemplified the complex of essential pragmatism, calculation, and restraint that characterized their eating habits. He found these habits in striking contrast to those of his gentry neighbors and friends in St. Petersburg. While cuisine as consumption in the village supported Engelgardt's vision of the moral pragmatism of the peasants of Batishchevo, cuisine as consumption among privileged Russians illustrated the very opposite.

On several occasions in his letters, Engelgardt described what he clearly considered to be dissipation among the rural gentry. During a trip to the provincial capital for elections of delegates to local councils of self-government, he found that eating and drinking were the real business of the day, while the elections themselves were subsidiary. From the time he arrived at a relative's estate through their journey to Smolensk and their two days at the elections, they did nothing but wine and dine. At home, *en plein air* as they drove to town, and at the assembly, they indulged in Rhine wine and burgundy, punch, appetizers, and other fine gentry fare. He concluded that "if there had been anything of interest at the assembly, I would not have been aware of it. . . ."[28]

After he had lived in the country for several years, Engelgardt found that his constitution could no longer tolerate such excesses. In one of his rare forays off the estate, he attended the name day party of one of his relatives. He recounted the day's entertainment:

> At one o'clock in the afternoon we had breakfast—at home I would have already eaten lunch and lain down for a nap—of course, first of all there were vodka and various hors d'oeuvres. We drank and ate. We began to eat lunch: paté with truffles, we ate them, we drank a burgundy wine, a real one, not the kind they sell in district towns with the label "Burgundy Night." Then something else. We ate and drank for two hours. Then napped. At seven o'clock in the evening we had dinner. Here it was the same, we ate and ate, drank and drank, to the point of nausea even.[29]

A good vomit would have been a relief for Engelgardt, who was so sick that he decided he might actually die, and considering it "better to do it at home . . . I left the next day for home." Salvation came at a common posting inn, where a peasant acquaintance urged him to cure himself with some "solid Russian food." After a glass of vodka, cold fish soup, and thick *kasha,* his ills "vanished like magic." This experience only strengthened his conviction that "we educated people eat less rationally than cattle who have a good master" and that doctors really knew nothing about the fundamentals of nutrition and digestion.[30] The consumption habits of the wealthy literally made Engelgardt sick, and he used his experience to demonstrate the distance between the appropriate, constrained diet of the peasants and the inappropriate, unconstrained appetites of the rich.

Embedded in his binary opposition of constraint versus excess there also lay the opposition between native Russian food and imported foreign food. He noted not only the amounts of food eaten at gentry gatherings but also the types, which invariably included such items as paté with truffles and German and French wines. Indeed, in recounting his decision to attend an agricultural exhibition sponsored by the Smolensk Agricultural Society during the third year of his exile, he confessed that, being a "sinful person," he wanted "to see civilized people who eat various kinds of *fines herbes,* and not adulterated bread. . . ." He went so far as to admit that he longed for the most emblematic of foreign delights, oysters.[31] Foreign, refined foods thus constituted one of the major attractions for Engelgardt when he described himself as being "drawn to town." And their antidote when he could no longer tolerate them was "solid Russian food." Once again, food served as a cultural marker recognizabale to readers of *Notes of the Fatherland* who read his letters as part of a larger discourse in which virtually all discussion of the countryside and peasant culture fit into some kind of binary category.

As the digger's statement Engelgardt chose to quote about the effects of too much good food suggests, he was also attuned to the linkage between sexuality and eating, which many anthropologists and literary critics have noted.[32] While Engelgardt did not attribute sexual properties to specific foods, he did link gluttony and lust. These companions entered his physiognomy of the engorged country gentleman. In a description of a ceremonial luncheon attended by members of the local gentry, Engelgardt drew a direct line between gluttony and sexuality. The luncheon was the final event at the Smolensk agricultural exhibition, which Engelgardt generally found to be a waste of time and money because he learned nothing useful there. He resolved to attend the luncheon in the hope that at last something substantial would come of his trip to the capital. He was disappointed.

> It was simply a luncheon. At first, of course, we drank and ate appetizers, then we sat down at the table; there was no time for conversation until we had satisfied our hunger. Then, when we were drinking, we got lively, and about halfway through the lunch began to demand that the fellow playing music during the meal play "something from *La Belle Hélène.*" Then we drank again, then came the champagne, the telling of off-color stories, and finally dancing. . . .[33]

Engelgardt's disappointment prompted him to compare the luncheon to gatherings of peasants around his estate in Batishchevo.

> I have never heard anything off-color at these luncheons, nothing outrageous: everyone decorously gets seated at the table, sits staidly. They talk about farming, about the weather, about anticipated harvests and work on the side, about local interests. They drink, they begin to get rowdy, the conversation livens up, but never does it take an immodest turn; they start dreaming about that wonderful time when grain will grow well; even so, there is nothing off-color or immodest.[34]

Even in a mood of celebration and indulgence, peasants did not descend into the lower form of sensual pleasures that Engelgardt attributed to the local gentry. The reason for this distinction in Engelgardt's explanation lay in the fact that peasants were genuine workers, practical people engaged in real, living labor, while the gentry farmers had no genuine interests or occupations. Instead, they were fatuous gluttons who continued to live off the labor of the local peasants and whose very idleness led them to indulge all of their appetites to the extreme.

Not only were gentry appetites excessive. They were also artificial, in Engelgardt's view. From the beginning of his construction of two food cultures in Russia, Engelgardt had drawn the connection between labor, appetite, and consumption. In trying to convey the reality of hunger in the countryside to his urban readers, he wrote that he doubted their ability to understand real hunger, given that they had to take a stroll to stimulate their appetite before dining.

It was not only the prosperous, rural gentry whose eating habits contrasted with those of the peasants. Essentially, all nonpeasants profited in some way from the peasants' labor and poverty and from the subsistence nature of their eating habits. Whereas peasants ate *kasha,* the others ate meat. In a brief but telling statement, Engelgardt made an explicit connection in his seventh letter between the subsistence economy and diet of the peasantry and the meat-eaters who were not peasants. Here he reminded his readers that "I speak the truth: the rich bureaucrat who has enjoyed a juicy filet mignon, and the poor student who chews gristle in eating-house soup, and the driver who uses five-kopek salted beef in his soup have meat only because most agricultural workers eat an exclusively vegetarian diet and the children of these agriculturalists do not have enough milk."[35] Even within the village community, only the prosperous peasants could eat meat, and Engelgardt's description of them also suggested that exploitation was involved: "if one person has enough land and others do not have enough, then, of course, one can buy beef for two or three kopeks a pound from those in need, and he can sell them his grain for the same price."[36] Meat thus became another marker of the cultural divide between the haves and have-nots in Russian culture, between those who exploited and those who were exploited, between those who consumed and those who were figuratively consumed. Engelgardt did not acknowledge the discrepancy between his disquisition on the absence of meat as a feature of the rational peasant diet and the absence of meat as a feature of restraint caused ultimately by exploitation.

Engelgardt's comments about food and exploitation were part of broader currents of thought in Russian culture. The most obvious one was populism. His comment about the common privilege of the rich bureaucrat and the poor student who could eat meat while the peasant could not resonated with the message of Petr Lavrov's *Historical Letters,* one of the founding works of Russian populism, in which Lavrov reminded educated youth that they were all indebted to the Russian peasant for the privilege of being cultivated. Lavrov's entire argument stressed both the debt owed to the underprivileged and the Darwinian struggle for existence which had shaped human as well as natural history.[37]

Darwinism, with its images of competition both between and within species for territory and food, pervaded Engelgardt's writing as it did that of many of his contemporaries. Such concepts as natural selection, adaptation, and mutual aid recur throughout Engelgardt's letters, feeding into the vocabulary of Darwinian struggle that permeated public debate about rural culture in Russia during the 1870s and 1880s. This was particularly acute in his discussion of the village strongman, the *kulak*.

By the time Engelgardt wrote his tenth letter from Batishchevo for *Notes of the Fatherland,* he had concluded that the Russian countryside was a scene of perpetual competition and exploitation. This conclusion was evident in his statement "Every peasant has a bit of the kulak in him; with the exception of those who are stupid, and especially goodhearted people and the 'carps' in general. Every *muzhik* is a *kulak,* a pike, to a certain extent, who is in the sea so that the carp will not doze. . . . everyone is proud of being a pike and tries to eat up the carps."[38] The "pikes" of the Russian village were those peasants who no longer simply fed off the land but who also fed off their fellow peasants. They were the winners in the struggle for existence.

While every peasant had a bit of the *kulak* in him, not every peasant became a full blown *kulak* in Engelgardt's assessment. For him, the critical issue was labor. Any peasant who continued to work with his own hands, who continued to sweat and toil over the land, continued to be a peasant, a genuine agriculturalist, a *krest'ianin*. "Of course, he makes use of another man's need, he makes him work for him, but he does not build his well-being on the need of others, but builds on his own labor." Such a peasant crossed over from the moral, nonexploitative labor of *krest'ianstvo* into the immoral, individualistic, exploitative activities of *kulachestvo* when his sole goal became profit and he no longer labored for his sustenance. He became a *kulak* when he crossed two moral boundaries in Engelgardt's mental universe. The first was that he no longer labored. The second was that he moved from subsistence to profit and overconsumption. Again, an eating metaphor served to illustrate his point. Of the genuine peasant, he said, "He expands his farm not with the goal of profit alone; he works to the point of exhaustion, he does not get full, he does not eat his fill. Such a peasant of the land never has a big gut the way a real *kulak* does." Of the genuine *kulak,* he said, "This one prides himself on his fat gut, he prides himself on the fact that he himself does little work."[39] In sum, Engelgardt's *kulak* was an early form of the fat capitalist who would later dominate Soviet political imagery.

What were the sources of Engelgardt's sensitivity and aversion to consumption beyond subsistence? Was it primarily a product of his own experience in Batishchevo and his first confrontation with limited food resources there? Was it a product of populist ideology? Did it violate his chemist's preference for equilibrium in the consumption of energy as calories and the expense of energy through labor? Is there something peculiarly Russian, or at least non-Western, at play here?

I think we can dispose of the final suggestion on one level rather quickly. One has only to read Elena Molokhovets' prescriptions for evening tea in the most popular cookbook for the middle and upper classes of post-Emancipation Russia to be assured that Russians of her class had no objection to overconsuming.[40] In *A Gift to Young Housewives,* Molokhovets recommended for a late-evening gathering a spread that included vases full of fresh fruit, pastries, cookies, sherbet, jams, various breads, "veal, ham, beef, breasts of hazel grouse, turkey or chicken, tongue, hare, Swiss cheese, Russian or homemade cheese, some grated green cheese," various butters, and an assortment of ciders, teas, liqueurs, cognac, rum, and mulled wine. Was such overconsumption solely a product of Westernization, one might ask? Again, the answer is no, for accounts of travelers to Muscovy described sumptuous, one may even say outrageous, banquets as features of Russian court culture that struck their Western sensibilities.[41] Indeed, Adam Olearius wrote of Russian men in the seventeenth century, "They place great store by long beards and large stomachs, and those who have them are held in high regard."[42] These aspects of Russian culture assumed almost fantastic dimensions during the reigns of Elizabeth (1741–1762) and Catherine the Great (1762–1796) and came to be associated with their Frenchified excesses, but they were not a uniquely Western import. By Engelgardt's day, there seems to have been a long history of eating beyond one's fill and having a fat belly in Russia. So why did he come to despair of these practices?

He was certainly not alone; Tolstoy, for one, would eventually develop a moral philosophy centered on the rejection of overconsumption with vegetarianism as the hallmark of virtue.[43] Darra Goldstein's chapter in this volume ("Is Hay Only for Horses?") offers striking examples of other educated Russians who equated the diet of people of their class with immorality and ill health. In Engelgardt's case, the personal experience of constraint in Batishchevo was crucial. His avowed astonishment over the calculations in the diggers' diet and his surprise over the role that begging for crusts of bread played in saving the peasant population in lean years testify to the impact that living within the rural world had on his vision of food, diet, and consumption. His own forced economizing and adaptation to the local food supply were part of his personal transformation. He learned that he could live on less. Having learned this lesson, he became an outsider on the occasions when he sat at gentry tables and an insider at peasant tables. What had been pleasure before became physical misery and a source of moral discomfort.

His moral discomfort, in turn, issued from his constant interaction with men and women who were hungry and whose hunger drove them out into the cold to beg for bread or to barter away their future labor for grain. As a landowner himself and, furthermore, a landowner who required peasant laborers to work his fields, he became aware of the extent to which the entire Russian, post-Emancipation agricultural economy depended on the availability of cheap, desperate labor. This, in essence, meant hungry peasants. Having confronted this reality, he came to see food and patterns of consuming as the fulcrum of social and economic relations in Russia. A name day at a relative's house was no longer simply good company and good food; it became a symbol of the exploitation, degradation, and forced hunger of the majority of the population who worked the fields and slept in the izbas beyond his relative's demesne. The emaciated, darkened peasant woman with her bloody and cracked lips Engelgardt imagined painting became a ghost who floated behind the well-dressed and well-fed members of his family as they toasted each other with burgundy and champagne.

Engelgardt's perceptions were undoubtedly shaped, in turn, by populist currents in Russian thought and by their antecedents in Western thought. Faith in reason and science, based fundamentally in the Scientific Revolution and the Enlightenment, characterized the thinkers of Engelgardt's generation. He was speaking their language when he framed his discussion of food cultures in terms of rationality and irrationality. While his conclusion that the gentry diet was immoral matched the conclusion of peasants (see chapter 5 in this volume), the language he used was secular, not religious. In this sense Engelgardt was laying claim to his complicated inheritance as a privileged intellectual in Russia. As a man of position and wealth, he had indulged his own appetites on the foreign foods of Frenchified, upper-class cuisine before his exile to Batishchevo.[44] Once stripped of his position and consigned to the economies of constraint, he was intellectually prepared to perceive and represent the food cultures of rural Russia through the filter of science-based Enlightenment ideals which assigned virtue to natural, rational equilibrium and restraint and assigned corruption to artificial, irrational, and unbalanced excess.

As an authority in the rational discourse of the 1870s and 1880s, Engelgardt was able to impress upon his readers the seasons of plenty and want in the countryside and to suggest the physical discomforts of constrained consumption, culminating in a diet of adulterated bread and dried crusts or starvation. As a chemist, he could not resist offering an analysis of the chemical and nutritional properties of the ideal peasant diet of fat, acid, and dense foods. These aspects alone of his treatment of the food culture of the villages around Batishchevo deepened contemporary understanding of rural life.

By going beyond description to analysis and commentary, Engelgardt also contributed to the tradition of the binary conceptualization of Russian culture by setting the peasants' diet against that of the gentry in his verdict on consumption and exploitation in Russian culture. Again, he offered visual images to illustrate cultural distinction and moral disparity. On one hand there were lean, often emaciated peasants whose eyes either reflected careful calculation or betrayed their desperation grown of hunger. On the other stood those with fat guts, gentry and peasant exploiters alike, who not only ate and drank their fill but also overate and overdrank to become swollen artifacts of their dissipation and exploitation.

NOTES

I first presented this paper at the conference "Food in Russian History and Culture," Russian Research Center, Harvard University, October 1, 1993. I would like to acknowledge the bibliographic and editorial assistance I received from Ronald LeBlanc and Joyce Toomre, both of whom contributed to the conceptualization and development of this piece. My work on A. N. Engelgardt was supported by a National Endowment for the Humanities Translation Grant, the International Research and Exchanges Board, Rutgers University, and the University of New Hampshire.

1. A. N. Engelgardt, "Iz derevni," *Otechestvennye zapiski,* vol. 202 (May 1872), 44-45.

2. This was Geroid T. Robinson's term to describe the post-Emancipation village; see his *Rural Russia under the Old Regime: A History of the Landlord-Peasant World and a Prologue to the Peasant Revolution of 1917* (New York: Macmillan, 1949), 94 ff.

3. Under the terms of his exile, Engelgardt could not travel abroad or live in any city in the Russian Empire where there was an institution of higher education. Within those limits, he was able to choose his own residence. He and visitors to his estate were also subject to constant police surveillance. He was able to subscribe to Russian and foreign publications, to have personal and professional correspondence, and to receive visitors. Thus, although cut off geographically from his professional life as chemist and professor, he was able to pursue his intellectual and practical interests.

4. See, for example, Aleksandr Nikolaevich Radishchev, *A Journey from St. Petersburg to Moscow,* trans. Leo Wiener, ed. Roderick Page Thaler (Cambridge: Harvard University Press, 1958), 219-221.

5. For a discussion of Tolstoy's use of food as metaphor, see Ronald LeBlanc, "Unpalatable Pleasures: Tolstoy, Food, and Sex," *Tolstoy Studies Journal,* vol. 6 (1993): 1-32; Lynn Visson, "Kasha vs. Cachet Blanc: The Gastronomic Dialectics of Russian Literature," in Robert L. Belknap, ed., *Russianness: Studies on a Nation's Identity in Honor of Rufus Mathewson, 1918-1978* (Ann Arbor: Ardis, 1990), 60-73; Paul Schmidt, "What Do Oysters Mean?" *Antaeus,* vol. 68 (1992), 105-111.

6. On the earlier binary structures in Russian thought, see Iurii M. Lotman and Boris A. Uspenskii, "Binary Models in the Dynamics of Russian Culture (to the End of the Eighteenth Century)," in Alexander D. Nakhimovsky and Alice Stone Nakhimovsky, *The Semiotics of Russian Cultural History* (Ithaca: Cornell University Press, 1985), 30-66.

7. R. E. F. Smith and David Christian made use of Engelgardt's information in their fundamental study, *Bread and Salt: A Social and Economic History of Food and Drink in Russia* (Cambridge: Cambridge University Press, 1984), 258-261, 278, 337, 349-50. Engelgardt served as one of Smith's and Christian's most consistent sources on nineteenth-century peasant diet.

8. For the best biographical study in English on Engelgardt, see Richard Wortman, *The Crisis of Russian Populism* (Cambridge: Cambridge University Press, 1967). For Engelgardt's place in debates about the peasant, see Cathy A. Frierson, *Peasant Icons: Representations of Rural People in Late Nineteenth Century Russia* (New York: Oxford University Press, 1993). For an abridged translation of Engelgardt's letters, see Cathy A. Frierson, trans. and ed., *Aleksandr Nikolaevich Engelgardt's Letters from the Country, 1872-1887* (Oxford: Oxford University Press, 1993).

9. A. N. Engelgardt, "Iz derevni," *Otechestvennye zapiski,* vol. 206 (January 1873), 85.

10. Ibid.

11. Ibid., vol. 202 (May 1872), 45-46.

12. Ibid., vol. 206 (January 1873), 83.

13. Ibid., vol. 202 (June 1872), 174.

14. Ibid., vol. 242 (January 1879), 102.

15. Ibid., 105.

16. Ibid.

17. Ibid., 106. Engelgardt's reference to the general opinion that meat was the measure of a good diet was consistent with ideas about the need for meat protein in a healthy diet held throughout Europe during his time; see Smith and Christian, *Bread and Salt,* 260.

18. Engelgardt, "Iz derevni," *Otechestvennye zapiski,* vol. 242 (January 1879), 106.

19. Ibid.

20. Ibid., 111.

21. Ibid., 112.

22. Ibid., 105.

23. Ibid., 113.

24. Ibid.

25. Ibid., 114.

26. As Smith and Christian explain (*Bread and Salt,* 173), by the eighteenth century, "Upper class diet had long differed from that of the mass in terms of quality and quantity, now it also came to differ in style."

27. Engelgardt, "Iz derevni," *Otechestvennye zapiski,* vol. 242 (January 1879), 103.

28. Ibid., vol. 202 (June 1872), 180-81.

29. Ibid., vol. 242 (January 1879), 108.

30. Ibid., 109.

31. Ibid. vol. 212 (February 1874), 295.

32. Jack Goody provides a survey of anthropological literature on this topic in *Cooking, Cuisine, and Class* (Cambridge: Cambridge University Press, 1982), 11, 114-115. See also LeBlanc, "Unpalatable Pleasures," and Leonid Heretz's contribution to this volume (chap. 5).

33. Engelgardt, "Iz derevni," *Otechestvennye zapiski,* vol. 212 (February 1874), 330-331.

34. Ibid., 331.

35. Ibid., vol. 242 (January 1879), 117.

36. Ibid., 119.

37. Peter Lavrov, *Historical Letters,* trans. James P. Scanlan (Berkeley: University of California Press, 1967), 135.

38. Engelgardt, "Iz derevni," *Otechestvennye zapiski,* vol. 254 (January 1881), 411.

39. Ibid., 412.

40. Joyce Toomre, trans., *Classic Russian Cooking: Elena Molokhovets'* A Gift to Young Housewives (Bloomington: Indiana University Press, 1992), 114-115.

41. Visson, "Kasha vs. Cachet Blanc," 62; Smith and Christian, *Bread and Salt,* 112-118.

42. Samuel H. Baron, trans. and ed. *The Travels of Olearius in Seventeenth-Century Russia* (Stanford: Stanford University Press, 1967), 126.

43. See LeBlanc, "Unpalatable Pleasures," and his contribution on Tolstoy's vegetarianism in this volume (chap. 6).

44. See Toomre, *Classic Russian Cooking,* 20-22, for a brief discussion of the French influence on Russian cuisine.

FIVE

LEONID HERETZ

The Practice and Significance of Fasting in Russian Peasant Culture at the Turn of the Century

For any general survey of the role of food in prerevolutionary Russian popular culture, one of the most important problems is fasting, the religiously dictated periodic abstention from certain types of food. An examination of the practice of fasting in late Imperial Russia will enhance our feeling for the shape and texture of everyday life in that era, and an analysis of the thinking which motivated it will show a number of essential characteristics of the popular conception of the divinely ordained order of the universe and humanity's place in it.

This chapter examines fasting as conceived of and practiced by the Russian people. The concept of "the people" is a fundamental category of Russian thought and, through the influence of Russian writers and scholars, of foreigners' analysis of Russia as well. The idea of "the people" has rightly been criticized for its absolute and metaphysical tendencies and for its obscuring of the diversity of Russian popular life. Nevertheless, the concept retains an inescapable and profound significance if placed in the context of the problem of modernization. From this point of view, "the people" refers to the great mass of the Russian population—primarily peasants but also hereditary townspeople and the lower orders of the ecclesiastical establishment—which continued to live within the confines of the traditional culture, based, as are all traditional cultures, on a religious understanding of the world and its phenomena. "The people" is thus defined in distinction to the Westernizing elite (usually termed "educated society" or "the intelligentsia" in the broader sense of the word), which was the product and carrier of the modernity, i.e., the secular and rationalist world view, in Russia. This chapter focuses on fasting on the part of the people and will be an attempt to use fasting as a means of gaining insight into the traditional culture and understanding it on its own terms.

Chronologically, this chapter concentrates on the end of the nineteenth century and the beginning of the twentieth. This is for two reasons, one practical and the other conceptual. On one hand, the high stage of development achieved by Russian scholarship and journalism by the turn of the century produced a substantial body of observation of popular life which provides a pool of source material for the analysis of the largely nonliterate traditional culture. On the other hand, the period is most interesting in analytical terms because by that time the traditional culture, the carriers of which had been subjected to an accelerating pace of far-reaching socioeconomic and cultural change in the aftermath of the Emancipation and as a result of increasing urbanization, industrialization, and, perhaps most important, improved communications (both in the physical and the psychological sense), began to show unmistakable signs of crisis and incipient disintegration. This aspect of crisis and conflict with the dominant modern culture brings out the fundamental characteristics of the traditional culture in exceptionally sharp relief. Since fasting was an essential part of the order of life for traditional Russia and was motivated by the basic ideas of the old religious world view, it offers a sharp focus for analysis with broad implications.[1]

Fasting in the Laws and Teachings of the Orthodox Church

Fasting was not an original discovery of the Russian peasantry but, like all else in the traditional culture, was introduced to it by the Orthodox Church and its civilization, the ultimate source of most of the notions of the folk culture.[2] To provide a basis for further discussion it might be worthwhile to summarize Orthodox regulations regarding fasting and the ideas which lay behind them.[3]

In dietary terms, Orthodox fasting is essentially the abstention—in degrees of severity which vary with the seasons of the church calendar—from animal products and from oils.[4] Meat and dairy products are to be refrained from on Wednesdays (in commemoration of Judas's betrayal and of the Cross) and Fridays throughout the year, except for the weeks, *sploshnye sedmitsy,*[5] following the greatest holy days—Easter (*Paskha* in Orthodox terminology), Trinity (Pentecost), and Christmas ("Nativity")—and one week in the run-up to Great Lent. They also are to be refrained from during the relatively mild fasts leading up to Christmas (the *Rozhdestvenskii post*, six weeks; in Russian popular usage it is called *Filippov post* and *filipovka*, since it begins the day after the feast day of Saint Philip, November 14) and to the feast day of Saints Peter and Paul (June 29; the length of this fast—the *petrovki*—varies according to the date of Easter, since it begins one week after Trinity) and on the eves of major holidays. The preparation for Lent begins with a week during which all food is allowed, followed by one in which dairy products and fish may be eaten (this is *maslenitsa*, analogous to the Western Carnival, albeit marginally more ascetic, for there is no meat as in Mardi Gras). During Great Lent, *Velikii post* (forty days), and Holy (*Strastnaia*, "Passion") Week (counted separately, contrary to the Roman Catholic tradition), and the nearly-as-stringent two-week fast preceding Dormition (*Uspenie*, August 15, the "Assumption" in Western parlance), fish is foresworn, as is vegetable oil on certain days of heightened penitence (*sukhoiadenie*, "dry eating," the highest stage of dietary asceticism). In popular usage, the days preceding major fasts are called *zagoven'e*, for that is when one prepares to fast (*govet'*), while periods without fasting are called *miasoedy* ("meat-eating").[6]

The total number of fast days (with the varying degrees of severity just sketched out) in the Orthodox calendar comes to about 180 (depending on the length of the fast of Peter and Paul), or half the year. Weddings were forbidden on these days (and married couples were enjoined to refrain from marital relations), as were displays of merriment, such as dances and popular festivities. The Russian Empire, in the best style of Enlightened Absolutism, assigned the compartment of religion and certain basic social functions to the church. Ecclesiastical rules regarding the timing of matrimony were therefore strictly enforced for Orthodox Russians, and public life followed the church calendar to a large extent, with both holidays and fasts being officially observed.[7] Without an awareness of the church calendar and of the schedule of fasts and feast days we cannot sense something as fundamental as the rhythm of communal and personal life in prerevolutionary Russia.

In theoretical terms, Orthodox fasting may be examined on several levels. At the risk of simplifying and distorting a body of thought of great complexity and depth, one might sketch the theoretical underpinnings of fasting as follows. At its most basic level, fasting is a means of penitence and purification. At the same time, it is a manifestation of the Christian attitude toward the body and its functions and of the asceticism which permeates the Orthodox Christian world view. Although Orthodox Christianity, unlike the other religions which produced the ascetic ideal or offshoots which took it to extremes, does not teach that the body itself is evil, it nevertheless assigns the body a decidedly secondary importance in comparison to the spirit and views it as a potential source of trouble as the concrete tie to the fallen, "sensual" world. Therefore the body must be controlled and subordinated to the spirit and become a vehicle for the attainment of the higher values of the faith and communion with God. Fasting is the means by which the flesh is tamed. It should be stressed that it is not the forbidden food itself which is bad (as in *kashrut*—traditional Jewish dietary law—or in the Muslim injunction against pork) but the effects of its immoderate consumption. In the physiology of late antiquity (from whence came the regulations in force up to the present day), fats and oils were seen as the fuel of bodily passions, especially sexual, and as sources of spiritual intemperance, of anger and self indulgence. Fasting is therefore also directed toward taming the sexual aspect of human nature, not only by enjoining periodic celibacy but also by restricting the consumption of what are seen as the fuels of sexual desire. Thus Orthodox monks and the hierarchy—according to church practice, all bishops are from the ranks of the monastics, as opposed to the married "secular" priesthood in the parishes—are not only supposed to be celibate but also to abstain from meat. Indeed, the fasting regulations—as well as the order of church services—are derived from monastic rules, generated in Christian Egypt and Syria, brought to their final form in Byzantium, and subsequently applied to the church as a whole, including the lay majority. [8] Thus, Russians fasting at the turn of the century (like all practicing Orthodox up to the present day) were continuing a mode of behavior deriving from the very distant past according to rules drawn up in late antiquity.

In theoretical terms it should also be stressed that fasting is not an act of individual inspiration or motivation but a function of an order established by the church. The timing of the fasts reinforces the rhythm of the sacred calendar, which, in its cyclical quality, is an image of eternity, of the plane of existence outside the confines of mundane time. The fact that people fast not as individuals but as members of the church underscores the communal aspect of the Orthodox tradition, by which believers are not just individuals, facing God alone (as in Protestantism and the modern individualism made possible by it), but members of the church as a body.

Although the Russian peasantry and other traditional segments of the population at the turn of the century were innocent of high theology (and of the letters needed to achieve even mechanical access to it), an examination of popular beliefs regarding fasting shows that the people understood or sensed the meaning of the theological assumptions sketched out here, although, to be sure, it made a number of interesting shifts in emphasis and application. Fasting as a manifestation of popular life is an invaluable case study of the ways in which the people assimilated ideas from the old Orthodox high culture and applied them in circumstances determined by the predominance and force of the modern culture of the Westernizing Empire and its elite.

🌑 The Practice of Fasting in Prerevolutionary Peasant Society

The single most important fact regarding fasting in prerevolutionary Russian popular culture is that it was practiced well-nigh universally by the peasantry and other traditional groups within the population (in sum, by the subject population, as opposed to the ruling elites both in government and society), and to a degree of stringency exceeding even the ascetic standards of the monastically derived Church rules. The prevalence of fasting as well as its relative severity is most revealing with regard to the religious and cultural perceptions of the peasantry.

Ethnographic accounts dating from the turn of the century all point to the strictness with which fasts were observed in the villages of Russia. Moreover, this observation is confirmed by the results of a systematic survey of peasant life undertaken at the end of the nineteenth century.[9] As S. V. Maksimov, the eminent ethnographer who directed the study, summarized the findings, "Our people not only observes fasts according to the full strictness of church regulations, but even goes further in this respect, setting fast days unknown to the church."[10] The most common form of self-imposed additional fasting was the so-called *ponedel'nichan'e* ("Mondaying"), by which pious laymen imitated the monastic rules for *sukhoiadenie* and added a third day of strict abstention to their week. Although *ponedel'nichan'e* was practiced by a minority, most often older people in a penitential frame of mind, it was a significant factor in popular culture and was looked upon with admiration by the peasant society as a whole.

Ponedel'nichan'e was a means of marking yet another day of the week and setting it outside profane time. The same impulse was manifested more broadly by the peasantry as a whole with regard to the official fasts. Dietary restrictions were not the only means by which this was achieved; for the duration of the major fasts, mundane social life was suspended. Here is a typical description: "During Great Lent all forms of communal amusement come to an end and songs may not be sung under any circumstances. At that time all they sing is [religious] verses, and these are sung slowly and mournfully."[11] The reference to "verses" is significant, for it points to how the peasantry used the sacral time of the fast for contemplation of higher things.

It was then that the explicitly religious genres of the folklore were put to use, and the "verses" and "psalms" sung at that time were among the main vehicles for the preservation and transmission of popular religious beliefs.

One of the most characteristic examples of popular religious creativity (involving, as always, the application of ideas and images derived ultimately from the old apocryphal literature) was the set of beliefs concerning specific fast days. Most often in the form of the "epistle" or the "sermon" "On the Twelve Fridays," and attributed to "Clement, Patriarch of Jerusalem," or "Pope of Rome," it was circulated on manuscript sheets or chanted by itinerant religious singers. Each Friday—*Piatnitsa*, often personified as a woman in folk belief—promised a special blessing for those who honored it or, in other versions, a curse for those who failed to do so. Some Fridays, especially those before a major holiday, offered protection from disease, hail and lightning, and drowning, while others promised such blessings as inscription in the book of life.[12] This belief in Fridays typifies the way the peasantry infused the church regimen with folk meaning.

The peasantry's attitude toward the foods which were periodically forbidden—called *skorom'*, adjective *skoromnoe*—shows a fundamental divergence from the church's approach. Here the people manifested an essentially magical mode of thinking. During a fast, meat or eggs became *skorom'*—a taboo substance. For those rebellious souls reckless enough to taste of it, their act was charged with all the significance of defying God's power.[13] Maksimov notes that vegetables grown from seeds soaked in milk are *skorom'* and adds:

> On similar grounds the peasants consider it to be an unforgivable sin to drink tea with sugar during a fast: tea itself is a semisinful drink [because it is a luxury and of heathen origin], while sugar is unconditionally *skorom'*, because, in the understanding of the peasants, it is made out of animal [often dog] bones. In light of this harshly ascetic attitude toward fasting it is not surprising that mother's milk is also considered sinful *skorom'*, although, in contrast to the not-too-distant past, the peasants no longer deny infants milk during fasts.[14] Once they are weaned, children are made to observe fasts as strictly as adults. . . . The same is expected of seriously ill people. . . . In general, the peasants, especially the elderly . . . would sooner die than defile their souls with *skorom'* food.[15]

The peasants' zeal for fasting went beyond the requirements set by the church, and their dread of *skorom'* clearly shows the influence of archaic modes of thought. This severity reflected a number of the strongest and deepest tendencies of the traditional folkway of understanding the world.

🌼 *Fasting and the Traditional Folk World View*

At root, fasting was a means of taming the flesh and providing evidence of adherence to God's law. This essentially ascetic impulse points to the cardinal fact of the old world view, namely, its strongly dualist tendency. Dualism in the context of traditional Russian religiosity refers to the belief that good, identified with God, and evil—Satan and his legions—are engaged in combat with the world and mankind as their battleground.[16] In the traditional Russian view, heaven is the realm of God, while Satan holds sway over the earth and humanity (in the classic Russian apocryphal formulation, the Devil tells God "The heavens are thine, but the earth is mine"),[17] having spoiled the world[18] and mankind[19] at the moment of creation. By extension, the body represents the means by which evil, preeminent in the physical world, drags down the soul and thwarts its strivings for release into the spiritual realm. This set of beliefs, although certainly not Orthodox, is derived from Christian civilization, since it represents a failure to resolve some of the most difficult and apparently ambiguous questions posed by Christianity itself (regarding the relationship between God and Satan, the spiritual and the physical). It was, moreover, not merely the result of observation of the sorry state of the world as it existed but also had a firm textual basis in medieval Russian high culture, from whence it seeped down into the peasant milieu.[20]

The dualist tendency meant that popular fasting was, to a certain extent, an expression of hostility toward the body.[21] More important, if evil was predominant in the present age, then the means of combating it and struggling to escape its grip—religious observance, especially as given concrete form in fasting—were necessarily of an especially severe nature and charged with great significance.

🌼 *Fasting and the Identification of God's People (and of His Enemies)*

In the traditional world view, religious observance—including, above all, fasting—was the means by which the community of the faithful manifested its allegiance to God and to good in the circumstances of the present evil age. This method of identification is made explicit not so much by positive self-description, which would require a degree of distance and introspection alien to the traditional mindset, as by contrast to those who were not pious. In the concrete historical circumstances of Imperial Russia the educated classes represented the social group marked by its severance from the traditional religiosity, which, it should be stressed, involved not only belief (in the manner of the modernizing Protestant distinction between the essential—faith—and nonessential—ritual) but also an integral and all-encompassing way of life and behavior based on religion. Insofar as peasants expressed a consciousness of group identity at the turn of the century it was in the context of distinguishing themselves from the nobility, above all in terms of piety, in which fasting played such an essential role.

In the popular perception and the lexicon which gave words to it, educated society as a whole was composed of "the nobles" (*bare*) or "the lords" (*gospoda*). Thus a government official, a university professor, a doctor, and a student revolutionary were all "lords," subsumed in one functional designation. There is a certain undeniable logic to this usage, for regardless of the development of and differentiation within the intelligentsia, it was in fact an organic outgrowth of the nobility forcibly set on the path of modernization by Peter and, more important, it was the carrier of the ruling elite culture. At the outset of the imperial period the nobility broke with the outer trappings of the old identity, and from the point of view of the holistic traditional culture this alone sufficed to mark a complete break with God and the order which he had ordained. Over time the intelligentsia as a whole did in fact turn from religion, and ruling class expressions of atheism also made an impression on the people, albeit not as deep as that of the plain fact of its impiety in observance and morality. Thus, in Russia, relations between masters and subjects, fraught with the possibility of enmity and conflict by their very nature, were infinitely complicated by the chasm between the rationalist, secular modernity of the "lords" and the religion-based traditional culture of the people. The peasantry made sense of the oppression it suffered at the hands of "the nobility," i.e., the dominant culture and its carriers, by pointing to the godlessness of its tormentors.

A typical example of peasant philosophizing at the turn of the century makes special reference to fasting as an expression of piety and shows the complex of evil behavior and its consequences associated with the nobility and its laxity in religious observance.

> We peasants have gone to the dogs . . . but God protect us from what goes on among the lords—almost all the lords eat *skorom'* each day throughout the year and don't honor any of the fasts or pray to God. . . . Most have forgotten about God and others say he doesn't exist, and they treat us like dogs, tricking us at every step and punishing us for nothing. . . . And a lot of them have never married but live with young

girls—as soon as one gets old he finds another. . . . They run after other men's wives and girls . . . like dogs chasing bitches.[22]

Thus impiety, manifested in a refusal to submit to God's law concerning fasts, is explicitly associated with sexual immorality and exploitation. The crimes listed are standard in peasant complaints against the nobility, but in another folkloric theme the lords are accused of feeding on the very flesh of the people.[23] Such beliefs can be seen as the most emphatic way in which the peasantry could express its perception of the lords' depravity and total divorce from the laws of God.

In order to explain the vehemence of such perceptions, it should be stressed that "godlessness" was not a neutral category from the point of view of the traditional culture. One could not doubt the existence of God and still be an honorable person, as is the case in modern society. Given the absolute and holistic nature of the traditional world view and also its pronounced dualist tendency, turning away from God (failure to observe the fasts being sufficient evidence of such a step) necessitated entry into the camp of the Devil. This is a major factor in explaining the difficulties faced by educated Russians when they turned their benevolent attentions to the long-suffering people. A doctor (whose profession was the object of particular loathing on the part of the traditionalist segments of the population) or a teacher might devote an entire lifetime to the betterment of the peasantry, but if he failed to cross himself before icons or abstain from meat on Fridays, he would be viewed by many as an agent of the Devil.

In a more positive sense, religious observance with fasting as its centerpoint served as a means by which the Russian people affirmed their own worth in the midst of perceived oppression and degradation. As one saying put it, "Even though the peasant's coat is plain, at least the Devil hasn't eaten his brain."[24] Despite the paternalistically propeasant stance of the late imperial administration and the usually sincerely expressed populism of Russian educated society, the people remained a socially and culturally inferior group in the context of the empire's civilization and could not escape consciousness of this inferiority. However, by the categories of his own culture, the peasant was superior to his impious and inhuman oppressor, whose moral degradation was made plain by religious impiety—according to one folk saying, "Lords and dogs eat *skorom'*."[25] In circumstances of the decadence of the rich and the powerful, the task of doing God's will fell to the humble folk: "Only we little peasants can fulfill the fasts, because the learned people and the nobles won't —they couldn't last a day without tea and beef."[26] From the point of view of the traditional culture, the peasants, insofar as they remained pious, were the people of God on earth and played a crucial role in the great scheme of things.[27]

The Cosmic Significance of Fasting in the Traditional World View

In the traditional view, fasting was not merely the means by which the community of the faithful manifested its allegiance to God and his law and thereby achieved the hope for salvation. It was also necessary for the proper functioning of the world, above all agriculture, the preeminent concern of most of the traditional Russian population.

As in the case of group identification, the development of the conception of fasting proceeded negatively—the people did not see good things happening because it observed the fasts, but rather found the cause for all manner of disasters in religious laxity and impiety. This is of course a classic theme of traditional cultures throughout the world; but for the sake of illustration from our place and period, here is how one ethnographer described the villagers' understanding of the causality of events: "The peasants view every misfortune which befalls the people—whether fire, or failed harvest, or epidemic disease—as God's punishment, the inevitable result of infractions against the religion."[28]

There is a great body of material concerning popular expectations of imminent doom at the turn of the century. By means of rumors, contemporary legends, chain letters, and the like, the traditional culture spread the message that God was gravely displeased with the world and would soon visit his wrath upon it. One of the most popular chain letters, the "Scroll of the Sign from Above in Jerusalem" [Svitok Ierusalimskogo znameniia], which had a wide circulation over the years,[29] was presented as an epistle from Christ, who had sent it inside "a stone small and cold, but exceedingly heavy," which fell to earth in Jerusalem. The scroll tells of the impending judgment of impious and immoral humanity and contains the following admonition and warning:

> Love one another; do not curse [*maternoiu bran'iu ne branites'*] and do not commit fornication. . . . For he who falls into fornication not only destroys his soul but also makes defilement with his whole body and with all of his members. . . . Live in love and harmony, and honor the holy days, and Wednesday, and Friday, and Sunday [or] I will loose heathen nations upon you, and send down great frosts and hail upon you.[30]

The main theme of the scroll is ritual observance—with fasting as its center point—the lack of which is directly linked to fornication and defilement. Thus the connection between fasting and controlling the flesh is made explicit, and the consequence of the loss of control is the disruption of the world order and the final judgment. The common theme in this material is that laxity in religious observance—the equivalent of godlessness and therefore of allegiance to the force of evil—was spreading inexorably and that God would surely punish and cleanse the wicked world.

Peasant moralists saw a drastic decline in the piety of the people themselves, and not only in that of "the nobility," long the embodiment of evil and depravity. It is important to contrast this with the observations of outsiders, such as ethnographers and others who dealt with the peasantry. By all accounts, the people still observed the fasts strictly as of 1900, although there had been some relaxation of the almost self-destructive ascetic zeal which had ostensibly been the general norm only a decade earlier. How, then, is the perceived decline to be explained?

It is an essential characteristic of the traditional world view that the motion of history (or the condition of the world, if "history" seems too abstract in our case) is seen as proceeding downward from an original perfection to ever-lower depths of debasement. Thus by definition the past is superior to the present, and value is of course assessed in religious moral terms. As one proverb put it, "That which is older is better [more just, virtuous]."[31] It is possible that this assumption was at work at the turn of the century—the people of that day were, by definition, the sorry descendants of ancestors who had excelled in piety and virtue.

Objective factors also came into play. Through a disorienting array of changes—urbanization, industrialization, improved literacy and communication, universal military service—increasing numbers of peasants were removed from the self-enclosed world of the traditional village, and piety, part of an all-encompassing complex of beliefs and behaviors, necessarily suffered as a result. Although by the turn of the century relatively few peasants had made a complete break with the past, the concerns of traditional moralists were aroused, and they were in their own way prescient, given the subsequent complete disintegration of the traditional culture as war and revolution accelerated the pace of disruptive change.

NOTES

1. This chapter also is intended to give the reader who might be unfamiliar with the subject a sound body of general information which will enhance his or her understanding and appreciation of classic Russian literature and descriptions of popular life, where references to fasting crop up frequently.

2. This is not to say that the traditional culture was entirely "orthodox" in the strict sense; rather, ideas emanating from the Orthodox higher culture were filtered down and adapted in various ways. For a forceful statement of this general approach to the origins of the ideas and images of Russian popular culture, see A. B. Strakhov, "Stanovlenie dvoeveriia na Rusi" [The emergence/creation of dual faith in Rus'], *Cyrillomethodianum*, vol. 10 (1987), 33–44.

3. Orthodox practice will at times be contrasted to that of the pre-Vatican II Roman Catholic Church, which might be familiar to many readers. This tactic might, however, cause some confusion and interference in perception. Although Orthodox fasting is analogous to that practiced in traditional Catholicism, it varies significantly in terms of extent and in some aspects of theological motivation.

4. The traditional Roman Catholic fast involved abstention from meat, while fish and dairy products were generally allowed. In Russian popular usage the Catholic method was therefore given the disparaging designation of "the forbidden-food [i.e., not real, fake, anti-] fast," *skoromnyi post*. See V. Dal', *Tolkovyi slovar' zhivogo velikorusskogo iazyka* [Dictionary of the living Great Russian language] (St. Petersburg, 1882), "Skoromnyi."

5. I am providing the Russian/Slavonic terms for the fasts and related concepts as an aid to the reader who might encounter them in Russian texts.

6. For a more detailed and authoritative presentation of Orthodox fasting regulations, see *Polnyi pravoslavnyi bogoslovskii entsiklopedicheskii slovar'* [Complete Orthodox theological encyclopedic dictionary] (reprint: Moscow, 1992), "Posty" (Fasts).

7. This, along with the fact that Catholic Europe followed an analogous schedule, is the reason why the Russian aristocracy's social "season," familiar to any reader of the great Russian novels, was in January, after the pre-Christmas fast and before Great Lent.

8. This argument was advanced most forcefully by M. M. Tareev, crusader against what he saw as the alien, non-Slavic heritage of Byzantine asceticism in the Russian Orthodox Church, and reiterated in such works as G. Feodotov's *Russian Religious Mind* (Cambridge, Mass: Harvard University Press, 1946). For a summary and appraisal of Tareev's ideas, see G. Florovskii, *Puti russkogo bogosloviia* [Paths of Russian theology], 2d ed. (Paris, 1981), 439–444.

9. This survey, known by the name of its sponsor, Prince Tenishev, consisted of a questionnaire formulated by ethnographers and sent to the "village intelligentsia" (to use Soviet terminology), i.e., teachers, medical personnel, agronomers, priests, throughout Russia.

10. S. V. Maksimov, *Krestnaia sila* [The power of the Cross], *Sobranie sochinenii* (St. Petersburg, n. d., c. 1900), vol. 17, 84.

11. E. Peredel'skii, "Stanitsa Temizhbekskaia, i pesni, poiushchiesia v nei" [The cossack settlement of Temizhbek and the songs sung in it], *Sbornik materialov dlia opisaniia mestnostei i plemen Kavkaza* [Collection of materials for the description of the localities and tribes of the Caucasus], no. 3 (1883), part 2, 42.

12. For an example, see the copy reproduced in A. Semilutskii, "Selo Pokoinoe, Stavropol'skoi gubernii, Novogrigor'evskogo uezda" [The village of Pokoinoe, Stavropol' Province, Novogrigor'evka District], *Sbornik materialov dlia opisaniia mestnostei i plemen Kavkaza*, no. 23 (1897), part 2, 332–334. This version is particularly concerned with sexual relations, calling them "defilement" on Friday, "even if between husband and wife."

13. The Russian peasant idea of *skorom'* is highly reminiscent of the notion of *tref* (Yiddish for nonkosher food) in traditional Jewish popular culture.

14. This would seem to be physiologically impossible. If this statement is based on peasant testimony rather than on the observations of objective outsiders, it might be that

the villagers were ascribing heroic piety to their ancestors, in accordance with the traditional world view, in which the past is by definition superior to the present.

15. Maksimov, *Krestnaia sila,* 85.

16. This discussion focuses on Russia. For the sake of perspective, however, it should be stressed that dualist tendencies were characteristic of the traditional peasant cultures of most of Europe and, with qualifications, of much of the rest of the world as well.

17. "Tvoia nebesa, a moia est' zemlia," from "The Lord's Disputation with the Devil" [Prenie Gospodne s diavolom], in N. Tikhonravov, ed., *Pamiatniki otrechennoi russkoi literatury* [Relics of forbidden Russian literature] (St. Petersburg, 1863), vol. 2, 286. These words are a twisting of a verse—frequently invoked in Orthodox services—from the Psalms in which the heavens and the earth are the Lord's. The heretical formula appears quite often in the folklore.

18. In the mythology of the Slavs and many other peoples the story of creation bears no resemblance to that of Genesis. In the Russian version—recorded throughout the country and well into the twentieth century—the Devil creates the land by diving into the primordial sea and bringing up soil in his mouth. For a discussion of the Russian folk creation myth with an extensive survey of analogies in the traditional cultures of other peoples, see A. N. Veselovskii, "Dualisticheskie pover'ia o mirozdanii," [Dualist beliefs regarding the creation of the universe], *Razyskaniia v oblasti russkogo dukhovnogo stikha* [Investigations in the field of Russian spiritual verse], part 5 (1889), 1–116. For a consideration of the immense significance of this myth for the development of the religious world view of the European peasantry, see M. Eliade, *A History of Religious Ideas* (Chicago, 1978-1985), vol. 3, 36.

19. In most Russian versions of this myth, the Devil tampers with the body of Adam before God has gotten around to giving him a soul. For some typical examples, see E. Barsov, "Narodnye predaniia o mirotvorenii," [Folk traditions/legends about the creation of the world], *Chteniia v Imperatorskom Obshchestve Istorii i Drevnostei Rossiiskikh* [Readings in the Imperial Society for Russian History and Antiquities], October–December, 1886, *Materialy istoriko-etnograficheskie* [Historico-Ethnographic Materials], 1–7.

20. Dualist ideas entered into medieval Russian culture along with the Orthodox faith and the Church Slavonic language because the textual baggage of the new religion contained Bulgarian Bogomil heretical writings. On the Bogomils' dualist theology and religious writings, as well as a survey of their spread to Russia, see I. Ivanov, *Bogomilski knigi i legendy* [Bogomil books and legends] (Sofia, 1970). Originally part of the monastic high culture, Bogomil ideas filtered down into the popular religion, and in the ethnographic recordings of the twentieth century one can find numerous examples of ideas and even phrases drawn from the ancient heretical texts.

21. The dualist tendency present in the traditional culture was taken to the extreme by the so-called *khlysty*, who, alongside the Old Belief in its myriad factions (which also showed strong dualist inclinations, albeit for different reasons), constituted the preeminent native Russian religious dissident movement. Although *khlystovstvo* was a diverse and complex phenomenon, a number of generalizations can be made: the *khlysty* believed evil to be absolutely predominant in the material world. The chosen few, the *khlyst* "Israel," could hope to avoid the mortal perils of the present age by communion with God through ecstatic worship and allegiance to the Christ incarnate in their leaders, and, of more direct relevance to the subject of this chapter, by the most extreme mortification of the flesh. Thus the *khlysty* were complete vegetarians and developed an entire lore about the demonic and repulsive qualities of meat and eggs, and, to make the connection between fasting and sexuality explicit, they strove for total celibacy, viewing the sexual

act as the very embodiment of capture by the world and perdition. In the vulgar view, the *khlysty* were orgiasts, but whether this reputation was a result of slander or of the special pitfalls of ecstatic religion, their teachings are among the most harshly antisexual of any religion known to man. The *skoptsy* "self-castrators" took the ascetic drive to its conclusion. Both groups have generated an extensive literature. For an introduction to the subject, see A. I. Klibanov, *Istoriia religioznogo sektantstva v Rossii* [History of religious sectarianism in Russia] (Moscow, 1965), and A. S. Prugavin, *Religioznye otshchepentsy* [Religious renegades] (St. Petersburg, 1904).

22. A conversation between two middle-aged peasant men recorded in Kursk Province, in M. Dikarev, "Tolki naroda v 1899 godu" [Popular interpretations of events in 1899], *Etnograficheskoe obozrenie* [Ethnographic survey], no. 1 (1900), 165.

23. For example, "there is a tradition that in the village of Gai there once lived a lord who, when hearing of the birth of a baby plump and clean in body, would take the baby away from its parents, feed it and raise it like a calf, and then eat it." V. Bondarenko, "Ocherki Kirsanovskogo uezda Tambovskoi gubernii" [Sketches of Kirsanov District, Tambov Province] *Etnograficheskoe obozrenie*, no. 3 (1890), 76.

24. "U muzhika kaftan khot' i ser, da um u nego ne chert s"el." Ia. Kuznetsov, "Kharakteristika obshchestvennykh klassov po narodnym poslovitsam i pogovorkam" [The characterization of social classes in folk proverbs and sayings], *Zhivaia starina* [Living antiquity], no. 3 (1903), 397.

25. "Skoromnichaiut bary da sobaki." Dal', "Skoromnyi."

26. Maksimov, *Krestnaia sila,* 86.

27. The traditional Russian understanding of fasting is highly reminiscent of the Jewish *kashrut*, another cultural system in which the religious regulation of food is essential to the group's identity and the assertion of its centrality in God's plan. This similarity is not merely a coincidence deriving from the sacral aspects of food in all traditional cultures. Rather, it stems from the position which Russia occupied in sacred history as understood in Orthodox Christian terms. The Russian people did not think on such a level of abstraction, but it did see itself as the unique carrier of faith and proper religious observance, and therefore its beliefs and practices show marked affinities to those of traditional Judaism.

28. Bondarenko, "Ocherki Kirsanovskogo uezda Tambovskoi gubernii," 74-75.

29. P. Bezsonov, *Kaleki perekhozhie* [Wandering singers of spiritual verse] (Moscow, 1861-1863), part 6, 74-96, gives similar texts (of a pronounced Old Believer cast), with the same title, dating back to the eighteenth century. This is a good example of how the process of modernization could work to spread antimodern ideas: the "Jerusalem Scroll," a manifestation of militantly traditionalist thinking, gained wide circulation as a result of increasing literacy and improved communications.

30. V. Balov, "Ocherki Poshekhon'ia," [Sketches of the Poshekhon'e region], *Etnograficheskoe obozrenie*, no. 4 (1901), 91-92.

31. "Chto staree, to pravee." F. Buslaev, "Russkii byt i poslovitsy" [The Russian way of life in proverbs], *Istoricheskie ocherki russkoi narodnoi slovesnosti i iskusstva* [Historical sketches of Russian folk literature/verbal expression and art] (St. Petersburg, 1861), vol. 1, 102-103.

SIX

RONALD D. LeBlanc

Tolstoy's Way of No Flesh: Abstinence, Vegetarianism, and Christian Physiology

It is not necessary to make vegetarianism the main goal of your efforts. The goal worthy of man and attributable to him is overall perfection in his moral life. Vegetarianism is only one of the results of moral perfection.

—L. N. TOLSTOY

. . . there is more love for mankind in electricity and steam than in chastity and abstention from eating meat.

—A. P. CHEKHOV

Much like George Bernard Shaw in England and Mohandas Gandhi in India, Lev Nikolaevich Tolstoy is generally acknowledged to be his country's most famous vegetarian. In the Russian popular consciousness, one critic notes, "the name 'Lev Tolstoy' and the concept 'vegetarianism' have long been conflated and inextricably linked together."[1] Tolstoy was certainly not the first vegetarian in Russia, however. Socioeconomic conditions in tsarist Russia, as well as the religiously dictated practice of fasting, had long made de facto vegetarians out of the peasantry, who subsisted mainly on a diet of black bread, potatoes, cabbage soup, and *kasha*.[2] But vegetarianism did not truly become a cause in Russia, as Janet Barkas observes in her book on the history of the vegetarian movement, until the highly celebrated Count Tolstoy voluntarily decided to adopt a meatless diet sometime during the 1880s.[3] And while the Russian author himself might not have been the actual founder of the vegetarian movement in his homeland, his advocacy of a meatless diet certainly supplied a tremendous stimulus to its growth and development there, since his example inspired many of his fellow countrymen to reform their "carnivoristic" ways and adopt more "humane" eating practices. Thus Peter Verigin, for instance, the leader of the Dukhobors, reportedly reintroduced the ban on meat eating for the members of his religious sect after he had become acquainted with some of Tolstoy's moral writings, and a number of Tolstoyan vegetarian colonies would be founded at the turn of the century in England, Holland, and America.[4] Indeed, vegetarianism eventually came to be one of the essential tenets of "Tolstoyism," the ideology of radical Christianity that informed the lifestyle of thousands of people worldwide who became converts to the moral and religious teachings of the apostle from Yasnaya Polyana. Along with pacifism, temperance, chastity, anarchism, antimilitarism, and nonviolent resistance to evil, vegetarianism came to constitute a basic component of the message of Christian love that Tolstoy's followers sought to incorporate into their daily lives.[5]

It is difficult to determine exactly when—and, more important, why—it was that Tolstoy initially decided to give up fleshly foods and converted to a vegetarian diet. According to his son Sergei, Tolstoy was convinced to become a vegetarian by William Frey (Vladimir Konstantinovich Geins), a strong advocate of Auguste Comte's Positivist philosophy, who had traveled to America and lived in several agricultural communes in the United States but later returned to Russia and visited Tolstoy at Yasnaya Polyana during the autumn of 1885.[6] As early as 1882, however, Tolstoy had indicated his resolve to adopt a meatless diet; and as late as 1887, two years after he had first met Frey, Tolstoy would find himself still lapsing back occasionally from vegetarianism to carnivorism. Barkas is no doubt correct, therefore, when she asserts that Tolstoy's conversion to an exclusively vegetarian diet was a long and gradual process and that "he struggled with the decision for several years, vacillating back and forth."[7] We do know for a fact that during the last two decades of his life Tolstoy adhered quite rigidly to a vegetarian diet, one that he claimed never consciously to have betrayed and that he alleged never cost him any effort or deprivation.[8] Some have argued that this new meatless diet greatly aided Tolstoy's failing health at the time and served well his lack of teeth.[9] The author's wife, however, believed that this "abominable" and "senseless" diet was having a decidedly ruinous effect upon her husband's once

*I. E. Repin, Lev Nikolaevich Tolstoi
(Barefoot), 1901.
State Russian Museum, St. Petersburg.*

robust constitution. In addition to complaining about the daily burden such a special diet placed upon her as a homemaker (by forcing her to have two menus prepared for every meal instead of just one), Sophia Andreevna claimed that her husband's vegetarian diet did not provide him nearly enough nourishment. To her mind, his refusal to eat meat contributed directly to his constant bouts with digestive ailments; and, indeed, doctors diagnosed Tolstoy at this time as suffering from severe catarrh of the stomach. "An old man of sixty-nine," she objected, "really shouldn't be eating this sort of food, which just bloats him up and doesn't give him any nourishment at all!"[10] Sophia Andreevna was not the only one who questioned the nutritional value of her husband's vegetarian diet. I. S. Listovsky, one of Tolstoy's more ardent critics at the time, went so far as to suggest that the artistic talent of the author of *War and Peace* and *Anna Karenina* was in sharp decline largely because of his meatless diet.[11]

Tolstoy's Renunciation of the Flesh

Tolstoy's decision to abstain from the use of meat in his diet, in any case, seems to have been prompted not by health considerations but rather by moral and ethical concerns. As he himself once observed in a letter to his wife,

RONALD D. LEBLANC

"Vegetarianism, as long as it does not have health as its object, is always associated with high moral views on life" (LXXXIV, 152). Tolstoy's advocacy of vegetarianism, therefore, has traditionally been viewed in an ideological light and understood mainly in a humanitarian context. His conversion to a vegetarian diet is usually associated with his decision to give up hunting, a favorite outdoor pastime that over the years had provided him with a large amount of pleasure and had served as a great source of relaxation (it had also enabled him as a writer to depict so convincingly such fictional sportsmen as Dmitry Olenin, Nikolai Rostov, and Konstantin Levin). Tolstoy swore off eating meat at about the same time that he gave up hunting, and it is generally agreed that he came to condemn these two activities as morally evil because both involved the cruel treatment of animals.[12] As V. I. Porudominsky observes, Tolstoy's path to vegetarianism—understood as a step leading to a new moral life—is unavoidably connected with his renunciation of hunting, an evil pastime "in which our killing habit and, consequently, our meat-eating habit merge together."[13] Tolstoy, in other words, apparently subscribed to what would today be called "ethical" or "philosophical" vegetarianism: that is, he seems to have abjured the use of meat in his diet not on the basis of any health concerns or religious beliefs but rather because eating meat contributed directly to an unjustifiably cruel and inhumane exploitation of animals.[14]

The key text that is invariably cited as spelling out Tolstoy's motivation for having become a vegetarian is the essay "Pervaia stupen'" [The first step] (1891), which he wrote as the preface to a new Russian translation of a book by the British vegetarian Howard Williams, *The Ethics of Diet: A Catena of Authorities Deprecatory of the Practice of Flesh-Eating* (1883).[15] Williams's book, which contains short biographical essays that summarize the dietetic theories and eating practices of a whole host of famous philosophers, poets, and thinkers (from Porphyry and Pythagoras in classical antiquity to Shelley and Schopenhauer in the modern period), no doubt provided Tolstoy with additional motivation for deciding to become a vegetarian.[16] In his introductory essay to *The Ethics of Diet*, an essay that has been characterized as one of "the most thorough, soul-searching modern treatments of the moral reasons for vegetarianism," Tolstoy describes in particularly graphic detail the bloody scene he had witnessed during his recent visit to a slaughterhouse in the nearby city of Tula.[17] The cruelty toward animals that Tolstoy observed there seems to have confirmed his belief that meat should be eliminated from the human diet. To quote Coral Lansbury, the author of a recent history of the antivivisection movement, "a visit to an abattoir would make a vegetarian of the most convinced carnivore among us."[18] And, indeed, Tolstoy's gruesome description of the Tula slaughterhouse in "The First Step" helped to forge in his mind—as well as in the minds of many readers—what one student of the vegetarian movement in Russia has called "the logical link between violence towards animals and violence towards men."[19] Vegetarianism now became for Tolstoy an essential component of a nonviolent way of life (in accord with what Buddhists call *ahimsa*) and thus an inextricable part of his efforts to make the world a better and more peaceful place to live.

The main purpose of my chapter, however, is to offer an alternative—if not revisionist—account of Tolstoy's conversion to a meatless diet and thus, in effect, to demythologize this traditional view of his vegetarianism as being essentially "ethical" or "philosophical" in nature. I intend to examine Tolstoy's avoidance of meat within a different context than that of nonviolence and animal rights. While I would not dispute the assertion that Tolstoy's decision to adopt a meatless diet was reached to some extent on these humanitarian grounds, I would argue that his conversion to vegetarianism cannot be properly understood unless it is viewed in terms of his lifelong quest for ascetic discipline and moral self-perfection. To be more specific, I situate Tolstoy's vegetarianism within the context of the personal struggle he waged throughout his life between the flesh and the spirit, a context that shares many affinities with the one that surrounded the health reform movement in the United States during the nineteenth century, when modern physiological concerns about the human body were closely interwoven with traditional Christian anxieties about sins of the flesh. As I have argued elsewhere, Tolstoy—in his life as well as in his works—came increasingly to regard the carnal pleasures of both the flesh and the palate as sinful temptations that lure people away from the strait and narrow path of moral righteousness.[20] Tolstoy, the so-called "seer of the flesh" and earthy pagan who once celebrated the joys of the natural life in his portrayal of characters such as the robust Daddy Eroshka in *The Cossacks* (1863) and the vivacious Natasha Rostova in *War and Peace* (1869), eventually became transformed from a hedonist to an ascetic. In the process he came more and more to believe that our physical appetite for both food and sex must somehow be moderated if we hope ever to transcend our base animal nature and attain spiritual grace.[21] Thus we can see already in *Anna Karenina* (1877), through the contrastive pair of Konstantin Levin and Stiva Oblonsky, how the satisfaction of both gastronomic and sexual desire has become closely identified in Tolstoy's mind with a sinful appetite for sensual pleasure that must be strictly regulated.

During the period following his spiritual crisis, Tolstoy even came to question the effectiveness of this puritanical ethos of moderation and restraint in curbing libidinal appetites. He no longer considered Levin's highly functional, utilitarian approach to food and sex in *Anna Karenina* an effective way to combat lust. More radical measures were deemed necessary in order to help men resist the sweet allure proffered by these libidinal pleasures and thus to liberate them from their enslavement to carnal desire. In his *Confession* (1882), therefore, Tolstoy categorically condemns the way of life of his entire social class, the Levins and the Oblonskys alike. The conditions of luxury, idleness, and epicurean indulgence under which the "parasites" from the upper class in Russia live, he maintains, make it virtually impossible for them ever to understand the true meaning of life. In order to live according to the ways of God, one must renounce entirely the gentry way of life—as well as the sensual pleasures traditionally associated with it—and adopt instead the more genuine, morally authentic lifestyle of the simple, hard-working peasants, who have never strayed from their religious faith. "We must renounce the sensual pleasures of life," the author writes, "we must labor, suffer, and be kind and humble" (XXIII, 47). Tolstoy's Victorian assault upon the pleasure principle in general—and upon gentry idleness (*prazdnost'*) in particular—finds perhaps its most explicit artistic expression in the highly controversial *Kreutzer Sonata* (1889), a work that seems to have grown out of the author's own personal disillusionment with married life. In his attempt to deromanticize people's idealized notions of love, the story's central character, Pozdnyshev, manages to strip love of any emotional or spiritual value that it might have, reducing it to mere sexual passion and a brutish animal lust. In addition, he condemns the institution of marriage as a moral fraud perpetrated by the members of his decadent social class: he exposes it as a sham whose main purpose is actually to legitimize man's wanton sexual desires.

Wishing to leave no doubt in the reader's mind that the extreme opinions on sexuality, love, and marriage expressed by his deranged protagonist accurately reflect the author's own views, Tolstoy wrote an "Afterword to the *Kreutzer Sonata*" (1889–1890), in which he asserts that sexual continence, "which constitutes an indispensable condition of human dignity in the unmarried state, is still more essential in the married one" (XXVII, 81). For our purposes, what is particularly relevant about the views expressed by Pozdnyshev in the *Kreutzer Sonata* is that excesses of sexual debauchery are linked in a cause-and-effect manner with gastronomic indulgence. Eating rich and fleshly foods, Tolstoy's hero asserts, leads directly to the arousal of sexual desire. "You see," Pozdnyshev explains,

> our stimulating superfluity of food, together with complete physical idleness, is nothing but the systematic excitation of lust. The usual food of a young peasant lad is bread, *kvas*, and onions; he keeps alive and is

vigorous and healthy; his task is light agricultural work. When he goes to perform railway work, his rations are buckwheat *kasha* and a pound of meat a day. But he works off that pound of meat during his sixteen hours wheeling around thirty-pound barrow-loads, so it is just enough for him. But we, who consume two pounds of meat every day, and game, and fish, and all sorts of hot foods and drinks—where does all that go? Into excesses of sensuality. (XXVII, 23)[22]

When he accounts for the origins of his own infatuation with the woman he would later wed (and subsequently murder), Pozdnyshev asserts that this love was largely the result of "the excess of food I consumed while living an idle life" (XXVII, 24). This direct cause-and-effect relationship between gastronomic excess and sexual excitation is reiterated when Pozdnyshev claims that had he lived in circumstances normal to man, "consuming just enough food to suffice for the work I did," he would not have fallen in love and "none of all this would have happened" (XXVII, 24). In a variant version of the *Kreutzer Sonata* that circulated privately in Russia in manuscript form, Pozdnyshev puts it even more bluntly. "All of our love affairs and marriages," he asserts, "are, for the most part, conditioned by the food we eat" (XXVII, 303).[23]

✹ The First Step: Curbing Carnal Appetite through Abstinence

In view of Tolstoy's artistic representation of food in several of his later works of fiction as a dangerous stimulant that can excite sexual lust, it should not surprise us terribly to find that among the radical measures against sensual pleasure the author comes to advocate late in his life he would also include vegetarianism. Since the spiritual ideal that Tolstoy believed we should all be striving to attain is absolute sexual continence, it follows that we should avoid eating meat, because fleshly food, he maintained, arouses in us sexual passion and carnal desire. As the epigraph to this chapter suggests, Anton Chekhov, who openly admitted that Tolstoy's philosophy had informed his own thinking for a number of years, likewise came to see this ascetic connection that Tolstoy makes between abstinence from sex (chastity) and abstinence from fleshly food (vegetarianism).[24] Indeed, it is precisely this commitment to a rigid brand of Christian asceticism—more than any compassion he may have felt for creatures from the animal kingdom—that initially prompted Tolstoy to adopt a vegetarian diet. Eating fleshly foods is wrong, Tolstoy writes unequivocally in "The First Step," because it "serves only to develop animal feelings, to excite lust, to promote fornication and drunkenness" (XXIX, 84). In this so-called "Bible of vegetarianism," Tolstoy contends that a carnal diet stimulates a carnal appetite, that eating animal food arouses our animal passions.[25] Tolstoy argues, in fact, that people should abstain from eating not just meat but any rich and tasty food item from which one might conceivably derive gustatory enjoyment. After all, gastronomic pleasure, in Tolstoy's chain of reasoning, leads directly and ineluctably to sexual pleasure. Accordingly, he inveighs strongly in this essay against the sin of gluttony (overeating), and he encourages his readers to practice strict abstinence and fasting in matters concerning the consumption of food and drink. Although "The First Step" was written as the preface to a book on vegetarianism, it turns out that Tolstoy's introductory essay is hardly about vegetarianism at all. It is essentially a moral tract that warns about the dangers of gluttony and preaches the need to practice abstinence.[26]

This orientation toward gluttony is already evident in the opening sections of the essay, where Tolstoy asserts that it is impossible for one to lead a good and moral life—whether as a Christian or a pagan—unless one begins with abstinence and self-abnegation. The indispensable "first step" up the ladder of virtues, Tolstoy writes, involves the renunciation of our basic physical appetites and our liberation from the animal lusts that plague us. Although the abstract language that Tolstoy employs in the early part of this essay might lead one to think that he is speaking about our sexual appetite and our lust for the pleasures of the flesh, it soon becomes clear that the author has in mind mainly our gastronomical appetite and our lust for the pleasures of the palate.[27] When he finally does specify the three basic "lusts" that torment human beings, Tolstoy identifies them as "gluttony, idleness, and carnal love" (XXIX, 73). Not unlike Pozdnyshev in the *Kreutzer Sonata,* Tolstoy in "The First Step" posits a direct causal link between food and sex. "The gluttonous person," he writes, "is not equipped to struggle against laziness, nor will the gluttonous and idle person ever be strong enough to struggle against sexual lust. Therefore, according to all moral teachings, the striving for abstinence commences with the struggle against the lust of gluttony; it commences with fasting" (XXIX, 73-74). In the same way that the first condition for a good life is abstinence, Tolstoy explains, "the first condition for a life of abstinence is fasting" (XXIX, 74). Just as gluttony is the first sign of a bad life, so is fasting "the essential condition for a good life" (XXIX, 74). What lends particular urgency to this need to fast, according to Tolstoy, is the fact that the main interest of the vast majority of people is to satisfy their craving for food. "From the poorest to the wealthiest levels of society," he writes, "gluttony is, I think, the primary aim, the chief pleasure of our life" (XXIX, 74). The educated classes in Russia, he points out, wrongly imagine happiness and well-being to reside in "tasty, nutritious, and easily digestible food" (XXIX, 75). Even destitute working-class people, Tolstoy sadly notes, seek to follow the example of the decadent upper classes; they too strive to acquire "the tastiest and sweetest foods, and to eat and drink as much as they can" (XXIX, 74).

The only effective way to curb our voracious sexual appetite, Tolstoy asserts in his "Afterword to the *Kreutzer Sonata*," is to eliminate any pleasure we might possibly derive from the act of sexual intercourse.[28] Only in this way can we succeed in our efforts to make ourselves what he elsewhere calls voluntary "eunuchs" and thus to conquer our carnal lust.[29] This would explain, of course, why Tolstoy was so favorably impressed by the American Shakers, whose practice of complete sexual abstinence seemed to corroborate perfectly his own austere views on chastity.[30] The same antihedonistic, antiepicurean reasoning that Tolstoy applies to the issue of human sexuality seems to inform the solution that he advances in "The First Step" for curbing our basic animal craving for food: one should strive as much as possible to remove all pleasure from the act of eating. As long as a person continues to enjoy the pleasure that eating provides, Tolstoy maintains, there can be no limit to the increase of the desire or appetite for that pleasure. One can keep this gastronomic lust under control only when one does not eat except in obedience to necessity. "The satisfaction of a need has limits," he writes, "but pleasure does not have any limits. For the satisfaction of one's needs, it is necessary and sufficient to eat bread, *kasha*, and rice. While for the augmentation of pleasure, there is no end to the flavorings and seasonings" (XXIX, 77). In a lengthy passage that ensues, Tolstoy proceeds to illustrate in considerable detail how, if we continue to eat tasty and spicy comestibles (rather than these three bland food items—bread, *kasha,* and rice), our appetite for gustatory pleasure will never be satisfied but will instead keep growing larger and larger; we will be seduced into piling one more delicious entrée on top of another at a meal. "And so there is the meal," Tolstoy writes,

> a modest meal. One could augment the pleasure to be derived from this meal even more and more. And people do augment it, and there are no limits to this augmentation: hors d'oeuvres meant to whet the appetite, and entremets, and desserts, and various combinations of tasty treats, and flowers, and decorations, and music played during the meal. And the surprising thing is that the people who gorge themselves every day on such meals—compared to which Belshazzar's feast, which evoked the prophetic warning, is nothing—naïvely believe that for all that they can still lead a moral life. (XXIX, 77)

Since eating rich and tasty foods stimulates our desire for additional physical pleasures (both gastronomical and sexual), Tolstoy's solution is thus for us to practice abstinence by striving as much as possible to make "unpalatable" the pleasures of the palate and thus to subscribe to a program of gastronomic asceticism that provides, in effect, the "pleasure of no pleasure."[31] Our main purpose in eating, after all, should be to provide healthy nourishment for the body, not to derive enjoyment from, or stimulation for, our taste buds.[32] Nourishment, rather than gustation, ought to be the primary physiological aim of the activity of eating; and a sort of gastronomic "chastity" constitutes the spiritual ideal toward which we should strive in matters concerning the palate. Our Christianity, according to Tolstoy, ought to be one of fasting and privations, not of beefsteaks and self-indulgence.[33]

After spending twenty pages of this twenty-seven-page essay sermonizing about the sin of gluttony and the virtue of abstinence, Tolstoy turns at last to the topic of vegetarianism per se. He mentions how reading Williams's "wonderful" book had prompted him to go visit a slaughterhouse in order to observe firsthand what it was that propelled the vegetarian movement (XXIX, 78). For the next five pages Tolstoy switches from his authoritative language and homilitic mode of discourse as a moral preacher to his incomparable narrative style as a verbal artist, depicting for the reader in gruesome naturalistic detail the manner in which innocent, terrified cattle are brutally slaughtered at the modern abattoir in Tula. The pages describing this gruesome slaughterhouse scene, R. F. Christian asserts, make more painful reading than any others we encounter in all of Tolstoy's oeuvre.[34] Finally, on the last two pages of the essay, Tolstoy at last addresses directly the issue of the fledgling vegetarian movement. "What is it that I wish to say? That for people to be moral they need to stop eating meat?" the author asks rhetorically. "Not at all," he continues. "I simply wished to say that for a good life a certain sequence of good actions are necessary" (XXIX, 84). The indispensable "first step" in this sequence of steps leading to the attainment of the morally good life, he reiterates, is abstinence:

> If he earnestly and sincerely strives to lead a good life, the first thing that a man will abstain from, while fasting, will always be the use of animal food, because, not to mention the arousal of passions produced by the food, its use is directly immoral since it necessitates killing, an act that is repugnant to moral sensibility, and it is provoked only by avarice and the desire for gourmandism. (XXIX, 84)

As we see, even here Tolstoy condemns the use of fleshly food in one's diet on ascetic as well as humanitarian grounds: eating meat is wrong not merely because it involves the slaughter of animals but also because it stimulates in human beings their base animal personalities and excites their sinful sexual lust. Tolstoy continues to advocate abstinence from meat because it will facilitate abstinence from sex.

🏵 *Christian Physiology: Graham, Alcott, and Kellogg*

Tolstoy's belief that diet can help shape morality seems to echo the view promulgated by key figures in the health reform movement in the United States in the nineteenth century, men such as Sylvester Graham (1794-1851), William Alcott (1798-1856), and John Harvey Kellogg (1852-1943), all of whom warned of the highly disturbing influence—even debilitating effect— that meat and other rich food products have upon the male sexual organs. Vegetarianism was regarded by these reformers, much as it would be by Tolstoy, mainly as a remedy for what they considered to be the dangerously uncontrollable male libido: the absence of meat in one's diet was promoted as a way of bringing about male sexual abstinence. Indeed, one scholar refers to Graham and other nineteenth-century health reformers as founders of "the male purity movement" in the United States, since these were men whose Victorian fears about male orgasm and whose obsessive concern with sexual purity led them to advocate behavioral reforms that involved bodily as well as social control.[35] As was true of the temperance movement, the brand of vegetarianism that held sway in the nineteenth-century United States was initially a religious one whose health reform program relied heavily upon scriptural authority—in particular, biblical injunctions against hurting, kill- ing, and eating animals. The origins of the vegetarian movement in the United States are usually traced back to late eighteenth-century England, where the Reverend William Cowherd (1763-1816), a Protestant minister, founded the Bible Christian Church and included abstinence from meat as one of the basic tenets of his teaching. In 1817, one of Cowherd's disciples, the Reverend William Metcalfe (1768-1862), assembled a group of Bible Christians and left with them for Philadelphia, where he established a new branch of the church. Shortly thereafter, Metcalfe published an essay, "Absti- nence from the Flesh of Animals" (1823), which attracted the attention of two men who would become instrumental in organizing and shaping the vegetarian movement in the United States: Graham and Alcott. Both of these reformers, as James Whorton has pointed out, sought to provide a "physio- logical" rationale to help support the moral superiority of a vegetarian diet that Cowherd and Metcalfe had advocated mainly on religious grounds: they preached, in short, that proper diet would save not only man's soul but also his body.[36]

Graham, a Presbyterian minister, became a fervent hygiene crusader who delivered public lectures up and down the Atlantic seaboard during the 1830s, inveighing against the pernicious aftereffects that an improper diet can have upon man's physical and mental well-being. Ill health, Graham firmly believed, results primarily from sexual overindulgence, which debilitates the body by robbing it of vital bodily fluids, thus diminishing its ability to resist illness. People can eliminate the cause of lust, however, by means of scrupulous attention to their daily diet and physical regimen. "For Graham," writes Stephen Nissenbaum, "a healthy freedom from sexual desire followed directly from the careful regulation of personal regimen, especially dietary practices—just as improper regimen inevitably led to unnaturally intense prurience."[37] Thus we find that some of Graham's most prominent ideas about vegetarianism were first articulated in a lecture he delivered about the dangers of masturbation (what was then more politely called "self-pollution") and marital sexual excess. In his *Lecture to Young Men* (1834), Graham proclaims:

> All kinds of stimulating and heating substances; high-seasoned foods; rich dishes; the free use of flesh; and even the excess of aliment; all, more or less,—and some to a very great degree—increase the concupiscent excitability and sensibility of the genital organs, and augment their influence on the functions of organic life, and on the intellectual and moral faculties.[38]

Like Tolstoy, Graham associates abstinence from animal food with sexual continence, but where Tolstoy's concern seems to have been mostly spiritual, Graham's was primarily physiological.[39] Indeed, in his study of the U.S. health reform movement, Whorton refers to Graham, Alcott, Kellogg, and other purity advocates from the nineteenth century as "Christian physiologists," since they sought to promote godliness by teaching their followers how to suppress their animal appetites and sexual passions mainly through a strict regimen of diet, exercise, and hygiene.[40]

Although William Alcott was by vocation a schoolteacher rather than a minister, he too brought a religious fervor and Christian perspective to his pronouncements on dietary reform. A cousin of Louisa May Alcott's rather eccentric father, Amos Bronson Alcott, William was an educator turned food crusader who helped to organize the first vegetarian society in the United States and served for a while as its president. At the banquet concluding the inaugural meeting of the new American Vegetarian Society held in New York in 1850, Alcott rose to propose a toast (of cold water, of course) to the fledgling movement, proclaiming that "a vegetable diet lies at the basis of all reform, whether civil, social, moral, or religious."[41] Invigorated by the same evangelical zeal that characterized Graham's advocacy of radical dietary and hygienic practices, Alcott firmly believed that human physiology provides the cornerstone upon which a Christian society can erect a heavenly kingdom on earth. Christian physiology, Whorton notes, served as Alcott's prescription for the coming millennium; to his mind, proper personal hygiene and a meatless diet promised an exalted moral purification and spiritual sanctification for those Christians who were willing to stop indulging their depraved bodily appetites and adopt correct living habits instead.[42] Properly educated and regulated physical appetites, Alcott confidently maintained, "are a means of lifting us toward the Eden whence we came."[43] One critic correctly observes that "in emphasizing the contribution of a healthy, beautiful body to Christian conduct, Alcott effectively made hygienic obedience prerequisite to moral progress."[44]

The name of John Harvey Kellogg is perhaps best remembered today in connection with cornflakes and his role in the rise of the breakfast cereal industry in our country, but he too was active in the moral reform movement. Like Graham and Alcott earlier, Kellogg sought to cleanse the souls of the members of his generation of Americans by purging their debauched bodies of the toxic poisons that meat, fat, and other elements of their "unnatural" diet had deposited within them. He also sought, again like Graham and Alcott, to advance a scientific theory of sexual abstinence, since he firmly believed that the legacy of sexual overindulgence is the spread of health-destroying effects throughout the human anatomy.[45] But whereas his two predecessors had concentrated their efforts on regulating the sorts of food that people ingest into their bodies through their mouths while eating, Kellogg focused his attention primarily on the digestive and eliminative processes that take place in bodily organs at the opposite end of the alimentary canal. Serving as director of the Battle Creek Sanitarium that Ellen White of the Seventh-Day Adventist Church had founded in Michigan in 1866, Dr. Kellogg became famous for his rigorous program of hydropathic therapy (the so-called "water cure") and frequent enemas, both of which were applied in an effort to clean out the human bowels and thus rid the intestines of the debilitating toxins that he claimed (in accord with the theory of "autointoxication") had accumulated there as a result of a highly carnal diet.[46] As a Christian moral reformer who had actually received some formal medical training, Kellogg was able to provide what seemed to be greater scientific support for the strict dietary rules and chaste sexual conduct that had also been advocated by earlier religious vegetarians such as Metcalfe, Graham, and Alcott. Dr. Kellogg, who referred to the high-fiber, antitoxic diet followed by the patients at his sanitarium as "scientific" or "biological" eating, believed that sexual immoderation—triggered primarily by a carnal diet—caused a myriad of mental and physical problems: sexuality, like hunger, was seen as an unhealthy urge that produced a harmful irritation within the human body, overstimulating and ultimately debilitating its vital organs. Sexual morality, for Dr. Kellogg, was essentially a problem of physical hygiene—a problem that could be remedied medically through a scientifically sound regimen of vegetarian diet and hydropathic cleansing of the bowels. As one critic notes, Kellogg at his sanitarium essentially "institutionalized and popularized the dietary and sexual principles which Graham first articulated in the 1830s."[47]

🌀 *The Meatless Diet: Purity Crusade or Food Faddism?*

Although Tolstoy does not appear to have been directly acquainted with the writings of Graham, Alcott, or Kellogg, and although his argument for converting to a vegetarian diet may well lack the scientific grounding or coherence of the physiological rationale provided by these American health reformers, he too associates abstinence from animal food very closely with abstinence from sexual activity. Tolstoy shares another important similarity with these purity crusaders from the United States: namely, a disdain for the civilizing process of socioeconomic modernization. All four of these men—Graham, Alcott, Kellogg, and Tolstoy—developed their rather eccentric views on diet and chastity during a period in the history of their respective societies when the pressures and artificial conditions of modern urban life had made the public extremely apprehensive about human sexuality. Graham's food theories, for example, emerged during the Jacksonian era largely as a way to deny the power of the new values of the capitalist marketplace, which was rapidly replacing the family household as the primary locus for economic activity and social relationships in the early nineteenth-century United States.[48] The traditional homemade bread—baked with unadulterated whole wheat flour—that Graham championed so passionately in his writings (what has come to be known as "Graham bread") was itself mainly a symbolic protest against the growing commercialization of grain agriculture in the United States during a period of vanishing economic self-sufficiency. "The transformation of American sexual ideology and behavior," Jayme Sokolow points out, "coincided with the modernization process. During the nineteenth century, urbanization, commercialization, industrialization, and increased geographical mobility made antebellum America appear disorderly and dangerous to many reformers."[49] Later in the century, Dr. Kellogg would likewise crusade against the artificial conditions and enervating effects of urban life, urging the well-to-do patrons at his Battle Creek Sanitarium not only to adopt a more natural diet but also to incorporate a daily regimen of bodily exercise into their largely sedentary and sybaritic lives. "Kellogg's advocacy of extreme self-denial," Sokolow writes, "was related to his vision of the city, the center of luxury, corruption, and sexual indulgence. His books and sanitarium were designed to counteract urban civilization by re-creating rural life and habits, which were synonymous with natural health and sexual restraint."[50]

In the case of Tolstoy, he and some of his fellow countrymen began to voice their deep anxieties about human sexuality and the perceived decline of morality in Russian society only near the end of the century, when the modernizing process accelerated sharply following the reforms of Alexander II. As recent studies devoted to this topic have shown, the debate on sexual morality in Russia intensified greatly during the 1890s and early 1900s, when public discourse began to occupy itself with such controversial social and moral issues as rape, divorce, abortion, venereal disease, prostitution, homosexuality, and masturbation.[51] Tolstoy's own literary output during this period—works such as *The Devil* (1890), *Father Sergius* (1898), and *Resurrection* (1899)—amply reflect this general anxiety over male sexual desire felt within educated Russian society at the turn of the century, when the ideology of extreme sexual moderation became a dominant attitude.[52] As Laura Engelstein notes, "the Russian adoption of a (modified) Victorianism coincided with the revolt against Victorianism in the West."[53] Tolstoy's own hostility to modernization led him to identify ever more closely with the traditional, unspoiled way of life of the Russian peasant, whose dietary habits and hygienic regimen roughly approximated those advocated by the purity crusaders.

Present-day historians of the vegetarian movement in Russia tend to ignore the close association between abstinence from meat and abstinence from sex posited by Tolstoy. Instead they emphasize the progressive, humanitarian aspects of Tolstoy's vegetarianism: how his refusal to eat meat stems from his ethical refusal to commit violence upon any of God's living creatures. Dudley Giehl, for example, disregards the direct testimony of the Tolstoy family governness, Anna Sauron, who maintained that "the Count took up these manias only in the spirit of penitence, to subdue his flesh and elevate and enlighten his spirit."[54] "Notwithstanding Anna Sauron's comments," Giehl writes, "it is quite apparent that Tolstoy had adopted the vegetarian diet out of his compassion for animals."[55] It is not difficult to understand why historians of vegetarianism would prefer to emphasize the humanitarian rather than the Christian, ascetic, or physiological side of Tolstoy's avoidance of meat. For one thing, the ascetic and religious considerations that prompted Tolstoy's decision to adopt a meatless diet resonate with an antisexualism that was not likely to attract many converts to vegetarianism during the twentieth century. Like both Graham and Kellogg, Tolstoy displayed a traditional

Christian distrust of the flesh, viewing sexual desire as a pathological disorder that unleashed the animal nature in man, an instinctual side of human beings that needed to be controlled, in part, through extreme dietary measures.[56] Like them, he believed that concupiscence represents not merely the sin but also the disease of a lustful appetite.[57] To his mind, the craving for meat, like the craving for sex, was more than just a depraved habit that stupefied man's sensibilities; it was a pathological condition that must be remedied through diet and physical labor.

In addition to its Victorian antisexualism, Tolstoy's ascetic argument for vegetarianism rested on the rather shaky foundation provided by a kind of physiological pseudo-science that proved very popular during much of the nineteenth century. Modern advances in medicine (and especially nutritional science) during the past hundred years have invalidated most, if not all, of the physiological premises on which the nineteenth-century health reformers based their views on diet and sexuality. There is, as a result, a quite legitimate fear among true believers in vegetarianism that the movement as a whole is seriously discredited, or at least greatly trivialized, when it is associated with this so-called "Christian physiology," since a meatless diet will likely be treated as yet another outdated food fad that lacks scientific validity.[58] This is exactly what happens, for example, in a popular paperback written in the 1970s by Ronald M. Deutsch entitled *The New Nuts among the Berries: How Nutrition Nonsense Captured America*, which humorously tells the story of various food faddists during the first two hundred years of our country's history—"all the nutty people who have exploited our desire for better health," as the author puts it. Among those "nutty" people whom Deutsch profiles in his book are Graham, Alcott, and Kellogg, whose physiological arguments for adopting a meatless diet are, of course, thoroughly discredited.[59] More recently, the popular film based on T. Coraghessan Boyle's satirical novel *The Road to Wellville* (1993) broadly ridicules Kellogg's advocacy of a meatless diet by treating it as yet another bizarre food fad advanced by a neurotic fitness fanatic.

It is no doubt in an effort to prevent a similar charge of food faddism and nutritional quackery from being leveled against the eccentric Tolstoy that his vegetarianism has been closely identified with the issues of pacifism, nonviolence, and animal rights. Thus we read in a recent Russian book entitled *Vse o vegetarianstve* [Everything about vegetarianism] (1992) how Tolstoy's essay "The First Step" is mainly devoted to the question of the immorality of killing other living creatures: "the first step in the moral perfection of man, in the author's opinion, ought to be the refusal to take part in violence toward helpless creatures."[60] Tolstoy's gruesome depiction of the Tula slaughterhouse is then paraphrased, with lengthy citations taken from the final section of "The First Step." Indeed, it has become a rather common practice within vegetarian publishing circles to reprint only the final section of Tolstoy's essay, where he describes his visit to the abattoir, and to exclude the main part, where he discusses at length gluttony, fasting, and carnal appetite.[61] In this way, Tolstoy's ascetic notions about diet and sexuality can be conveniently muted and safely distanced from his moral and ethical grounds for advocating vegetarianism. At the same time, however, we are deprived of the full meaning of Tolstoy's "way of no flesh," since his vegetarianism is seriously decontextualized when it is severed from two of its most defining philosophical bases: abstinence theory and Christian physiology.

NOTES

Research for this project was supported by a grant from the International Research and Exchanges Board, with funds provided by the U.S. Department of State (Title VIII) and the National Endowment for the Humanities. I also wish to acknowledge the generous support provided by the Kennan Institute for Advanced Russian Studies, the Summer Research Laboratory on Russia and Eastern Europe at the University of Illinois, as well as the Center for the Humanities and the Office of the Dean of the College of Liberal Arts at the University of New Hampshire. None of these organizations is responsible for the views expressed. Finally, I wish to thank two of my UNH colleagues, Cathy Frierson and Sam Smith, for reading and critiquing earlier versions of this manuscript.

1. V. I. Porudominsky, "L. N. Tolstoi i etika pitaniia" [L. N. Tolstoy and the ethics of diet], *Chelovek* [Man], vol. 2 (1992), 106.

2. Cathy Frierson discusses the diet and "involuntary" vegetarianism of the Russian peasants in chap. 4 of this volume and in a paper, "The Meatless Peasant Diet in Late Nineteenth-Century Russia," that she delivered at a panel on Russian vegetarianism at the annual meeting of the New England Slavic Association held at the Russian Research Center of Harvard University in Cambridge, Mass., in April 1994. Leonid Heretz examines how the absence of meat in the diet of the Russian peasant was dictated in part by the Orthodox religious practice of abstinence; see chap. 5 in the present volume.

3. Janet Barkas, *The Vegetable Passion* (New York: Charles Scribner's Sons, 1975), 154.

4. For Tolstoy's influence upon Peter Verigin, see chap. 9, "Tolstoy and the Doukhobors," of Barkas, *The Vegetable Passion*, 154–165, and Colin Spencer, *The Heretic's Feast: A History of Vegetarianism* (London: Fourth Estate, 1993), 289–290.

5. For a synopsis of the influence of Tolstoy's moralistic writings worldwide, see William B. Edgerton, "The Artist Turned Prophet: Leo Tolstoj after 1880," in *American Contributions to the Sixth International Congress of Slavists* (Hague-Paris: Mouton, 1968), vol. 2, 61–85.

6. Sergei Tolstoy, *Tolstoy Remembered by His Son*, trans. Moura Budberg (London: Weidenfeld & Nicolson, 1961), 145. For an informative biographical sketch of Frey, see N. V. Reingardt, *Neobyknovennaia lichnost'* [An extraordinary person] (Kazan', 1889).

7. Barkas, *The Vegetable Passion*, 157.

RONALD D. LEBLANC

8. In response to a letter from A. D. Zutphen, a Dutch medical student who had read in a newspaper about Tolstoy's frugal meals and wrote to inquire about the writer's diet, Tolstoy wrote, "My health not only has not suffered; it has in fact improved significantly since I have given up milk, butter, and eggs, as well as sugar, tea and coffee." See L. N. Tolstoi, *Polnoe sobranie sochinenii* [Complete collected works] (Moscow: Khudozhestvennaia literatura, 1928-1958), vol. LXVII, 32. All further quotes from Tolstoy's novels, stories, diaries, essays, and letters will come from this ninety-volume jubilee edition of his complete works. These references will be listed parenthetically in the text by volume (Roman numerals) and page (Arabic numbers).

9. See, for instance, Barkas, *The Vegetable Passion*, 157.

10. S. A. Tolstaia, *Dnevniki v dvukh tomakh* [Diaries in two volumes] (Moscow: Khudozhestvennaia literatura, 1978), vol. 1, 359.

11. See I. S. Listovsky, *Zametki na "Kreitserovu sonatu" grafa L. N. Tolstova* [Notes on Count Tolstoy's "Kreutzer Sonata"] (Moscow, 1891), 9-10. Such a sentiment is no doubt what underlies the comic episode in Il'f and Petrov's *Dvenadtsat' stul'ev* [The twelve chairs] (1928), in which Kolya Kalachov, a zealous vegetarian, attempts to convince his wife, Liza, of the nutritional value of such inexpensive meals as "fake rabbit," carrot roast, and vegetarian frankfurters. Kolya invokes the name of Count Tolstoy, pointing out that the famous Russian author did not eat meat either. Liza reminds him that Tolstoy did indeed eat meat while he was writing *War and Peace* and that he positively stuffed himself while he was writing *Anna Karenina*. "And I suppose that while he was writing the *Kreutzer Sonata* he also stuffed himself?" Kolya shoots back venemously. "The *Kreutzer Sonata* is a short work," Liza explains. "But just imagine him trying to write *War and Peace* on a diet of vegetarian frankfurters!" See Il'ia Il'f and Evgenii Petrov, *Sobranie sochinenii v piati tomakh* [Collected works in five volumes] (Moscow: Khudozhestvennaia literatura, 1961), vol. 1, 166-167.

12. T. von Galetsky, for example, linked Tolstoy's conversion to a meatless diet very closely with the evils of hunting and cruelty toward animals. In *Leo Tolstoi und der Vegetarismus* (Frankfurt, 1906), von Galetsky asserts that for Tolstoy compassion is one of man's highest ethical principles and forbids us from killing others. The author then proceeds to discuss Tolstoy's description of terrible scenes of cruelty toward animals witnessed during hunting trips and in visits to slaughterhouses. See the Russian translation of this essay, *L. N. Tolstoi i vegetarianstvo* [L. N. Tolstoy and vegetarianism] (Moscow: Posrednik, 1913). Vladimir Chertkov, who is credited by Iurii Perper with having introduced Tolstoy to vegetarianism, had himself authored a pamphlet that condemns the evils of hunting: *Zlaia zabava: Mysli ob okhote* [An evil pastime: Thoughts about hunting] (Moscow: Posrednik, 1890). Tolstoy, who suggested the title of the pamphlet to Chertkov, agreed to write a preface for it (XXVII, 290).

13. Porudominsky, "Tolstoy and the Ethics of Diet," 116.

14. For a discussion of the moral and ethical grounds for vegetarianism, see R. G. Frey, *Rights, Killing, and Suffering: Moral Vegetarianism and Applied Ethics* (Oxford: Basil Blackwell, 1983).

15. Tolstoy first received a copy of Williams's *Ethics of Diet* from Chertkov in April 1891 and informed him, in a letter of 29 April 1891, that he would like to write a preface to it (LXXXVII, 84). In a letter of 6 May 1891, Tolstoy tells Chertkov that his daughters have already started translating it (LXXXVII, 85). "The First Step" appeared originally in the journal *Voprosy filosofii i psikhologii* [Questions of philosophy and psychology], vol. 13 (1892), 109-144; it was republished a year later as the introductory essay to the Russian translation of Williams's book. See *Etika pishchi; ili, Nravstvennye osnovy bezuboinogo*

pitaniia dlia cheloveka: sobranie zhizneopisanii i vyderzhek iz sochinenii vydaiushchikhsia mys-litelei vsekh vremen [The ethics of food; or, the moral bases of a meatless diet for man: A collection of biographical sketches and excerpts from the writings of prominent thinkers of all times] (Moscow: Posrednik, 1893), v–xxxi.

16. According to R. F. Christian, reading Williams's book effectively resolved all Tolstoy's hesitations about following a meatless diet. See "Tolstoy and the First Step," *Scottish Slavonic Review*, vol. 20 (1993), 8.

17. Barkas, *The Vegetable Passion*, 158. Tolstoy's wife noted his visit to the slaughter-house in her diary: "He went to the slaughterhouse again and told us in great agitation what a frightful spectacle it was: how the cattle are afraid when they are being led in and how their skin is flayed off of them, starting from the head, while their legs are still kicking and they have not yet died." See *Dnevniki*, vol. 1, 191.

18. Coral Lansbury, *The Old Brown Dog: Women, Workers, and Vivisection in Edwardian England* (Madison: University of Wisconsin Press, 1985), 177.

19. Isaac Skelton, "The Vegetarian Tradition in Russian Literature," manuscript, 42.

20. See my article, "Unpalatable Pleasures: Tolstoy, Food, and Sex," *Tolstoy Studies Journal*, vol. 6 (1993), 1–32. My discussion of Tolstoy's attitude toward food and sex here largely repeats the arguments that I made in this earlier article.

21. As René Fueloep Miller notes, "When Tolstoy, the sensualist, turned moralist, the body with its carnal desires ceased to be the subject of ectasy and became the target of scorn. Tolstoy, who had once glorified the body, now preached that the flesh had to be forcibly broken to bring about the liberation and salvation of the soul. He demanded the mortification of the body, and he was no less insistent in this demand than Saint Anthony or the pillar saints in the Lybian desert." See René Fueloep Miller, "Tolstoy the Apostolic Crusader," *Russian Review*, vol. 19, no. 2 (1960), 101–102.

22. Listovsky accuses Tolstoy of somewhat idealizing the peasant diet as healthy and wholesome. "We do not know of those localities," the critic writes, "where peasants are satisfied with bread, *kvas*, and onion, and where, moreover, they are hale and hearty" (*Zametki na "Kreitserovu sonatu" grafa L. N. Tolstova*, 31).

23. In *Die Pfennig-Sonate* (1890), one of the several parodies of the *Kreutzer Sonata* that arose as part of the counterliterature that appeared in the wake of Tolstoy's controversial tale, Sigmar Mehring pokes fun at this causal connection that Tolstoy makes between sexual and gastronomic abstinence. In Mehring's parodic sequel, the narrator once again meets Pozdnyshev on a train and listens to his account of how he killed a second wife. "His account of his second conjugal murder," one critic writes, "is interwoven with a series of nonsensical arguments in favour of total abstinence—from food!" See Peter Ulf Møller, *Postlude to the Kreutzer Sonata: Tolstoj and the Debate on Sexual Morality in Russian Literature in the 1890s*, trans. John Kendal (New York: E. J. Brill, 1988), 169. "We should never eat," Pozdnyshev asserts in Mehring's sequel. "We should return again to primitive abstinence—that is the ideal condition for all those who are possessed by cultural catarrh. How many wails and how many wants would disappear from the world if only we would free ourselves from the ridiculous habit of eating." I am quoting here from the Russian translation, *Groshevaia sonata* [The Half-Kopeck Sonata] (St. Petersburg, 1890), 9.

24. For a discussion of Chekhov's flirtation with Tolstoyism, see Josephine M. New-combe, "Was Čexov a Tolstoyan?" *Slavic and East European Journal*, vol. 18, no. 2 (1974), 143–152, and Harold Schefski, "Chekhov and Tolstoyan Philosophy," *New Zealand Slavonic Journal*, 1985, 81–88.

25. Iurii Perper, among others, refers to Tolstoy's "The First Step" as the "Bible of vegetarianism." See Perper, "Dobavlenie k stat'e, 'Lev Nikolaevich Tolstoi kak vege-

tarianets'" [Supplement to the essay, "Lev Nikolaevich Tolstoy as a vegetarian"], *Vegetarianskoe obozrenie* [Vegetarian review], vol. 2, no. 2 (February 1909), 24.

26. This is exactly the way that Tolstoy himself refers to the essay in his diary and correspondence during the summer of 1891 while he was engaged in writing it. "Last night I was still thinking about the preface to the vegetarian book, that is, about abstinence, and I wrote not badly all morning," Tolstoy records in his diary on June 25 (LII, 43). On July 13 he writes that he has finished writing the "article about gluttony" (LII, 44). And again on August 27 he mentions how for the past two days he has been making corrections to the "article about gluttony" (LII, 50).

27. In a diary entry of 25 June 1890, Tolstoy writes: "I ought to write a book called GORGING: Belshazzar's feast, bishops, tsars, and taverns. Meetings, partings, and jubilees. People think that they are occupied with various important matters, but they are occupied only with gluttony" (LI, 53).

28. To show that engaging in sexual intercourse for purposes of pleasure is morally wrong, Tolstoy resorts in his essay to a gastronomic analogy. He writes that "the attainment of the goal of union with the object of love, whether in marriage or outside of marriage, no matter how poeticized that union might be, is a goal unworthy of man, just as is unworthy of man the goal of acquiring for oneself sweet and abundant food, which is imagined by many people to be the highest blessing" (XXVII, 82).

29. See Leo Tolstoy, *The Relations of the Sexes*, trans. Vladimir Chertkov (Christchurch, England: Free Age Press, 1901), 37–38.

30. "I read the Shakers," Tolstoy records in his diary on 9 April 1889. "Excellent. Complete sexual abstinence" (L, 64). Tolstoy mentions these Shaker brochures in a letter to Chertkov written the very next day (LXXXVI, 224).

31. Focusing primarily on eating disorders among women in contemporary society, Margaret R. Miles examines how, paradoxically, ascetic practices could actually be said to be "pleasurable." See her essay, "Textual Harassment: Desire and the Female Body," in *The Good Body: Asceticism in Contemporary Culture*, ed. Mary G. Winkler and Letha B. Cole (New Haven: Yale University Press, 1994), 49–63.

32. Tolstoy makes quite explicit his utilitarian attitude toward food and eating in *Chto takoe iskusstvo?* [What is art?] (1897–1898): "If we were to analyze the question of food, it would not occur to anyone to see the importance of food to reside in the pleasure that we receive from eating it. Everyone understands that the satisfaction of our taste can in no way serve as the basis for our determination of the merits of food, and that we therefore have no right to suppose that the dinners with cayenne pepper, limburger cheese, alcohol, etc., to which we are accustomed and which please us, constitute the very best human food. To see the aim and purpose of art in the pleasure we derive from it is like assuming . . . that the purpose and aim of food consist in the pleasure derived from consuming it. People came to understand that the meaning of food resides in the nourishment of the body only when they ceased to consider that the aim of that activity is pleasure. And the same is true with regard to art. People will come to understand the meaning of art only when they cease to consider that the aim of that activity is beauty, i.e., pleasure" (XXX, 60–61).

33. In "The First Step," Tolstoy mentions how an evangelical, who had attacked monastic asceticism, once boasted that his brand of Christianity had nothing to do with fasting and privations; instead it was based on beefsteaks. "Christianity and virtue together with beefsteaks!" Tolstoy exclaims rather incredulously (XXIX, 78).

34. Christian, "Tolstoy and the First Step," 12.

35. Carroll Smith-Rosenberg, "Sex as Symbol in Victorian Purity: An Ethnohistorical

Analysis of Jacksonian America," in *Turning Points: Historical and Sociological Essays on the Family*, ed. John Demos and Sarane Spence Boocock (Chicago: University of Chicago Press, 1978), 213.

36. James C. Whorton, "'Tempest in a Flesh-Pot': The Formulation of a Physiological Rationale for Vegetarianism," *Journal of the History of Medicine and Applied Sciences*, vol. 32, no. 2 (April 1977), 115-139.

37. Stephen Nissenbaum, *Sex, Diet, and Debility in Jacksonian America: Sylvester Graham and Health Reform* (Westport: Greenwood Press, 1980), 32. For additional biographical background on Graham, see Richard Harrison Shryock, "Sylvester Graham and the Popular Health Movement, 1830-1870," *Medicine in America: Historical Essays* (Baltimore: Johns Hopkins University Press, 1966), 111-125.

38. Sylvester Graham, *Lecture to Young Men* (Providence, R.I., 1834; reprint, New York: Arno Press, 1974), 18-19.

39. Some of Tolstoy's contemporary critics, however, accused the author of reducing human beings to their basic physiological instincts. According to A. Gusev, for example, "Count Tolstoy sees absolutely no difference whatsoever between man and animals." Gusev cites the opinion of Elizabeth Fields, an American writer, who insisted that "Tolstoy's psychology is mere physiology." See Gusev, *O brake i bezbrachii. Protiv "Kreitserovoi sonaty" i "Poslesloviia" k nei grafa L. Tolstogo* [On marriage and celibacy: Contra Count Tolstoy's "Kreutzer Sonata" and the "Afterword" to it] (Kazan, 1891), 9-10, 128-129.

40. James C. Whorton, *Crusaders for Fitness: The History of American Health Reformers* (Princeton, N.J.: Princeton University Press, 1982). See esp. chap. 2, "Christian Physiology," 38-61.

41. *American Vegetarian*, vol. 1 (1851), 25.

42. James C. Whorton, "'Christian Physiology': William Alcott's Prescription for the Millennium," *Bulletin of the History of Medicine*, vol. 49, no. 4 (1975), 466-481.

43. William Alcott, *The Laws of Health; or, Sequel to "The House I Live In"* (Boston, 1859), 187.

44. Whorton, "'Christian Physiology,'" 474.

45. For background information on Kellogg, see Richard W. Schwartz, *John Harvey Kellogg, M.D.* (Nashville: Southern Publishing Association, 1970), and Gerald Carson, *Cornflake Crusade* (New York: Holt, Rinehart, and Winston, 1957). In his writings, Kellogg frequently cites Graham, whom he credits with being "the founder of the modern movement for dietetic reform." See, for example, *The Natural Diet of Man* (Battle Creek, Mich.: Modern Medicine Publishing Co., 1923; reprint, Imlaystown, N.J.: Edenite Society, Inc., 1980), 89.

46. See, for example, J. H. Kellogg, *Autointoxication; or, Intestinal Toxemia* (Battle Creek, Mich.: Good Health Publishing Co., 1919), and *Colon Hygiene: Comprising New and Important Facts concerning the Physiology of the Colon and an Account of Practical and Successful Methods of Combating Intestinal Inactivity and Toxemia* (Battle Creek, Mich.: Good Health Publishing Co., 1915).

47. Jayme A. Sokolow, *Eros and Modernization: Sylvester Graham, Health Reform, and the Origins of Victorian Sexuality in America* (Rutherford, N.J.: Farleigh Dickinson University Press, 1983), 163.

48. Nissenbaum, *Sex, Diet, and Debility*, 4.

49. Sokolow, *Eros and Modernization*, 14. Sokolow adds, however, that the U.S. health reformers were confident that "individual morality and proper physiology could counteract the ruinous temptations of contemporary urban civilization and lead to a moral revolution" (14).

50. Ibid., 163.

51. In addition to Møller's *Postlude to The Kreutzer Sonata,* see Laura Engelstein, *The Keys to Happiness: Sex and the Search for Modernity in Fin-de-Siècle Russia* (Ithaca, N.Y.: Cornell University Press, 1992), esp. chap. 6, "Eros and Revolution: The Problem of Male Desire," 215–253.

52. John M. Kopper discusses some of these texts in his essay "Tolstoy and the Narrative of Sex: A Reading of 'Father Sergius,' 'The Devil,' and 'The Kreutzer Sonata.'" in *In the Shade of the Giant: Essays on Tolstoy,* ed. Hugh McLean (Berkeley: University of California Press, 1989), 158–186.

53. Engelstein, *Keys to Happiness,* 6.

54. Quoted in Aylmer Maude, *The Life of Tolstoy,* vol. 2 (London: Oxford University Press, 1917), 213.

55. Dudley Giehl, *Vegetarianism: A Way of Life* (New York: Harper and Row, 1979), 135. Giehl adds that "it is the ethical aspect of vegetarianism that is emphasized in Tolstoy's writings which deal with this subject" (136).

56. Dmitry Merezhkovsky, Vasily Rozanov, and other religious modernists in Russia at the turn of the century maintained that this renunciatory brand of Christianity was responsible for placing Tolstoy, who was by nature a robust hedonist, in direct conflict with his own flesh. Rozanov describes the visit he made in 1905 to Tolstoy's estate in the essay "Poezdka v Iasnuiu Polianu" [A trip to Yasnaya Polyana]. According to Rozanov, Christianity derived not only from Golgotha but also from fasting: "to be more exact, Golgotha did not begin to conquer the world until it united with fasting; it discovered the secret way to influence the souls of people by means of mushrooms, *kasha,* and soup." See *O Tolstom. Mezhdunarodnyi tolstovskii almanakh* [On Tolstoy: An international Tolstoyan almanac], ed. P. Sergeenko (Moscow, 1909), 288.

57. On the antisexualism of the American health reformers, see John Money, *The Destroying Angel: Sex, Fitness, and Food in the Legacy of Degeneracy Theory, Graham Crackers, Kellogg's Corn Flakes and American Health History* (Buffalo, N.Y.: Prometheus Books, 1985), esp. chap. 2, "The Diet That Cured Sex," 17–27, and chap. 8, "Sylvester Graham's Concupiscence Disease," 61–67. Nissenbaum likewise discusses the antisexualist views of Graham and Kellogg in *Sex, Diet, and Debility,* esp. chap. 7, "Sex: The Pathology of Desire," 105–124. One of Tolstoy's contemporaries, Vladimir D. Vol'fson, attempted to provide a physiological basis for the author's austere views on sexuality; see his *"Kreitserova sonata" grafa L. N. Tolstogo s tochki zreniia gigieny. Gigiena vozderzhaniia* [Count Tolstoy's "Kreutzer Sonata" from the point of view of hygiene: The hygiene of abstinence] (St. Petersburg, 1899).

58. This fear is expressed by Carol J. Adams, who maintains that the tendency in our culture to trivialize vegetarianism (by reducing it to merely a food fad) constitutes a deliberate strategy for delegitimizing a valid reform movement and thus for preserving patriarchal attitudes and male dominance. See Adams, *The Sexual Politics of Meat: A Feminist-Vegetarian Critical Theory* (New York: Continuum, 1990), 154–155.

59. Ronald Deutsch, *The New Nuts among the Berries: How Nutrition Nonsense Captured America* (Palo Alto, Calif.: Bull, 1977).

60. I. L. Medkova, T. N. Pavlova, and B. V. Bramburg, *Vse o vegetarianstve* (Moscow: Ekonomika, 1992), 230.

61. This practice seems to have originated with Chertkov, whose Posrednik press published Tolstoy's depiction of the Tula slaughterhouse in "The First Step" as a separate pamphlet entitled *Na boine* [At the slaughterhouse] (1911).

SEVEN

DARRA GOLDSTEIN

Is Hay Only for Horses?
Highlights of Russian Vegetarianism
at the Turn of the Century

The subject of vegetarianism in Russia inevitably conjures up Lev Tolstoy, a guru for vegetarians of all stripes even today. As author of "Pervaia stupen'" [The first step], an impassioned preface to the 1891 Russian translation of Howard Williams's tract on vegetarianism,[1] Tolstoy publicly associated himself with the vegetarian cause, and by linking his name with the vegetarian crusader's, he directly influenced the development of vegetarianism in Russia. Vegetarian promoters repeatedly invoked Tolstoy's name; and so forcefully did Peter Verigin, the leader of the Dukhobor religious sect, preach Tolstoy's method to his followers that they willingly gave up meat, alcohol, and tobacco.[2] Meanwhile, Tolstoy's own disciples practiced vegetarianism in the communities they founded based on their understanding of his teachings.

Yet despite such wide-ranging and profound influence, nowhere in his work does Tolstoy espouse vegetarianism per se. Rather, for him the disavowal of meat is simply one step in his quest for moral self-perfection. Although Tolstoy was mythologized as a vegetarian pacifist, in truth his abstinence did not initially arise from ethical considerations, the eloquence of his famous slaughterhouse description in "The First Step" notwithstanding. Tolstoy struggled against carnal and gustatory temptation alike, the renunciation of sex and meat being equally important for attaining moral purity. Thus his treatise on the first step toward ethical living shows far greater concern with the rigors of asceticism than with compassion for animals.[3] In a letter written near the end of his life, Tolstoy made his views explicit: "It is not necessary to make vegetarianism the main goal of your efforts. The goal worthy of man and attributable to him is overall perfection in his moral life. Vegetarianism is only one of the results of moral perfection. If man sets this overall goal for himself, then in all likelihood he will discover many shortcomings in himself and will first direct his efforts toward eradicating them before becoming a strict vegetarian."[4]

Such subleties were lost, however, on a public that yearned for a ready way to emulate the master. The disingenuous myth of Tolstoy as a compassionate vegetarian was further diffused by his principal disciple, Vladimir Chertkov, largely through publications from the Posrednik Publishing House, which Tolstoy and Chertkov founded in 1885. As Posrednik's first editor, Chertkov formulated its mission "to communicate to the public in selected literary and popular scientific works the Christian world view at which Tolstoy arrived after long and agonized searching."[5] In espousing humanitarian goals, the editorial staff made clear that one way for readers to achieve "a pure bright life" (*chistaia svetlaia zhizn'*)[6] was through good eating habits. Thus, in the 1890s, Posrednik began to publish numerous books on vegetarianism. Posrednik billed itself as a publishing house "for cultured readers" (*dlia intelligentnykh chitatelei*), and a vegetarian diet was meant to appeal precisely to them. No one expected to make converts of the Russian peasantry, who practiced vegetarianism perforce.[7] It was the overfed, gouty, leisured class that needed not only to eat less but also to develop a social conscience against the slaughter of helpless animals, as well as a sense of justice in the face of widespread hunger.

Largely through the efforts of Posrednik, the Russian vegetarian movement in its early years attempted to cover all grounds, in order to appeal to the greatest number of people. Thus Posrednik's publications represented vegetarianism not only as ethically based but also as grounded in religious thought. Practical and dietary considerations were similarly important. Therefore anyone suffering from malaise, whether physical or spiritual, could turn to vegetarianism for revival. And indeed, several prominent groups of the time embraced vegetarianism, even without Tolstoy as direct inspiration. The theosophists, following Rudolf Steiner, practiced vegetarianism. So did the Esperantists, who found vegetarianism entirely in keeping with their internationalist goals. A separate League of Vegetarian Esperantists vowed "to make esperantists vegetarians, to esperantize vegetarians, and to be of practical benefit to one another."[8] Esperanto was often used as the official language for speeches and debates at international vegetarian congresses.[9]

Two of Posrednik's greatest proselytizers were the husband and wife team of Aleksandr Petrovich and Ol'ga Konstantinovna Zelenkova. A practicing biologist and physician, Aleksandr Petrovich published books on homeopathy and the biological sciences and edited a translation of Plato's writings on vegetarianism. He is perhaps best known as a founder and chairman of Russia's first vegetarian society. An ideological pioneer, he simultaneously crusaded against alcohol, and, as may well be imagined, his temperate stance did little to enhance the popularity of vegetarianism in Russia. Although his wife held the same sober beliefs, she wisely chose to approach vegetarianism as any conscientious housewife would, by emphasizing its benefits. Ol'ga Konstantinovna can thus be given much of the credit for popularizing the vegetarian way. Writing in a chatty manner quite dissimilar to her husband's tendentious theorizing, she published four pamphlets and a lively cookbook, *I Don't Eat Anyone,* under the pseudonym "Vegetarianka" [A Vegetarian].[10]

Zelenkova's first pamphlet, only sixteen pages long, is the most engaging. Here we find brief articles about Tolstoy's vegetarianism and the ease of realizing a vegetarian diet, a list of suppliers to the St. Petersburg Vegetarian Society, a menu from a vegetarian cafeteria, and the minutes of the first meeting of the society. Zelenkova knowingly appeals to the housewife's point of view by pointing out that not only are vegetarian food products always fresh (*tovar ne zalezhivaetsia*), but their prices are "strikingly" lower than those in small shops, because they can be purchased in bulk.[11] Vegetarian ideology is important to Zelenkova, but so are the way food tastes and the ease with which it can be prepared. She admits that "of course, keeping house is generally not interesting, it's monotonous and boring, even very boring, but if we're convinced that the well-being of our family depends on the successful resolution of this question, then we'll find enough good will and endurance to do it: we have only to want to."[12] As Zelenkova knows, however, emotional appeals are not enough. What will truly help is good cookware, in this case "Peterson's Patent Reform Cooker" with its nearly hermetic seal. Imported from Baden Baden, this early version of a pressure cooker does not require the copious (and hence economically exploitative) amounts of firewood needed to stoke the massive Russian stove. Since the cooking is accomplished by steam, vegetables retain their flavor and nourishment. Although this modern appliance is largely unavailable in St. Petersburg, Zelenkova hastens to assure her readers that an everyday potato cooker can be substituted.

Zelenkova remains unbending in her imprecations against alcohol. As elsewhere in Europe, the Russian temperance and vegetarian movements were generally allied,[13] and Tolstoy's admonitions against intoxicants of all kinds are well known. Zelenkova goes further, however. In addition to alcohol, she condemns all sorts of spices and singles out coffee, tea, kola nuts, and guarana seeds as especially dangerous. She seems to have a particular prejudice against America and its uncivilized inhabitants, citing the addiction of American women to coffee, which she compares to American men's need for whiskey.[14] America even gets blamed for the lowly potato—neither a spice nor an intoxicant—which she anathematizes for its relatively high content of potassium and sodium. Zelenkova concludes: "One can only regret the initial export of the potato from America and its introduction onto European soil."[15]

Such diatribes notwithstanding, the founding of the St. Petersburg Vegetarian Society early in 1902 ushered in an era of intense activity and interest in vegetarianism in Russia. Within a decade similar societies had been formed in Moscow, Kiev, and Poltava. Individuals in cities as far-flung as Saratov, Vologda, and Ekaterinoslav expressed interest in forming local chapters.[16] With their idealistic agenda, perhaps it is inevitable that the vegetarians, like other groups, would fall prey to factional fighting, particularly since each party was desperately in need of funds. As the first vegetarian society, the St. Petersburg chapter wrote into its charter that if other groups wanted to form elsewhere, they had first to receive permission from the mother organization.[17] This elitist attitude caused considerable dismay, and friction seems to have been particularly acute between the St. Petersburg society and the highly active Kiev group. Not only did the St. Petersburg beau monde see Kiev as terribly provincial, but a number of the most active members of the Kiev group, including I. O. Perper and E. O. Dymshits, had names that were obviously Jewish. This factor suggests that the tension between the parties reflected societal divisions extending well beyond any ethical considerations of vegetarianism.

Thanks to two journals published in the early years of this century, the activities of the various societies and the trends in vegetarianism can quite easily be traced. Eighteen issues of *Vegetarianskii vestnik* [The vegetarian herald] appeared in St. Petersburg between 1904 and 1905; *Vegetarianskoe obozrenie* [Vegetarian review] was published in Kiev from 1909 to 1915.[18] The journals define three stages of vegetarianism. The first, or "literary," period occurred before 1901. The second, or "theoretical," stage lasted from 1901 to 1907 and represented a time of organization surrounding the founding of the St. Petersburg Vegetarian Society, when the guiding issues behind vegetarianism were discussed under its leadership. The final, or "practical," stage began in 1908, when vegetarian societies were formed throughout Russia and cafeterias were set up.[19] Each stage concentrated on different facets of vegetarian life, which to the most fervid proponents inevitably meant that some important aspect of the movement was being overlooked. Thus in 1914 the

Kiev society challenged vegetarians to awaken from the "ideological hibernation" into which they had fallen through their wholehearted devotion to such practical matters as the organization of cafeterias, public lectures, and conferences.[20] The St. Petersburg society remained a notable exception here: true to its mission of ideological purity, it had never ceased educational work.

In its final, prerevolutionary phase, vegetarianism in Russia was also associated with the green city movement (*goroda-sady*), a concept subsequently revived in the early Soviet years as a means of increasing worker productivity and health. Urban life was generally viewed as unwholesome; Zelenkova, in one of her early pamphlets, urges apartment dwellers whenever possible to find lodging on the top floors of buildings, in order to avoid harmful fumes and to get the most light and ozone.[21]

A decade later, Zelenkova's work was widely known. Journals of the time reveal that the publishing of vegetarian cookbooks had in fact become an established industry, and a profitable one at that. In 1915 Zelenkova, in a letter to the editor of the *Vegetarian Herald*, informed readers that her book, *I Don't Eat Anyone*, was in its third edition, with 13,000 copies sold. She warned that a certain Belkov had plagiarized her title; worse, he had included in his book such "harmful elements" as cinnamon, cloves, pepper, vinegar, mustard, wine, even meat, giving an entirely false picture of a vegetarian diet.[22]

Zelenkova was one of the liveliest of the vegetarian writers, and from her we learn a good deal about the Russian situation. For the most part, however, the early issues of the *Vegetarian Herald* contained little information specific to Russia. The majority of articles are translations and reviews from the foreign press or descriptions of discoveries in Europe, where vegetarians had been active for half a century. But as the movement grew in Russia, the journals began to address questions of special pertinence to Russian society, such as the harsh northern climate, the role of vegetarianism in the Russian Orthodox Church, and Russia's role in World War I. The editors of the journals were so enthusiastic and committed that one gets the sense that the vegetarian world was quite large and growing daily. However, close inspection reveals that the same names reappear through each issue, so in reality only a handful of devotees kept the journals alive.[23] Nevertheless, the vegetarian cafeterias that the societies organized developed a reputation for good, fresh, and inexpensive food and were frequented by surprisingly large numbers of people.

Russia's entry into World War I caused considerable anguish within the vegetarian community: most vegetarians were pacifists opposed to any sort of killing. In addition to the obvious moral dilemma, the war caused economic hardship for the vegetarian societies, putting a strain on their ability to finance their publications. The journals were ultimately forced to close down for a time, although the cafeterias continued to function. The first issue of the *Vegetarian Herald* to appear after a year's hiatus reports that in November 1916 the Kiev Vegetarian Society provided 53,215 dinners at its two cafeterias.[24]

In its reincarnation, the *Vegetarian Herald* was notably more political; it also included sentimental literary sketches and poems in an attempt to garner more readers. While an overall sympathy toward revolutionary aims is evident, many of the articles simultaneously betray an overtly religious, even messianic, tone. At the same time, the new *Vegetarian Herald* does not neglect to address issues of practical import to vegetarians. For instance, after praising the success of the February revolution, the April 1917 issue calls attention to such problems as the adulturation of foods and the danger of painting rooms without proper ventilation. Of special interest is an article entitled "Toward the Second Step" (following Tolstoy's first), which hails the government's abolition of capital punishment and calls for abolishing capital punishment for animals as the next step.[25] The July issue is disheartening in its report that capital punishment has been reintroduced into Russia.[26]

Despite the genuine social value of many of the articles in the journals, the vegetarians generally come across as a strange lot. Aware of public perception, the authors of the vegetarian cookbooks strive to make their practice seem quite normal. *Vegetarian Cuisine*,[27] published by Posrednik as early as 1894, offers three categories of meals to appeal to the widest range of consumers: "simple, cheap, and healthy"; "more complicated, but equally healthy"; and "more complicated and expensive, [but] less healthy." The recipes offered are not only Russian; in fact, the title page gives Russian dishes second billing after foreign foods, no doubt to make the vegetarian diet appear worldly. This feature was calculated as a selling point, as Russians were likely bored with the vegetarian dishes familiar to them. Without actually calling them vegetarian, the Russians already enjoyed a wide variety of meatless dishes, which they prepared on a regular basis according to the strictures of the Russian Orthodox Church. Some 180 days of the year were considered fast days by the church, each requiring varying degrees of abstention. During the four major fast periods, lasting up to forty days at a time, all meat and dairy products were proscribed.[28] Thus the meatless meal was hardly a radical innovation to a Russian, particularly a religious one.

All of the cookbooks of the time reflect the division of the Russian table into feast-day (*skoromnoe*) and fast-day (*postnoe*) meals. Notably, however, the 1901 edition of Elena Molokhovets' *A Gift to Young Housewives* offers not only a complete selection of *postnoe* variations for favorite dishes but a separate vegetarian section as well. Her notes for "The Vegetarian Table" show a thorough familiarity with the rules of the strictest vegetarian diet.[29] She also marks vegetarian dishes in the regular table of contents with an asterisk "to aid vegetarians in finding appropriate foods."[30] Molokhovets' sensitivity to changing public taste did not mean, however, that Russians had embraced vegetarianism en masse. People generally believed that a meatless diet was not suitable for Russia's severe climate. And besides, meatless meals were far less prestigious, and many households chose not to serve them.

Though no figures are available, women seem to have been more receptive to the idea of vegetarianism than men—whether for reasons of personal sensibility, kitchen economy, or morality. In her 1848 autobiography, for instance, Nadezhda Sokhanskaia (Kokhanovskaia) confesses to an acute sensitivity which makes it impossible for her to kill animals for her supper.[31] Similarly, the religious poetess Anna Pavlovna Barykova (1839–1843), whose works the Chertkovs published, fills her letters with descriptions of the salutary effects of a vegetarian regimen.[32]

Perhaps the most fascinating Russian vegetarian of all was Natalia Borisovna Nordman-Severova (1863 –1914).[33] In public lectures and printed volumes Nordman argued for the liberation of domestic servants from excessive labor, the liberation of the housewife from the kitchen, and the abolition of world hunger. Significantly, all of these grand social schemes were contingent upon vegetarianism, which became Nordman's main platform. Yet her brand of vegetarianism was unlike any other. Progressing from a standard meatless diet, she gradually excluded all dairy products from her meals and eventually came to eat almost all of her food raw.[34] In her most extreme period of vegetarianism, she touted the diet for which she became famous: a regimen based almost entirely on grass and hay. Despite the obvious asceticism of her program, Nordman expressed great joie de vivre both in person and in her writings, always emphasizing the pleasure and well-being to be gained from her diet.

The daughter of a Swedish admiral and Russian mother, Nordman had a childhood marked by poverty following her father's untimely death. Nevertheless, her mother managed to give her an aristocratic upbringing consisting of little formal education but excellent training in manners and foreign languages.[35] Frustrated by her lack of useful skills and without the means to engage in charity work, Nordman at the age of twenty-two ran away from home to America, where she felt she would find a meaningful "life of labor."[36] There she spent a few months, working variously as a chambermaid and dairymaid. But America was unable to provide her with the métier she sought, and so she returned to Russia. In her autobiographical tale *Beglianka* [The fugitive], Nordman portrays herself as an independent, idealistic young woman. This picture differs from the portrait painted by her close friend the Princess Tenisheva, who saw herself as the idealist and Nordman as an irredeemable cynic. In her memoirs, Tenisheva writes of their meeting: "She was a crude and very free-and-easy girl of sixteen or seventeen, in a short dress, who acted like a spoiled child. Her eyes, which were hardly naive, and her thick, sensitive lips were not in keeping with her affected childishness. In this unnatural girl one sensed depravity, a lack of moral foundations. Although we were nearly the same age, we presented a striking contrast: I, with my broken dreams, having already known deep disappointment, and this unbalanced and affected girl."[37]

Despite these harsh judgments, Tenisheva and Nordman remained intimate,[38] and their association ultimately determined the course of Nordman's life. In 1891 Marianna Verevkina, a student of the Realist painter Ilia Repin, arranged for Repin to meet Tenisheva, hoping to distract him from his infatuation with Elizaveta Zvantseva. When they met, Nordman was with Tenisheva.[39] Repin was immediately taken with Tenisheva, whose portrait he wanted to paint. By contrast, his first impressions of Nordman were far from positive, yet he gradually became more interested in her, and by 1899 he had purchased a small house in her name in the Finnish village of Kuokkala, not far from St. Petersburg. Nordman moved to Kuokkala in 1900; Repin followed in 1903.[40] There they set up house together in the beautiful, newly-renovated *dacha* that Nordman named Penaty after the Roman gods of the household.

Repin appreciated the comfortable domesticity of his new life, lacking ever since he had separated from his wife. Many of his friends, however, could barely tolerate Nordman and considered her influence over Repin deleterious. While conceding that the artist seemed more content than ever in his personal life, they nevertheless resented his companion's conservative taste in literature and art. Some even attributed the decline in Repin's talent to her uncompromising views. Virtually all those who recall Repin's life at Penaty have harsh words for Nordman. Although her strongly articulated opinions could be infuriating, one also suspects a modicum of envy, especially on the part of Repin's erstwhile models: in his devotion to Nordman, Repin executed more portraits and drawings of her than of anyone else. *Gratsioznaia* (graceful) to Repin,[41] Nordman's figure appeared *gromozdkaia* (cumbersome) to others.[42] As for her influence over him, Repin publicly declared that thanks to the enforced vegetarian diet at Penaty, he had never felt better: "I am experiencing an unprecedented surge of health and my energy has soared."[43]

At Natalia Nordman's famous round table in Penaty, 1915. Ilya Repin is fourth from the left.
Vladimir Mayakovskii is standing, third from right. Next to him are Kornei Chukovskii and
Nikolai Evreinov. A portrait of Nordman by Repin is visible at right. Photo from I. E. Grabar' and
I. S. Zil'bershtein, eds., Repin, *vol. 1 (Moscow-Leningrad: Izdatel'stvo Akademii nauk, 1949).*

Repin's enthusiastic acceptance of vegetarianism indicates the degree to which Nordman did in fact hold sway over him, for she succeeded in converting him after the great Tolstoy had failed. Repin had visited Tolstoy more than once to paint his portraits, and like others before him was deeply moved by the writer's beliefs. For a time he had tried "to live by some of Tolstoy's moral precepts," if only out of infatuation with Tolstoy's daughter, Tatiana.[44] In his memoirs Repin claims that he could do nothing but "submit to Tolstoy's will,"[45] yet despite several attempts at vegetarianism, he was unable fully to embrace it.[46] In the end he succumbed only to Nordman's earnest suasion.

Nordman worked to convert not only Repin but all visitors to Penaty as well, holding an open house each Wednesday afternoon[47] that provided the perfect opportunity to proselytize. The guests included some of the most gifted writers and artists of the time: Vladimir Mayakovsky, Leonid Andreev, Maxim Gorky, Vsevolod Meyerhold. The rules Nordman established at Penaty were highly original, and even those visitors who did not care for the hostess could hardly help being amused, even charmed, by her regulations. As part of her larger social agenda, Nordman had revolutionized the household. Repin's close friend Kornei Chukovsky writes that "everywhere the pompous and despotic taste of the [hostess] of Penaty—Natalia Borisovna—was felt."[48] But less critical guests could enjoy the surprises with which they were met and allow themselves to be drawn into the household's prevailing spirit of play.

It all began in the front hall, where guests were immediately confronted with a bold sign proclaiming, "Take off your own coats and beat on the tom-tom!"[49]—the first indication that egalitarianism reigned. This directive applied to everyone: even Repin was once chastised for breaking the rule when he helped a guest off with her coat.[50] The ethos of self-service extended into the dining room, where it reached a brilliant intensity. A prominently placed sign reminded everyone that *Ravnopravie i samopomoshch'* (equality and self-help) were the order of the day.[51] To put her rules into effect, Nordman set up a separate table at which guests were expected to cut their own bread with a special machine of her own devising.[52] But her greatest innovation—truly the talk of the town—was the dining table itself, a large round table with a sort of lazy susan in the center that enabled guests to help themselves without being waited on by servants.

While such a system might seem unduly rigorous for diners accustomed to the finest in mealtime service, Nordman's dining room was always beautifully appointed. The table was covered with red lacquer and bordered in green, so that no tablecloth was necessary.[53] Fine china, crystal, and flatware sparkled, and fresh flowers or leaves of the season were always strewn decoratively across the table.[54] For placecards Nordman used postcards with photographs of a painting by Repin or another artist.[55] But the real ingenuity of the table lay in its two-tiered construction. The central, upper tier turned by means of nickel-plated hooks that were positioned all along the edges so that each person could take hold of a hook and turn any portion of the table toward himself to reach whatever he needed. On the lower tier, in front of each place setting, stood two small, interior shelves holding clean plates, so that the diner could exchange his dirty plate for a clean one without the aid of a servant. Guests were expected to adhere rigidly to the motto about self-help and were not even supposed to serve one another. If someone, most likely a newcomer, made the mistake of offering a dining partner food, he or she was forced to make a speech, which could be short or quite long, depending on the seriousness of the infraction. The more infractions, the livelier the dinners at Penaty, so newcomers were always welcome.

The food, all vegetarian, was artistically arranged in the middle of the lazy susan, with the symbol of the Repins—a large turnip[56]—rising as a center-piece above all. Nordman seems to have had a special fondness for *trompe l'oeil* presentations: to their surprise, diners found mashed bananas in the butter dishes instead of what had looked like butter from a distance.[57] On the table also stood various *zakuski,* or hors d'oeuvres, *pirozhki,* or pies, and miniature barrels holding sauerkraut and pickles. All of these delights alternated with bottles of port, madeira, and other fine wines carrying the name "Sun's Energy."[58] Unlike most of her fellow vegetarians, Nordman eschewed neither spices nor wine; in fact, she considered wine "the energy of the sun" and a necessary accompaniment to any meal. As "the blood of the sun," wine caused all of the human juices to flow.[59]

Before sitting down to a Penaty dinner, other rituals had first to be observed. Nordman would put on music to "heighten the mood and stimulate the appetite,"[60] and all of the guests were expected to begin "plastic dancing" with exaggerated gestures and steps. In probable imitation of Isadora Duncan, Nordman would wave a white scarf and flirtatiously float like a swan past Repin, who kept his arms taut at his sides while stamping his feet like a Cossack dancer. These "plastic dances" were an integral part of Nordman's program for health, as were cross-country skiing and *Schneetreten,* the practice of walking barefoot on snow,[61] which she apparently accomplished with "a beatific look" on her face.[62] Not everyone enjoyed the compulsory exercise. Furthermore, these outdoor rituals likely exacerbated the tuberculosis that eventually caused Nordman's death in 1914. As for the dancing, Tolstoy's son recalls one visit Repin and Nordman made to Yasnaya Polyana. Although pleased by Repin's conversion to vegetarianism, Tolstoy was greatly distressed by the "dancing orgies to a gramophone" that took place in the room above his and could hardly wait for the eccentric couple to leave.[63]

Even after Nordman's death, Repin preserved the order she had established at Penaty. The meals served at the Wednesday salons were vegetarian, and the lazy susan still revolved. When the Futurist poets David Burliuk and Vasily Kamensky visited Penaty in 1915, Nordman's precautionary signs still hung on the walls. Burliuk recalls the difficulties of self-service at the dining table. As the Futurist frantically tried to move a tasty-looking tub of sauer-kraut garnished with cranberries and lingonberries in their direction, Kornei Chukovsky suddenly decided he wanted a helping of salted mushrooms and grabbed the table's hooks, jerking it back. Burliuk also remembers the pop-ping of corks for sparkling water and Bavarian beer but is unable to recall whether the famous *"borshch* made of hay" was served.[64]

More than an advocate for healthy living, Nordman truly believed she could save the world.[65] In a tireless crusade she presented public lectures, published articles and brochures, and organized courses for women workers in Kuokkala, at which Repin himself sometimes lectured. The essence of Nordman's teachings lay in a reverence for all forms of life: we should not eat eggs lest we upset the mother hens; similarly, we should avoid honey because its retrieval destroys the bees' home.[66] Milk, as the product of a sad creature whose baby has been taken away, will inevitably upset our stomachs.[67] Nordman dreamed of transforming the entire world into an Edenic garden free of malady and pestilence. By working the land himself, without servants, a man could be healthy growing the fruits and vegetables needed for sustenance; at the same time, his nonexploitative approach to life would ensure the happiness of his fellow creatures.[68] As Nordman contemplated the problem of eradicating widespread hunger, her views crystallized into the solution that made her at once famous and notorious: her diet of grass and hay. This discovery came in a moment of epiphany as she watched her favorite workhorse Liuba hungrily munching hay. She suddenly realized that man, too, could benefit from this produce, becoming as healthy and strong as a horse.[69] And Russia would never again have to suffer from hunger, since hay was not only abundant, but also free.

In 1911, Nordman published a cookbook in which she explicitly presents the merits of her hay diet: *Povarennaia kniga dlia golodaiushchikh* [A cookbook for the hungry]. She purposely had the book printed on cheap gray paper to make it accessible to the poor. She dedicated it, however, to the "overfed" (*presyshchennym*), explaining that "vegetarianism is necessary for the very rich and the very poor. The poor need it because it is cheap and nourishing, the rich to cleanse all the poisons from the corpses that have accumulated in their overfed organism." The book methodically details a comprehensive method for changing the human diet, including an important "project for feeding the hungry," in which every large apartment house or yardman's lodge would daily provide a huge kettle of free soup for the poor. The soup would be free in both senses of the word. The indigent would not have to pay for it and neither would the providers, since the ingredients would consist of the discards (*otbrosy*) from wealthy kitchens. Kindergartens and factories could establish similar soup kitchens, and thus, without spending a cent, the rich could feed the needy.[70]

Nourished by grass in the summer and hay in the winter, everyone would be healthy. Other greens would supplement the diet. City dwellers could easily get scraps from cooks and shopkeepers who regularly discarded cabbage stalks, beet tops, and turnip greens as unfit provender. They could also take delight in the rejected greens from carrots, cauliflower, celery, parsley root, rutabaga, jerusalem artichokes, potatoes, radishes, beans, and peas. A search for greens could turn into a summer holiday with an excursion to the countryside to pick the freshest and tastiest grasses—a special treat for the children. Like the fruit of the vine, grasses kissed by the sun and wind give humans vitality. They also provide important nutrients, and Nordman cites chemical analyses of different grasses to show just how nourishing each variety is. A further advantage of cooked grass or hay is that the broth rapidly quells hunger, so that a hearty bowl at noon satisfies the body for virtually twenty-four hours. One need only partake of a cold, light snack in the evening if the stomach begins to complain.

In keeping with her expansive theory, Nordman adduces further benefits to the simple consumption of broth made from hay: by not having to toil endlessly in the kitchen, the cook can be liberated from the most menial tasks and return home to her family at four o'clock. Close reading reveals that this liberation still entails an eight-hour day (instead of seventeen), but even if the liberation is only partially complete, it is still a significant "first step."

Here I should note that the idea of using hay in the kitchen is not as farfetched as it may sound. Good Russian cooks took advantage of the aromatic properties of hay in many ways. For instance, Molokhovets advocates tossing hay into the water in which fresh ham is boiled to add extra flavor. She also uses it to impart a special taste to fish as it smokes and often spreads it on the floor of the wood-fired Russian oven when baking cabbage or bread.[71] But Nordman appears to have been the first to brew hay systematically into an edible broth. And this she did with a vengeance, forcing distinguished visitors to Penaty to swallow what must have seemed a bitter brew. Still, her cookbook offers a number of intriguing recipes, and Nordman explains how a standard hay broth can be used in combination with other ingredients to make a variety of delicious soups. Here is her recipe for the basic "Hay Soup in a Teapot":

> Take a teapot, depending on the number of people either a small porcelain one or a huge tin one for a whole workers' cooperative, toss in two *zolotniks*[72] of hay per person, chop an onion, add some bay leaves (one leaf for every three people) and two peppercorns per person, pour on rapidly boiling water, simmer for ten minutes, and the soup is ready."[73]

Nordman admits that hay can smell a bit medicinal (*nemnozhko aptekoi pakhnet*), but cheerfully adds "but that's not so bad" (*a to nichego*). If you really can't stand it plain, simply add it to other soups for the nutritional value and you won't even notice its presence.[74] Better yet, follow Nordman's advice for making a vegetable *rassol'nik*: take the discarded peels of potatoes and other root vegetables, as well as the water in which the vegetables or grains were cooked. Throw in some fruit peels for exceptional flavor (these can be had for the asking from prosperous shopkeepers). If you're lucky enough to have half a cucumber, mince and add it, too, or ask for cucumber peelings which would otherwise go to waste. Boil all of this up, add a bit of salt, purée the mixture, and the soup is ready to enjoy. Nordman claims that this soup is very popular in her household: her yardman and joiner can eat three bowls apiece.[75]

Ever concerned with expenses, Nordman offers in her book an economical weekly menu for which she provides the cost per person. For instance, the Tuesday menu calls for "simple oatmeal, served as a purée. This soup is made at absolutely no cost, since the oats are strained for the purée and given to the horse. Baked turnip with bread crumbs and onions. Fried celery."[76] This meal costs only five kopecks per person. The real feast is reserved for Wednesdays, when expenses reach a full sixteen kopecks a head. Here Nordman suggests "lentils, a *borshch* of greens, and compote."[77] At some Penaty dinners, at least in the earlier stages of her vegetarianism, Nordman would serve a soup of freshly mown hay from the Penaty meadows, flavored with carrots, potatoes, and other vegetables, offering on the side such tasty dishes as vegetable ragouts, *pirozhki* with rice or cabbage, fruit puddings (*kisel'*), and compotes.[78] In her later, more extreme period everything at Penaty was served raw and cold on the beautiful round table. One guest recalls a Wednesday meal of turnip pastry with barley filling, olives, raw grated celery, and the like.[79]

Nordman insisted that a Russian meadow with its many grasses could provide a more varied and nutritious diet than any in Italy, where produce is available only in season.[80] In Russia, for a quick and tasty meal, one need simply go out into the summertime fields and pick fresh grasses like lady's mantle, goutweed, angelica, mountain sorrel, yarrow, timothy grass, and canary grass, then sauté them with celery, parsley, dill, and onion in a little olive oil.[81] As the gentle season draws to a close, dry the grasses and tie them in cheesecloth to make an instant boullion to have on hand for a variety of soups throughout the year. After the soup has boiled, the grasses can be strained from the bag and mixed with an equal portion of flour to make an excellent dough. Cabbage pies made from strained, cooked turnip mixed with flour are particularly delicious, claims Nordman.[82] To make lovely black currant, raspberry, and rhubarb puddings, dry the young leaves of these plants in summer. As a substitute for black tea, use dried wild strawberry blossoms and leaves. Replace coffee with dried beets and chicory.[83] Nordman emphasizes that nothing need ever be thrown away. Leftover broth can be boiled up several times with various new additions, and even used tea leaves can be dried and brewed again several times.

Lest the foregoing sound too unappetizing, I hasten to add that in her book Nordman includes many recipes from Zelenkova's *I Don't Eat Anyone*, which seem delicious by any standards. Chestnut purée with jerusalem artichokes, stewed green peppers with tomatoes, onions, and olive oil, and "vegetarian herring" of olives and potatoes dressed with a mustard vinaigrette are all sophisticated and appealing. Because Nordman genuinely wants people to enjoy being vegetarian, she takes pains to include recipes for the ritual Easter dishes of *paskha* and *kulich*, both of which are traditionally made with enormous amounts of eggs, curd cheese, and butter (Molokhovets' recipe for "Royal *Paskha*," for instance, calls for five pounds of *tvorog*, or curd cheese, ten eggs, one pound of sweet butter, and two pounds of sour cream).[84] Nordman's *kulich* uses two pounds of flour, two cups of water, and one cup of olive oil. She recommends mixing these ingredients into a yeast dough, then flavoring it with saffron, cardamom, sugar, vanilla, salt, raisins, and almonds to taste. Although likely heavy in texture, this *kulich* is no doubt aromatic and pleasing. For *paskha* Nordman mixes together puréed chestnuts, almond milk, and olive oil,[85] creating a delightful, if nontraditional, pudding.

Strident and eccentric, Nordman was too unappealing to garner a following, and her views never really caught on in her native land. Rich and poor alike found the thought of eating discards too distasteful. In the aftermath of revolution and civil war, with the severe food shortages, her ideas might have gained a following, if not outright popularity, but she was no longer alive to expound them. And although vegetarian cafeterias continued to flourish in the twenties,[86] for most of the Soviet period meat represented a status symbol, its procurement an obsession. Thus Nordman's grand vision fell into obscurity. No one remembered the special footwear she had invented or the winter jackets stuffed peasant-style with wood shavings so that she could avoid wearing fur; her innovative comforters stuffed with hay (what else?) in place of goose down were similarly forgotten.[87]

One rare sympathetic memoirist recalls Nordman as the only woman of her time unafraid to state publicly her bold views on the deplorable position of the woman worker. However, such articles as "Down with Servants!" and "Down with Slavery!" did little to endear her to her own class. Yet even though her views were extreme, she worked hard to live by her moral precepts and use her ideas in the service of others. It is unfortunate that no one paid closer attention to the "magic chest" she insulated with pillows. An early version of a crockpot or slow-cooker, this chest was designed to ease the busy housewife's burden. Half-cooked food placed in the chest would finish cooking unattended. "Just think," said Nordman, "any working woman can start fixing soup or *kasha*, put it in my magic chest, and calmly go off to work, to her job. Returning home, she'll find everything ready! Just think how this will liberate women!"[88] The possibility of an "instant meal" was extremely important to Nordman: "It seems as though the magical fairytale tablecloth (*skatert'-samobranka*) has laid itself, and that at last the time has come for women's liberation from the yoke of endless domestic cares that humiliate her."[89] In her commentary to recipes for dried soup powders, Nordman expressed the hope that this sort of instant soup would become widespread in Russia.[90]

It hasn't yet. Soviet housewives labored for decades without the benefit of Nordman's labor-saving devices. And even if they had been exposed to her vegetarian ideas, they would have had no patience with her unconventional diet, preferring instead to dream of extravagant dining à la Molokhovets. Now, however, vegetarianism is rising again in Russia, to judge from the recent spate of vegetarian books published.[91] So Nordman's egalitarian vision may yet find an audience in this new age. As of now, however, no apostle stands ready to fill the role.

NOTES

1. Howard Williams, *The Ethics of Diet: A Catena of Authorities Deprecatory of the Practice of Flesh-Eating* (London, 1883).

2. Verigin was responsible for the religious revival of the sect, and his 1893 message to his people came directly from Tolstoy's preachings. Ironically, however, Verigin himself had never read Tolstoy's writings but simply absorbed ideas in the air at the time. In 1895 the Dukhobors split, with the "Butcher's Party" rejecting vegetarianism and the "Fasting Party" accepting it. When later that year they began to be persecuted for refusing conscription into the Russian army, Tolstoy took up their cause, helping them to emigrate to Canada. For the relationship between Tolstoy and the Dukhobors, see Aylmer Maude, *A Peculiar People: The Doukhobors* (New York: Funk & Wagnalls, 1904); Janet Barkas, *The Vegetable Passion: A History of the Vegetarian State of Mind* (New York: Charles Scribner's Sons, 1975), 154–165; and Colin Spencer, *The Heretic's Feast: A History of Vegetarianism* (London: Fourth Estate, 1993), 288–290.

3. The question of Tolstoy's attitude toward vegetarianism is investigated by Ronald LeBlanc in chap. 6 of this volume and in his paper "The Way of No Flesh: Tolstoy's 'First Step' toward the Righteous Life," presented at the New England Slavic Association meeting, April 16, 1994.

4. Cited in *Vegetarianskoe obozrenie*, 1912, no. 1, 33.

5. Ibid., 1915, no. 4, 120.

6. See ibid. This formula sounds uncomfortably like the Soviet slogan touting the "radiant future" (*siiaiushchee budushchee*) awaiting all once the goals of socialism were met.

7. For more on the meager diet of the Russian peasant, see Cathy Frierson, chap. 4 in this volume and *Peasant Icons: Representations of Rural People in Late Nineteenth-Century Russia* (New York: Oxford University Press, 1993).

8. Cited in *Vegetarianskii vestnik. Organ Kievskogo vegetarianskogo obshchestva*, no. 2 (27 June 1914), 7.

9. Ibid.

10. [Ol'ga Konstantinovna Zelenkova], *Ia nikogo ne em. 365 vegetarianskikh meniu,* ed. I. P. Tret'iakova (Moscow: Moskovskii rabochii, 1991); *Nechto o vegetarianstve,* vyp. I, St. Petersburg, 1902; vyp. II, III, and IV, St. Petersburg, 1903. All four pamphlets were published by the printer associated with the Poor Children's Home.

11. *Nechto o vegetarianstve,* vyp. I, 16.

12. Ibid., 7.

13. On the European movements, see Sarah Freeman, *Mutton and Oysters: The Victorians and Their Food* (London: Victor Gollancz, 1989), esp. 95 and 250, and Spencer, *Heretic's Feast.*

14. *Nechto o vegetarianstve,* vyp. II, 13.

15. Ibid., 17–18.

16. *Vegetarianskii vestnik,* no. 1 (15 May 1914), 2, 6.

17. Ustav S.-Peterburgskogo vegetarianskogo obshchestva, utverzhdennyi G. Ministrom vnutrennykh del 21 okt. 1901, *Vegetarianskii vestnik,* no. 2 (February 1904), 33.

18. There were two *Vegetarianskii vestnik*s. The first, published in St. Petersburg by Doliachko, appeared monthly for 18 months in 1904 - 1905. The second, in a less hefty format, was published by the Kiev Vegetarian Society between 1914 and 1917, excluding 1916, when World War I caused funds to dry up. *Vegetarianskoe obozrenie,* billed as "the only vegetarian journal in Russia," appeared in Kiev between 1909 and 1915. *Biulleteni vegetarianstva v S-Peterburge* also appeared in 1914. It was intended to come out ten to thirty times a year, but apparently the proceeds from the Vegetarianstvo cafeteria on Nevsky Prospekt could cover only the costs of a single issue. Published by N. P. Evstif'ev and K. S. Drozdov, who had set up the cafeteria, this bulletin was meant to offer practical advice to St. Petersburg vegetarians.

19. These categories are enumerated in *Vegetarianskii vestnik,* no. 1 (15 May 1914), 2.

20. Ibid.

21. *Nechto o vegetarianstve,* vyp. 2, 31.

22. *Vegetarianskoe obozrenie,* 1915, no. 1, 34.

23. *Bulletins of Vegetarianism* reports that after twelve years of existence, only thirty-nine persons had joined the St. Petersburg Vegetarian Society, including residents of St. Petersburg and other cities. See *Biulleteni vegetarianstva,* no. 1 (January 1914), 5.

24. *Vegetarianskii vestnik,* no. 1 (January 1917), 12.

25. Ibid., no. 4 (April 1917), 2.

26. Ibid., no. 7 (July 1917), 1.

27. *Vegetarianskaia kukhnia. Nastavlenie k prigotovleniiu bolee 800 bliud, khlebov i napitkov dlia bezuboinago pitaniia, so vstupitel'noi stat'ei o znachenii vegetarianstva i s prilozheniem raspisaniia obedov trekh razriadov na dve nedeli. Sostavleno po inostrannym i russkim istochnikam.* Izdanie "Posrednika" dlia intelligentnykh chitatelei (Moscow: I. D. Sytin, 1894).

28. For more on feast and fast days in Russia, see Joyce Toomre, trans., *Classic Russian Cooking: Elena Molokhovets' A Gift to Young Housewives* (Bloomington: Indiana University Press, 1992), 13.

29. Elena Molokhovets, *Podarok molodym khoziakiam ili sredstvo k umen'sheniiu raskhodov v domashnem khoziaistve* (St. Petersburg: N. N. Klobukov, 1901; reprint, Moscow: Polikom, 1991), section XXIII, 681.

30. Ibid., 639.

31. Sokhanskaia's autobiography was commissioned by the famous critic Pletnev, who was asssociated with Pushkin's journal *Sovremennik*. The manuscript was not published until 1896, however, since Sokhanskaia did not want it made public during her lifetime (she died in 1884). See the introduction by S. I Ponomarev to *Avtobiografiia N.S. Sokhanskoi* (Moscow: Universitetskaia, 1896), 1–11. Sokhanskaia's comments regarding the killing of animals are on 188.

32. Vladimir and Anna Chertkov, "Zametki o zhizni i lichnosti A.P. Barykovoi," in Barykova, *Stikhotvoreniia i prozaicheskie proizvedeniia* (St. Petersburg: A. A. Porokhovshchikova, 1897), 3–11.

33. Severova is the pen name under which Nordman wrote. Her fiction includes the novella *Beglianka*, serialized in the journal *Niva* in 1900 with nine watercolors by Repin. It appeared in book form under the title *Eta* in 1901; a third edition, renamed *K idealam*, was issued in 1912. Nordman published *Krest materinstva*, a "secret diary" with three drawings by Repin, in 1904 and *Intimnye stranitsy*, for which Repin provided the cover illustration, in 1910. She also published numerous proselytizing essays and pamphlets, including *Sleduet raskrepostit' prislugu*, 1912, and *Raiskie zavety*, 1913.

34. We know this today as a vegan, or macrobiotic, diet.

35. E. Kirillina, *Repin v Penatakh* (Leningrad: Lenizdat, 1977), 13.

36. Ibid.

37. Larisa Zhuravleva, *Kniaginia Mariia Tenisheva* (Smolensk: Poligramma, 1994), 21–22.

38. Quoting from archival material, Tenisheva's biographer states that Nordman was in love with Tenisheva; see ibid., 22.

39. This account is based on Nordman's memoirs, and it seems to be the most accurate. See ibid., 92-93. Other reports state that the meeting occurred under different circumstances. The art historians Grabar' and Zil'bershtein, in their comprehensive volume on Repin, report that he met Nordman at an international exhibition in Paris; see I. E. Grabar' and I. S. Zil'bershtein, eds., *Repin. Khudozhestvennoe nasledstvo* (Moscow-Leningrad: Akademii nauk, 1949), vol. 2, 244. Repin's biographer believes that they met at the Princess Tenisheva's (Kirillina, *Repin v Pentakh,* 14); this information is repeated by the American art historian Elizabeth Valkenier in her *Ilya Repin and the World of Russian Art* (New York: Columbia University Press, 1990), 161. Repin's apparent infatuation with Tenisheva is confirmed by Grabar' in his monograph on the artist, *Repin. Monografiia v dvukh tomakh* (Moscow: Nauka, 1964), vol. 2, 89.

40. Kirillina, *Repin v Penatakh,* 17, 26.

41. Cited in *Ia nikogo ne em,* 49.

42. This memoirist T. L. Shchepkina-Kupernik goes on to describe Nordman's face as "a poorly baked bun [*bulka*] with small eyes" in Grabar' and Zil'bershtein, *Repin,* vol. 2, 266.

43. Cited in *Ia nikogo ne em,* 50, from a letter published in *Vegetarianskoe obozrenie*. Repin's devotion to vegetarianism was apparently fitful. Shchepkina-Kupernik's memoirs, "O Repine i ego nekotorykh modeliakh," states that whenever Repin would visit his old friends the Tarkhanovs, he'd ask them to prepare "good vegetarian. . .*bifshteks!*" for him and then make them promise not to tell Nordman; see Grabar' and Zil'bershtein, *Repin,* vol. 2, 268.

44. Valkenier, *Ilya Repin,* 161.

45. Repin writes: "For me the spiritual atmosphere of Lev Nikolaevich always gripped and seized me. In his presence, as if hypnotized, I could only submit to his will. In his

presence, each sentence he uttered seeemed incontrovertible to me." I. I. Repin, *Dalekoe blizkoe* (Leningrad: Khudozhnik RSFSR, 1986), 365.

46. See Repin's account of his on again, off again vegetarianism in *Vegetarianskoe obozrenie*, no. 2 (February 1912), p. 64.

47. In 1909 the Wednesday open houses were replaced by Sunday afternoon "cooperative" teas and dinners, attended by guests from all classes who paid a nominal fee for refreshments and listened to lectures, danced, and sang. The impetus for these gatherings came from the ideas of the French political economist Charles Gide, who advocated the organization of classless cooperative societies. See Kirillina, *Repin v Penatakh,* 91.

48. Quoted in Grabar', *Repin,*, vol. 2, 273.

49. A. I. Mendeleeva, "Iz davnikh vospominanii," in Grabar' and Zil'bershtein, *Repin,* vol. 2, 182. Other visitors to Penaty recall a gong or drum instead of a tom-tom, but whatever the instrument, it was meant to be struck loudly.

50. Ibid.

51. K.A. Morozova, "V Penatakh s Nikolaem Aleksandrovichem Morozovym," in Grabar' and Zil'bershtein, *Repin,* vol. 2, 250.

52. V.V. Verevkina, "Pamiati uchitelia," in Grabar' and Zil'bershtein, *Repin,* vol. 2, 196-197.

53. Shchepkina-Kupernik, "O Repine," 266.

54. Morozova, "V Penatakh," 248.

55. Ibid., 250.

56. The Russian word for "turnip" is *repa*, from which the name Repin derives.

57. Mendeleeva, "Iz davnikh vospominanii," 182. Shchepkina-Kupernik, "O Repine," 267, considers Nordman hypocritical here: since Nordman is so concerned with hunger among the needy, she should not make bananas, fruits, and nuts such an important part of her own table, especially in winter, when they are unavailable to most people.

58. Morozova, "V Penatakh," 250.

59. Shchepkina-Kupernik, "O Repine," 267. Nordman lyrically describes a dinner at the poet Yasinsky's, when he served a "wonderful nectar, a one-hundred-year-old white wine. It courses through my blood with a gentle warmth. It seems as though the sun is warming me." She goes on to compare Yasinsky to Zeus and states that this meal represented "the realization of my dream—triumphant vegetarianism, creatively alluring." See N. B. Severova, *Raiskie zavety. Stat'i i zametki* (Moscow ?, 1913), 25. The idea of warming of the blood is significant for vegetarianism. As Zelenkova points out, "it is not fat that warms us, but pure blood"; hence a fatty diet is not necessary even in a cold climate (though for Zelenkova pure blood is untainted by alcohol). See *Nechto o vegetarianstve*, vyp. 3, 34-35.

60. Morozova, "V Penatakh," 249.

61. This practice had been advocated as early as 1903 by Zelenkova, who stresses the importance of fresh air and hence of winter sports. By extension, she considers sandals or bare feet preferable to the "unbreathing leather" of boots, even in winter. Zelenkova goes so far as to state that "walking barefoot on freshly fallen snow, across dew, across shallow water (*Schneetreten, Wassertreten*) . . . protects one from catching cold, destroys excessive sensitivity to cold and highly stimulates the circulation." See *Nechto o vegetarianstve*, vyp. 4, 44-46. For similar reasons of health, Repin always slept in an unheated room, a practice Nordman lauds in her essay "Why Is It Healthy to Sleep without a Shirt?" See *Raiskie zavety*, 68-69.

62. Kornei Chukovsky, cited in *Ia nikogo ne em*, 47. Nordman called her ideas "ecstasies of the soul," ibid.

DARRA GOLDSTEIN

63. See Grabar', *Repin,* pp. 190-192, and S. L. Tolstoi, "Moi vospominaniia o Repine," in Grabar' and Zil'bershtein, *Repin,* vol. 2, 116.

64. David Burliuk, "Fragmenty vospominanii," in Grabar' and Zil'bershtein, *Repin,* vol. 2, 280-281. When Burliuk saw a tattered sign advertising one of Nordman's lectures still hanging in Kuokkala when he visited there in 1915, he turned the visible fragments into a Futurist poem:

> . . . .verova
> Se. . . . . .
> pitanie. . . . . . .
> Normal'noe.

65. Chukovsky called her an "apostle" of Russian vegetarianism. See *Ia nikogo ne em,* 47.

66. *Raiskie zavety,* 14.

67. N. B. Severova, *Povarennaia kniga dlia golodaiushchikh* (St. Petersburg: Tipografiia pervoi Sankt-Peterburgskoi trudovoi arteli, 1911), 52.

68. *Raiskie zavety,* 4.

69. Severova, *Povarennaia kniga,* 38.

70. Ibid., 56.

71. For more on Molokhovets' use of hay, see Toomre, *Classic Russian Cooking,* 39.

72. A zolotnik is equal to 4.26 grams.

73. Severova, *Povarennaia kniga,* 56.

74. Ibid., 61.

75. Ibid., 55.

76. Nordman has a special fondness for celery because it is "cheap, filling, aromatic, and tasty." Surprised that it is not better known in Russia, she offers an entire section on the sorts of dishes that can be prepared from celery. The twenty recipes include *zakuski,* soups, and stews; Nordman also suggests an interesting meal of fried celery cutlets with tomatoes and chestnuts (ibid., 84–87).

77. Ibid., 59-60.

78. Shchepkina-Kupernik, "O Repine," 267.

79. Morozova, "V Penatakh," 250.

80. Severova, *Povarennaia kniga,* 41.

81. Ibid., 83.

82. Ibid., 63.

83. Ibid., 63-64.

84. Molokhovets, *Podarok,* part 2, 41 (recipe # 3216).

85. Severova, *Povarennaia kniga,* 87-88.

86. Note the existence of a vegetarian cafeteria in Il'f and Petrov's *Twelve Chairs.*

87. At a lecture she gave in 1912, "What the Poor, Fat, and Ill Should Know," Nordman exhibited some of her inventions: "In addition to N. B. Nordman-Severova's vegetarian buffet, a small vegetarian exhibit was organized. Vegetarian books, shoes, tea, soap, overcoats stuffed with shavings, a magic chest, an almond grinder, a comforter of hay, and many other things were exhibited." The event was reported in *Vegetarianskoe obozrenie,* 1912, no. 7, as cited in *Ia nikogo ne em,* 48. Chukovsky reports seeing Nordman in one of her special jackets: "She was freezing . . . [yet] she assured herself and others that she was very warm and comfortable. " See ibid., 47.

88. Shchepkina-Kupernik, "O Repine," 266.

89. *Raiskie zavety*, 64.

90. Ibid., 61.

91. A sampling of recent vegetarian books includes, in addition to *Ia nikogo ne em*: I. L. Medkova et al., *Vse o vegetarianstve* (Moscow: Ekonomika, 1992); G. I. Molchanov, ed., *Tselebnaia vegetarianskaia kukhnia* (Moscow: SP Interbuk, 1992); *Vegetarianskaia kukhnia* (Moscow: Raduga, 1993); M. A. Vorob'eva, *Neobychnye bliuda iz obychnykh ovoshchei* (Moscow: Kolos, 1993); and Adiradzha das, *Vedicheskoe kulinarnoe iskusstvo* [The Hare Krishna book of vegetarian cooking (Russian)] (Borehamwood, Herts.: Bhaktivedanta Book Trust, 1993).

EIGHT

RONALD D. LeBLANC

An Appetite for Power:
Predators, Carnivores, and
Cannibals in Dostoevsky's Fiction

In a rather fanciful American novel set in the late 1960s entitled *The Abortion* (1970), Richard Brautigan describes a public library in California that accepts books from its patrons rather than lends them out. One of the titles brought to this mythical library is *The Culinary Dostoevsky*, written by a man named James Fallon, who refers to his literary creation as "a cookbook of recipes" culled from Dostoevsky's novels and who claims to have eaten everything the Russian author ever cooked.[1] "Brautigan's fancy is delightful," Simon Karlinsky observes in regard to this fictitious Dostoevsky cookbook, but in actual fact his character would end up very poorly nourished. Gogol, Tolstoy, and Chekhov, among Russian writers, have written lovingly and at length about various foods eaten by their characters. But Dostoevsky, who can be so magnificent in his own realm of irrational passions and spiritual insights, had very little interest in the physical basis of human life or in man's natural surroundings. The only kinds of food that it would occur to him to use for literary purposes are a crust of dry bread someone denies to a starving little boy or a pineapple compote that a neurotic young girl dreams she would eat if she were witnessing the crucifixion of a child.[2]

Few readers, I think, would dispute the validity of this analysis; nor would they seriously challenge Karlinsky's additional claim that "for the flavor and the feel of actual life as it was lived in Russia, reproduced with all the fidelity and subtlety that literary art is capable of," we have to turn to other Russian authors than Dostoevsky.[3] The "culinary Dostoevsky," therefore, turns out to be a rather ironic (if not oxymoronic) choice of title for a cookbook, since the novels by this author seem an unlikely site to explore in search of tasty recipes, kitchen expertise, or cooking tips.

It seems to me, however, that we can account for the rarity — not to mention the perversity—of descriptions of food and scenes of eating that we observe in Dostoevsky's fiction by more than merely what Karlinsky calls the Russian author's putative lack of interest in "the physical basis of human life" or in "man's natural surroundings." Dostoevsky, I would argue, simply utilizes food motifs and eating metaphors for different narrative purposes than do most Russian writers; moreover, the "poet of the underground" proceeds to encode these gastronomic images with a peculiar symbolic significance. Visits to inns, taverns, and restaurants in a Dostoevsky novel serve not as an opportunity for the author to paint a picture—rich in physical detail and pictorial expressiveness—of contemporary culinary practice in Russia; they instead provide him with an opportunity to orchestrate memorable scandal scenes and impassioned dialogic encounters between his characters. As a verbal artist, Dostoevsky seems eminently more interested in appropriating the discourse of gastronomy as a trope for depicting the emotional state or psychological motivation of his characters than in providing readers with the artistic representation of actual meals. Accordingly, he tends to exploit the act of eating not as a mimetic device for representing the details of everyday life in nineteenth-century Russia but rather as a metaphor for illustrating human conflicts in modern life between the sexes, the generations, and the social classes.

Moreover, in Dostoevsky's fictional world, where many of the characters

Hellish Monster, *lubok (popular print), nineteenth century. State Historical Museum, Moscow.*

are portrayed as highly volitional creatures who seem obsessed with a desire to dominate and control each other, the act of eating serves less as a paradigm of pleasure than as a paradigm of power. For his characters (especially the pathological ones to whom Karlinsky alluded), the ingestion of food—whether it be as a mimetic or metaphoric act—tends to indicate not taste, enjoyment, and nourishment but rather violence, aggression, and domination. Dostoevskian characters such as these do not merely eat; they seek to devour, digest, and destroy. Indeed, they seem to share the same pathology of desire that Pechorin experiences in Lermontov's *A Hero of Our Time* (1841), when he confesses to satisfying a strange inner need that compels him, vampirelike, to "feed" upon the feelings and emotions of other people. "I have an insatiable craving inside me that consumes everything," the hero explains, "and that makes me regard the joys and sufferings of others only in their relationships to me, as food to sustain my spiritual powers."[4] Food, like sex, comes to serve in Dostoevsky's novels as an object of desire that is coveted not for the libidinal satisfaction it can bring but rather for the sense of autonomy, domination, and control it can bestow. Both eating and fornicating thus come to signify acts of violence rather than of pleasure in Dostoevsky's fictional universe, where carnal desire seems to manifest itself primarily as a rapacious appetite for power.[5]

What I wish to explore in this chapter is how Dostoevsky conveys the will to power within people in large part through the language and imagery of eating. Like Dickens in England, this nineteenth-century Russian writer repeatedly uses different kinds of animal imagery (birds of prey, insects, reptiles) to help convey how the dynamics of various relationships of power—sociological, sexual, and psychological—operate between human beings.[6] To help reinforce this imagery, he selects certain masticatory terms (such as "to swallow" and "to devour") whose literal meanings and etymological origins are designed to compete semantically with what seem to be their more neutral figurative value. I will seek to show, in addition, how the carnivoristic appetite that develops within some people—a metaphorical hunger that Dostoevsky identifies closely with the psychological desire to dominate and control others—can ultimately devolve into anthropophagy (or man-eating), especially when this will to power is fueled by a highly competitive social and economic environment, such as the one that was taking shape in post-Emancipation Russia, a country that was undergoing a process of rapid industrialization and capitalist development. Filtered through his unique artistic imagination, his abiding Christian faith, and his profoundly apocalyptic vision of mankind's future, the bestial carnivorism that Dostoevsky saw at the basis of human relations in the modern secular world threatens to make people degenerate eventually into bloodthirsty cannibals intent upon devouring one another.[7]

⚜ *Eating as Devouring: Dostoevsky, Darwin, and the Discourse of Predation*

The carnivoristic nature of human appetite that Dostoevsky represents in his major novels coincides with the critical reaction within Russian intellectual circles to the appearance of Darwin's theory of evolution, which was enthusiastically received by the young radical activists of the 1860s, members of a burgeoning secular intelligentsia who worshipped the natural sciences. Intellectuals from across the political spectrum in Russia may generally have revered Darwin as a scientist, but they were almost equally unanimous in their condemnation of Darwinism as an ideological movement that they associated primarily with the pessimistic social theories of Malthus.[8] Darwin himself maintained that his famous metaphor, the "struggle for existence," was merely the social doctrine of Malthus applied to the animal and vegetable kingdoms. Most Russian thinkers, however, objected strongly to the contention made by Darwinists that the laws of nature were not fundamentally different from the laws of society—that biology, in other words, could join hands with political economy and social theory to help explain the human condition. As Daniel Todes has observed, the Russians' sense of communitarianism, their cooperative social ethos, and their vision of a cohesive society emblematized by the traditional peasant commune (*mir*) were seriously threatened by Darwin's Malthusianism, which to them exalted individual conflict at the expense of cooperation, brotherhood, and mutual aid.[9] Indeed, the conservative Slavophiles and the radical socialists in mid-nineteenth-century Russia found themselves in rare agreement over this issue, since both groups shared the belief that the ideological underpinnings of Darwin's theory were inappropriate for Russian historical conditions and cultural values. To their minds, the ideology of Social Darwinism championed what were essentially "alien" values for Russians: mainly, a European respect for bourgeois egoism and individualism in general and a British enthusiasm for competition in particular. Although most Russians thus accepted Darwin while rejecting Darwinism, the debate that ensued immediately following the publication in 1864 of a Russian translation of *On the Origin of Species* (1859) prompted widespread discussion about the nature of human beings and their social relations. Indeed, the controversy over Darwinism in Russia, one critic notes, "acquired the character not of a scientific, but of a philosophical dispute."[10]

For many of Dostoevsky's contemporaries, it is true, the drive to obtain food that Darwin posited as underlying the struggle for existence among animals in the natural world seemed a not entirely appropriate metaphor for human behavior within a civilized society, even a society that found itself increasingly being affected by the free economic competition that characterized the era of growth capitalism. Nonetheless, the debate over Darwinism in Russia often prompted mention of the open warfare that is perpetually being waged between predators and their prey in the animal kingdom. As a result, it was not uncommon in Russia during the 1860s and 1870s to encounter naturalistic metaphors about people behaving like "wolves" and "sheep" (or "pikes" and "carps")[11] as well as animal idioms such as "homo homini lupus est." Indeed, the public discourse during this period of sudden and rapid capitalist development on Russian soil fairly resonates with predatory imagery and carnivoristic language of this sort.[12] Aleksandr Ostrovsky, for instance, explicitly foregrounds predation as a trope in his play *Volki i ovtsy* [Wolves and sheep] (1875), where the dynamics of human relations are shown to be dominated almost exclusively by socioeconomic coercion and sexual duress. In the opening act of Ostrovsky's rather bleak comedy about marriages arranged through economic blackmail and extortion, the landowner Lynyaev observes that it is not human beings who live all around them but rather wolves and sheep. "The wolves devour the sheep," Lynyaev notes, "and the sheep peacefully let themselves be devoured."[13] Likewise, Aleksei Pisemsky's drama *Khishchniki* [The predators] (1873), makes it clear that the new wave of capitalist entrepreneurs living in Russia during the 1860s and 1870s constitute little more than predatory beasts possessed of an almost insatiable appetite for material comfort, economic power, and worldly success.[14] In Nikolai Leskov's antinihilist novel, *Na nozhakh* [At daggers drawn] (1870-71), the opportunistic swindler Gordanov, who at one point in the narrative is characterized as "a wolf in sheep's clothing," openly admits that he is merely seeking to put into practice in his own life Darwin's famous theory about the struggle for existence, which to his mind is accurately summed up by the adage: "Swallow up the others or they will swallow you up."[15] Even in Lev Tolstoy's *Anna Karenina* (1878) we find that one of the dark thoughts that enters the heroine's troubled mind just prior to her suicide is Yashvin's cynical view that "the struggle for existence and mutual hatred are the only things that unite people" (pt. 7, chap. 30).

Since Dostoevsky was acutely attuned to the dominance hierarchies that operated in his society, he clearly saw in the Russian life around him a world dominated by the ruthless struggle for survival and inhabited by human beings whose bestial nature and carnivoristic appetite for power predisposed them toward devouring each other. It is not surprising, therefore, to find that in his novels he too makes extensive use of imagery derived from the animal kingdom, frequently portraying the dynamics of human relationships in terms of animal predation. In Dostoevsky's fictional world the pyramidal food chain from zoology seems to have invaded human society and made it into a wild kingdom where one must either eat or be eaten. Indeed, Dostoevsky once noted sardonically that in Russia Darwin's theory about the fierce nature of the struggle for existence was not merely considered an ingenious hypothesis but had already long ago become axiomatic.[16] As we know from some of his letters and notebook entries, Dostoevsky firmly believed that in a godless universe—in a secular world that believes in Darwin and science rather than in Christ and religion—there can be neither love nor compassion. "There is only egoism," he writes, "that is, the struggle for existence."[17] As a verbal artist, Dostoevsky adds a compelling psychological and religious dimension to this public discourse in Russia during the 1860s and 1870s that centered upon the issue of predation of a social and economic nature. In the famous essay in which the populist critic Nikolai Mikhailovsky attacks Dostoevsky's so-called "cruel talent," he acknowledges the author's keen insight into human psychology, noting that "no one in Russian literature has analyzed the sensations of a wolf devouring a sheep with such thoroughness, such depth, one might say with such love, as Dostoevsky."[18] This writer's specialty, Mikhailovsky notes, is his ability to dig "into the very heart of the wolf's soul, seeking there subtle, complex things — not the simple satisfaction of appetite, but precisely the sensuality of spite and cruelty."[19]

Dostoevsky's notebooks for *A Raw Youth* bear witness to this abiding concern with what the author calls the "predatory" (*khishchnyi*) character, a personality type that we encounter in many of his novels.[20] Thus in *The Devils*, for instance, the strong-willed Countess Varvara Petrovna Stavrogina is described as pouncing upon Shatov's sister Darya "like a hawk" (pt. 1, chap. 2), and later she grabs the arm of the Bible-selling Sophie Ulitkina (another of Stepan Trofimovich's female friends) much "as a kite seizes a chick" (pt. 3, chap. 7). "Well, here she is, I haven't eaten her up," Varvara Petrovna reassures Stepan afterward. "You thought I had eaten her, didn't you?" (pt. 3, chap. 7). Likewise, Marya Lebyadkina notes that her tyrannical mother-in-law "would have been glad to devour me" (pt. 2, chap. 3). In *The Brothers Karamazov*, meanwhile, the voluptuous Grushenka is characterized as a "hyena" and "tigress" who promises to "devour" (*s"est'*) (bk. 3, chap. 4) and "swallow up" (*proglotit'*) (bk. 7, chap. 3) the docile Alyosha by taking away from him his monkish virginity. Lise Khokhlakova, another predatory female who has sexual designs upon Alyosha, cannot understand how it is that she has scared off the youngest of the Karamazov brothers, wondering aloud at one point, "Surely I will not eat him up?" (bk. 2, chap. 4).[21]

Much has already been written about the "insectology" at work in Dostoevsky's novels and about how the Russian author — in order to foreground the bestial nature of human beings — consistently links his characters with lower forms of animal life, especially with those from the insect realm: spiders, ants, flies, cockroaches, lice. Readers of Dostoevsky are apt long to remember Svidrigailov's haunting vision of hell as a bathhouse filled with spiders in the corners (pt. 4, chap. 1) as well as the Hamlet question that Raskolnikov poses to himself when he asks whether he is "a man or a louse" (pt. 5, chap. 4).[22] Ralph Matlaw correctly notes how Dostoevsky associates the image of the spider with evil, in particular with morally dissolute behavior on the part of his more demonic characters, some of whom are rumored to have committed such heinous acts as the sexual violation of children. "The spider," Matlaw writes, "is inevitably connected with evil, not only in a sensual but also in a broader, ethical and moral sense."[23] What has not been emphasized sufficiently enough about Dostoevsky's use of insect imagery, however, is the highly predatory nature of many of the crawly creatures he does mention, especially spiders and tarantulas, who trap and then devour the other (invariably weaker) insects that have been caught in their sticky webs. Insect imagery of this kind helps to reinforce the dynamics of power relationships between human beings in Dostoevsky's fictional universe, which—according to Gary Cox—can be seen as being polarized between "tyrants" and "victims," between masters and slaves.[24]

In *The Devils*, for example, the political conspirators who make up Petr Verkhovensky's local group of five are correct to feel trapped—in a legal as well as a moral and psychological sense—"like flies in the web of a huge spider" (pt. 3, chap. 4). In *Crime and Punishment*, when Raskolnikov speculates as to what he might have done with the pawnbroker's money after murdering her, the alternatives he poses are either to have become a generous benefactor to mankind or to have spent the rest of his life "like a spider catching everybody in my web and sucking the lifeblood out of them" (pt. 5, chap. 4). Predatoriness of a socioeconomic nature is likewise the target of the mad speaker's harangue at the fête in *The Devils*. The speaker accuses Western-style capitalism of preying upon his homeland; the modern railways, he asserts, have "eaten up" all of the country's economic resources and now cover Russia "like a spider's web" (pt. 3, chap. 1).[25] In *The Idiot* Ippolit feels that, in a broader metaphysical sense, we are all trapped in the clutches of a dark and evil nature, which he envisions as an enormous tarantula that devours Christ and thus destroys all that is good in life. Ippolit protests plaintively, "Can't I simply be devoured without being expected to praise what has devoured me?" (pt. 3, chap. 7). Quite frequently in Dostoevsky's novels images of predatory insects are used to characterize the dynamics of personal relations between individual human beings, especially their sexual relationships.[26] Thus Dmitry Karamazov, that self-proclaimed "noxious bug" who senses that his own heart has been bitten by a phalange spider, feels inclined to take advantage of Katerina Ivanovna, who is completely at his mercy when she comes to him for the money she needs to cover her father's alleged embezzlement of government funds. Stung by a "venomous" thought whose voluptuous appeal he can hardly resist ("My first thought was a Karamazov one" [bk. 3, chap. 4]), Dmitry is strongly tempted to exploit the young lady's position of acute economic and sexual vulnerability, to act toward her, in his words, "like a bug, like a venomous tarantula, without a spark of pity" (bk. 3, chap. 4).[27]

Dostoevskyism: From Carnivores and Predators to Cannibals

In addition to spiders, tarantulas, and birds of prey, reptiles constitute another species of animal that Dostoevsky at times invokes as a way to convey to readers the highly rapacious nature of some of his fictional characters. *The Crocodile*, written in 1865 as a satirical and allegorical lampoon against Chernyshevsky and contemporary nihilism, tells the story of how a certain gentleman is swallowed alive by just such an enormous reptile. The notebooks for *A Raw Youth* reveal the thoughts of a female character (Liza) who looks upon her male lover "like a crocodile wanting to swallow its prey alive."[28] At the famous scandal scene with which part 1 of *The Devils* comes to a climactic conclusion, Captain Lebyadkin suddenly stops dead in his tracks at the threshold to the drawing room, directly in front of Stavrogin, "like a rabbit in front of a boa constrictor" (pt. 1, chap. 5).[29] But perhaps the most memorable instance of Dostoevskian reptile imagery occurs in *The Brothers Karamazov*, where Ivan is confronted with the very real possibility that the competition being waged between his father and his older brother over Grushenka's affection may well result in the heinous crime of parricide. With regard to this volatile love triangle, Ivan remarks, more with indifference than disgust, "One reptile will devour the other" (bk. 3, chap. 9), an utterance that proceeds to echo, with significant reverberations, throughout the remainder of the novel. For Alyosha, these words are disconcerting mainly because they indicate that Ivan looks upon Dmitry as nothing more than a lowly, disgusting animal.[30] For readers of *The Brothers Karamazov*, however, Ivan's words signal not merely a recognition of man's innate carnivorism and predatory instincts. They also reveal his very real potential for committing the taboo crime of cannibalism, for devouring not simply another species of animal but one of his very own kind. Understood in the terms of insect predation, the spider is no longer just eating flies; he is now eating other spiders as well. Dostoevsky broaches this idea of man's cannibalistic nature with just such an insect metaphor in his *Notes from the House of the Dead* (1860), where the narrator remarks that without work to keep them busy, prisoners at the Siberian prison camp "would eat each other up like spiders shut up in a bottle" (pt. 1, chap. 1). Likewise in *The Devils* Captain Lebyadkin depicts artistically, in his playful verse allegory *The Cockroach*, how when flies crawl into a glass in summer, they turn into "cannibal flies" (pt. 1, chap. 5).[31]

It is human cannibalism—as opposed to cannibalism of the insect or reptile variety—that serves as the topic of Lebedev's memorable anecdote in *The Idiot* about the sinful (and hungry) monk from the famine-plagued twelfth century who confesses at last to having survived for many years on a largely "clerical" diet: he admits to having killed and consumed by himself some sixty monks and (for the sake of "gastronomic variety") six lay infants (pt. 3, chap. 4). Human cannibalism also serves as an important component within the narrative structure of *The Brothers Karamazov*, where the competition between fathers and sons, as Michael Holquist has shown, is built directly upon the Freudian paradigm of the primal horde myth and thus replicates the psychosexual dynamics of the Oedipal complex.[32] According to this myth, a despotic father, who for a long time obstructs the sexual desires of his sons as well as their craving for power, is eventually killed and then promptly devoured by his male offspring. August Strindberg provides a compelling modern statement of this myth, explicitly utilizing its concomitant metaphor of cannibalism, in his play *The Father* (1887), in which a tyrannical patriarch at one point shouts angrily at his child:

> I am a cannibal, you see, and I'm going to eat you. Your mother wanted to eat me, but she didn't succeed. I am Saturn who devoured his children because it was foretold that otherwise they would devour him. To eat or to be eaten—that is the question. If I don't eat you, you will eat me—you've shown your teeth already.[33]

In Dostoevsky's novel, it is Fyodor Pavlovich who acts out the primal role of the tyrannical tribal despot, "depriving his sons of power, money, and women, better to prosecute his own lusts."[34] Although each of the Karamazov sons has sufficient grounds for hating this despotic father and desiring his death, Dmitry's case seems best to fit the Freudian scheme, for the eldest Karamazov son competes most overtly with his father both for disputed property (the power of money) and for the sexually enticing Grushenka (carnal desire). It is his brother Ivan who recognizes that the struggle between a tyrannical father and his rebellious sons is an archetypal one, universal in scope and cannibalistic in nature, that all men are fated to share. "Who does not desire his father's death?" Ivan asks rhetorically at his brother's trial. "My father has been murdered and they pretend they are horrified . . . they keep up the sham with one another. Liars! They all desire the death of their fathers. One reptile devours the other" (bk. 12, chap. 5). The Oedipal rivalry that Freud describes in the psychoanalytic literature can thus be understood as the repression of a desire for oral cannibalism: it reenacts a mythological fall from grace and harmony in which primal sons seek to eat the original father in an attempt to incorporate his power and authority. "In literature, cannibalism is not anthropological (still less gustatory)," Mervyn Nicholson reminds us; "it is a metaphor for power."[35]

This Oedipal struggle for power in Dostoevsky's novels can be extended beyond the boundaries of the immediate family to include the socioeconomic dynamics at work in the larger society as well, whereby empowered groups attempt to cannibalize those who are disenfranchised. Such socioeconomic cannibalism is, after all, the point behind all the predatory imagery that we find in Ostrovsky's *Wolves and Sheep*, Pisemsky's *The Predators,* Leskov's *At*

Daggers Drawn, and numerous other literary works from the 1860s and 1870s that dramatize the deleterious effect that the entrepreneurial spirit of capitalism was having upon social relations in post-Emancipation Russia. Dostoevsky likewise attacks the social, economic, and political ideologies that accompanied the rise of modern capitalism, blaming them for having created the ruthlessly competitive atmosphere of modern life, a pernicious social environment that severely exacerbates man's materialistic lusts as well as his carnivoristic inclinations. Thus the members of the current generation of Russian nihilists, who have been nurtured on the liberal ideas of atheism, secular humanism, and utopian socialism preached by their fathers, the "European" Russians of the 1840s, are often described as cannibalistic creatures. "Madmen! Conceited creatures!" Mrs. Yepanchin screams at the members of Burdovsky's gang who have come to Prince Myshkin "seeking their rights" in *The Idiot*. "They don't believe in God, they don't believe in Christ! Why, you're so eaten up with vanity and pride that you'll finish up by devouring each other" (pt. 2, chap. 9). Similarly, in part 1 of *Crime and Punishment*, in the scene where Raskolnikov witnesses a fat dandy trying to proposition a young prostitute who is sitting drunk on a park bench, Dostoevsky's hero changes his mind about intervening on the poor girl's behalf and we hear him exclaim instead, "Let one devour the other alive" (pt. 1, chap. 4). In the "Necessary Explanation" that he reads at Prince Myshkin's nameday party in *The Idiot*, Ippolit conceptualizes the modern world as a place that could not exist without the lives of millions of human beings being sacrificed daily: "I agree that otherwise—that is to say, without the continual devouring of one another—it would be quite impossible to organize the world" (pt. 3, chap. 7). In *The Devils*, when attempting to explicate Shigalyov's paradoxical social theory, Petr Verkhovensky asserts that "once in thirty years Shigalyov resorts to a shock and everyone at once starts devouring each other, up to a certain point, just as a measure against boredom" (pt. 2, chap. 8).[36]

As we have come to discover during our own violent century, it often turns out to be but a short step from theory to practice: in this instance, from Shigalyov's philosophical system to Stalinist political reality. Tatyana Tolstaya, who recently characterized the long years of oppressive totalitarian rule in her homeland as "cannibalistic times," compares this barbaric period of twentieth-century Russian history with the reign of Ivan the Terrible during medieval times, when someone is quoted as having said: "We Russians do not need to eat; we eat one another and this satisfies us."[37] What underlies such "Asiatic savagery," Tolstaya explains, is "the sense of sin as a secret and repulsive pleasure," or what she calls "Dostoevskyism."[38] The creator of this "Dostoevskyism" was, of course, simply providing commentary (highly prophetic commentary, if you will) upon the workings of the human mind, especially the darker recesses of the psyche, where our deep-seated urges for cruelty and brutality lie hidden. Projecting from the prevailing trends of human isolation and social fragmentation that he observed in the world around him, Dostoevsky envisioned a gloomy apocalyptic future for mankind, a dark and somber period of the Antichrist that would be characterized by widespread cannibalism. This apocalyptic vision of a godless human society, plagued by widespread anthropophagy, is sometimes communicated symbolically in Dostoevsky's novels through microbe imagery. In the epilogue to *Crime and Punishment*, for instance, Raskolnikov has a frightful dream about a devastating pestilence—"a new strain of trichinae, microscopic parasitic creatures"—that infects mankind and makes people act like men possessed: "Men killed one another in a senseless rage . . . they bit and ate one another" (chap. 2). Likewise in the "Dream of a Ridiculous Man," the narrator contaminates the happy and innocent inhabitants of the harmonious utopian land he visits "much like a filthy trichina or pestilential germ infecting whole countries" (chap. 5). This evil, pestilent germ, according to Dostoevsky, is nothing other than the cruel carnality that is being nurtured in people by the current social and ideological climate in Russia. "We are approaching materialism," the author warned in an entry for March 1877 in his *Diary of a Writer*, "a blind, carnivorous craving for personal material welfare, a craving for personal accumulation of money by any means" (chap. 2). The main ethical tenet of the nineteenth century, Dostoevsky insisted in this entry, proclaims the Hobbesian slogan "Everybody for himself and only for himself, and every intercourse with man solely for one's self" (chap. 2).

🌾 *Anthropophagy, Antichrist, and Apocalypse*

People are themselves becoming acutely aware of the serious consequences that will result from the current "chemical decomposition" of society, Dostoevsky maintained, and therefore they are desperately searching to find any form of universal solidarity in order to avoid cannibalism. In the bleak, apocalyptic description of modern London's urban blight provided in *Winter Notes on Summer Impressions* (1863), Dostoevsky declares quite unequivocally that man's craving for even an artificial and synthetic unity of mankind—his yearning to bow down collectively in worship of Baal—arises out of a desperate effort to find an alternative to human cannibalism and mutual annihilation:

> And yet there too [in London] the same stubborn, silent and by now chronic struggle is carried on, the struggle to the death of the typically Western principle of individual isolation with the necessity to live in

some sort of harmony with each other, to create some sort of community and to settle down in the same ant-hill; even turning into an ant-hill seems desirable—anything to be able to settle down without having to devour each other—the alternative is to turn into cannibals. (chap. 5)[39]

In *The Brothers Karamazov*, it is Ivan's Grand Inquisitor who recognizes the hidden potential for cannibalism that lies dormant within modern man, a primordial urge that he believes must be restrained through the institution of the Roman Catholic Church. "Oh, ages are yet to come of the confusion of free thought, of their science and cannibalism (*antropofagiia*)," he predicts to a silent Christ. "For having begun to build their Tower of Babel without us, they will end, of course, with cannibalism. But then the beast will crawl to us and lick our feet and spatter them with tears of blood" (bk. 5, chap. 5). For Dostoevsky, this new "Tower of Babel" constitutes—like the Crystal Palace—but another misguided attempt undertaken by human beings to construct a harmonious "anthill" as a way to satisfy their craving for a community of worship and for universal unity.

For Father Zosima, who voices some of Dostoevsky's own most cherished ideas about the messianic role of the Russian Orthodox faith, the worrisome tide of modern men's mutual envy and ruthless rivalry with one another can only be stemmed by means of the model that Christ has provided us: that is, the Russian Orthodox idea of salvation through a moral brotherhood of man and active Christian love. "They aim at justice," Zosima says of those secular humanists and socialist dreamers who scorn his deeply Christian views of brotherhood and love, "but, denying Christ, they will end by flooding the earth with blood, for blood cries out for blood. . . . And if it were not for Christ's covenant, they would slaughter one another down to the last two men on earth" (bk. 6, chap. 3). According to Zosima, those who deny Christ "feed upon their vindictive pride like a starving man in the desert sucking blood out of his own body" (bk. 6, chap. 3). Zosima's final exhortations thus acquire decidedly apocalyptic overtones as he warns prophetically of the cannibalism (even to the point of self-cannibalism) that is certain to visit human beings if the affairs of men on earth are allowed to continue to be dominated by the modern spirit of "isolation" (*uedinenie*) rather than "communion" (*edinenie*), by the spirit of worldly materialism rather than spiritual love. Zosima sadly predicts that today's egoistic "gluttons" (*plotougodniki*), who live only for mutual envy, "soon will drink blood instead of wine" (bk. 6, chap. 3).

A similarly dire apocalyptic prediction is made elsewhere in the novel by Dostoevsky's intellectual paradoxicalist, Ivan Karamazov, who is reported to have argued that there is nothing in the whole world to make men love their neighbors. That there exists no law of nature that man should love mankind, and that, if there had been any love on earth hitherto, it is not owing to a natural law, but simply because men have believed in immortality . . . that the whole natural law lies in that faith, and that if you were to destroy in mankind the belief in immortality, not only love but every living force maintaining the life of the world would at once be dried up. Moreover, nothing then would be immoral, everything would be lawful, even cannibalism. (bk. 2, chap. 6)

When Smerdyakov at last confesses that it was indeed he who committed the murder of Fyodor Pavlovich (acting upon the belief that Ivan wished him to kill their despicable father), he reminds his brother—whom he idolizes so much—of those fateful words he had uttered earlier: "You yourself said, 'everything is lawful'" (bk. 11, chap. 8). However, when Ivan's devil quotes back to him excerpts from the poem he had once written, *The Geological Cataclysm*, we are presented with a much more hopeful vision of the future. Belief in God and the immortality of the soul need to be replaced with a benign and brave humanism, one that in many respects echoes the atheistic notion of the "man-god" that Kirilov had preached in *The Devils*.

There are new men . . . they propose to destroy everything and begin with cannibalism. Stupid fellows! They didn't ask my advice! I maintain that nothing need be destroyed, that we only need to destroy the idea of God in mankind, that's how we have to set to work. That's what we must begin with. Oh, blind race of men who have no understanding! As soon as men have all of them denied God—and I believe that period, analogous with geological periods, will come to pass—the old conception of the universe and, more importantly, the old morality will fall of itself, without cannibalism, and then everything will begin anew. Men will unite to take from life all it can give, but only for joy and happiness in the present world. Man will be lifted up with a spirit of divine, titanic pride and the man-god will appear . . . and he will love his brother without need of reward. (bk. 11, chap. 9)

Thus the goal of brotherly love, according to Ivan, can indeed be achieved without the necessity of believing in the Christ of Zosima and Alyosha; it can be reached instead through the development of purely human (what Nietzsche would call "all too human") potentialities. Dostoevsky is able to discredit Ivan's dream of utopian humanism largely through the irony of having it be the devil who—with a highly sardonic reaccentuation—recites the words of this poem back to its half-crazed author. Moreover, Ivan's lofty and highly abstract goal of brotherly love seems quite ludicrous to readers of the novel when it is considered within the context (and against the dialogizing background) of the markedly inimical relationships that he has managed to develop with his own flesh and blood, his actual Karamazov brothers—Alyosha, Dmitry, and Smerdyakov. Ivan's dream of a future utopia is destined to fail, Dostoevsky strongly implies, because it is based not upon a solid and authentic Christian foundation of love but upon a counterfeit humanist one. As Lebedev, the author's interpreter of the Apocalypse in *The Idiot*, makes clear, without Christian morality even such an ostensible "friend of humanity" as Malthus can just as quickly turn from a putative benefactor of mankind into a human "cannibal" (pt. 3, chap. 4). Indeed, the whole point of Lebedev's anecdote about the conscience-stricken cannibal monk seems to be to convey to his listeners the point that only the compelling spiritual force of a "binding idea," instilled in people during the Christian Middle Ages, could have driven this repentant sinner to make a free confession of his terrible transgression. Such a powerful "binding idea" is conspicuously absent in the contemporary age of growth capitalism, a cannibalistic age of railways, banks, and commodity trading. "Lebedev tells the tale of a real cannibal," Robin Feuer Miller rightly observes, "to underline the worse horror existing in a spiritual cannibal (Malthus)."[40]

Redemption: Christian Love, Polyphony, and Communion

Through his use of predatory, carnivoristic, and cannibalistic imagery Dostoevsky is suggesting that in a world that has foresaken Christ and his message of love—in an atheistic world that believes instead in Darwin and the laws of science—human beings will behave no differently than insects, birds of prey, or reptiles. Reduced to his most primitive animal instincts, man will indeed act in accord with the Malthusian paradigm of struggle, conflict, and competition. What then constitutes, to Dostoevsky's mind, a viable solution to this problem of the predatory instincts that lurk within human beings? What can possibly curb their innate carnivorism, their apparently insatiable appetite for power, control, and domination? How can man's bestial nature—the insect lust of Karamazovism—be overcome and his truly human face restored? And what can be done to prevent the realization, in the very near future, of a gruesome apocalyptic nightmare of human cannibalism and mutual annihilation?

Dostoevsky's journalistic writings suggest that the solution to all these pressing human problems consists in somehow stemming the tendency toward what he called the "chemical decomposition" of society.[41] According to Dostoevsky the journalist, human isolation and social atomization only further aggravate the bestial tendencies within human beings—their innate predatoriness, carnivorism, and cannibalism. Modern efforts to reverse the prevailing trends toward increasing social fragmentation by means of an ideology that champions human solidarity—whether it be the ideology of secular humanism, utopian socialism, or Roman Catholicism—have all been misguided, he would argue, because in their neglect of Christ and their rejection of his ethical model they have considered only man's material needs and not his spiritual demands: they have considered mainly man's belly rather than his soul. Since it lacks a firm moral basis for its actions, even the humanistic philanthropy of Malthus (emblematized in Dostoevsky's novels by the rumble of carts bringing "bread" to a starving mankind) is in his eyes most decidedly inferior to true spiritual peace and harmony. For Dostoevsky, an authentic utopia can only be the result of a Christian brotherhood—more specifically, a Russian Orthodox brotherhood (*sobornost'*)—that is based on spontaneous active love and on voluntary self-sacrifice rather than on law, calculation, and self-interest, which serve as the foundation for the secular utopias of Western socialism. In some of the later entries of his *Diary of a Writer*, where Dostoevsky concerned himself in great part with issues of international politics (especially the so-called "Eastern question"), the Russian author repeatedly prophesied the rapidly approaching collapse of Europe and the imminent establishment of an Orthodox utopia, a millennium of Christian brotherhood, just as soon as Russia recaptured the ancient capital of Constantinople from the heathen Turks.[42]

In Dostoevsky's artistic texts, meanwhile, this prophetic and polemical voice from the realm of journalism (the voice that champions a politics of Russian nationalism, messianism, and Panslavism) is considerably muted and modulated as it merges polyphonically within a broad matrix of other dialogized voices. Dostoevsky the artist, in other words, predominates over Dostoevsky the ideologue. Or, as Mikhail Bakhtin puts it, "the social and religious utopia inherent in his ideological views did not swallow up or dissolve in itself his objectively artistic vision."[43] The way to overcome both human carnivorism and social atomization, according to Dostoevsky the novelist, is through the inner spiritual transformation of individual human beings. As Joseph Frank observes, Dostoevsky's fictional characters are invariably faced with the choice between a Christian doctrine of love and a secular doctrine of power.[44] The discovery and subsequent liberation of the "man within man" is what compassionate, kenotic characters such as Sonya Marmeladova, Prince Myshkin, Marya Lebyadkina, Father Zosima, and Alyosha Karamazov all seek to effect. Considered metalinguistically, in Bakhtinian terms, all these characters point toward Dostoevsky's dream of attaining a true polyphony by means of their "penetrative" words and their "hagiographic" discourse: "a firmly monologic, undivided discourse, a word without a sideward glance, without a loophole, without internal polemic."[45] They champion a polyphony not of battling and internally divided (dialogized) human voices but rather of harmoniously reconciled and merged voices. Dostoevsky's ideal, as a religious thinker if not as a literary artist, seems to have been to transform social heteroglossia, with its wide diversity of different speech patterns and tonalities, into one harmonious and melodious chorus in which, as Bakhtin puts it, "the word passes from mouth to mouth in identical tones of praise, joy and gladness."[46] Redemptive polyphony would come in the form of a specifically Russian chorus, in which the voices of the intelligentsia and the *narod* would merge together at last to sing a joyful hymn to God and proclaim aloud, "Hosanna!"

In gastronomical terms, a genuine brotherhood of man will come about, according to Dostoevsky, only when the wolves lie down peacefully with the sheep, when human beings start to live for their souls rather than their bellies, and when people begin to find joy in the sense of commensalism that results from sharing communally in the banquet of life rather than in the false sense of superiority that they seem to derive from egoistic acts of cruel, bestial sensuality. A true utopia of universal harmony will be realized only when we finally lose our carnivoristic appetite for power, when we decide to stop devouring each other (as well as our own selves), and when we turn at last from the individualistic struggle for self-preservation that engenders human cannibalism to a joyful communion through Christ with all other human beings.[47] Darwin's clever theory of natural selection, with its Malthusian notion of the "struggle for existence," may well help to explain predatory human behavior in a modern world that is becoming increasingly secularized, capitalistic, and atheistic. But Darwinism, Dostoevsky insisted, can never impart to us the profounder spiritual truth about the human condition that Christ endeavored to teach us: that man can be a brother—rather than a wolf—to his fellow man. Indeed, it is only by learning to share—chorally and communally—in the spiritual banquet of life, such as the one that Alyosha is beckoned to join in the "Cana of Galilee" chapter of *The Brothers Karamazov*, that humankind can ever hope to avoid an otherwise inevitable and terribly destructive banquet: the anthropophagic feast of Thyestes.

NOTES

Research for this project was supported by a Summer Research Fellowship from the National Endowment for the Humanities. I would also like to thank Donald Fanger, Gary Saul Morson, Robin Feuer Miller, Michael Katz, and Eric Naiman for their comments on an earlier version of this essay.

1. Richard Brautigan, *The Abortion: A Historical Romance* (New York: Pocket Books, 1972), 28.

2. Simon Karlinsky, "Dostoevsky as Rorschach Test," in Dostoevsky, *Crime and Punishment*, ed. George Gibian (New York: W.W. Norton, 1964), 636. The Dostoevsky character who would deny a crust of bread to a starving little boy is no doubt Arkady Dolgoruky's friend Lambert in *A Raw Youth*, who claims that when he becomes wealthy, he will derive great pleasure from feeding his dogs bread and meat while the children of the poor starve to death (pt. 1, chap. 3). The "neurotic young girl" who dreams of eating pineapple compote while witnessing the suffering of a crucified child is, of course, Lise Khokhlakova in *The Brothers Karamazov* (bk. 11, chap. 3).

3. Karlinsky, "Dostoevsky as Rorschach Test," 636.

4. Mikhail Lermontov, *Sobranie sochinenii v chetyrekh tomakh* [Collected works in four volumes] (Moscow-Leningrad: Akademiia nauk, 1958-1959), vol. 4, 401, 438.

5. In his study of Molière's *L'Ecole des femmes* (1662), Ronald W. Tobin interprets the central romantic plot as a semiotic collision between the code of power, communicated by the verb *manger* ("to devour"), and the code of pleasure, with its concomitant notion of *goûter* ("to taste"). Whereas the carnivoristic and predatory Arnolphe seeks to "devour" Agnes, hoping to dominate and control her as soon as she becomes his wife, Horace wishes instead to enjoy a "taste" of Agnes's sexuality and tender affection as a love partner. See Tobin, "Les Mets et les mots: gastronomie et sémiotique dans *L'Ecole des femmes*," *Sémiotique*, vol. 51 (1984), 133-145. This same paradigm of eating as power and violence seems to operate in the works of one of Dostoevsky's polemical arch-enemies, Mikhail Saltykov-Shchedrin. In a paper entitled "The Myth of Nourishment in *The Golovlyov Family*" delivered at the annual meeting of the American Association for the Advancement of Slavic Studies, in Washington, D.C., in October 1990, Darra Goldstein demonstrates quite convincingly how in Saltykov-Shchedrin's novel "food and eating are used both symbolically and structurally to dramatize the gluttonous appetite for power that the family members share" (p. 2).

6. "Not only is eating itself of huge importance in the Dickens world," John Bayley points out about the British novelist, "but in a broad sense all his characters are engaged in eating each other, or being eaten." See "Best and Worst," *New York Review of Books,* January 19, 1989, 11. For a more detailed study of Dickens's purported obsession with human carnivorism, an obsession rooted in his earliest childhood days and stimulated in large part by his boyhood reading of fairy tales, travel accounts, and "penny dreadfuls," see Harry Stone, *The Night Side of Dickens: Cannibalism, Passion, Necessity* (Columbus: The Ohio State University Press, 1994).

7. In *Dostoyevsky: The Novel of Discord* (New York: Harper & Row, 1976), Malcolm V. Jones examines the trope of "cannibalism" as a recurring theme in Dostoevsky's fiction and as one pole of the author's vision of humanity. Unfortunately, Jones's fine study came to my attention only after this chapter had been written.

8. See Alexander Vucinich, *Darwin in Russian Thought* (Berkeley: University of California Press, 1988); Daniel Todes, *Darwin without Malthus: The Struggle for Existence in Russian Evolutionary Thought* (New York: Oxford University Press, 1989); James Allen Baker, "The Russian Populists' Response to Darwin," *Slavic Review,* vol. 22, no. 3 (1963), 456-468, and "Russian Opposition to Darwinism in the Nineteenth Century," *Isis*, vol. 65, no. 229 (1974), 487-505; and George L. Kline, "Darwinism and the Russian Orthodox Church," in *Continuity and Change in Russian and Soviet Thought*, ed. Ernest J. Simmons (Cambridge, Mass.: Harvard University Press, 1955), 307-328.

9. Todes, *Darwin without Malthus*, 29. As Peter K. Christoff points out, one of the leading Slavophiles maintained that "the best way to constrain man's animal, jungle

RONALD D. LEBLANC

proclivities was to raise him in a commune." See *K. S. Aksakov: A Study in Ideas*, vol. 3 of Christoff's monumental study, *An Introduction to Nineteenth-Century Russian Slavophilism* (Princeton, N.J.: Princeton University Press, 1982), 368. The peasant commune, according to another Slavophile, "does not comprehend the personal freedom of man alone, which for it is a wolf's freedom, not human freedom." See A. Gilferding, *Sobranie sochinenii* [Collected works] (St. Petersburg, 1868), vol. 2, 478. Gilferding, in Christoff's words, "saw in the Russian communal principle salvation from jungle-like individualism and social Darwinism" (368 f.).

10. Theodosius Dobzhansky, "The Crisis of Soviet Biology," in *Continuity and Change in Russian and Soviet Thought,* ed. Ernest J. Simmons (Cambridge, Mass.: Harvard University Press, 1955), 338. James Allen Rogers voices a similar opinion. "The Darwinian controversy in Russia as in Europe," he writes, "went quickly beyond the world of science and became a focal point of philosophical and political disputes." See "Darwinism, Scientism, and Nihilism," *Russian Review*, vol. 19, no. 1 (1960), 16.

11. Describing peasant culture in post-Emancipation Russia, the populist A. N. Engelgardt remarks that "everyone is proud of being a pike and strives to devour the carp." See Cathy Frierson, *Peasant Icons: Representations of Rural Life in Late Nineteenth-Century Russia* (Oxford: Oxford University Press, 1993), 141.

12. "In literature Darwinism became a topic of direct concern or a target of endless allusions," Alexander Vucinich writes. "References to the letter or the spirit of Darwinian thought, sometimes of the most subtle nature, became an infallible way of depicting the world outlook and ideological proclivities of the heroes of literary masterpieces. Individual heroes of Dostoevsky's and Tolstoy's literary works provided graphic examples of the myriads of prisms refracting Darwinian science and showing the multiple strands of its impact on current thought and attitudes. More often than not, these heroes were alter egos of their literary creators, giving added scope to Darwinism as an intellectual and social phenomenon. A literary figure took note of Darwinian evolutionism not only by commenting on its scientific principles but also by making use of its metaphors." See Vucinich, *Darwin in Russian Thought*, 4.

13. Alexander Ostrovsky, *Sobranie sochinenii* [Collected works] (Moscow: Khudozhestvennaia literatura, 1960), vol. 7, 121–223.

14. Aleksei Pisemsky, *Sobranie sochinenii* [Collected works] (Moscow: Pravda, 1959), vol. 9, 285–359.

15. Nikolai Leskov, *Polnoe sobranie sochinenii* [Complete collected works] (St. Petersburg, 1903), vol. 23, 90. Gordanov advises one of his acquaintances, "Living with wolves, act in a wolflike fashion."

16. Dostoevsky, *Diary of a Writer*, May 1876 (chap. 1). "Perhaps Dostoevsky's extensive, and often biting, use of naturalist allegories," Vucinich writes, in *Darwin in Russian Thought*, 110, "owed some debt to Darwin's suggestive ideas."

17. "Notebook for *Diary of a Writer*, 1875–76," in Dostoevsky, *Polnoe sobranie sochinenii* [Complete collected works] (Leningrad: Nauka, 1982), vol. 24, 164. Everything in a such a world, Dostoevsky adds, is reduced to "despotism" over a piece of bread. "Too much spirit," he sadly notes, "is being exchanged for bread" (164). For a brief discussion of Dostoevsky's reaction to Darwinism, see G. M. Fridlender, *Realizm Dostoevskogo* [Dostoevsky's realism] (Moscow-Leningrad: Nauka, 1964), 157–163.

18. N. K. Mikhailovsky, *Dostoevsky: A Cruel Talent*, trans. Spencer Cadmus (Ann Arbor: Ardis, 1978), 12.

19. Ibid. Mikhailovsky maintains that during Dostoevsky's early career the Russian writer's talents were devoted mainly to studying the psychology of the sheep being

devoured by the wolf, while in his later career Dostoevsky turned his attention almost exclusively to the psychology of the wolf devouring the sheep.

20. Fyodor Dostoevsky, *The Notebooks for "A Raw Youth,"* ed. Edward Wasiolek, trans. Victor Terras (Chicago: University of Chicago Press, 1969), 21–28. Jacques Catteau discusses *A Raw Youth* as "the novel of the predator" in *Dostoyevsky and the Process of Literary Creation,* trans. Audrey Littlewood (Cambridge: Cambridge University Press, 1989), 265–268.

21. Dostoevsky's portrayal of "predatory" character types resembles in a number of important ways that of Dickens. J. R. Kincaid, in *Dickens and the Rhetoric of Laughter* (Oxford: Clarendon Press, 1971), writes that the narrator in *David Copperfield* "speaks of good people as harmless domestic animals and evil people as predatory beasts" (168). In a similar vein, R. D. McMaster examines the extensive use of predatory imagery in another of Dickens's novels. See his essay "Birds of Prey: A Study of *Our Mutual Friend,*" *Dalhousie Review,* vol. 40, no. 3 (1960), 372–381. Speaking of the avaricious world of mercantile London that Dickens describes in the novel, McMaster notes that "character after character is a bird, a beast, or a fish of prey in this swamp" (373).

22. Renato Poggioli explores this spider imagery as a symbol for modern man's existential alienation in his essay "Kafka and Dostoyevsky," in *The Kafka Problem,* ed. Angel Flores (New York: Gordian Press, 1975), 107–117. In the essay "Piccola Bestia," Dostoevsky relates how a tarantula once crawled about all night in his rented flat in Florence. He then proceeds to use this spider imagery in his ensuing discussion of international politics. See *Diary of a Writer* for September 1876 (chap. 1).

23. Ralph Matlaw, "Recurrent Imagery in Dostoevskij," *Harvard Slavic Studies,* vol. 3 (1957), 206.

24. See Gary Cox, *Tyrant and Victim in Dostoevsky* (Columbus, Ohio: Slavica, 1984). S. K. Somerwil-Ayrton employs Cox's notion of "dominance hierarchy" in Dostoevsky's fictional world as the foundation for a study in literary sociology entitled *Poverty and Power in the Early Works of Dostoevskij* (Amsterdam: Rodopi, 1988) that examines the power hierarchy along what is called "the *tyrant-victim axis*" (see p. 1). Martin P. Rice, meanwhile, explores the origins of Dostoevsky's concept of a power hierarchy in Hegelian philosophy in "Dostoevskij's *Notes from Underground* and Hegel's 'Master and Slave,'" *Canadian-American Slavic Studies,* vol. 8, no. 3 (1974), 359–369.

25. In the chapter devoted to *The Idiot* in *The Shape of the Apocalypse in Modern Russian Fiction* (Princeton, N.J.: Princeton University Press, 1989), David Bethea discusses how Dostoevsky came "to associate the railroad with the spread of atheism and the spirit of the Antichrist" (p. 77).

26. "Dostoevsky's view of sexual relationships," Alex de Jonge observes, "is distorted by intensity, and operates along an axis of violence and pain." See *Dostoevsky and the Age of Intensity* (New York: St. Martin's Press, 1975), 179. "Even more or less normal sexual relationships," de Jonge adds, "tend to be founded in sadism" (185). See also Robert L. Jackson, *Dialogues with Dostoevsky: The Overwhelming Questions* (Stanford, Calif.: Stanford University Press, 1993), esp. chap. 8, "Dostoevsky and the Marquis de Sade: The Final Encounter," 144–161.

27. When discussing Pushkin's *Egyptian Nights* in his "Response to *Russkii vestnik*" [Response to *The Russian Messenger*], Dostoevsky characterizes Cleopatra as a black widow spider "who devours her male after mating." See Dostoevsky, *Polnoe sobranie sochinenii,* vol. 19, 136. In his famous Pushkin Speech, he notes how the author of *Egyptian Nights* portrays the ancient gods as desperately seeking diversion "in fantastic bestialities, in the voluptuousness of creeping things, of a female spider devouring its male." See *Diary of a Writer* for August 1880 (chap. 2). In *The Romantic Agony,* trans. Angus Davidson (New

York: Oxford University Press, 1970), 214-216, Mario Praz discusses literary representations of Cleopatra as an algolagnic woman by writers such as Gautier and Pushkin.

28. Dostoevsky, *The Notebooks for "A Raw Youth,"* 159.

29. During the Soviet period, Fazil Iskander wrote a novel that thoroughly exploits this
particular predatory metaphor in the form of a satiric beast fable. See his *Rabbits and Boa
Constrictors,* trans. Ronald E. Peterson (Ann Arbor: Ardis, 1989).

30. Alyosha's response would seem to parallel Sonya Marmeladova's consternation (and
indignation) in *Crime and Punishment* at Raskolnikov's assertion that in murdering the
pawnbroker Alyona he had killed not a human being but a foul, noxious "louse" (pt. 5,
chap. 4).

31. Leonid Grossman surmises that Dostoevsky got this image of cannibal flies from
Balzac's *Père Goriot*, where Vautrin at one point is heard to remark, "Il faut vous manger
les uns les autres, comme des araignées dans un pot." See Grossman, *Tvorchestvo
Dostoevskogo* [Dostoevsky's oeuvre] (Moscow, 1928), 89. It is entirely possible, however,
that Dostoevsky took the idea of cannibal insects from Vladimir Odoevsky's beast fable,
"Novyi Zhoko," which appeared in 1833 as part of a cycle of stories called *Pestrye skazki*
[Motley tales].

32. Michael Holquist, "How Sons Become Fathers," in *Fyodor Dostoevsky's* The Brothers
Karamazov, ed. Harold Bloom (New York: Chelsea House 1988), 39-51. Gary Cox
likewise examines the Oedipal rivalry depicted in *The Brothers Karamazov* in chap. 9
("Primal Murders") of his *Tyrant and Victim,* 86-101. Michael André Bernstein expropri-
ates Mikhail Bakhtin's theory of carnival in an innovative way and discusses Ivan
Karamazov's murderous intent toward his father as the manifestation of a modern cultural
development. See Bernstein, "'These Children That Come at You with Knives': *Ressenti-
ment*, Mass Culture, and the Saturnalia," *Critical Inquiry,* vol. 17, no. 2 (1991), 358-385.
The classic study on this topic remains Freud's "Dostoevsky and Parricide," reprinted in
Russian Literature and Psychoanalysis, ed. Daniel Rancour-Laferriere (Amsterdam-Philadel-
phia: John Benjamins, 1989), 41-57.

33. August Strindberg, *Six Plays,* trans. Elizabeth Sprigge (New York: Doubleday,
1955), 52.

34. Holquist, "How Sons Become Fathers," 40.

35. Mervyn Nicholson, "Eat—or Be Eaten: An Interdisciplinary Metaphor," in *Diet and
Discourse: Eating, Drinking, and Literature,* ed. Evelyn J. Hinz (Winnipeg, Manitoba:
Mosaic, 1991), 198. For a study that provides a historical overview of the theme of
cannibalism in Western literature (from Swift, Flaubert, and the Marquis de Sade to
Artaud, Genêt, and Mailer), see Claude J. Rawson, "Cannibalism and Fiction: Reflections
on Narrative Form and 'Extreme Situations,'" *Genre,* vols. 10 (1977), 667-711, and 11
(1978), 227-313.

36. According to one of the petitioners who comes to visit the holy fool Semyon
Yakovlevich in part 2 of *The Devils*, contemporary youths are already "cannibals" (*liudoedy*)
for having issued a writ against this poor old widow (pt. 2, chap. 5).

37. Tatyana Tolstaya, "In Cannibalistic Times," *New York Review of Books,* April 11,
1991, 3. Roger Dadoun discusses the connection between cannibalism and Stalinism in
his essay "Du cannibalisme comme stade suprême du stalinisme," in *Destins du cannibalisme*, ed. J.-B. Pontalis, special issue of *Nouvelle Revue de Psychanalyse,* no. 6 (Fall
1972), 269-272. For anthropological studies of cannibalism, see the following: William
Arens, *The Man-Eating Myth: Anthropology and Anthropophagy* (New York: Oxford University Press, 1979); Marvin Harris, *Cannibals and Kings: The Origins of Culture* (New York:
Random House, 1977); Eli Sagan, *Cannibalism: Human Aggression and Cultural Form* (New

York: Harper, 1974); Reay Tannahill, *Flesh and Blood: A History of the Cannibal Complex* (New York: Stein and Day, 1975); and Peggy Reeve Sanday, *Divine Hunger: Cannibalism as a Cultural System* (Cambridge: Cambridge University Press, 1986).

38. Tolstaya, "In Cannibalistic Times," 3.

39. "Men all clamor for unity," Kyril FitzLyon writes in paraphrasing Dostoevsky's view of this human desire for solidarity, "and, in default of genuine brotherhood, are all too eager to accept a counterfeit model in the shape of socialism or the Catholic Church, which can offer nothing but the brotherhood of an 'ant-hill.'" See his Introduction in Fyodor Dostoyevsky, *Winter Notes on Summer Impressions*, trans. Kyril FitzLyon (London: Quartet Books, 1985), vii–viii.

40. Robin Feuer Miller, *Dostoevsky and* The Idiot: *Author, Narrator, and Reader* (Cambridge, Mass.: Harvard University Press, 1981), 202. The scene where Lebedev relates the cannibal anecdote is examined by Leon Burnett in "Hors d'oeuvre: Catering for the Consumer in *The Idiot*," *Essays in Poetics*, vol. 15, no. 2 (1990), 68–93.

41. See, for instance, *The Notebooks for "A Raw Youth,"* 38, as well as *Diary of a Writer* for March 1876 (chap. 1).

42. See, for example, chap. 1 ("Once More on the Subject That Constantinople, Sooner or Later, Must Be Ours") for March 1877 and chap. 3 ("Peace Rumors. 'Constantinople Must Be Ours'—Is This Possible? Different Opinions") for November 1877 of Dostoevsky's *Diary of a Writer.*

43. Mikhail Bakhtin, *Problems of Dostoevsky's Poetics*, trans. Caryl Emerson (Minneapolis: University of Minnesota Press, 1984), 250.

44. Joseph Frank, "The World of Raskolnikov," in Dostoevsky, *Crime and Punishment*, 570.

45. Bakhtin, *Problems of Dostoevsky's Poetics*, 249.

46. Ibid.

47. In a recent study of what she calls metaphors of "incorporation," Maggie Kilgour posits a whole spectrum of tropes for the process of ingestion, ranging from the pole of communion, which indicates a relationship that encompasses unity, identity, and harmony, to the opposite extreme of cannibalism, which represents, in her words, "the most demonic image for the impulse to incorporate external reality." See Kilgour, *From Communion to Cannibalism: An Anatomy of Metaphors of Incorporation* (Princeton, N.J.: Princeton University Press, 1990), 16.

NINE

PAMELA CHESTER

Strawberries and Chocolate: Tsvetaeva, Mandelstam, and the Plight of the Hungry Poet

Marina Tsvetaeva (1892–1941) and Osip Mandelstam (1891–1938) are two of the greatest poets of our century. They were not only contemporaries but also friends, and in 1916 their friendship resulted in a remarkable poetic dialogue. Although they drifted apart soon afterward, Tsvetaeva took exception to a sloppy 1931 memoir about Mandelstam and replied with her own "History of a Dedication," explaining the true origins of his final poem to her. She crystallizes their different views on life, death, and immortality in the unlikely figure of strawberries and chocolate. She takes as her own emblem the perennially fruiting strawberry and assigns the confection to Mandelstam.

Food was not a popular theme even in the modernist verse of Mandelstam and his fellow acmeists, who were engaged in writing about the things of this earth, demystifying the symbolist idealism of the preceding generation of poets. Yet Tsvetaeva, always at odds with her contemporaries and their literary schools, returns repeatedly to images of food. She links food and physical hunger with spiritual and psychological drives, especially the poet's desire and need to create immortal poetry.

The distinction between strawberries and chocolate may reflect the poets' identities as, respectively, Muscovite and Petersburger. Moscow was the Russian capital from the fifteenth century until 1703, when Peter the Great constructed his Italianate city on the Gulf of Finland to serve as his "window on the West"; in their exchange of lyrics in 1916, both poets make much of their identity with their native cities. Chocolate, like St. Petersburg, is a manufactured product imitated from a Western original; strawberries, like Moscow, grow from the rich soil of central Russia. At one concentrated period in each year, they offer a free and abundant source of pleasure to children and adults alike.

If we gather Tsvetaeva's scattered references to these delicacies and read the texts for clues to her understanding of human life and of poets' lives in particular, we find that she weaves a rich representation of poets' mortal and immortal parts. She represents both Mandelstam and herself as hungry poets; that is, they crave both physical food and poetic generativity. The flesh and the spirit are not readily separable, especially in her own case, and both are fed by strawberries. Mandelstam's case, she seems to argue, though, is less straightforward and less satisfactory. His unsatisfied appetite for exotic sweets, like his discomfort in the face of death and its aftermath, parallels or perhaps even produces his relative lack of poetic productivity. He is ill at ease and dislocated even in his own country.

Three of the key texts dealing with the hungry poet are her early poem "You walk by; you are like me" (1913);[1] the short prose piece "Flagellant Women" (1934);[2] and the longer prose work written in 1931, "The History of a Dedication" (159–189), in which she offers her reading of Mandelstam's "Not Believing in the Miracle of Resurrection" (1916). The first text uses the image of wild strawberries[3] growing on her grave to describe her connection with her future reader. The second describes the luscious fruits, especially the garden strawberries,[4] slipped to her by sectarian women during her childhood summers. The third ties together the motif of summer and strawberries with her friendship with Mandelstam and his plaintive demands for a bar of chocolate.

The foods of childhood, like its other pleasures and pains, take on deep meaning for every human. In a nation where famine and deprivation have come to play such a prominent part, it would not be surprising if food took on a heightened meaning in the life and art of Russia's writers. The contrast between the security and plenitude of Tsvetaeva's or Mandelstam's early years and the dire need of their adult life only intensifies the impact of their remembered images of food and of hunger.[5] Yet Tsvetaeva resists any such simple bifurcation; she hungered for things of art and the spirit, as well as for sweets, during the relative comfort of childhood and bore without complaint the starvation of the civil war period. Ultimately, both for her and for Mandelstam, inner freedom was dearer than any physical food, although (at least in Tsvetaeva's representation of him) Mandelstam lacks the ease granted by her confident expectation of a life beyond the grave.

Tsvetaeva's equivocal attitude toward food and toward death and immortality figures even in her earliest verse. In this 1913 lyric, she evolves an image which ties her experiences of eating and feeding to sharing her poetry with an audience, even across the boundary between life and death. She speaks from her grave to a passer-by:

> You walk; you are like me,
> Casting down your eyes.
> I lowered mine, too!
> Passer-by, stop!
>
> Read—having gathered a bouquet
> Of poppies and buttercups,
> That my name was Marina,
> And how old I was.
>
> Don't think that there's a grave here,
> That I'm going to appear, threatening. . .
> I myself was too fond
> Of laughing when it wasn't allowed!
>
> And my blood flushed my skin,
> And my curls curled. . .
> I too was, passer-by!
> Passer-by, stop!
>
> Pick yourself a wild stem
> And a berry with it,—
> There's nothing bigger and sweeter
> Than a wild strawberry from the cemetery.
>
> Only don't stand there gloomily,
> With your head sunk to your chest.
> Think lightly of me,
> Lightly forget me.
>
> How the sunbeam illuminates you!
> You're all covered in golden dust. . .

Strawberries and Chocolate

—And may my voice from beneath the earth
Not trouble you.

3 May 1913
Koktebel'[6]

Here the young poet takes on the mask of her dead self, speaking to a living person strolling past her grave. In death she retains not only her voice, with which she begins and ends the poem, but also her vision; as the last stanza demonstrates, she can see her listener clearly. Perhaps Tsvetaeva is making reference to the Russian custom of attaching a portrait of the deceased to the grave marker, embossed on a ceramic plate or sealed under glass. From this vantage point, the eyes of the portrait could take in all the details of this unwitting visitor. Further, she knows exactly which plants grow in a cemetery, and she invites the passer-by both to pick a bouquet of flowers and to pick and eat the wild strawberries growing on her grave.

Another feature of Russian cemeteries which, like the ubiquitous portraits of the dead, may strike the Western visitor is the prevalence of food among the objects which are left at the graves of loved ones. Bouquets of flowers and plants, familiar from our own tradition, are common, certainly, together with seasonal decorations like the pussy willows with which Russians celebrate Palm Sunday. Evergreen boughs may be arranged over the whole surface of the grave, a reminder that the life of the soul, at least, is immortal and unchanging like the greenery of coniferous plants. Often, however, small pretzel-like *bubliki*, hard-boiled eggs, even hard candies will be left by the graves. Sometimes a vase will hold a small sheaf of ripe wheat in place of flowers. Nineteenth-century Russian ethnographers saw in such practices a direct link to the pagan roots of Russian culture; after all, in a country where Christianity took firm root only after A.D. 988, they reasoned, the seemingly unchanging life of the peasantry must retain traces of the ancestor worship practiced by the Slavs in prehistory.[7] Feeding the spirits of the ancestors kept them appeased and helped ensure that they would bring the rain and sun in good season and not break nature's cycles of sowing and reaping.[8] Orthodox church manuals offer an alternative explanation, accommodated to their own theology: small wheaten cakes mirror the bread of the Eucharist, sweets symbolize the good things God provides for believers. The funerary feasts held at Russian funerals and again at memorial services, with their ceremonial consumption of *kut'ia* (a dish made of rice or other grains with honey and sometimes with raisins), extend also to more substantial meals.[9] In the nineteenth century, great emphasis was laid on the charitable act of

This photograph of the cemetery in Yelabuga where Marina
Tsvetaeva is buried was taken in 1960 when Tsvetaeva's sister,
Anastasia, and Sofia Isaakovna Kagan were searching for the poet's
unmarked grave. In the unintentional double exposure two churches
appear to hover over the graveyard. From Kagan family archive.
Courtesy of S. I. Kagan.

feeding the hungry and uninvited (Romanoff, 229, 238-239); at the commemorations of Parents' Days on the second Tuesday after Easter and the
Saturday after Ascension Day, Russians of the lower classes "bestowed eggs,
coloured and raw, cakes or fried dough, or curd tarts" on the beggars who
lined the approach to the cemetery (Romanoff, 245). Some Slavic burial
customs, Kotliarevskii reports, also included scattering flowers over the

corpse in the coffin, "it seems, not only out of a desire to beautify the dead person, but also out of a sense of a connection between vegetative nature and his soul" (p. 210).

Given these varied traditions, I read in Tsvetaeva's boast of big sweet berries near her grave, ripe for the picking, a reference to this vegetative cycle of immortality. Although she retains vision and voice even after her death, her body lies under the earth; her soul and her verse may be deathless, but she is still subject to physical decay. Yet this very decomposition forms part of the cycle of seed, flower, fruit, and decay which produces new growth in the natural world with each passing year. She fully accepts both her physical and her spiritual nature, and implores the passer-by not to be discomfited by her ability to speak from beyond, or more literally beneath, the grave. Far from seeking vengeance, as she imagines her addressee fears, she takes on the role of comforter and nurturer, offering flowers and fruits even from her burial place. After death, she hungers for recognition of her humanity, for a listener who will acknowledge her voice. Yet, as her familiarity with berry-picking in graveyards implies, in childhood she helped herself to the fruit of the cemetery, aligning herself with the beggars receiving alms rather than with the pious mourners bringing in the ritual food which Russian tradition demanded.

The references to berries in "Flagellant Women" confirm and expand this reading. Here Tsvetaeva is recounting her childhood summers at the family dacha in Tarusa, during the comparatively peaceful time before her mother fell ill with tuberculosis in 1902. She describes the fascination she and her siblings find in the local sectarian community, which consists of a single man who is called "Christ," and a large band of women, almost all of whom seem to be called "Mary" or its affectionate form "Masha" ("<Kirillovny>," 491–492) or "Mother of God" (79); even Tsvetaeva herself will be rechristened "Masha" if she joins them (83). Collectively they are called Kirillovny (literally, daughters of Kirill) (77). The band lives in a house near the town of Tarusa, tending a large garden in which, as Tsvetaeva remembers it, "every fruit ripened all at the same time, strawberries, for example, at the same time as rowanberries, . . . it was always summer, the whole summer at once, with everything that is red and sweet in it, where all you have to do is go in (but we never went in!) and everything is at hand at the same time: strawberries, and cherries, and red currants, and especially elderberries" (79). Strawberries generally ripen in late spring and early summer, while the rowan tree's berries turn red in late summer or early autumn, but the memory of childhood endows this spot with an abundance which transcends nature. This enchanted kingdom offers the little girl a way out of everything that fetters her, "from my own name, from my own skin, a way out! From any flesh into wide open spaces" (78). She uses here the untranslatable Russian *prostor* (wide-open space), a word devoid of any negative connotations.

The sectarian women also call at the Tsvetaevs' dacha, bringing great heaps of ripe fruit for the mistress of the house, and their visit provides a glimpse of the confinement Tsvetaeva endures. The children hide behind their mother and peek out from behind her skirts, not because they are shy in front of a stranger; they are, in Tsvetaeva's recollection, afraid of their mother's sharp eye. If she catches them casting greedy looks at the berries, her glance alone is enough to impose an interdiction on the forbidden pleasure.

Their visitor is equally acute, however, and understands without a word the children's desires to glut themselves on her fruits:

> You would tear yourself away at last from the heap of strawberries and suddenly you would meet the sectarian woman's gaze, only just barely lifted from the ground (we were so little!), with her understanding smile. And while the berries were being poured from colander to dish, Kirillovna (which one? they were all one and the same! one with all thirty faces, under all thirty kerchiefs!), not taking her still-lowered eyes off mother's departing back, calmly and unhurriedly she would pop berry after berry into the nearest, boldest, greediest mouth (most often—mine!), as if into a pit. How did she know that mother didn't let us eat that way, before dinner, a lot all at once, all in all—to be greedy? The same way we did—mother never forbade us anything with words. With her eyes—[she forbade] everything. (81)

This fearsome godlike mother is described further on in Tsvetaeva's autobiographical prose cycle as the jealous defender of the forbidden fruits on the Tree of the Knowledge of Good and Evil, and of course since the young Tsvetaeva is a future poet, the fruits in her case are literary texts, mostly poetry. At this earlier period of her childhood, the fruits are literal ones, from a literally Edenic garden inhabited by her beloved Kirillovny. Like the Devil of her very earliest childhood memories, the women joke about adopting their *Marina-malina* (Marina-Raspberry) (83) for themselves. For one breathless moment she believes that they will carry out their plan, and she will truly belong to a loving, understanding, and indulgent surrogate family. She quickly realizes that this can never be, and yet she closes this celebration of earliest childhood and its luscious berries with the wish that she be buried in Tarusa's sectarian cemetery "in one of the graves with a silver dove, where the reddest and largest wild strawberries in our parts grow" (84).

Soon after Tsvetaeva wrote "You walk" at Koktebel', her host, the poet

Maks Voloshin, invited the young Mandelstam to join the Bohemian company of artists and writers whom he had gathered around him at his house in the eastern Crimea. Mandelstam, a year older than Tsvetaeva, was born to Jewish parents in Warsaw but was raised in St. Petersburg. He had received an excellent education at the Tenishev School. In order to gain admission to the university he was baptized.[10] She, by contrast, was the granddaughter of a Russian Orthodox priest and had been given the conventional religious training of the day, although her own spirituality was highly idiosyncratic. From the time her mother first fell ill in 1902, Tsvetaeva's childhood tranquillity was shattered, and when her mother returned from European sanatoria to die at Tarusa in 1906, her childhood was abruptly ended. Voloshin and Koktebel' offered shelter and encouragement to both of these young poets, although they seem to have been unimpressed with each other initially.

In the early winter of 1916, they renewed their acquaintance in St. Petersburg, and Mandelstam visited Tsvetaeva often in Moscow. During the spring of 1916, she was living in Aleksandrov, a village not far from Tarusa, with her daughter and her nephew Andrei. In part 2 of "History of a Dedication" she recounts incidents from his final visit to her, and in part 3 she offers an analysis of his poem based on her private knowledge of its background and creation, imbued with affectionate irony at the demands of the hungry poet.

She herself is content with her own poetic productivity, describing "a balcony, and on the balcony on a small pink tablecloth—an enormous dish of strawberries and a notebook with two elbows. The strawberries, the notebook, the elbows are all mine" (170). Here, as in her 1913 lyric, Tsvetaeva again links strawberries and poetry, if only by their physical proximity, and reduces her own material presence to the two elbows which recline on either side of her manuscript.

In this still-idyllic countryside, in spite of soldiers in their midst, undergoing training, and entraining for the front, they take daily walks. One of the children's favorites is a visit to the graveyard across the road, where one of the crypts has collapsed, allowing them a glimpse of the icons inside. Although the sight is fascinating to three-year-olds, it terrifies the visiting Mandelstam, and Tsvetaeva asserts that "it was because of this crypt that Mandelstam left Aleksandrov so quickly" (171). Whereas she from early childhood has seen graveyards as places to pick the best and biggest wild berries, he worries that the dead may be angered by their visit, may rise to haunt him, to visit his dreams (171). She is comfortable here, while he is increasingly uneasy. This may be related to his early experiences in the Jewish religion, where graveyard etiquette dictates that no one is to step on or over a grave, and frowns upon eating or drinking in the cemetery. It is even forbidden to pick any flowers which may be growing there.[11] One can only imagine what poor Mandelstam would have made of Tsvetaeva's fondness for graveyard berry-picking.

In a long passage devoted to a comparison of their attitudes toward the dead, their graves, and their own mortality, Tsvetaeva emphasizes her own positive attitude, and her guest's fearfulness. She finds walks in the cemetery quite absorbing; while he would prefer to recite poems, she recites the data on the headstones, and calculates the ages of those who are buried in the graves and of those who are "growing on them" (171), just as she hopes others will do for her in "You walk." She even announces that it would be nice to be buried. Mandelstam contradicts her sharply: "It wouldn't be nice at all: you'd be buried, and I'd be walking on you." She protests that by then he himself would be only "a soul" with neither feet nor boots which could trample her. This is no comfort, however; he cries, "That's exactly what I'm afraid of! Of the two—a naked soul and a decaying body—I don't know which is more frightening" (172).

> "What do you want then?" asks Tsvetaeva. "To live forever? Without even the hope of an end?"
> "Oh, I don't know," he replies in distress. "I only know that it's frightening me and that I want to go home." (172)

Tsvetaeva reflects on this further, concluding that "some people come to the cemetery to learn, others come to be afraid, and still others (I) come to be comforted. All of them come to try it on for size." She as a poet, with a family history of early death, does not see the realms of the living and the dead as entirely separate or the line dividing them as impermeable.

By contrast, she depicts a Mandelstam who sees a corpse in every corner. When a nun comes to the house to sew new shirts for the family (seamstressing, especially the making of linens and undergarments, was a common activity for Orthodox nuns in the late nineteenth century), he somehow connects the woman with the broken vault and the bones within. He even implies that the nun may be sewing a burial dress for Tsvetaeva, whispering, "Won't you be afraid to wear these shirts?" She rises to the bait, saying, "Just you wait, dear friend! I'm going to die, and in this very shirt—good thing it's a nightshirt—I'll come and haunt you" (172).

Mandelstam cuts a rather pathetic figure, especially in the eyes of Nadia, little Andrei's nanny. Tsvetaeva even reproduces her peasant speech in the narration, and her condescending description of his envy for the little boy's hot cereal and nicely darned socks reinforce Tsvetaeva's own observations: "Madam! Why is our Osip Emil'ich so peculiar? I'm feeding little Andrei his *kasha*[12] and he says to me, 'Little Andrei is so lucky, Nadia. His *kasha* is always ready, and all the holes in his socks are darned, but nobody'—he says—'feeds me *kasha*, and nobody'—he says—'darns my socks.' And he sighed so dee-eeply, poor orphan" (174).

A little later Tsvetaeva alternates the voices of Nadia and Mandelstam to narrate a still more telling episode. He comes to her complaining that the nanny is a she-wolf or perhaps some kind of witch. He continues, "I asked her for some tea—you had gone out with little Ariadna—and she tells me that it's all gone. 'Buy some more!'—'I can't leave little Andrei.'—'Leave him with me.'—'With yoo-ou?' And that offensive laugh. Her eyes are slits, her teeth are enormous!—She's a wolf!" (176).

Nadia's voice picks up the story. "Then I poured him a glass[13] of hot water, madam, and I bring it to him. And he says to me so pathe-etically, 'Nadia! Isn't there any chocolate?' —'No, I say, but there's some jam.' And how he moaned! 'Jam, jam, all day I'm eating jam, I don't want your jam. What kind of house is this, with no chocolate?'—'There is a bar of chocolate, Osip Emil'ich, only it's little Andrei's.'—'Little Andrei's! little Andrei's! The cookie is little Andrei's, the chocolate is little Andrei's . . .'—'I'll bring you some nice jam.' So he drank up his hot water—with jam," concludes Nadia (176). So Mandelstam finds himself consuming the fruits of the Russian countryside after all, and his longing for the children's more exotic confections is left unsatisfied.

Very shortly afterward he decides to flee from the Russian village back to Koktebel'. Tsvetaeva explains the habitual suddenness of his departures by his feeling of rootlessness: he is restless whenever he is not composing poetry. His decision is a surprise even "for him, with his childish homesickness for a home from which he was always running away" (176).

This departure produces the poem dedicated to Tsvetaeva, which in turn forms the pretext for her whole loose narrative in "History," as she explains at the very end of part 1. In 1931 she finds among her papers a clipping from a Paris newspaper, a badly distorted account of the circumstances surrounding the writing of this short lyric. She goes on to explain in part 3 that the author (Georgii Ivanov) purports to remember Mandelstam in the Crimea, smitten by a "pretty, rather vulgar lady doctor, who is the mistress of an Armenian merchant"! In this version, Mandelstam is writing his verse amid general scorn and mistreatment at the hands of his hosts. The memoirist asserts that they "torture" the poet for nonpayment of his debts by withholding water and feeding him only "leftovers" (180). Tsvetaeva has great fun with the improbable image of the woman doctor as kept woman[14] and stoutly defends the generosity and hospitality of Voloshin and his mother. No one ate richly at their home, but the fault lay with the meagerness of "our hostess the earth" (184) in this desert land, not with the human hosts.

The critic, by contrast, invents a sympathetic elderly Jewish lady who keeps a shop in the tiny village of Koktebel' (in reality, Tsvetaeva says, the shop was run by a sympathetic and open-handed but young and flourishing Greek man!); even this fictional woman refuses Mandelstam his coveted chocolate bar:

> The old woman (perhaps he reminded her of her own grandson, some Yankel or Osip or other) out of the goodness of her heart gave Mandelstam "credit": she allowed him to take a roll and a glass of milk every morning. . . . Sometimes he even got a pack of second-quality cigarettes from her, or matches, or a postage stamp. But if he, losing his delicacy, absentmindedly reached for something more expensive, a box of cookies or a bar of chocolate, the kind old lady, courteously deflecting his hand, would say, sadly but firmly, "Excuse me, Mr. Mandelstam, but that's beyond your means." (183)

Although Tsvetaeva does not admit it, this part of Mandelstam's behavior is at least consistent with the portrait she and Nadia have painted of him.

She goes on to show the obvious absurdity of contending that Mandelstam's poem describes the landscape of the Crimea, when it not only refers to features of the countryside around Aleksandrov but even specifies proper names: in the second stanza he speaks of the *vladimirskie prostory* (wide-open spaces of Vladimir) and in the seventh describes how passionately she had kissed the icon of the Savior in Moscow.

Although in his opening lines he attributes the same beliefs about resurrection to both parties ("Not believing in the miracle of resurrection / We strolled in the cemetery"), Tsvetaeva has already described their widely divergent convictions about, and instinctive reactions to, those who lie in that cemetery. She has tied together her own eccentric sense of how welcome death will be with a fearlessness in the face of ghosts and a willingness to eat the fruits of the graveyard. Tsvetaeva frames this account of her relations with Mandelstam in 1916 and her recollections of him triggered by the newspaper clipping of 1931 with a story about more incorporeal hunger, which also has its roots in her childhood.

Part 1 opens at the home of a friend, a young Russian émigrée who is about to leave Paris to marry a Canadian. Together the women are burning the accumulated papers and manuscripts which the bride will not be able to take with her across the ocean. Tsvetaeva confesses that the one thing she finds it impossible to burn is "white paper" (160); just as others could not bring themselves to burn money, she treasures the blank page. Giving away an empty notebook, for her, is like giving away the poems "which would have been written in it" and the work which "now will never come into being" (161). She terms this her "hunger for white paper" and declares that it is "pre-Teutonic and pre-Soviet: all my childhood, my pre-school, pre-seven-year-old childhood, all my early childhood is one solid cry for white paper" (161). Her recollection is that her mother did not give her paper because she was determined to make a musician out of her, and resisted her early inclination toward poetry.

Tsvetaeva paints a picture of her household in which physical hunger for treats which the children must not covet too eagerly and her own spiritual drive to produce poetry are inextricably linked:

> A circular table. The family circle. A dark blue serving dish with the Sunday pastries from Bartles.[15] One for each of us.
> "Children, help yourselves!"
> I want the meringue and take the eclair. Confused by the all-seeing glance of my mother, I lower my eyes and drop them completely in the face of:
> Fly, my restive steed . . . (161)

In the span of this last sentence, Tsvetaeva jumps from childhood confections to her own first poems. Then she describes how her mother leads the household in a round of laughter at the expense of little Marina's imperfect efforts at versifying. As the sudden shift of topics in this last paragraph demonstrates, there is no separation in Tsvetaeva's mind between the mother's interdiction of eating for pleasure and her ban on writing for pleasure.

"In our house no one had the right to make a request. Not even a request with their eyes." Just the contrary, in fact; if the children so much as looked at a sausage, they could be sure they would not receive any. Desire was the most basic reason for denying paper to the future poet: "They didn't give it to me *because I wanted it so much*" (Tsvetaeva's emphasis, 162).

Tsvetaeva acknowledges that now, when she herself is roughly as old as her mother was when she died, she is the living reincarnation of her mother, except in one respect: "I recognize her in everything except other people's requests" (162–163). In this area, Tsvetaeva contends, she is unfailingly generous, even in the direst of circumstances. Paradoxically, she has also absorbed her mother's prohibitions, valuing in herself austerity and an ascetic disdain for overindulgence, as the passage quoted above shows: before the age of ten she had been trained not to take a pastry, simply because it was the thing she wanted most.

A sense of threat and isolation stayed with Tsvetaeva throughout life, in her own family circle, in the tumultuous days of the revolution and civil war,[16] in the émigré communities of Prague and Paris, then back in the Soviet Union with the dual threats of Stalinist terror and World War II. Similarly, Mandelstam became an "internal émigré" long before his actual exile and imprisonment in the mid-1930s.

Ironically, whereas Mandelstam never left the USSR after 1917, Tsvetaeva wrote both "History of a Dedication" and "Flagellant Women" while living on the alien soil of France; this may explain the lyrical intensity of her memories of strawberries and her concern that she be buried in her motherland. Some of her retrospective scorn for Mandelstam may flow from the complex and conflicting love she felt for Russia: she eagerly claims for herself, an exile from the motherland, the "eternal" strawberries, with their intimate link to the Russian earth, and assigns the merely temporal food, chocolate, to him.

Ultimately Mandelstam and Tsvetaeva, different as she herself perceives them to be, occupy much the same position in relation to the society around them. They share an unyielding resistance to the social forces which would dictate how the poet eats or writes. Tsvetaeva rebels against her mother's control of her hunger, first by allying herself with the sectarian women who feed her berries and later by preempting her mother's sternness by her own even greater internal renunciation. Mandelstam, according to many legends which have surfaced about his final days,[17] starved to death in a prison camp rather than accept government rations which, in his paranoid state, he believed were poisoned. This suggests that at least in Russia and perhaps in all societies, the poet must make a choice between the freedom of the poetic word and the pleasures of food. One scholar argues that "since language must compete with food to gain the sole possession of the mouth, we must either speak and go hungry, or shut up and eat."[18]

Tsvetaeva, by contrast, embraces her physical hungers as she does her spiritual compulsions, unapologetically. In the context of the social and political repression in which both Tsvetaeva and Mandelstam lived, however, neither poet could be nourished by Mother Russia. We may even say that they chose death, because their need for poetic integrity was an even more intimate part of their psyches than the remembered delights of strawberries and chocolate.

NOTES

I would like to thank the many people and institutions who have supported my work on this chapter. It was drafted during my NEH fellowship year and polished during two visits to the University of Illinois Summer Research Laboratory on Russia and Eastern

Europe. I am especially grateful to the superb staff at the Slavic Library there and to the participants in the Workshop on Women in Slavic Culture and Literature in 1994 and 1995 for their help and guidance. Musya Glants and Joyce Toomre, whose work on food history is breaking new ground in Slavic studies, offered insightful comments on several drafts of this chapter.

1. Marina Tsvetaeva, "Stikhotvoreniia i poemy v piati tomakh," (New York: Russica, 1980–1990), Vol. I, 139. Hereafter cited in the text by volume number and page number.

2. Under the title "<Kirillovny>," the piece appears in Marina Tsvetaeva, *Sochineniia v dvukh tomakh, Vol. 2, Proza* (Moscow: Khudozhestvennaia literatura, 1980), 77–84. Hereafter prose works are cited in the text by page number.

3. In Russian the word is *zemlianika*, or "earth-berry"; the etymology is the same as the German *Erdbeere*. This variety of strawberry grew wild throughout the territory of Russia as well as in other parts of Europe. Picking wild berries continues to be an important part of Russian culture even today, a pleasure of the brief northern summer. These small, intensely flavored berries are almost never cultivated; they grow in the grass of open meadows and forest clearings. See, for example, the entry "Zemlianika" in Academy of Sciences, *Slovar' russkago iazyka sostavlennyi vtorym otdeleniem imperatorskoi Akademii Nauk* [Dictionary of the Russian language compiled by the second division of the imperial Academy of Sciences], vol. 2, no. 9 (St. Petersburg: Akademiia nauk, 1907), 2575. The Brokgauz-Efron *Entsiklopedicheskii slovar'* [Encyclopedic dictionary] gives more extensive technical information, pointing out that both *zemlianika* and *klubnika* are used imprecisely in the vernacular and may refer to the same botanical specimens; see *Entsiklopedicheskii slovar'*, vol. 12 (St. Petersburg: I. A. Efron, 1894), 467–469. See n. 4 for a discussion of garden strawberries.

4. The *klubnika* is a larger berry, a hybrid of native European types with strains imported from South America. These berries have been cultivated in Europe only comparatively recently, beginning in the fifteenth or sixteenth century. In Russia, cultivation began in the early nineteenth century, and then only in the areas around Moscow and St. Petersburg and in the western areas of the Russian Empire. They were cultivated in gardens, as Tsvetaeva describes, and also in fields and under glass for the wealthy urban consumer. See *Encyclopedic Dictionary*, 467–469.

5. Both poets' lives have by now been extensively documented. A brief description of their lives and works is available in D. S. Mirsky, *History of Russian Literature* (New York: Random House, 1958) and in Evelyn Bristol's *A History of Russian Poetry* (Oxford: Oxford University Press, 1991). For further information on Mandelstam, see the memoirs of Mandelstam's widow, Nadezhda, published in English as *Hope against Hope* and *Hope Abandoned* (New York: Atheneum, 1970 and 1974), and critical biographies of Mandelstam by Jane Gary Harris, *Osip Mandelstam* (Boston: Twayne, 1988), and Gregory Freidin, *A Coat of Many Colors: Osip Mandelstam and His Mythologies of Self-Presentation* (Berkeley: University of California Press, 1987). For Tsvetaeva, see Simon Karlinsky, *Marina Tsvetaeva: The Woman, Her World, and Her Poetry* (Cambridge: Cambridge University Press, 1986); Jane Taubman, *A Life through Poetry* (Columbus, Ohio: Slavica, 1988); Viktoria Schweitzer, *Marina Tsvetaeva* (New York: Farrar, Strauss and Giroux, 1992); and Lily Feiler, *Marina Tsvetaeva: The Double Beat of Heaven and Hell* (Durham: Duke University Press, 1994).

6. Koktebel' was the home of the poet and painter Maksimilian Voloshin (1877–1932) and his mother. It was located in the Crimea, but not in the lush subtropical area popular with tourists then and now; they built a house on the eastern shore of the peninsula, a rocky and sunscorched land which afforded few amenities beyond its own austere beauty and the joy of the Bohemian company of artists and writers whom the Voloshins invited

to stay with them each summer. Tsvetaeva met her future husband there in 1911, and she and Mandelstam first crossed paths at Koktebel' in 1915.

7. In his *O pogrebal'nykh obychaiakh iazycheskikh slavian* [On the burial practices of the pagan Slavs] (Moscow, 1888), the scholar Kotliarevskii remarks, for example, "We can judge how the ancient Slavs prepared the corpse for burial both from the short account of Ibn-Fotslan [a contemporary written source] *and from many folk customs*" (209; my emphasis).

8. See, for example, the *Entsiklopedicheskii slovar'* entry "Pominki," which describes how these commemorations placate the possibly vengeful spirits of the dead by feeding them (vol. 24, 502).

9. In *Sketches of the Rites and Customs of the Greco-Russian Church,* 2d ed. (London: Rivingtons, 1869), the author, H. C. Romanoff, apparently a foreign woman married to a Russian, describes in elaborate detail the feasts served to mourners, relatives, and beggars alike during the days before, during, and after the burial of the dead. She also tells of an occasion when she carried *kut'ia* to the grave of an acquaintance's mother (244–249) and adds, "In what manner this dish can bring to memory a departed friend is more, doubtless, than any of my readers can suggest. It is, however, thus explained by Bishop Benjamin: 'The rice (or, as in ancient times ordained, wheat-grain) typifies the deceased Christian, who will hereafter rise again like the buried seed (John xii, 24). The honey implies that on resurrection a sweet and delicious existence awaits us in the kingdom of heaven. The raisins, dried up as they are now, will, on coming up, be beautiful, and lovely, as the glorified Christian will be (I Cor. xv, 43–44)'" (243). The "working men's wives and daughters," she continues, were not content with a token spoonful of *kut'ia*; they "made a sort of table of the [grave] mounds by spreading a handkerchief like a tablecloth, and laying gingerbread, eggs, curd tarts, and even vodka, on it. . . . The mourners set to to commemorate the departed by partaking of his favorite dainty; and if he were fond of a glass, the vodka was sipped, with the ejaculation: 'The kingdom of Heaven be his! he loved a drink, the deceased'" (248–249).

10. Various sources give Mennonite (Mirsky, *History of Russian Literature,* 490), Lutheran (Schweitzer, *Marina Tsvetaeva,* 129), and Methodist (Bristol, *History of Russian Poetry,* 215) as his denomination; Freidin adduces evidence that he was indeed baptized Methodist (*Coat of Many Colors,* 30). All agree at least that he did not choose Russian Orthodoxy, although it was the state religion of the Russian Empire and the usual choice for Jews seeking baptism so that they could enroll in university or enter government service.

11. See, for example, the section "Cemetery Etiquette" in Maurice Lamm's *The Jewish Way in Death and Mourning* (New York: Jonathan David, 1969), 74–75. He argues that the cemetery is as holy as the sanctuary of the synagogue, and specifically directs that "eating and drinking may not take place on the cemetery. . . . One may not step over or sit on the gravestone which directly covers a grave. . . . Flowers which, perchance, have blossomed on the grave itself may not be picked for use at home."

12. This Russian term refers to a wide range of hot cereals, including our oatmeal and something resembling our cream of wheat; the buckwheat "kasha" sold in U.S. supermarkets in the kosher foods section is only a single representative of this staple food of the Russian peasant diet.

13. Russians traditionally drink tea from a glass tumbler rather than a ceramic teacup or mug.

14. Medicine was one of the first careers taken up by Russian feminists when they began seeking higher education in the mid–nineteenth century. Many young women traveled to Switzerland to attend medical school and returned to practice medicine in their

homeland. A woman so independent in both her convictions and her income would hardly be likely to become anyone's mistress.

15. A famous Moscow bakery and sweet shop which operated at the turn of the century.

16. She passes over in silence the years she spent trapped in Moscow with Ariadna and their second child, Irina, born in April 1917, and in particular the fact that her younger daughter had starved to death during the terrible winter of 1919-1920; this personal experience of the tragedy of hunger gets no mention in "History" and very little elsewhere in her writings.

17. See in particular Pavel Nerler, *"S gur'boi i gurtom": Khronika poslednego goda O. E. Mandel'shtama* ["In a crowd and in a throng": A chronicle of O. E. Mandelstam's last year of life] (Moscow: Mandel'shtamovskoe obshchestvo, 1994), 30-59, for a sifting of the various reports of fellow camp inmates collected by Nadezhda Mandelstam and others.

18. Maud Ellman, *Hunger Artists: Starving, Writing, and Imprisonment* (Cambridge, Mass.: Harvard University Press, 1993), 46.

TEN

MAURICIO BORRERO

Communal Dining and State Cafeterias in Moscow and Petrograd, 1917–1921

In the first years after the October 1917 revolution, the Bolshevik government embarked on an ambitious program of radical social transformation that extended beyond the traditional arenas of political struggle. The Bolsheviks saw no limits to their attempts to revolutionize the ways in which people lived and related to each other. Even dining, an activity of seemingly little political consequence, became a part of the Bolshevik program to construct a new, radically different society. Thus the Bolshevik revolutionary agenda came to include plans for communal dining establishments to replace private restaurants and family kitchens in urban Russia.[1]

The new Bolshevik government inherited a food crisis that threatened its own survival, just as the same crisis had contributed to the downfall of the tsarist government in February 1917 and its successor, the Provisional Government, in October.[2] The Bolsheviks had used food shortage as an issue to criticize the Provisional Government, but their revolution only exacerbated the crisis. Throughout the civil war (1918–1921) that followed this revolution, far more severe shortages became a permanent feature of Russian urban life. Rationing of bread, the staple of the Russian diet, which had been introduced by the Provisional Government in March 1917, was continued by the Bolshevik government until 1921. But whereas in the spring of 1917 the daily bread ration had been set at one pound, by the summer of 1919 it had dropped to as little as one-eighth of a pound.

In this environment of widespread hunger and revolutionary idealism, state dining grew rapidly after 1917. State cafeterias and communal kitchens were built on the sites of former restaurants, hotels, student dormitories, even private homes. By 1921, state dining facilities had become an integral part of a new urban landscape that included closed churches, new monuments, renamed urban places, and communalized mansions.[3]

🌼 Visions of Communal Dining

To its advocates, communal dining was the form of dining most appropriate for a communist society. Not only would state cafeterias and communal kitchens inculcate collectivist values among the population, but they would also utilize scarce food resources in the most efficient manner. The preparation of food by private restaurants or individual families entailed an unnecessary waste of human effort, fuel, food, and money. This was true even in times of peace and abundance; all the more so at times of war and scarcity as was the case of civil war Russia. Moreover, advocates of communal dining maintained that under a system of centralized preparation of food, it was easier to watch out for the quality of the food and to rationally account for its nutritional content.[4]

As socialists, the Bolsheviks valued highly the advantages of planning in the area of food distribution. But the Bolsheviks also saw communal dining as inherently superior to its opposite, private dining. The development of communal dining in revolutionary Russia cannot be fully understood without considering the entire range of images and values associated with private restaurants and kitchens. Private restaurants served as a foil for state cafeterias. In the contrast between private restaurants and state cafeterias we see signs of the broader contrast between "old" and "new," "wasteful" and "efficient," "individual" and "collective," and "bourgeois" and "proletarian" that was supposed to distinguish prerevolutionary from postrevolutionary society.

Not only were many cafeterias established on the premises of former private restaurants, but the advantages of communal dining were often defined in terms of the shortcomings of private restaurants. Restaurants were at fault because they wasted scarce resources and because they catered almost exclusively to the propertied classes. This was a point that both Mensheviks and Bolsheviks agreed on. Reporting to the Moscow Soviet in August 1917, Mikhail Shefler, a leading food supply official with Menshevik sympathies, advocated the closing of major restaurants on the grounds that they used up a lot of products.[5] In a speech given a few weeks before the October revolution, Aleksandr Shlikhter, a Bolshevik spokesman on food matters, charged that while the masses were on the verge of starvation and could afford only rationed goods, the propertied classes enjoyed the possibility of unlimited consumption at restaurants. He added: "Restaurants not only double food prices but also divert available resources away from the general population for the exclusive use of the well-to-do." Thus, for Shlikhter, not only was there a sharp contrast in the type of foods that the masses and the propertied classes ate, but more important, the propertied classes ate at the expense of the masses. The solution to this problem was to immediately requisition all restaurants and organize state cafeterias where food would be distributed in equal quantities to all.[6]

While the Bolshevik attack on private restaurants was made in the name of a more equitable distribution and rational utilization of scarce products, the attack on the private kitchen was first made in the name of women's emancipation.[7] The Bolsheviks defended the establishment of communal kitchens and state cafeterias as measures that would expedite the liberation of women from the burden of domestic duties. Here, Bolsheviks drew on the nineteenth-century socialist tradition for inspiration. Followers of the French socialist Charles Fourier had created utopian communities known as phalanxes where women performed the traditional household duties of cooking, laundry, and child care on a communal basis. Members of American utopian communities, such as New Harmony, established by followers of Robert Owen, also dined and socialized in common rooms. Closer to home, many members of the Russian intelligentsia had formed a positive impression of communal living arrangements from Nikolai Chernyshevsky's influential novel *What Is to Be Done?* (1863), in which the heroine, Vera Pavlovna, finds personal liberation through communal living in the heart of St. Petersburg.[8] To the utopian socialist tradition of communalism, the Bolsheviks added the Marxist emphasis on the state's role in promoting the creation of communal facilities. Karl Marx and Friedrich Engels approached the issues of household labor as part of a broader critique of the individual family. It was not enough for women to perform household labor on a communal basis; it was necessary to take household labor out of the home and into the public sphere. The belief that the individual family was a source of oppression lay at the heart of the more radical communal proposals advanced by the Bolsheviks after 1917.

Influenced by the utopian socialist and Marxist traditions, Bolsheviks approached the issues of the household economy from the basic proposition that the source of women's oppression lay in the drudgery of daily housework. State-run facilities such as communal kitchens, nurseries, laundries, and dining rooms would free women from this domestic slavery. The liberating potential of communal household arrangements was perhaps most forcefully articulated by Inessa Armand and Alexandra Kollontai, the first two directors of the Women's Section (*Zhenotdel*) of the Russian Communist Party. At the First All-Russian Congress of Women, held in Moscow in November 1918, Armand delivered a rousing attack on "pots and pans" while Kollontai argued that "housework was doomed to extinction with the victory of communism." Kollontai's speech, later published as a pamphlet entitled "Communism and the Family," presented a vision of a society in which working women would be "surrounded by the same ease and light, hygiene and beauty, that previously only the rich could afford." To make this possible, communist society would provide communal kitchens and dining rooms, laundries, and clothes-mending centers, as well as people who would clean rooms.[9]

Vladimir Lenin, leader of the Bolshevik Party, recognized the connection between communal arrangements and the emancipation of women. In a short speech at the Congress of Women, he echoed the themes already developed by Armand and Kollontai. But Lenin was also aware of the broader potential of communal household and dining arrangements. In a subsequent pamphlet entitled "Velikii pochin" [A great beginning], he wrote more extensively in favor of communal arrangements such as state-sponsored dining. Published in the summer of 1919, *Velikii pochin* is above all a celebration of *subbotniki* (volunteer Saturdays) as examples of how workers can contribute through small deeds to the defense of the revolution.[10] *Subbotniki,* as well as communal cafeterias, were to Lenin invaluable "shoots" of communism, living examples of communism in practice.[11]

Although prominent Bolsheviks such as Kollontai, Armand, and Lenin spoke favorably of communal dining arrangements, none of them elaborated on the practical details of implementing their vision. One of the more extensive descriptions of the potential of communal cafeterias in a communist society is found in a unique pamphlet entitled *Obshchestvennyi stol* [The public table]. The pamphlet's author, identified only by the initials F. Sh., begins with an evocation of the Last Supper as an example of communal dining in history, discusses the achievements and shortcomings of communal dining in Soviet Russia as of 1919, then concludes with a compelling vision of ideal communal dining in a communist society.[12]

In addition to serving affordable and nourishing meals to the general population, the author argued that communal dining should have an educational, socializing role. The theme of communal dining as a family event surfaces at several points in the pamphlet. "In order for communal dining to truly become a 'communal' event, bringing together people as in a family, going to the cafeteria must not feel like a necessary evil to be avoided whenever possible," the author noted. Here we see a statement of the Bolshevik goal of replacing private, family dining with state communal cafeterias.

In elaborating the ideal of communal dining, F. Sh. did not entirely reject the accumulated experience of private commercial dining. For example, managers of communal cafeterias had much to learn from private restaurant owners, who knew how to attract and keep customers as long as possible by means of aesthetic accompaniments such as music, painting, sculpture, even ballet. In a private restaurant or tavern, a piano or a gramophone enticed and held visitors as much as the food and the drink. The best of these restaurants or taverns became "a cross between a temple [khram] uniting a community of worshippers and a cozy, family hearth."

Although there were lessons to be learned from private restaurants and taverns, F. Sh. did not doubt that communal cafeterias would work on a superior plane. Through their furniture and decoration, communal cafeterias would lift customers beyond the "banal, bourgeois tastes" of taverns and restaurants, creating a truly beautiful setting that would provide educational and cultural enlightening. The author suggested that paintings and sculptures be displayed in cafeterias rather than museums. In museums, these works of art would be available to only those few who already knew about them. In cafeterias, they would be constantly seen, even by those who had no particular interest in the arts, and thus contribute to the cultural development of the customers. Communal cafeterias would also provide visitors with music, newspapers, and illustrated magazines.[13]

From Visions to Realities

In F. Sh.'s blueprint, state cafeterias were to be at the center of an extensive state dining network that would also include teahouses, canteens, communal kitchens, and food distribution points. Of these, cafeterias would be the main staging point of the government's attack on private commercial restaurants and home dining. For this purpose, Bolshevik officials carefully laid out guidelines for the establishment and functioning of these cafeterias. But in the grim civil war days these guidelines more often than not were a statement of ideological aspiration rather than a reflection of reality.[14] Even F. Sh. readily admitted that communal dining as it existed in 1919 was only an "emergency version," whose main task was to feed half-starving people. Only after the civil war crisis was over would the real communal dining be able to flourish.

In the meantime, the development of state cafeterias revealed the same tremendous gap between idealistic visions of the future and the harsh reality resulting from an unparalleled social and economic collapse that characterized daily life during the civil war.[15] Communal dining programs encountered the same obstacles that other social engineering programs encountered in the early Soviet period: lack of money, lack of trained personnel, and inadequate infrastructure. Women did not rush to embrace communal cafeterias, visions of the "ideal" cafeteria were far removed from what customers dealt with on a daily basis, food was barely edible, and ultimately state cafeterias did not replace home cooking or outside dining.[16]

The greatest advances in public dining took place in Petrograd and Moscow, where municipal governments created a network of state cafeterias from an assortment of canteens, cafeterias, and private restaurants. Although statistics for this period are not always precise, they are consistent enough to provide a reliable overall picture. In 1918–1919, the number of state cafeterias tripled in Moscow and quadrupled in Petrograd. Each city served about 900,000 persons in the span of a year.[17]

Some state cafeterias may have initially matched the promise of state-sponsored communal dining. Lynn Mally's account of the Proletkult clubs, where workers could find "food, warmth, and conviviality at a time of great social dislocation," suggests that these clubs may have come close to realizing the dreams of communal dining idealists. Mary McAuley describes the Bear Cafe in Petrograd, which attempted to create the atmosphere of an "educational-aesthetic" dining establishment: "experienced waiters would serve customers . . . there will be a separate room for smoking, and the character of the music will encourage the development of musical taste." However, it seems that this was a short-lived experiment of little impact.[18]

The cafeterias run by consumer societies in Moscow may also have come close to the goal of fulfilling the less ambitious, basic promise of feeding large numbers of people adequately.[19] A report published in *Kooperatsiia,* the newspaper of the consumer society of the same name, provides a glimpse into the daily life of five cafeterias opened during 1918. The most popular of Kooperatsiia's new cafeterias seems to have been number 3, located on the site of a former private restaurant. It catered primarily to workers and employees of retail establishments. The quality of the meals was apparently good, for the cafeteria was very crowded during lunch hours. Also popular was number 5, located near the downtown Arbat Square on the site of a former student dormitory. Here, the customers were primarily from the intelligentsia. Cafeteria number 1, located on the second and third floors of a former private home in the Zamoskvorech'e district across the Moscow River from the

MAURICIO BORRERO

Text by Vladimir Maiakovskii and graphics by Aleksandr Rodchenko, advertisement for Mossel'prom's public dining rooms in Moscow, 1924. Left: "Everyone needs to eat lunch and supper. Where to go? There is nowhere else but Mossel'prom." Right: "Dining rooms no. 20 (the former Praga restaurant, Arbat 2) and no. 34 (Arbat 24) open until 2 A.M. for dinner and supper with variety orchestra." Private collection.

Kremlin, catered primarily to clerical employees. Although described as clean and roomy, it had the lowest attendance figures of the five, possibly because a large proportion of meals were issued to go. The least popular, number 4, described as "uncomfortable and dirty" in the report, was located on a site that doubled as an auditorium for performances.[20]

Other descriptions of cafeterias present a far less favorable picture than Kooperatsiia's self-evaluation. Although Lenin complained of the excessively negative descriptions of state cafeterias in the Soviet press, the truth was that few cafeterias actually lived up to basic health and culinary standards, let alone the more grandiose images of cafeterias as a "public hearth."[21] As early as December 1918, government inspections of cafeterias in Moscow and Petrograd revealed that most of them lacked suitable places for food preparation and storage and that nearly all of them lacked adequate ventilation.

Unsanitary conditions and the large numbers of daily customers made state cafeterias a breeding ground for various diseases, such as typhus, which reached epidemic proportions during 1919 and 1920.[22] Although conditions were especially dismal in the underfunded cafeterias run by the cities' district soviets (as opposed to the central soviets), even the cafeterias serving the newly privileged bureaucrats of the Soviet government could not provide well-balanced meals.[23] In a case that received some public exposure, in the summer of 1920 several people dining at the Kremlin cafeteria for employees of the Council of People's Commissars (Sovnarkom) and the cafeteria of the Second Moscow House of Soviets fell victim to scurvy.[24]

There may have been exceptions to the overall pattern. At the Kooperatsiia cafeterias, for example, customers received a choice of meals of one or two courses. For the first course, the cafeterias offered a choice of soup: sometimes *borshch* made from canned preserves or dried roots, sometimes pea, fish, or rice soup. For the second course customers could choose from among such items as ham with beans, shepherd's pie, *kasha*, and cutlets. In addition to the main courses, the majority of cafeterias served tea, coffee, sour milk, (*prostokvasha*) and cookies (*lepeshki*). Tearooms provided cold and warm snacks (*zakuski*) in addition to tea.[25]

Readers who have sifted through the thick menus of Soviet-era restaurants may wonder what proportion of the dishes listed on the Kooperatsiia menus was actually available. The sources do not tell. More typical of the meals available to most urban residents at state establishments were perhaps those described by Alexandra Kollontai. Kollontai had to lobby hard for extra rations for women attending the First All-Russian Congress of Working and Peasant Women, held in November 1918. And yet her efforts yielded only "tiny plates of barley gruel, slivers of bread, and thin soup with thin pieces of dried roach (*vobla*) floating on top."[26] Almost two years later the picture remained distressingly similar. A delegate to the Eighth Congress of Soviets, held in Moscow in December 1920, later recalled meals that consisted of "soup with herring head or rotten sour cabbage and for the main course moldy millet gruel or a piece of old herring." The bread that accompanied the meals was "sodden and heavy, like clay."[27]

The great hunger of the civil war years was evident not only in terms of decreased rations and reduction in number of calories consumed but also in terms of the deteriorating quality of the food itself. Food surrogates and adulterated and spoiled foods all found their way into the state cafeterias and black markets, where consumers were most likely to obtain their food.[28] Sometimes the line separating accepted surrogates from adulterated products was very thin. The "tea" or "coffee" served at cafeterias had little resemblance to real tea or coffee. For residents of Moscow and Petrograd, the Soviet government's beverage trust, Tsentrochai, had developed drinks that contained no more than 35 percent coffee or chicory mixed with cereals, dried vegetables, and acorns.[29] Horse flesh was common, an accepted wartime meat surrogate. By 1919 it had long been available at markets, such as the Sukharevka, the largest open-air market in Moscow. But hunger and necessity were such that longstanding taboos, such as that against dog meat, were broken. Newspaper items announcing the open sale of dog meat at the Sukharevka were accompanied by articles that attempted to reason customers out of their cultural inhibitions against such foods.[30]

Cases of dangerously spoiled and adulterated foods were found in both the food issued through the state dining network and that sold on the black market. Toward the end of the civil war, for example, an investigation of state cafeterias in the Presnia district of Moscow uncovered widespread use of spoiled products, such as rotten fish and cabbage. Black market customers sometimes found that they had purchased milk diluted with water or flour mixed with powdered sugar. In one case a nutritionist reported that the cottonseed oil he had purchased was actually industrial oil colored with yellow paint and that beverages sold as tea were made from birch and twigs.[31]

Conditions at cafeterias were a source of concern to food officials, who feared they would reflect poorly on the revolution as a whole. In the summer of 1919, the poor quality of cafeteria food had triggered strikes in Petrograd.[32] At a time when the revolution's very survival was in doubt, few could be as optimistic as F. Sh., who even in the darkest moments of the civil war could envision "hungry and dirty communal cafeterias and teahouses" becoming places where people could eat appetizing food while receiving cultural and collectivist education.[33] More common was the fear expressed by a Bolshevik food official in commenting on the conditions of state cafeterias: "Ten counterrevolutionary agitators cannot cause us as much harm as one director of the cesspools that go by the name of soviet cafeterias."[34]

However, strikes and other forms of protest on the grounds of poor food conditions were not as dangerous as feared. By 1919, almost six years of increasingly greater hunger had decreased people's desire or ability to protest. The hungry masses of 1919 were not the same ones of 1917. Political protest was not as important as the struggle for survival. People made up for the shortcomings of the state dining system as best they could: through informal agreements, travel to the countryside, obtaining extra ration cards legally or illegally, barter, and the ever-present black market.[35]

🌣 *The Old World of Dining Survives*

In late 1920, the editors of *Krasnaia Moskva* [Red Moscow], an official survey of Moscow's economy and society in the first three years of Soviet rule, noted that private trade had disappeared from the streets of Moscow.[36] Private trade had indeed been abolished by decrees issued in the summer and fall of 1918, which capped a process of government encroachment and which sharply altered the prerevolutionary commercial landscape known to Moscow and Petrograd residents. In Moscow, for example, the fashionable Eliseev Brothers store on the downtown Tverskaia Street, one of Moscow's central arteries, became "Distribution Point No. 1," while the largest store of the Miur and Meriliz chain of department stores became "Universam No. 1." The famed "Yar" restaurant became a "kitchen-factory" that served almost 15,000 daily meals for children. By November 1918, the Bolshevik authorities had closed all private restaurants in Petrograd and replaced them with state cafeterias.[37]

The assessment of Krasnaia Moskva's editors was either premature or showed a certain degree of wishful thinking. The fact was that private trade was thriving in a variety of forms, despite the government's attempts to stamp it out. And there was no more powerful symbol of the survival of private trade than the Sukharevka market. In fact, the name "Sukharevka" became almost synonymous with illegal, private trade during the civil war. At the Sukharevka, consumers could find—at exorbitant prices—products such as meats, vegetables, and fruits which had long disappeared from state stores. In addition to its crowded market stalls, the Sukharevka housed a number of kiosks where prepared food could be bought.[38]

Private dining also survived in the form of underground restaurants or cafés attached to artistic establishments. Some of these restaurants were hidden away in private houses, open only to those who had the right connections and knew the correct password. The American correspondent Marguerite Harrison tells of such a restaurant located on an "out-of-the-way" street in Moscow.

> At the illegal restaurants, which were chiefly in private houses where no one could go without an introduction from a patron, delicious dinners were served at prices ranging from three to five thousand rubles. I was taken to one of these . . . by an employee of the Foreign Office. The hostess, who waited on us herself, assisted by her daughter and an old family servant, was an extremely elegant, very pretty woman from a distinguished Georgian family. Her husband was a trusted employee in a government office. The table appointments were all most attractive; we had delicious meals and most congenial company.

Harrison described meals that by 1920 had long since disappeared from the tables of the majority of Moscow's population: "Dinner . . . consisted of a good vegetable soup, followed by roast meat, cutlets, or chicken, with two vegetables. Real coffee, white roll, cakes, and tarts . . . and ices were extra."[39]

The sociologist Pitirim Sorokin has left an account of a similar underground restaurant in Petrograd. Arriving in Petrograd after a difficult journey, Sorokin waited in vain for his ration cards from the city's Supply Commissariat. Half-starved, he went to an "illegal" dining restaurant recommended to him by a friend. The hostess cautiously opened the door and, having heard the proper password, took him to a room where twenty men and women were dining. "Being given a bowl of millet gruel, I began to 'criminally' eat," he later wrote.[40] The difference in the underground meals served to Harrison and Sorokin can be partly explained by the more dire food crisis experienced in Petrograd and by Moscow's more extensive black market.

Not all the underground restaurants called for the elaborate cloak-and-dagger approaches described by Harrison and Sorokin. Some functioned quite openly, semitolerated by the authorities in the same way as the black market. Many were connected to the world of the arts and resembled the U.S. speakeasys of the 1920s. As Harrison became wiser to the ways of revolutionary Moscow, she discovered after-theater restaurants such as the Domino, a poets' hangout downtown on Tverskaya Street, where she found coffee, cakes, and ices. Another of her underground favorites was a Jewish restaurant where she and her friends had "'gefilte' fish, roast goose with apples and onions and other Jewish delicacies."[41]

Restaurants such as these were periodically condemned by the Soviet press as proof that "the majority, if not all, of the snack bars [*bufety*] in our theaters have turned into places of brisk trade in products made from flour, sugar, and other monopolized goods." Soviet reporters seemed to be willing to accept that in the snack bars of large theaters, profiteering in restricted food products undoubtedly accompanied art. But they reserved their strongest language for what they saw as a more recent phenomenon: the emergence of small theaters where art or entertainment was only the background to the food they served. These places posted alluring menus on their doors, promising two-course meals and coffee for prices that neither workers nor the average employee could afford.[42] In yet another example of the contrasts and ironies of the civil war, it was these places and not the state cafeterias that brought to life the visions of eating establishments as aesthetic meeting places, albeit in a distorted manner.

As the broader struggle against the black market repeatedly showed, it was almost futile to fight these expressions of private commercial dining. The fines imposed on the few owners who were caught barely made a dent in their rather profitable trade. They could easily cover the fines with the profits made in the course of one night from selling pastries and sandwiches at inflated prices. And as Harrison frequently witnessed, even when such establishments were shut down by the government, "their owners arrested and their supplies confiscated, others were always springing up to take their places."[43] The truth was that the extent of underground private commercial dining was tied directly to the failures of the state dining system, just as the growth of the black market was tied to the shortcomings of the state system of procurement and distribution.

With the end of the civil war in late 1920 and the inception of the New Economic Policy (NEP) in March 1921, the character of state dining changed significantly. As part of the NEP legislation, the Bolshevik government retreated from its attempt to become the sole supplier of food to urban populations. Restaurants were legalized, workers were taken off government supply rolls, and Narkomprod's state dining apparatus was transferred to the cooperatives. During the NEP years, the attempt to replace both private commercial dining and domestic home cooking with state-sponsored collective dining came to be seen as another example of the spartan and utopian civil war policies posthumously known as "war communism."

During the civil war, the Bolshevik attack on private restaurants and kitchens was driven by both utopian and pragmatic considerations. Of the two, the attack on private kitchens and domestic home cooking never really prospered. The attack on private commercial restaurants was more successful, as it was facilitated by the state's power to nationalize private restaurants and by the imperatives of survival during the hungry years of the civil war. After the NEP interlude, state dining received new life with the Stalin revolution of the 1930s.[44] For the remainder of the Soviet era, state cafeterias were places where the average citizen could obtain cheap, although unappetizing, meals. But for the overwhelming majority of citizens, home dining remained the source of the communality and hearth that writers like F. Sh. had once envisioned for state cafeterias.

NOTES

Research for this chapter was made possible by grants from the International Research and Exchanges Board (IREX) and the Hoover Institution's Title VIII program. I also wish to thank Phyllis Conn, Joyce Toomre, and Musya Glants for their comments and suggestions in the drafting of this chapter.

1. The study of communal dining is complicated by the often interchangeable use of

Russian terms that suggest different meanings, such as *obshchestvennoe pitanie* (public dining) and *kommunal'noe pitanie* (communal dining). The former generally suggests food eaten outside the home in a public setting, while the latter implies a more explicitly ideological and communal setting. In this chapter I use "state dining" to refer to the government's network of state cafeterias and "communal dining" to refer to its vision for an alternative to private dining.

2. On the food crisis, see Lars T. Lih, *Bread and Authority in Russia, 1914-1921* (Berkeley: University of California Press, 1990); Silvana Malle, *The Economic Organization of War Communism, 1918-1921* (Cambridge: Cambridge University Press, 1985); and Mauricio Borrero, "Hunger and Society in Civil War Moscow, 1917-1921," Ph.D. dissertation, Indiana University, 1992.

3. In Petrograd, for example, communal cafeterias became obligatory stopping points in the tours that Bolshevik officials gave to foreign visitors to publicize the achievements of the new Soviet republic. *Petrokommuna* [Petrograd Commune] (Petrograd: 1920), 55.

4. See "Kommunal'noe pitanie" [Communal dining], in *Izvestiia Narkomproda* [News of the Food Supply Commissariat], December 1918, 5, and Aleksandr Shlikhter, "Prodovol'stvennyi vopros kak ekonomicheskaia zadacha bor'by za vlast'," in *Agrarnyi vopros i prodovol'stvennaia politika v pervye gody sovetskoi vlasti* [The agrarian question and food supply policy in the first years of Soviet power] (Moscow 1985), 356-363.

5. Tsentral'nyi Gosudarstvennyi Arkhiv Moskovskoi Oblasti [Central State Archive of Moscow Oblast] (TsGAMO), f. 66, op. 12, d. 65, ll. 3-8.

6. Shlikhter, "Prodovol'stvennyi vopros," 358.

7. This discussion is drawn primarily from Wendy Z. Goldman, *Women, the State, and Revolution: Soviet Family Policy and Social Life, 1917-1936* (Cambridge: Cambridge University Press, 1993), 24-25, 32-35.

8. The literature on nineteenth-century utopian socialist communities is extensive. For two recent studies of Owenite communities in the United States, see Anne Taylor, *Visions of Harmony: A Study in Nineteenth-Century Millenarianism* (Oxford: Oxford University Press, 1987), and Carol A. Kolmerten, *Women in Utopia: The Ideology of Gender in the American Owenite Communities* (Bloomington: Indiana University Press, 1990).

9. Little was said about the workers (most likely women) who would staff these communal enterprises. See Goldman, *Women, the State, and Revolution*, 3-4; Richard Stites, *The Women's Liberation Movement in Russia: Feminism, Nihilism, and Bolshevism, 1860-1930* (reprint, Princeton: Princeton University Press, 1991), 330; Barbara Evans Clements, *Bolshevik Feminist: The Life of Alexandra Kollontai* (Bloomington: Indiana University Press, 1979), 153; Cathy Porter, *Alexandra Kollontai: The Lonely Struggle of the Woman Who Defied Lenin* (New York: Dial Press, 1980), 323-324. For a text of Kollontai's speech and pamphlet, "Communism and the Family," see *Selected Writings of Alexandra Kollontai*, translated with an introduction and commentaries by Alix Holt (Westport, Conn.: Lawrence Hill, 1977), 255.

10. V. I. Lenin, "Velikii pochin" [A great beginning], in *Polnoe sobranie sochinenii* [Complete works] (hereafter *PSS*), 5th ed., (Moscow, 1959-65), vol. 39, 1-29. In May 1919, workers at the Moscow-Kazan railway depot had volunteered their labor to help the cause of the revolution by unloading freight cars and other tasks. Other workers soon adopted this practice, in some cases spontaneously, in most cases with the encouragement of the Communist Party.

11. Lenin, "Velikii pochin," 24-25. *The ABC of Communism*, the explanation of the party's program intended for a popular audience, echoed this theme. See Nikolai Bukharin and Evgenii Preobrazhensky, *The ABC of Communism: A Popular Explanation of the Program of the Communist Party of Russia* (Ann Arbor: University of Michigan Press, 1967), 368.

12. F. Sh., *Obshchestvennyi stol. Kommunal'noe pitanie* [The public table: Communal dining] (Moscow: 1919).

13. F. Sh., *Obshchestvennyi stol*, 60–64.

14. Joyce Toomre has suggested that Soviet-era cookbooks can be read as utopian texts. A similar approach can be used for these cafeteria guidelines. See Joyce Toomre, "New Uses for Old Sources: Dusting Off Culinary Biographies," paper presented at the 1994 convention of the American Association for the Advancement of Slavic Studies (AAASS), Philadelphia, November 17–20. For cafeteria guidelines, see *Sbornik instruktsii i smet po oborudovaniiu i eksploatatsii obshchestvennykh pitatel'nykh punktov (stolovykh, chainykh, tsentral'nykh kukhon', razdatochnykh punktov i prochikh)* (Moscow: 1919), 2d ed.

15. As Daniel Brower has noted, long before 1921 "the stark contrast between utopian visions of the 'city of the future' and social reality" had refuted the Bolshevik government's "ability to impose a collectivist pattern of behavior on the urban population." Daniel Brower, "'The City in Danger': The civil war and the Russian Urban Population," in Diane P. Koenker, William G. Rosenberg, and Ronald Grigor Suny, eds., *Party, State, and Society in the Russian Civil War: Explorations in Social History* (Bloomington: Indiana University Press,1989), 75.

16. On women's responses to state dining, see Barbara Evans Clements, "The Effects of the Civil War on Women and Family Relations," in Koenker, Rosenberg, and Suny, eds., *Party, State, and Society in the Russian Civil War*, 112. Government statistical surveys showed that the majority of the population preferred to eat at home; see the surveys published by the Central Statistical Administration (Ts.S.U.) for March–April 1919, July 1919, December 1919, May 1920, and October–November 1920 in *Trudy Ts.S.U.*, vol. 8, pt. 2, 1–70.

17. For Petrograd, see P. P. Pakhnev, "Istoriia obshchestvennogo pitaniia v RSFSR" [A history of public dining in the R. S. F. S. R."], *Rabochii narodnogo pitaniia* [The popular dining worker], 1923, nos. 6–7, 19. For Moscow, see Pol'skii, *Leninskaia zabota*, 94–95.

18. Lynn Mally, *Culture of the Future: The Proletkult Movement in Revolutionary Russia* (Berkeley: University of California Press, 1990), 183–184; McAuley, *Bread and Justice*, 285.

19. Consumer or cooperative societies were autonomous voluntary associations of consumers which had grown dramatically since 1914. Financed by membership dues, consumer societies were able to purchase large quantities of food supplies and sell them to their members at reasonable prices. Consumer societies also ran their own independent network of cafeterias until March 1919, when the Bolshevik government nationalized them. See Catherine L. Salzman, "Consumer Societies and the Consumer Cooperative Movement in Russia, 1897–1917," Ph.D. dissertation, University of Michigan, 1977, and V. V. Kabanov, *Oktiabr'skaia revoliutsiia i kooperatsiia.* (1917 g. -marta 1919 g.) [The October revolution and cooperatives] (Moscow: 1973).

20. "Stolovye 'Kooperatsii' v 1918 godu" [Kooperatsiia's cafeterias in 1918], *Kooperatsiia* [Cooperation], no. 8 (September 1919), 23.

21. Lenin, *PSS,* vol. 39, 25.

22. F. Sh., *Obshchestvennyi stol,* 23–24.

23. "Kommunal'noe pitanie," *Izvestiia Narkomproda,* 8. In cities such as Moscow and Petrograd, there was a citywide soviet apparatus as well as one for each administrative district. As part of the overall process of centralization in the course of the civil war, the citywide soviets gained in importance at the expense of district soviets. For one example of this process, see Alexander Rabinowitch, "The Petrograd First City Soviet during the Civil War," in Koenker, Rosenberg, and Suny, eds., *Party, State, and Society in the Russian Civil War*, 133–157.

24. The Kremlin cafeteria served employees of the Council of People's Commissars (Sovnarkom) and the cafeteria of the Second Moscow House of Soviets served primarily employees of the All-Russian Central Executive Committee (VTsIK). See Gosudarstvennyi Arkhiv Rossiiskoi Federatsii [State Archive of the Russian Federation] (GARF), f. 1235, op. 96, d. 99, ll. 62–73ob. See also Pol'skii, *Leninskaia zabota*, 70.

25. "Stolovye 'Kooperatsii' v 1918 godu," *Kooperatsiia*, no. 8 (September 1919), 23.

26. Porter, *Alexandra Kollontai*, 324; Clements, *Bolshevik Feminist*, 154.

27. Mikhail Kotomkin, "Po ukazaniiu vozhdia," *Khleb i revoliutsiia. Prodovol'stvennaia politika Kommunisticheskoi Partii i sovetskogo pravitel'stva v 1917–1922 godu. Vospominaniia* (Moscow, 1972), 74. For other examples, see "Konferentsiia po voprosam pitaniia," *Izvestiia Narkomproda*, nos. 7–10 (April–May 1919), 21–25.

28. One example of this is the appearance of "war bread" (*golodnyi khleb*). For a brief discussion, see R. A. Omelianskii, *Khleb, ego prigotovlenie i svoistva. Popularnyi ocherk* (Moscow-Petrograd: "Priroda," 1918), 38–40. It is tempting to see the use of food surrogates and the presence of adulterated foods as examples of the extent of the civil war food crisis. However, analyses by food specialists at the time showed that adulteration of food sold in public places was a common practice even before the revolution. "Konferentsiia po voprosam pitaniia," *Izvestiia Narkomproda*, 22.

29. Residents of provincial towns received the beverage without the coffee or chicory. *Kooperatsiia,* July 27, 1919, 2–3.

30. *Kooperatsiia,* June 1, 1919, 3.

31. GARF, f. 4085, op. 9a, d. 306, l. 164; *Biulleten' Prodovol'stvennogo Otdela Moskovskogo Soveta*, August 2–3, 1919, 1, August 5–6, 1919, 1; *Kooperatsiia*, January 16, 1919, 5; *Vechernie izvestiia Moskvovskogo Soveta*, July 25, 1919, 3.

32. McAuley, *Bread and Justice*, 285.

33. F. Sh., *Obshchestvennyi stol*, 60–64.

34. Gr. G., "Kommunal'noe pitanie," *Izvestiia Narkomproda*, nos. 24–25 (December 1918), 9.

35. For more on these various survival strategies, see Borrero, "Hunger and Society in Civil War Moscow."

36. *Krasnaia Moskva* [Red Moscow] (Moscow: 1920), 302.

37. For Moscow, see *Biulleten' Prodovol'stvennogo Otdela*, June 21, 1919, 1; Pol'skii, *Leninskaia zabota*, 96. For Petrograd, see McAuley, *Bread and Justice*, 285.

38. For extensive firsthand descriptions of the Sukharevka at its peak, see Marguerite Harrison, *Marooned in Moscow: The Story of an American Woman Imprisoned in Russia* (New York, 1921), 150–157, and *Kooperatsiia*, June 14, 1919, 2.

39. Harrison, *Marooned in Moscow*, 157.

40. Pitirim Sorokin, *Leaves from a Russian Diary — and Thirty Years After* (Boston: Beacon Press, 1950), 210–211.

41. Harrison, *Marooned in Moscow*, 157–158.

42 "Iskusstvo ili spekuliatsiia?" *Biulleten' MPO*, November 16, 1919, 1. See also "Metsenatstvo," *Biulleten' MPO*, February 28, 1920, 1.

43. Harrison, *Marooned in Moscow*, 157.

44. The memory of communal state dining was kept alive among sectors such as the Food Workers' Union and in some cases briefly brought back to life in the late 1920s. See Pakhnev, "Istoriia obshchestvennogo pitaniia v RSFSR," 20; Goldman, *Women, the State, and Revolution*, 314–315.

ELEVEN

HALINA ROTHSTEIN AND ROBERT A. ROTHSTEIN

The Beginnings of Soviet Culinary Arts

The development of the culinary arts in the Soviet Union cannot be read simply as a history of cookbooks and cooking schools. In a society undergoing massive and wrenching change, a society struggling with hunger and deprivation, the effort to feed the population was affected by social and political issues and in turn had its effect on them. The great experiment of developing a large-scale system of public food service *(obshchestvennoe pitanie)* exerted the greatest long-term influence on culinary practice and popular consciousness about food and nutrition.[1]

The discussion that follows focuses on the 1920s, the decade that opened in the USSR under conditions of civil war and the rigors of "war communism" but soon saw the introduction of Lenin's New Economic Policy (NEP). Among other changes, the NEP period brought a loosening of restrictions on private production and trade, including publishing. By the end of the decade, NEP had been abandoned, Stalin was in charge (Lenin had died in 1924), and the country was embarking on a policy of forced industrialization and collectivization of agriculture. Although some of our sources are from the 1930s, we have based our comments largely on information about culinary publications of the 1920s and on examination of available publications from that decade.[2]

🌸 *The Women's Question*

It is impossible to discuss the development of the Soviet system of public food service and of culinary culture without touching upon the women's question. From the first postrevolutionary years one could observe two contradictory tendencies with respect to this issue. On one hand there was a continuation of revolutionary rhetoric about radicalizing the masses of women and about liberating women from domestic chores, while on the other hand there was pressure for women to be defined by their gender and to be tied even more closely to their traditional functions as mothers and wives, even when they were entering the work force. From the revolutionary perspective the kitchen and cooking *(striapnia)* were seen as a yoke holding back the moral, ethical, and political development of the female. In one of his 1923 articles Lev Trotsky astutely remarked that it is easy to achieve political equality between men and women, but real equality, equality in the family between husband and wife, is most difficult to achieve because that would require a total change in the conditions of everyday life *(byt)*. Without this kind of equality

> one cannot seriously speak of [women's] equality in society or in politics, for if a woman is tied to her family, to cooking, washing and sewing, then by that very fact her chances of influencing the life of society and the state are reduced to a bare minimum.[3]

The new family based on true equality between the partners was to be built on common interests, free from everything external, extraneous, incidental, while the state's function was to undertake collective care of children and to liberate the family from the kitchen and the laundry room.[4]

In the late 1920s, on the eve of the first Five-Year Plan, the emphasis shifted away from the ideology of equality of the sexes. Most authors, while paying lip service to the emancipation of women, were concerned primarily about bringing more women into the work force. The fight against the private kitchen, the development of communal kitchens and public food service enterprises, was a way to reach this goal while also solving the problem of food distribution and of feeding masses of people in the most economical and "scientific" way. N. A. Semashko, commissar of health, stressed that communal feeding contributes to the rise of worker productivity and accelerates the tempo of socialist construction, as well as helping to emancipate women from domestic drudgery.[5] Clearly ideologues who wanted public food service to supplant the private kitchen had a very negative view of women's labor at home. In 1923 P. Kozhanyi wrote in a popular brochure entitled *Down with the Private Kitchen!*: "The kitchen deforms a woman's body and soul. . . . In the interests of toiling women . . . the private kitchen should be buried as quickly as possible along with our entire dismal past."[6] And in 1931 kitchen chores are described by A. Khalatov as "a lot of fuss with pots and pans in a dark, stinking kitchen."[7]

At the same time, however, there were forces leading women back to the kitchen. The struggle against the individual kitchen presupposed the rapid development of public food service and its acceptance as a substitute for home cooking. The continued shortages and the failure of cooperatives to supply food, however, put more pressure on women to rely on traditional sources, the peasant market and the garden plot, which drew them even more into the sphere of domestic concerns. Other reasons, ironically, had to do not with the failures but with the successes of Soviet industry. As factories began to produce more inexpensive canning equipment, as sugar began to become more plentiful and cheaper, women were encouraged to do more canning and preserving. Furthermore, the educational activities of the various institutes, the teaching of hygiene, nutrition, etc., were beginning to pay off. A true revolution was taking place in the feeding of children, and mothers, not fathers, were encouraged to spend enormous energy and financial resources to feed the children properly.

Moreover, the greatest opposition to the proposed elimination of the individual kitchen came from women themselves. These attitudes were reflected in the pages of the popular magazine *Rabotnitsa* [The female worker], which was first published in Petrograd in 1914. The goal of the magazine was to raise women's revolutionary consciousness, to show that they shared the interests of the working class, and to bring working women into the proletarian movement. In the early 1920s there was a radical change in its orientation and this revolutionary political journal became a women's magazine. *Rabotnitsa* published articles by Trotsky and by the proponents of public food service, but also published the negative reactions of women workers who rejected the cafeterias not because they were expensive or bad but because they were a threat to the institution of marriage:

> We often hear from women workers . . . [that] if children are not going to be raised at home, if dinner is going to be prepared somewhere else, and laundry and mending as well . . . , then what sense will the family have. . . . No one will want to get married.[8]

The journal began to devote more and more space to advice on housekeeping and child care. In 1923 it introduced "The Housewife's Page," which included a column entitled "What and How to Cook." In 1926 the journal became a publication for women workers and housewives. A cooking column written by M. Zarina was introduced the same year. It is interesting to look at the recipes, to see how the working woman and housewife was supposed to feed her family. The children's diet included milk, eggs, vegetables, fruit, and cream, all things that were in short supply. Special preparation was required—pureeing, blanching, grating, frying. Adult recipes included homemade sausages, cold appetizers made from pumpkin, roast suckling pig with horseradish, apple cake, and cranberry-semolina pudding.[9] The journal's authors did not distinguish between working women and housewives, so all the recipes and advice on homemaking, i.e., everything that raised the family's living standard, would amount to an extra burden for the working woman.

Finally, those who called for the emancipation of women, for the expansion of communal services, frequently envisioned women in the very same roles from which they were supposed to be liberated. In the new utopian society envisioned by these (mostly male) authors, equality between the sexes was to be achieved not through a realignment of traditional roles within the family but by transforming the nuclear family into a communal unit and thereby shifting responsibility for cooking, cleaning, and child care to the newly created public service sector. The jobs in the new service industries were now filled by the very same women whom the revolution was supposed to emancipate from the three dreadful C's. So the woman continued to be a cook, only now instead of cooking for one family, she was cooking for "the masses." Instead of washing a few dishes in a dirty, unsanitary kitchen of her own, she was washing hundreds of them in dilapidated, unsanitary kitchens in communal cafeterias. Instead of doing laundry for one family, she was doing laundry for the entire neighborhood and being poorly paid for her labors. Since her family could not afford the communal services, she still had to come home and begin the infamous "second shift," to cook and wash and iron for her husband and children as before. The irony is that not only did the traditional sphere of women's activity not diminish, but—on the contrary—it became even more entrenched and expanded. The idea that women, thanks to their inherent traits, bring order, comfort, and cleanliness into family life and are most suited for child care became generalized into a notion of women's responsibilities in the country at large. Thus Semashko, appealing to workers, peasants, and soldiers to organize commissions to combat unsanitary conditions in public institutions, wrote:

> We know that Russia will continue to be dirty, that the Russian nation will not become free of lice and filth until the job is taken on by women—workers, peasants, homemakers. . . . [The Russian nation] will

have its lice washed off only when women keep a solicitous eye on cleanliness. . . . And what about the struggle for mothers' and children's health? Who can best lead that struggle? Mothers . . . , [who] will also pay heed to working conditions for women and children.[10]

🕎 *Public Food Service*

From the early days of the Soviet state and into the first half of the 1920s, the issue of public food service was framed by ideological issues—the transformation of the nuclear family into a communal unit, as already discussed, in the context of the ongoing search for a new Soviet culture. Moreover, the continuing and deepening food crisis gave a special urgency to the effort to introduce public food service. The opponents of individual kitchens often stressed the wastefulness and economic inefficiency of the individual household. It is cheaper, after all, for one kitchen to feed hundreds of people than for the same number of people to be fed in multiple kitchens: less food, fuel, and energy is used. (For a more detailed discussion of the antecedents and early days of the public food service, see chapter 10 in this volume.)

The decade of the 1920s was a heady period in Soviet history, when the young nation was trying to define itself, searching for new forms of art, a new Soviet way of life, and a new relationship between men and women and between the individual and the state. Likewise, the Soviet leadership from Lenin on was committed to developing a new Soviet science in all areas, including food, food delivery systems, and nutrition. This commitment can be seen in the establishment in 1920 of the Institute of the Physiology of Nutrition, which was part of the State Institute of Public Health. Public food service was deemed to be the most appropriate way to introduce scientific achievements to the population at large, to transmit the results from the laboratory to the table: "When each family eats by itself, scientifically sound nutrition is out of the question. What does the woman cooking for the family . . . know about such things when she learned to cook from a similar cook without any diploma?"[11]

The approach to establishing a new Soviet way of life changed dramatically with the inauguration of the first Five-Year Plan in 1928. The plan introduced an all-out effort to industrialize the nation, which was still nearly 85 percent rural. This entailed a wholesale restructuring of everyday life *(perestroika byta)* in which public food service was to play a crucial role. Here, just as in other areas targeted by the plan, the government moved from advocacy to enforcement. Millions of rubles were shifted from allocations for housing with private

HALINA ROTHSTEIN AND ROBERT A. ROTHSTEIN

Sketch by F. V. Antonov for a panel in a "factory-kitchen" in Fili. 1932.
State Russian Museum, St. Petersburg.

kitchens into public food service in a vast program that included not only new buildings, fixtures, and furnishings but also an array of educational courses for administrators, support personnel, and food preparers, and significant new investments in research. Between 1929 and 1932 seven new research institutes of nutrition were established, in Leningrad, Odessa, Khar'kov, Rostov, Novosibirsk, Voronezh, and Ivanovo. They conducted studies and experiments in synthetic food preparation (especially on finding ways to synthesize fat to alleviate fat shortages), nutrition, and developing new sources of protein and surrogates. They also developed diets for people of different sexes, ages, and professions and engaged in a vast educational campaign that changed the eating habits of the Soviet population.[12]

The prototypes of public food service existed abroad and in prerevolutionary Russia in the form of soup kitchens, restaurants, taverns *(traktiry)*, and especially tearooms *(chainye)*.[13] None of the prerevolutionary or foreign models, however, was viewed as adequate or particularly well-suited to Soviet conditions. Here public food service was intended to be a permanent feature of the everyday life of working people. The restructuring of the food system in the country, the elimination of individual kitchens, and the introduction of communal living were conceived on a colossal scale: by 1933, the end of the first Five-Year Plan, nearly 75 percent of the entire work force in critical industries was to be embraced by the new system. In this context the creation of gigantic food factories *(kukhni-fabriki,* or *tsekhi pitaniia)* and of automated cafeterias designed to serve thousands of customers a day was viewed as one of the important elements in the industrialization process. Between 1929 and 1933, the number of such factories increased from 15 to 105, and the network of cafeterias grew from 153 to 533.[14] The food factories and cafeterias boasted modern technology frequently borrowed from the West. The colossal cafeterias bore a striking resemblance to the large automated cafeterias in the United States such as New York's Automats, where the food was "untouched by human hands." The factories and cafeterias introduced crude dishwashers, which were described as an "American way for washing dishes."[15]

Efficiency and economy were not the only important features of the proposed system of public food service. The ideal system would provide an attractive and desirable alternative to the family kitchen. Specialists stressed that serving food with enough calories to be nourishing is not sufficient; the food should taste good and be served in a sanitary and appealing atmosphere. Here is a description of a model dietetic cafeteria that served twenty factories in the Moscow district, a cafeteria that had fresh flowers on every table and trees growing in planters:

> Alongside of the cafeteria there is a lounge where one can sleep or read. There are wide, comfortable couches along the walls, and in the center of the room there is a huge round table with newspapers and magazines. In this same room a doctor leads discussions on the principles of scientific nutrition, gets better acquainted with the patients, and gives advice.[16]

Just as in other Soviet endeavors, a deep chasm separated theory from practice. The overwhelming majority of cafeterias were places where food supplies were limited and the food was of low quality and inexpertly prepared, where chaos, flies, dirt, and terrible service reigned.[17] The customers' attitude was negative and often openly hostile. The workers refused to eat the food and often derisively called the cafeterias "grub-halls" *(obzhorki)*.[18] One specific problem was that the food factories were designed to use "thermoses" — insulated containers that were to serve both for delivery of food to distant eating halls and as a kind of slow cooker. Enthusiasts called the thermos *povar bednoty* (the poor man's chef) and *pishchevoi samovar* (the food samovar), since under ideal conditions, with zero heat loss, hot food would continue to cook with no additional input of energy. The results were less than ideal, however. In the crudely constructed containers the food from different compartments tended to get mixed together. The result was an unappetizing mess. By 1933 the government abandoned "thermos-based food delivery" in favor of an expanding network of cafeterias serving individual factories.[19] While such problems as unsanitary conditions, the severe lack of dishes and cutlery, and widespread pilfering could be (and were) dealt with by direct government intervention,[20] making food acceptable to the masses was a different matter. That required producing tasty food, something that neither the laboratories nor government directives alone were able to achieve.

🌣 *Cooking and Cookbooks*

We now turn our attention to cooking and cookbooks, tracing the development of Soviet culinary standards and ideals. We will examine the early trends that led ultimately to the publication of that exemplar of Soviet culinary culture, *Kniga o zdorovoi i vkusnoi pishche* [The book on healthful and tasty food], which first appeared in 1950. In examining these trends we are less concerned with a political or social message than with the standards of taste and culinary traditions that the various authors seemed to promote. During the turbulent 1920s and early 1930s, when the entire country was in the throes of the *Kulturkampf,* cookery too became the object of competing approaches. In one camp were the experts who wanted to make a clean break with the past. This radical group included those whom we shall here call "culinary ascetics" and "food futurists." Opposed to them were those whom we shall refer to as "traditionalists," who wanted to build on the experience of prerevolutionary Russian and classical Western cuisine.

Although published in the late 1930s, the following passage from the first Soviet encyclopedia reflects the views of the earlier radicals:

> Soviet culinary science is based on the application of the latest results from the study of food components as well as the data of chemistry, physics, and alimentary physiology. . . . Soviet culinary science encourages [the use of] high-quality foodstuffs, the stimulation of normal appetite through the appearance of food . . . and the full nutritional use of all valuable parts of foodstuffs. . . . In the preparation of food, foodstuffs must not be soaked in water . . . ; the water in which they have been cooked must not be poured out . . . ; foodstuffs must not be subjected to an excessively long action of high temperatures.[21]

Culinary ascetics were extremely hostile to culinary art, the goal of which was to transform commonplace products into refined, esthetically pleasing food. Their hostility extended to anything that aroused "excessive" appetite, which could lead to overeating and gluttony, then to moral dissolution. (See chapter 6 in this volume, on Tolstoy's view of vegetarianism.) They were opposed to the "misuse" of spices and condiments, to fancy sauces, and of course they were against alcohol. They viewed all of these as relics of the former capitalist society. Although they were sensitive to the importance of esthetically pleasing surroundings for the consumption of food—they recommended placing fresh flowers on cafeteria tables, decorating the walls with paintings and murals, etc.—they nevertheless looked askance at common ingredients like mustard, vinegar, and pepper used to make food more palatable.

These sentiments are echoed in M. P. Dubianskaia's 1929 cookbook, *Healthful Food and How to Prepare It.* Dubianskaia viewed taste enhancers and stimulating drinks like coffee and tea as something akin to poison: "An excessive amount of salt, pepper, mustard, vinegar, and other flavorings and spices harms not only the alimentary organs but the whole organism."[22] Dubianskaia's book was intended for a general audience. It was a product of an educational campaign undertaken by the publishers of the journal *Hygiene and Health,* which published Dubianskaia's work as a free supplement to the journal. The goal of such publications was to reeducate an entire generation of Soviet citizens, to wean them from poor eating habits, since inappropriate food was not only of no value to the human organism but also, like a narcotic, drew people into pernicious pursuits and aroused "unhealthy" instincts. As Professor Sulima-Samoilo wrote in her introduction to Dubianskaia's cookbook,

> In our country, especially in the cities, the state of nutrition is very bad. The monotonous and inadequate selection of foodstuffs [and] the incorrect preparation of food . . . undermine the health of the population, change the chemical composition of the body, lead to degeneration and to the perversion of healthy instincts, push people toward various stimulants and intoxicants—tobacco, alcoholic beverages—and toward unhealthily stimulating shows and amusements.[23]

Dubianskaia went even further: all refined food leads to overeating; overeating leads to excessive drinking of tea, coffee, and eventually alcohol; and all these things, separately or especially taken together, "ruin one's health and lead to degeneration and extinction."[24] Not all of Dubianskaia's ideas were so extreme. In fact, much of what she had to say has a very contemporary ring to it and would be familiar to today's reader. She was a natural-food advocate who deplored the use of refined, processed foods and foods "mutilated by the art of the cook." She favored a richly varied diet based on foods that were changed as little as possible during the cooking process. She advocated the principles of *syroedenie* (the use of uncooked food) and borrowed from the experience of vegetarian cooking. (See chapter 7 in this volume, on vegetarianism in Russia.)

HALINA ROTHSTEIN AND ROBERT A. ROTHSTEIN

More radical in their departure from the established culinary norms were the "food futurists," the food-surrogate enthusiasts and proponents of experimental and synthetic foods. For them the nutritional and caloric value and chemical composition of foodstuffs was the decisive factor in choosing foods and setting menus. One extreme example is provided by a brochure published in the Siberian city of Tiumen' in 1922, *How to Eat More Beneficially and Appropriately*.[25] The author, S. A. Ezerskii, advocated developing synthetic nutritional substitutes such as amino acids, which could be introduced intravenously. Ezerskii and other Soviet food technologists based their suggestions on the work and experience of German and Russian scientists who had studied the effects of starvation on the human organism. The conditions in post-revolutionary Russia—famine and economic ruin—provided the motivation for eager scientists to search for foods of the future. There were many obstacles on the path to developing synthetic food. The idea was to synthesize the components into which food was broken down in the process of digestion, but not all of them could be replicated in the laboratories of the time. The scientists found ways to synthesize amino acids and glucose but could not synthesize fats. Moreover, the synthetic nutrients were very expensive and turned out to be useful only as nutritional supplements in the clinical treatment of severely malnourished patients; they could not be used as a substitute for eating.

A less drastic and cheaper approach to widespread malnutrition was to seek out ways to increase the caloric value of common foods. One proposal involved the creation of food concentrates, such as concentrated milk. Another was to find naturally occurring food concentrates, and in the 1920s brewer's yeast seemed to fit the bill. The enthusiasm for food concentrates, however, was not shared by such culinary experts as Zarina, who suggested that the daily ration of bread and fats simply be increased to reach the desired level of caloric intake. The compilers of the *Culinary Handbook* devoted nearly two pages of detailed description and instruction on how to add yeast to sauces only to conclude that since only very small amounts of liquid yeast can be added without distorting the taste of food, the caloric and nutritional value of yeast as a nutritional additive is very small.[26]

Most of the attempts to find new solutions involved substitutes for the staples that were in short supply rather than supplements. The earliest work in this area, rushed into print in 1921, was Ia. Ia. Nikitinskii's *Surrogates and Food Sources . . . That Are Unusual in Russia*.[27] It is a straightforward compendium of food substitutes with brief explanatory notes and histories of their use. Nikitinskii based his work on the experience of earlier famines in Russia and on German observations of severe malnutrition during World War I, but he also drew on the habits of the Russian settlers and indigenous peoples of the Far East and northern regions. These populations used the flesh and oils of sea mammals in their regular diet. In 1923 Drs. L. A. and L. M. Vasilevskie published *Dietary Surrogates,* an expanded version of Nikitinskii's work.[28] Both books contained instructions for preparing such things as surrogate bread using mashed potatoes, apples, beets, etc. In addition to compendia like these, there were dozens of brochures aimed at the general public on how to produce surrogate coffee, sugar, etc. at home.

Recipes from nontraditional food sources were tried out at culinary workshops organized by the Scientific and Technological Department of the Supreme Economic Council and at a laboratory of the Moscow Institute of the Physiology of Nutrition. The government also promoted the raising of fast-growing and reproducing animals such as rabbits and the introduction of less common crops such as soybeans as a source of protein.[29]

Among the vegetable surrogates the soybean received the most attention. It was the subject of a large number of publications, including cookbooks with titles like *130 Soybean Dishes* and *The Mass Preparation of Vegetable and Soybean Dishes.*[30] The soybean, however, did not enter the culinary mainstream, even though it had been known and cultivated in the Russian Empire and modest quantities of soybean, soycake, and soy oil had been imported into Russia before the revolution. Moreover, most soya from northern Manchuria had reached Europe through Vladivostok in the Russian Far East. By the eve of the revolution soybean-growing regions had been established in Podolia in Ukraine and in the Samara region of Russia proper, which gave its name to one soybean variety. By that time soybean coffee was being sold in southern Russia.[31]

The introduction of soybean products into Soviet cafeterias was greeted with no great enthusiasm. Workers refused to accept strange-looking and strange-tasting food. More work had to be done before nontraditional foods like soya could be accepted by the general public. Some of this work was delegated to newly created research laboratories attached to public food service institutes. The task of these laboratories was to increase the variety of dishes, to find new food substitutes, and to develop new combinations of foodstuffs and efficient methods for preparing food for cafeterias.[32] They studied possible new surrogates (e.g., meat substitutes such as shark and seal meat), which were first tested on animals and medical students. In an effort to overcome consumer resistance to new dishes, the laboratories often established culinary courses and printed menus and recipes for general use (e.g., *The Mass Preparation of Soybean Dishes*).

Soybean cake was one of the most popular subjects of research, since it could easily be combined with other components. Recipes were developed in which it was mixed with ground meat and baked as a familiar meatloaf.[33] The use of soymilk in baking was less problematic, since it had little effect on taste and had the advantage of longer shelf life at room temperature. Despite the best efforts of soybean enthusiasts and the continuing commitment of resources by the government, the campaign to introduce soybean products on a large scale failed in the face of consumer resistance. Soybean recipes, so painstakingly developed in the laboratories, do not appear in the two compendia of food surrogates; nor is one likely to find recipes using soybean products in general cookbooks of the period.

The countervailing force to the radical trends that we have been discussing was represented by the efforts of "traditionalists" to adapt prerevolutionary Russian and sophisticated Western cuisine to the new conditions of Soviet society. There were various reasons for the persistence of this approach. Despite the drastic changes that had taken place and the difficult conditions that prevailed, the demand for refined cooking and for cookbooks did not disappear. During the NEP period cookbook authors could once again publish their works privately; here we will briefly consider two examples of such privately published cookbooks. *Bliny, Blintzes, Fritters, and Pancakes* was published privately in Moscow in 1925 by A. V. Markov, a self-described "food technologist" *(tekhnolog pishchevykh veshchestv)*. More than half of its forty-five pages is devoted to bibliography and an introduction to the recipes (historical background and information on how to judge the quality of foodstuffs and how to store them). Except for the insistence on the use of expensive, high-grade ingredients (the best flour, fresh eggs, whole milk, and cream) the eighty or so recipes for pancakes, etc., are rather unremarkable in contrast to the rest of the book. In the introduction the author declared his goal to be "to encourage the broad masses to study the details of everyday life carefully and to have an intelligent attitude towards them . . . , to bring science and life closer."[34] For Markov the recipes represented an opportunity to expound before a wide audience (the brochure was issued in two thousand copies) on a variety of topics, including Russian rituals and culinary traditions, and to make veiled comments about socioeconomic conditions in the country:

> Thus the simple question of *bliny* can provide a great variety of topics for elaboration: culinary questions, physiological ones, . . . questions dealing with living conditions; religious, economic, social questions, etc., and even philological or linguistic questions—should one write *maslianitsa* [Shrovetide] or *maslenitsa* . . .[35]

Very different, both in size and content, is Nikishova's, *Cookbook: A Handbook for the Domestic Table,* first published in the provincial capital of Tver' in

1928, with a second edition in 1929.[36] Like Markov's, this book was published privately by its author and was intended for home use. Nikishova's work, a direct descendent of prerevolutionary cookbooks, is an impressive collection of recipes with a brief introduction on how to organize a kitchen, given primitive Soviet living conditions. Her book, to be sure, does not call for truffles or for sides of beef or dozens of geese, but her recipes are quite extravagant. Some of the baba recipes require thirty to fifty eggs. To clarify fish stock she recommended the use of pressed caviar. Her recipes represent a gamut of traditional Russian dishes, but also Caucasian and Western specialties: from Russian *kulebiaka* (hot fish pie) to Georgian *chakhokhbili* (meat or vegetable stew) and Armenian *tolma* (stuffed vegetables or grape leaves) to a whole range of dishes, including desserts, characterized as being in American, French, Portuguese, or Polish style. She uses a wide array of condiments and spices and devotes a whole chapter to alcoholic beverages, including instructions on how to make them at home. Unlike Dubianskaia, Nikishova gives prominent place to sauces and dressings. She lists forty of them in her book, and there is hardly a recipe for meat, fish, or vegetables that does not call for some kind of a sauce or dressing. "Some lovers of sauces and gravies," Nikishova wrote, "even claim that the basic foods have no taste in and of themselves and that only the seasonings give them taste."[37]

Given Markov's veiled comments about the socioeconomic conditions and his emphasis on Russian traditions and Nikishova's unabashedly opulent menus that were a throwback to the "good old days," both books can be read not only as being in opposition to certain culinary trends but perhaps as a repudiation of the Soviet system itself. But the resistance to radical changes in diet and cooking extended to authors who were dedicated to the system; it can also be seen in books meant for public food service workers. M. Zarina was an influential and prolific author, whose prerevolutionary *Culinary Textbook* was reprinted after the revolution.[38] In the Soviet period she worked in the field of public food service. She headed culinary workshops, in which she directed efforts to improve the palatability of surrogates. She was the author of a brochure entitled *The Soybean in Mass Food Service* and many other works, among them *At the Common Table: How to Organize Public Food Service on the Collective Farm.*[39]

Zarina was the editor and chief contributor to the cooking column in *Rabotnitsa*. Despite her work with surrogates, she was a very practical and rather conservative author, as we can see from the columns and from her book *At the Common Table*. Both in recipes designed for home cooking and in those meant for the collective-farm kitchen, Zarina's main concerns were clear: economy, hygiene, nutritional value, and taste. Taste for her was the key to good nutrition, since bland, unpalatable food, even if made of the best ingredients, does not provide the maximal nutritional value: "A properly organized food service definitely requires the tasty preparation of food."[40] Variety and spices are necessary to arouse the appetite. One advantage of cooking in the *kolkhoz* (collective farm), she pointed out, was the easy availability of cheaper and nutritionally more important substitutes for spices, such as dill, garlic, onion, and horseradish. Zarina's sample weekly menus for the *kolkhoz* offer simple meals, high in caloric content but without sauces or fancy cakes. Each day's menu, however, includes at least one dish flavored with spices—bay leaf, pepper, mustard—and seasoned with vinegar or some other sour ingredient. (Sours were considered to be an important ingredient in the daily diet of Russian peasants.)[41]

Zarina's recipes are simple and look deceptively like traditional peasant fare based largely on one-pot meals with a few urban borrowings, such as vinaigrette salad. Here is a sample daily menu. For breakfast: a choice of buckwheat groats or potatoes with butter or cheese croquettes *(tvorozhnye lepeshki)*. For dinner: a choice of soup or *borshch*, and for the main course a choice of groats or noodles with butter. For supper: a choice of noodles with meat or braised goose with potatoes, and *kisel'* (a dessert pudding). The daily ration also included 800 grams of bread and 35 grams of sugar. If we compare this menu with the traditional peasant diet, we see that they share a high carbohydrate content and simplicity of preparation; neither includes baked desserts. Differences, however, are equally striking. Zarina's diet contains a much higher intake of animal fats; it offers more varied sources of protein— meat, fish, but also dairy products and lentils. (The introduction of dairy products is especially important, since fresh milk products were considered a luxury in many regions.) It has a high vegetable content and almost doubles the average daily sugar ration.[42] Also noteworthy is the fact that some of her menus omit potatoes, the staple of the Russian peasant diet.

In *At the Common Table,* as in her other popular writings, Zarina's commonsense approach to teaching basic principles of good nutrition comes through. Instead of grouping recipes in the traditional way, according to food categories or courses, she arranged them according to the method of preparation—in a cauldron, in the oven, on the stove—as a way of helping the cook whose choice of dishes is limited by the available equipment. She was frugal without being excessively so. Unlike the "radicals," she does not insist that water in which dried legumes were soaked overnight be reused in cooking. Taste consideration remained one of her primary concerns.

The lack of tasty food and poor food preparation more generally were responsible, as we pointed out earlier, for the difficulties that public food service institutions encountered from their very inception. Since the government was committed to the expansion of the food service network, steps were taken at the very highest levels to make food service offerings more acceptable to the general public. These steps included the introduction of quality control and the organization of culinary courses to train a new generation of chefs for food service establishments. There was also a need for new culinary textbooks. In the early 1930s Anastas Mikoyan, the commissar for food supplies, asked: "Do we have a book [called] a gift for the young chef? We don't have anything of the sort."[43] *A Culinary Handbook* was published in 1934 in response to Mikoyan's challenge. In general its menus, recipes, and instructions on food preparation differ little from those of such prerevolutionary professional cookbooks as P. A. Aleksandrova-Ignat'eva's *Handbook for Studying the Fundamentals of the Culinary Art*.[44] What differences there are involve the variety of dishes and the size of portions of meat and fish (sometimes only half as much as in the older books). The approach and the organization of the menu, however, are the same. *A Culinary Handbook* offers the following sample menu for a five-course meal, which consists of the classic procession of courses: consommé with meat patties, sturgeon in tomato sauce, veal with salad, cauliflower, coffee-flavored crème.[45] The handbook is a far cry from cookbooks like Dubianskaia's *Healthful Food*. The food here is refined, urban, and frankly Western. There are nearly fifty sauces, all classics like béarnaise, hollandaise, piquante, tatare, etc.. While there are no excesses such as fifty-egg babas or luxuries such as caviar, recipes are rich in eggs, butter, cream and spices. There are standard recipes for roast beef, steak, pheasant, and sturgeon but none for soybean products or seal meat. (Incidentally, unlike Nikishova's privately published book for homemakers [1929], *A Culinary Handbook* contains almost no "ethnic" recipes.) The only mention of food supplements is a brief discussion in an appendix on the use of yeast as an additive to sauces and soups.[46]

In its instructions for food preparation *A Culinary Handbook,* like Zarina's *Common Table,* departed from the doctrines of the culinary radicals.[47] The handbook advised cafeterias to attract and keep customers not only by creating tasty dishes but also by offering a choice in their menus in order to appeal to individual preferences. The book contains hardly any simple recipes that could be quickly prepared in a large kitchen; all recipes are complex and require special skills and equipment; they have to be individually cooked and garnished. Thus the ideal of public food service had changed. The communal table was now more like a bourgeois restaurant than a public cafeteria.

The primary driving force behind the tremendous changes in the eating habits of the Soviet population was the system of public food service. Despite its many defects and false starts, its public cafeterias and field kitchens were the places where the average worker became acquainted with new concepts and norms of eating. Recipes often traveled from public to private kitchens as cooks copied and disseminated favorite recipes learned on the job.[48]

An important role was also played by popular educational literature and by cookbooks, both those written for professionals and those for home use, which sold out as quickly as they were published. The influence of the important Soviet work on improving children's nutrition and on the public health aspects of nutrition cannot be addressed here because of limitations of space.

The process of eliminating the economic and cultural differences between the city and the country began in earnest in the 1920s. The effect on eating habits was gradual; old habits died hard. Although we earlier contrasted culinary radicals and traditionalists, it turns out that the traditionalists were the true revolutionaries in that their efforts to make traditional urban culinary and nutritional norms accessible to the population at large were in large measure responsible for the revolution in culinary consciousness and practice that culminated in the 1950s.

NOTES

1. We use the term "(system of) public food service" to translate the Russian expression *obshchestvennoe pitanie,* which literally means "societal feeding/nourishment."

2. The authors are grateful to Laszlo Dienes of the University of Massachusetts at Amherst and Stanley Rabinowitz of Amherst College for bringing from Russia materials without which this chapter could not have been written. Special thanks are due to Joyce Toomre for her valuable comments and for her exquisite patience.

3. L. Trotsky, *Voprosy byta: epokha "kul'turnichestva" i ee zadachi* [Challenges of everyday life . . .] (Moscow: Krasnaia Nov', 1923), 49.

4. Ibid., 53.

5. N. A. Semashko, *Health Protection in the USSR* (London: V. Gollancz, 1934), 57.

6. P. Kozhanyi, *Doloi chastnuiu kukhniu!* [Down with the private kitchen!] (Moscow, 1923), 7, 12.

7. A. Khalatov, *Rabotnitsa i obshchestvennoe pitanie* [The female worker and the question of public food service] (Moscow: Narpit, 1924), 5.

8. F. N-a, "Nuzhna li rabotnitse organizatsiia byta na obshchestvennykh nachalakh?" [Does the female worker need community organization of everyday life?], *Rabotnitsa,* 1923, no. 2, 17–18.

9. M. Zarina, "Kak i chto gotovit'" [How and what to cook], *Rabotnitsa* 1924, no. 23, 22; "Kulinariia" [Cooking], *Rabotnitsa* 1926, no. 24, 21–22.

10. N. A. Semashko, *Sovetskaia vlast' i narodnoe zdorov'e* [Soviet rule and the health of the people] (Moscow: Gosudarstvennoe Izdatel'stvo, 1920), 13.

11. Kozhanyi, 6.

12. W. H. Fitzpatrick, *Soviet Research in Nutrition,* I.C.R.S. Medical Reports, no. 4 (1963), 4; V. Val'ter, "Obshchestvennoe pitanie—vazhneishee zveno v bor'be za prom-finplan" [Public food service—the most important link in the struggle for the industrial and financial plan], *Voprosy truda* 1931, no. 11-12, 85–90; E. Zagorskaia, "Ratsional'noe pitanie" [Rational nutrition], *Nashi dostizheniia* 1931, no. 1, 93–95.

13. M. G. Rabinovich, *Ocherki material'noi kul'tury russkogo feodal'nogo goroda* [Studies on the material culture of the Russian feudal city] (Moscow: Institut Miklukhi-Maklaia, 1988), 243 ff.

14. *Bol'shaia sovetskaia entsiklopediia* (Moscow: OGIZ, 1940), vol. 45, 443–463; see also A. Khalatov, *Za pereustroistvo byta (Sbornik statei po voprosu obshchestvennogo pitania)* [For the restructuring of everyday life: A collection of articles on the question of public food service] (Moscow: Vsenarpit, 1930); Val'ter, 85–90.

15. A. Prints, "Industrializatsiia kukhni" [Industrialization of the kitchen], *Nashi dostizheniia* 1931, no. 10-11, 41–43.

16. E. Rikhter, "Fabrika-kukhnia" [The food factory], *Nashi dostizheniia* 1931, no. 1, 95–96.

17. Val'ter, 85–87.

18. Kozhanyi, 8.

19. *Bol'shaia sovetskaia entsiklopediia* vol. 45 (Moscow: OGIZ, 1940), 443 ff.; Val'ter, 88.

20. Val'ter, 86.

21. *Bol'shaia sovetskaia entsiklopedia* vol. 35 (Moscow: OGIZ, 1937), 454–455.

22. M. P. Dubianskaia, *Zdorovaia pishcha i kak ee gotovit'* [Healthful food and how to prepare it] (Leningrad: Leningradskaia Pravda, 1929), 11.

23. Ibid., 3.

24. Ibid., 5.

25. S. A. Ezerskii, *Kak pitat'sia vygodnei i tselesoobraznei: obshchedostupnoe izlozhenie osnov ratsional'nogo pitaniia i problemy iskusstvennogo pitaniia* [How to eat more beneficially and appropriately: An accessible presentation of the fundamentals of rational nutrition and of the problem of artificial food] (Tiumen': Tiumenskii Tekhnikum, 1922).

26. B. V. Vilenkin and G. A. Levin, eds., *Spravochnik po kulinarii* [A culinary handbook] (Moscow-Leningrad, 1934).

27. Ia. Ia. Nikitinskii, *Surrogaty i neobychainye v Rossii istochniki pishchevykh sredstv rastitel'nogo i zhivotnogo proiskhozhdeniia* [Surrogates and food sources of vegetable and animal origin that are unusual in Russia] (Moscow, 1924).

28. L. A. and L. M. Vasilevskie, *Pishchevye surrogaty* [Dietary surrogates] (Petrograd: Nauchno-Khimiko-tekhnicheskoe Izdatel'stvo, 1923).

29. Soviet efforts to raise rabbits as a meat substitute and similar harebrained ideas were satirized in R. O. G. Urch, *The Rabbit King of Russia* (London: Eyre & Spottiswoode, 1939).

30. E. M. Tsvetaeva, *130 bliud iz soevykh* [130 soybean dishes] (Moscow, 1930); P. I. Samokish and F. F. Tarasenko, *Izgotovlenie massovykh bliud ovoshchnykh i soevykh* [The mass preparation of vegetable and soybean dishes] (Voronezh, 1934).

31. C. V. Piper and W. J. Morse, *The Soybean* (New York: Peter Smith, 1943), 22–54, 227. An earlier version appeared in Russian as Ch. Piper, *Chto mozhno prigotovit' iz bobov* [What can be made from beans] (Khabarovsk, 1931).

32. Samokish, 4; Zagorskaia, 95; Fitzpatrick, 5.

33. Samokish, 24.

34. A.V. Markov, *Bliny, blinchiki, blintsy i olad'i* [Bliny, blintzes, fritters, and pancakes] (Moscow: Izdanie Avtora, 1925), 4.

35. Ibid., 4-5.

36. A. I. Nikishova, *Povarennaia kniga—rukovodstvo domashnego stola, zapasov i zagotovok* [Cookbook: A handbook for the domestic table . . .], 2d ed. (Moscow: Izdanie Avtora, 1929).

37. Ibid., 136.

38. M. Zarina, *Uchebnik kulinarii byvshei prepodavatel'nitsy i zaveduiushchei prakticheskimi znaniiami* [A culinary textbook . . .], 4th ed. (Moscow, 1918).

39. M. Zarina, *Za obshchim stolom: kak organizovat' obshchestvennoe pitanie v kolkhoze* [At the common table: How to organize public food service on the collective farm], 4th ed. (Moscow-Leningrad: Krest'ianskaia Gazeta, 1932), and *Soia v massovom pitanii* [The soybean in mass food service] (Moscow-Leningrad, 1931).

40. Zarina, *At the Common Table*, 10.

41. R. E. F. Smith and David Christian, *Bread and Salt: A Social and Economic History of Food and Drink in Russia* (Cambridge: Cambridge University Press, 1984), 286.

42. Ibid., 267-268, 286; Zarina, *At the Common Table*, 27-31.

43. B. V. Vilenkin and G. A. Levin, eds., *Spravochnik po kulinarii* [A culinary handbook] (Moscow-Leningrad: Snabtekhizdat, 1934), 3. Mikoyan was alluding to the classic pre-revolutionary Russian cookbook, Elena Molokhovets' *Podarok molodym khoziaikam,* published in 1992 in a translated and edited version by Joyce Toomre as *Classic Russian Cooking: Elena Molokhovets' A Gift to Young Housewives* (Bloomington: Indiana University Press, 1992).

44. P. A. Aleksandrova-Ignat'eva, *Rukovodstvo k izucheniiu osnov kulinarnogo iskusstva* [Handbook for studying the fundamentals of the culinary art] (Odessa, 1897).

45. Vilenkin, 234.

46. Ibid., 230.

47. Ibid., 79.

48. L. M. Saburova, *Kul'tura i byt russkogo naselen'ia Priangar'ia* [The culture and everyday life of the Russian population in the Angara Region] (Leningrad: Nauka, 1967), 161.

TWELVE

JOYCE TOOMRE

Food and National Identity in Soviet Armenia

You know what a *tonir* is? It's a place where you prepare the fire until it is hot and, then in a container, put it in a spot underneath, with ashes on top of it. Then you spread a large comforterlike blanket on top of it so that whoever wanted to would go and place his or her feet under the blanket and get warm. I remember, I'd place my feet under and lie down and sleep in the winter. Also, when guests would come, they'd each go around and find a spot to put their feet under, with the comforter pulled over them, sometimes all the way up to their waist. Then my mother would place all the winter goodies, like the raisins and dried food, on top of the blanket, and we would eat. In the winter, we then slept in the same room.[1]

In this passage an elderly Armenian evokes childhood memories of winter evenings when family and friends gathered around the *tonir* for warmth and companionship. The description suggests the emotional power of everyday rituals, a power that imbued the *tonir* with a significance far beyond its functionality. The *tonir* is merely a pit dug into the ground that was widely used for heating and cooking by Armenian families in rural Turkey at the beginning of this century. Although used less frequently in modern Armenia, it is still a central part of Armenian life and cooking. Now contrast the emotional power of the above passage with the laconic directions from a late Soviet cookbook for baking *lavash*, the traditional Armenian bread, in the *tonir*.

Women prepare lavash *for baking in a* tonir, *village of Gndevaz, Vayots Dzor province, Armenia, 1995. Photo by Sam Sweezy.*

Lavash *baked in a* tonir. . . . Form the prepared dough into small cakes, roll out and prick with a fork. Throw the rolled-out dough onto the hot inner wall of the *tonir* in a single easy gesture. Cover with a lid and bake for 3 to 5 minutes. Remove the baked *lavash* from the *tonir* walls and serve with either the first or second course.[2]

Passages like these are more than nostalgia or simple instructions for baking bread. Although sharply differentiated, each provides valuable clues about the society from which it emanates. The difference in genre and time period surely accounts for most of the contrast in the two passages—they refer to events nearly a century apart. Left over, however, is the question of cultural identity, which still peeps out from the interstices. Is the contrast a function of perspective dependent upon whether one is inside the culture looking out or outside looking in? In Soviet circumstances, this inside/outside perspective probably has a political coloration, in which case, does the flat prose of the cookbook suggest, however obliquely, an undue dominance of the republic by the Soviet central powers? Or perhaps the two passages reflect a growth in urbanization and the resultant opposition between private and public dining, between the fundamental warmth of one and anonymity of the other. This chapter explores some of these underlying issues in an effort to understand whether changes in Armenian foodways[3] over the past century can be traced to Soviet interference and whether these changes have affected the Armenian sense of national identity.

✦ *Methodology and Sources*

Modern Soviet Armenian cuisine is a hybrid based upon traditional foodways transformed by urbanization and industrialization and influenced by political decisions. Since materials for documenting culinary history are scarce, I have constructed this history using three disparate sources: memoirs, cookbooks, and oral histories. Each has its own strengths and limitations, which are reflected in the pages that follow.

My story begins in eastern Anatolia prior to the 1915 genocide of the Armenians by the Turks. Its inhabitants were known as Western Armenians, but few remain in Turkey today. Most of those who escaped the genocide fled westward; some, however, headed eastward, into territory then known as Eastern Armenia but which soon became Soviet Armenia. At first the living conditions there were nearly catastrophic; although economic conditions gradually improved over the next two decades, the quality of life deteriorated rapidly under the repression of the Stalinist years and the hardships of the Second World War. None of this was conducive for reflections on the quiet joys of home cooking and domestic celebrations. So, due to lack of materials, my narrative breaks for thirty years. The story resumes only in the late 1940s, not through memoirs but by looking at Armenian cuisine as mirrored through Soviet cookbooks. This method shows those aspects of Armenian cooking that migrated beyond the borders of the Armenian republic into a greater pan-Soviet cuisine. Cookbooks are an underutilized resource and can tell us much about the society, but they have their limitations—notably that as a genre they are unreliable witnesses for showing what actually happens within the home. For this information, I have turned to oral histories. My informants are few, but their accounts are vital, since they provide a continuum with the memoir literature while supplementing the limited information found in the cookbooks.

This chapter examines Armenian cuisine from two perspectives. The first views Armenian cuisine from within and focuses on its internal development, asking what changes occurred and why. Can any political influences be discerned and can they be separated from the forces of urbanization? The other, by questioning the role of Armenian cuisine as one element among many within Soviet cuisine, requires a shift in focus from an Armenian to a Soviet point of view. Although I offer no definitive answers, the very process of looking at these questions is informative. The evidence suggests that foodways are an exceptionally conservative arena of life, with changes so gradual, almost imperceptible, that they become apparent only in retrospect.

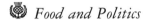 *Food and Politics*

I am looking at Armenian cuisine in the Soviet period in an effort to understand the role of nationalism in the lives of ethnic minorities in the former Soviet Union. I contend that people express their national identity through their manner of eating and drinking, that foodways define a people as much as their language, dress, or architecture. Armenian cuisine, as it has developed in Armenia SSR over the last seventy years, has changed dramatically from the cuisine practiced by Turkish Armenians in pre-1915 eastern Anatolia. Memories of that Western Armenian cuisine are tinged with nostalgia for a way of life that has disappeared forever. Armenians have suffered more than their share of tragedies and hardships, both natural and political, but the loss of their distinctive foodways has as much to do with modernization as with political machinations. Armenians, like people everywhere, have participated in a worldwide technological and industrial revolution that has affected daily life from Chile to China, from Austria to Australia. This process of change, however, was aggravated for people in the former Soviet Union by the meddling of the central political powers in the daily lives of the people in the constituent republics. These two strands of modernization and politicization are tightly interwoven; this chapter will highlight but not try to untangle some of the issues.

The primary question is whether any "Sovietization" of Armenian cuisine is discernible. By "Sovietization" I mean intent or coercion beyond mere influence. In Armenian terms, that means that what people ate and the circumstances in which food was consumed were affected by Armenia's position as a small constituent republic in a larger political entity. The macro issues which resulted from this political, economic, and social dependency have been studied in considerable detail. What has not been studied is the effect on traditional eating patterns in Armenian families of the enforced secularization and modernization of the society. Throughout the USSR, the Bolsheviks were intent on destroying bourgeois comforts and creating new Soviet citizens. Not only was the Orthodox Church deprived of its former authority, but women were sent to work and children to schools. For a patriarchal and deeply religious culture such as that in Armenia, these were revolutionary changes. These changes in turn affected foodways. Instead of eating at home, children ate at schools and adults at their workplaces. That led to a standardized and Sovietized diet, if for no other reason than the numbers of people served and the use of partially prepared foods that were manufactured in other republics. In addition, food shortages were common from 1917 onward. Stalinization took its toll, as did the Second World War. Khrushchev's "thaw" of the 1960s did not live up to its promise and the Brezhnev era brought new difficulties. All of these political factors hindered the normal expression of Armenianness, however that might be defined, and were *in addition to* the forces of industrialization and urbanization that were already making significant inroads into the traditional cultural patterns of Armenians, including their foodways.

🌰 *How Traditional Is Traditional?*

Cuisines are not immutable, but constantly evolve. Any cuisine needs to be defined in terms of time and place before one can attempt to assess outside influences. An analogous problem would be to try and characterize Italian or Thai food before the New World tomatoes or chile peppers became available. International, national, and domestic factors all affect what people eat and how they eat it. Who stirs the pot matters as much as what it contains. The society's level of technology and the presence or absence of electricity and running water materially affect the division of labor and the methods used to obtain, process, prepare, and store a family's provisions. In Armenian terms, different foods are prepared depending on whether the source of heat is a *tonir* or a microwave oven.

This chapter focuses on Armenian and Soviet domestic cooking, not the public cooking done for restaurants, institutions, or other communal establishments. A community's eating habits, or what we call its cuisine, evolve from a multitude of private, unrelated decisions made in response to public circumstances—economic, political, social, and religious. Home cooking is basically conservative and gradually evolves amid the rituals, traditions, and idiosyncrasies of the family group.

To derive past culinary norms and traditions from a contemporary cuisine is to walk through a minefield, since older traditions are often obscure and modern ones are unreliable in the sense that they may have no counterparts in the past. In traditional societies, where women were often illiterate, recipes were not written down but transmitted orally. Culinary practices from preindustrial households, although "reliable" in the sense that they may represent venerable traditions, are an endangered species. The skills and ingrained working habits that formerly required no explanation by their practitioners are now dying out. Cookbooks, even when available, must be treated cautiously, since they represent only the author's testimony, not what was actually prepared in the kitchen. Whether oral or written, accounts of past culinary practices are often unsatisfactory in that they tend to omit crucial culinary details as "too obvious" or not "high-minded" enough for inclusion. A related problem is that women's work was usually invisible in patriarchal societies (as in our own) and hence was excluded from the group's historical record.

By contrast with traditional societies, the eating patterns of contemporary urban families change rapidly. Where there is little collective memory beyond that of the immediate participants, impromptu responses to a given occasion can quickly assume an aura of tradition, unrelated to actuality. Although a favorite family dish may be heralded as genuinely authentic, as a beloved (or hated) vestige of earlier times, closer examination often reveals that the dish was nothing more than grandmother's inspiration of the moment. This may be a domestic version of the greater process dubbed by historians as "the invention of tradition."[4]

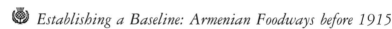 Establishing a Baseline: Armenian Foodways before 1915

Just as Armenians perennially debate what is Armenianness and who is an Armenian, the question "What is Armenian cuisine?" admits no easy answer. Armenian history is full of turmoil; geographical, cultural, and political factors all affected the development of the culture, just as they affected the cuisine. The present discussion focuses on the foodways of Armenians living in eastern Anatolia rather than those of their cosmopolitan cousins in Tbilisi and Constantinople. The sharp contrast between the rural lifestyle of the Turkish (Western) Armenians and the urban lifestyle of latter-day Soviet (Eastern) Armenians is useful, because it highlights the enduring features of Armenian cuisine at the same time that it exposes the enormous changes that have occurred over the last seventy years.[5]

A basic premise underlying this chapter is that cuisines are rooted in culture. Any dish taken out of its cultural context quickly loses its essential savor and integrity because then there is little to prevent randomness and expediency from overriding any historical circumstances that once determined the combination of ingredients and method of preparation. Armenian cuisine has particularly close ties to the history of the region. The English historian David Marshall Lang captured the complexity of the issues when he noted that contemporary Soviet Armenian "cuisine is rooted in ancient traditions of food technology, gastronomy, and hospitality characteristic of the Caucasian and Anatolian region."[6] In addition, the cuisine has been enriched over the centuries by Armenians who settled in many parts of the globe, including Iran, Syria, Western Europe, and America. The ancient culture, along with its attendant cuisine, developed in a mountainous area known for its harsh climate, hot summers, and severe winters.

Prior to the genocide of 1915, most of the two million Armenians who lived under Ottoman rule were clustered in small, self-sufficient mountainous villages of eastern Anatolia, where transportation was primitive and communication was limited.[7] The extended families who lived in these villages were strongly patriarchal; obedience was demanded "of the younger to the older and of the female to the male."[8] At mealtimes, the men ate first and were served by the women. Chastity, restraint, passivity, and obedience were demanded of the women. The youngest bride in the household had the least status. In many regions, she was not permitted to speak to anyone except when alone with her husband or the family's children. The birth of her first child signaled a reprieve from this "rule of silence." She was the first up in the morning and often the last to bed at night. She had to fetch the household water from the local fountain or stream; she also set the table for the men, waited on them silently while they ate, then cleared the table and set it for the women in the family.[9] She waited on her father-in-law and mother-in-law and was expected to wash the feet of the guests. Beyond these duties specific to the youngest bride in the family, men and women divided the household chores, with each sex sharing its tasks communally. "The women prepared meals, made the clothing for the family, attended to dairy animals and poultry, and made rugs, mats, bedding, soap, candles, and pottery for the household."[10] Individualism was not encouraged; a young woman seldom appeared in public alone, and then only if the lower half of her face was covered.[11] Given their limited economic resources and infrequent contact with other communities, few women had interests or goals beyond promoting the well-being of their family. Their kitchens, in these circumstances, were very conservative arenas, cut off from most outside influences.

The center of the hearth and household was the *tonir*, a hole for fire dug three to five feet in the ground of the main room of the house. The Armenian *tonir* resembled the Indian tandoori oven in both name and usage. In Armenia, the *tonir* was the primary device for cooking and for heating. Since wood was scarce, dried dung was the usual fuel. Some families had a second *tonir* outside in the courtyard for cooking and baking in the summer, and a few families also had an *ojakh*, a hearth, or recess in the wall, where a fire could be built. Some villages had communal ovens; to heat these huge ovens, the villagers contributed the wood and "each family had a special emblem which they used to identify their loaves."[12]

Echoes of ancient fire rituals were still found in Armenian folk beliefs at this period. When a new bride first entered her husband's home, she reverently kissed the *tonir* and piously circled it three times with her husband.[13] Often a bride brought a fire from her paternal home, and when an extended family broke into smaller units, every son first lit his own hearth with fire taken from his father's home.[14] Such Armenian expressions as "may your smoke not be extinguished" (= may your hearth and family endure) and "my smoke has died down" (= calamity has struck me) reflect the strong associations between hearth, fire, and family.[15]

Lavash, a thin leavened bread baked on the interior ceramic walls of the *tonir*, was consumed at almost all Armenian meals. Sometimes older widows earned money by going from house to house baking the *lavash*, which was arduous work requiring a quick, skillful hand. Usually a couple of women rolled out the dough while a third tended to the baking.

> Once the *tonir* was blazing hot and ready, the one doing the baking, appropriately dressed, wearing the baking mitt with wetted paw, squatted at the *tonir* with her *agish* [bread-handling tool], scraper, bowl of glaze, and vessel of water, and a little table all at hand. Two helpers sat opposite her and [after rolling out the dough] . . . tossed the opened dough onto the baker's table. The baker made a sign of the cross, spread the glaze and sesame over the dough, and with the mitted hand slapped the opened dough onto the hot wall of the *tonir*—with a "There, O Lord!" She did this one after another until all the wall of the *tonir* was covered with bread. The baked bread was removed from the *tonir* wall with the *agish*. Then the *tonir* wall was cleaned with a wet scraper. The process was then repeated.[16]

The bread kept well for months; it was either stacked in a barrel or hung in bags from the ceiling. Just before eating, people moistened the *lavash* with water until it was soft and pliable and used it to scoop up food from the communal bowls. Barring spoons, other utensils were not used; "forks were rare except in Constantinople."[17] At mealtimes, the food was placed on a large tray set on a low table or over the covered *tonir*. People sat on the ground or on cushions to eat. According to former inhabitants, Armenians "sat flat on the floor because they should not be higher than their food," or they "ate sitting on the ground because they knelt only in church." Reverence toward food (and the God who provided it) is also apparent in the saying "your table should be so low that you will bow to eat."[18]

Meals for the poorer villagers consisted of little more than bread, butter, and cheese; bulghur and lamb were holiday supplements.[19] Those with more resources typically ate tea, bread, *madzoon* (yogurt), and cheese for breakfast. For lunch they added pilaf, eggs, olives, beans, onion, and/or greens to the breakfast basics. Dinner was the same as lunch, but families that were better off also ate small quantities of fish or meat.[20]

Preserving foods was a major occupation of the women, since shops did not exist in many of these mountainous villages. The family's survival depended on the skills and resources of the women to preserve the bounty from the short growing season against the enforced isolation of the harsh winters. The writer Vahan Totovents recalled:

> The winters used to be long and severe. The snow would come down in flakes as large as petals, and it would fill the streets. It would rise; it would reach the windows; it would bury the houses into the depths of the earth. The front doors would no longer open. The streets would almost reach the level of the roofs, and people would walk from the streets straight on to the roofs and down into the houses below, through the doors there.[21]

To prepare for this snowy isolation, late summer and fall were seasons of intense labor. Bertha Ketchian, an Armenian from eastern Turkey, described her mother's preserving activities in Husenig in the late summer of 1919.

> Mama dried greens, like string beans, okra, peppers, and eggplant. She cooked tomato paste. She bought some nuts and she dried grapes into raisins and wished there were dried apricots, but she dried peaches, plums, and pears. From some of the grapes, Mama made *bastegh*, or fruit roll. We loved to sample the grape pudding [*malez*] before she spread it thinly and evenly on clean white sheets to dry into *bastegh*. Once it was dry enough on the roof, so that it would not drip, she would hang it up on a clothesline until it was dried thoroughly. Then she would dampen the backside with a wet cloth and gently pull it off in large pieces, which she would sprinkle with flour and keep. She also made *rojig*, long strands of strung walnut halves dipped and dried many times into the same hot grape pudding. All this work took some time, but the result was excellent, because the succulent grapes are so flavorful and sweet. No sugar was added.[22]

The most important and onerous autumn task was to turn wheat harvest into flour, cracked wheat (*bulghar*), and hulled wheat (*dzedzadz*). Animals were also slaughtered in the fall. The fresh meat was salted and dried in the sun, braised in its own fat in small pieces (*khavurma*), spiced, chopped, stuffed into casings, and dried (*sugugh*), or spiced and dried in large pieces (*basturma*).

Tomatoes are a New World fruit, but by the late nineteenth century, they had become an important ingredient of many Armenian dishes and needed to be preserved for the winter. The women spread sheets on the flat roofs and set out drained tomato pulp to dry in the sun. Sun-drying unquestionably enhanced the flavor of the fruit, but more important, it conserved scarce fuel. Like root vegetables, the more fragile tomatoes and peppers were also preserved by burying them in the ground. One Armenian remembered that his grandmother "would place a layer of tomatoes and cover them up with dirt; then she would place several more layers of tomatoes, each time with dirt on it. The tomatoes were preserved until winter, as long as no water got to them."[23]

Many varieties of fruits and nuts grew well in the climate and were important items in the traditional Armenian diet. Transcaucasia was the home of the wild grape, and Soviet excavations show that grapes were grown and wine produced in Armenia as early as 800 B.C.[24] The writer Totovents recalled: "Red, black, yellow, and white bunches of grapes would draw in light, color, and sweetness from the sun, concentrating it, drop by drop, into small globes, each hanging down like the brilliant, clear eye of a 'child."[25] Apples were also popular. Armenian folk tales traditionally end with a metaphorical gift of apples: "From the sky fell three apples: one to me, one to the storyteller, and one to the person who has entertained you."[26]

Church festivals and fast days shaped Armenian culture and diet. Armenians were proud of the fact that the Armenian kingdom had been the first nation to adopt Christianity as the state religion (A.D. 301). The church was of overweening importance in Armenian life and was responsible for maintaining the culture of the people during those long periods when "national political authorities ceased to function among Armenians."[27] The Church Synod established rules for fasting at Sis in 1243.[28] The Armenian equivalent of *Maslenitsa* and Mardi Gras was *Pareegentahn*. Like the Russians, the Armenians enjoyed ritual swinging at this festive time. In the Van basin, the wife of the head of the family would take "her daughter in her arms, or else a heavy stone mortar, [and] would sit on a swing and be pushed in order to obtain the equivalent weight in butter in the coming year."[29] Instead of consuming *bliny* as the Russians did, the Armenians feasted on rich food and *katah* (firm pastries, richer than bread, made of flour, eggs, and butter).[30] According to the early rules for fasting, fish, olive oil, and wine were forbidden during Lent and people were restricted to a diet of salt and bread. By the nineteenth century, the rules had relaxed considerably, but Lent was still observed very strictly; butter, cheese, milk, eggs, and meat were all prohibited. On Wednesdays and Fridays outside of Lent, the church forbade the consumption of milk, meat, and fish.[31] With more than 150 fast days per year, the Armenian cuisine developed an extensive repertoire of fast day dishes.

Easter was the greatest of the Armenian church holidays. Usually a young bride was allowed to visit her family for the first time after her marriage at Easter.[32] The church collected from the congregation and distributed meat to everyone, including the poor "on Easter Sunday, to break the fast before the doors of churches."[33] Eggs dyed in onion skins were exchanged on Easter Day. Like many other Christians, the Armenians played tapping games with the dyed eggs. Children were given a red egg nestled in a plait of baked *cheorig* dough.[34] Families customarily visited the cemetery on the Monday after Easter, taking baskets of food and drink. In the Caesarea area, the people included *paklava* in their baskets; they ate what they wanted and left the rest for the priest who blessed the graves.[35]

Political events destroyed this way of life forever in 1915. Those Armenians who fled from the atrocities of the Turks and landed in eastern Armenia spent the next thirty years enduring revolutions, civil wars, and international conflicts under the Soviets. Those years had a terrible cost. We pick up our story after the Second World War, when families were able to resume a more normal existence.

Cookbook Publishing in the Soviet Union, 1949 to 1989

From the richly nuanced memoir literature of the Turkish Armenians we now turn to the more impassive and "scientific" literature of Soviet cookery books. Owing to the tight government control of the publishing industry, Soviet cookbooks, unlike their Western counterparts, have a distinct political dimension. Nothing was published in the Soviet Union without the state's permission, and it is fair to say that little was published that did not serve the political goals of the government. Given this background, Soviet cookbooks are a good index for analyzing governmental attitudes toward domestic life in general and the minority populations in particular.[36]

In 1949, the Soviet Union published 37 books that could be called cookbooks; in 1989, the last year for which figures are available, 118 titles were published.[37] This growth is part of a worldwide phenomenon, but the bare figures are not as revealing as the shift in topics, which mirror societal trends and the change from socialism and communal dining to individualism and ultimately consumerism. The nationality question, that perennial thorn in Soviet life, also shows up in the list of cookbooks. The progression of titles suggests that the publication of national cookery books was a politically sensitive act in the Soviet Union, marked in part by a hostility toward domestic life and bourgeois comforts but also by larger political considerations. Any of several motivations may have determined the language, the size of the print run, and the subject matter, that is, which cuisine to showcase to which audience. The political climate may have been the overriding factor—in which case, publishing decisions may have reflected the shifting political balance of discrimination and favoritism among the nationalities and constituent republics. Or it could be argued that since cookbooks were at the bottom of the Soviet cultural hierarchy, the Soviets, despite their philosophical reservations, used the publication of national recipes as a sop to quiet restive nationals when other cultural outlets were denied or had been cut off. Finally, since many cookbooks were published outside of Moscow, the possibility of free-wheeling regional decisions must be considered.[38]

Most of the 37 books published in 1949 were small manuals for organizing communal food services, with instructions for everything from training waiters to running restaurants and buffets in train stations. Other topics include directions for operating equipment, preserving nutrients, using partially prepared foods, and learning about sanitation and bookkeeping. By 1989 books on domestic cookery had eclipsed books on communal dining. Not only had the total number of cookbooks published increased, but so had titles devoted to the national cuisines and published in the national languages. In 1949, one book was published in Armenian and another in Ukrainian; in 1989, nineteen cookbooks were published in the national languages. Interest in the national cuisines grew increasingly specialized during this period, a trend echoed in Western publishing, where increasing attention was paid to ever more exotic cuisines. In hindsight and given the value people place on preserving their traditional foodways, this burst of interest in national cuisines might be seen as another sign of the festering national tensions that flared up with the collapse of the Soviet empire.

Of the eighteen Soviet-Armenian cookbooks published since 1949, eleven are distinct titles and seven are reprints. Two separate titles are devoted to miscellaneous topics in domestic cooking, and three each concern preserving, professional cooking (including communal kitchens), and Armenian cuisine. The books on Armenian cuisine were reprinted several times and included five editions in Russian and three in Armenian.

Representation of Armenian Cuisine in Soviet Cookbooks

Anyone wanting to learn about Armenian cooking from Russian language cookbooks has three primary options. An experienced cook might recognize the occasional Armenian recipe in a general Soviet cookbook, but since these recipes are rarely identified by name or national origin, it is better to search for titles like *"Cuisines of Our Republics."* These books, which began to appear in the early 1970s, typically discuss a different national cuisine in each chapter.[39] The best choice, of course, is to consult one of the three titles devoted solely to Armenian cooking.

Armianskaia kulinariia [Armenian cuisine], a book of 272 pages and 500 recipes, represents the high end of these culinary materials.[40] Four editions were published (one in Armenian and three in Russian) over a twenty-five-year period, with a total print run of 305,000 copies, of which 60,000 were in Armenian. In addition, selected recipes were reprinted and sold as packets of postcards.[41] Separate chapters are devoted to soups, fish dishes, meat dishes, pastries, jams, etc. Sections on Armenian national breads, milk products, pastries, and sweets offer valuable information not readily available elsewhere. Essays on the history of natural food resources in Armenia and the development of a distinctive Armenian cuisine enhance the book's cultural value. A chapter on "Eastern" dishes—really Middle Eastern dishes—is especially helpful, as it allows Soviet-Armenian dishes to be compared with variations in Turkey and the Diaspora. The most intriguing section of the book, however, is called "The Armenian Culinary Heritage" and contains nearly sixty recipes for various kinds of sweets said to be taken from copies of an 1827 manuscript written by Ovanes Amiraian-Mamikonian.[42]

Armianskaia kulinariia is unusual for a Soviet cookbook because it calls attention to the richness and variety of traditional Armenian food and its role in the society. The effect of the miscellaneous chapters and recipes for Armenian dishes found in most Soviet cookbooks is to reduce Armenian cuisine to a core of commonly recognized preparations. These include *bozbash* soup (lamb soup), *shashlyk* (shish kebab), *plov* (rice pilaf, especially with pomegranates or sevruga), and *tolma* (stuffed vegetables or grape leaves). Other dishes commonly mentioned are string bean salad with vinegar and garlic, *Izmiri kiufta* (sautéed meatballs in tomato sauce), and grilled trout on a spit. Except for *gata* or *nazuk*, Armenian desserts and sweets are rarely included.

Given the limitation of the Soviet cookbooks, what do they tell us about Armenian eating habits? Although Soviet authors tend to avoid cultural issues in favor of nutritional or pseudo-scientific material, they do include a modicum of information about Armenian ingredients, cooking methods, and diet. From Reutovich we learn that Armenians in rural areas traditionally ate a light breakfast, a modest midday meal, and a heavy supper.[43] Other authors mention traditional Armenian foodstuffs—grains, fruits, nuts, yogurt, and cheese. V. V. Pokhlebkin describes Armenian cooking techniques as complex and labor intensive. He points out that the soft (rather than chewy or crunchy) consistency of many Armenian dishes depends on cooking and processing several different components before combining them into a single dish. Although better than nothing, these comments reveal little about either the people or their cuisine.

If the discussion finishes with the cookbooks, it will end on a somber note emphasizing what has been lost since 1915. Undoubtedly there were changes that occurred when the population shifted from country to city and from an oral to a written tradition. But perhaps the loss is more apparent than real. Perhaps we are merely seeing the poverty of the source—Soviet cookbooks—and not the poverty of the culture. *Armianskaia kulinariia* is not perfect, but its eighty-one recipes for different soups compare well with Pokhlebkin's twenty-one and the one or two that are occasionally found in ordinary Soviet cookbooks. Another serious issue, not addressed in this chapter, is the reliability of the individual recipes. Recipes change as they cross from one culture to another, and it would be remarkable if the national recipes had not been adapted for Soviet circumstances and Soviet products. Pokhlebkin, for one, warns that no Armenian grain dish is authentic unless made with grains processed by the distinctive Armenian methods.[44] So, given the loss of the cultural material, the paucity of recipes, and the inevitable modern adaptations and compromises, what is left of the traditional Armenian foodways? Have they vanished along with any mention of fasting in the Soviet cookbooks? Have they been relegated to holidays and special occasions?

🌾 An Oral Perspective on Soviet-Armenian Foodways

This story of Armenian foodways concludes with material drawn from oral interviews with six women who lived for varying periods in Soviet Armenia after the Second World War.[45] The number of informants is small, but their remarks underscore both the limitations of cookbooks as social documents and the durability of traditional foodways despite urbanization and political interference. I began this chapter suspecting that the Soviets had imposed changes on Armenian cuisine from the outside. Certainly the portrayal of Armenian cuisine in Soviet cookbooks suggests that the Sovietization of Armenian cuisine is a tale of diminishing options and fading identity. The word "Sovietization" alone is ominous, suggesting dark shadows that "menace" the "purer" indigenous cuisine. But informants tell a brighter tale than might be expected. The Soviets introduced changes that otherwise might not have occurred, but my informants view this positively rather than negatively. New ingredients are now available and numerous non-Armenian preparations have been introduced. Collectively, these are seen as broadening the range of possibilities, not as an imposition of Soviet power.

Armenia is a land-locked country and people traditionally consumed only freshwater fish. By the late Soviet period, frozen saltwater fish was sold widely in the Erevan markets. This fish had a mixed reception: it was cheap and enriched the diet, but the local population regarded it suspiciously as non-Armenian. The most prized local fish is the trout called *ishkhan* of which there are several varieties. Due to environmental problems with Lake Seven—the lake is in danger of evaporating—the *ishkhan* have become so scarce and expensive that they are reserved for very special occasions like wedding banquets, where they appear beside sturgeon and caviar, both Soviet specialties. Caviar is commonly available now, but H. Martirosian reports that her wealthy grandparents had never heard of it in the old days. She also said that when she was small, her mother forced her to eat caviar daily because of an old belief that caviar improves eyesight.

The pattern of meat-eating changed considerably in the Soviet period. Traditionally Armenians ate very little animal flesh. When they did, they preferred lamb; beef was too expensive and pork was not eaten at all. According to S. Ketchian, meat was scarce in Erevan from the end of the war until the mid-1960s. Supplies improved once pigs began to be raised locally and beef began to be imported regularly from Russia and the other republics. Instead of lamb, pork is now preferred for shish kebab. Turkeys raised in Georgia were another popular innovation by the Soviets. The adoption of Soviet-style sausages, however, was the biggest change, since they were not part of the traditional Armenian cuisine. According to N. Baratyan, Armenians still lack a sufficient vocabulary to cover all the varieties now available. H. Martirosian reports that after the Soviets built a sausage factory in Armenia in the 1950s, Soviet-style sausages suddenly became fashionable and were even served as a delicacy at weddings. But, Martirosian continued, "the fad faded quickly. It was purely a phenomenon of the 1950s."

Some Soviet dishes, such as *borshch* (beet soup), *bliny* (pancakes), and *pelmeni* (ravioli), are no longer even perceived as foreign by Armenians. Soviet citizens living in Armenia introduced some of these dishes, as did Armenian students and adults who had studied or worked in other republics and brought their newly acquired tastes back home. This is a significant factor, since only 66 percent of Soviet Armenians lived in their titular republic in 1989.[46] Breads from Georgia are now sold widely in Erevan, and a number of new *plovs* have been introduced from Azerbaijan and Uzbekistan (N. Baratyan).

Despite urbanization, preserving has lost none of its importance over the years. In Soviet times, home preserving was perceived as a necessity because foods were not always available when needed in the shops and commercially prepared foods were considered inferior—something between unhealthy and unappetizing. The city of Erevan still has close ties to the surrounding suburbs and countryside. Fruit is picked from trees in private gardens or bought when cheapest in the markets. Both fruits and vegetables are set out on the roofs or balconies to dry in the summer sun or are pickled and preserved in time-honored methods. Old-timers still boil down grape juice into a syrup for *bastegh* (grape leather) and spread the paste onto clean sheets to dry in the sun on the balcony. Home-preserved foods not only taste better, but are available for unexpected company. Hospitality remains important in Armenian society and great effort is made to treat guests well. Traditionally women would not frequent restaurants, and eating out is still not widely accepted; generally speaking, the food is considered inferior and the prices too high. The difficulty of storing home-preserved goods in city apartments is acknowledged, but people are willing to sacrifice precious closet space for jars of preserves, or they store the preserves with friends or family in the country and bring them into the city as needed. So the disproportionate number of Soviet Armenian cookbooks devoted to preserving may have served a real need in the community, although the reasons for the preserving are not elaborated for the reader.

The pattern of annual holidays in Armenia has changed somewhat over the last seventy years. Religious holidays have all but disappeared. Christmas is not observed and Easter has been reduced to the coloring of eggs. A special Easter pilaf with raisins is prepared and eggs are still colored for the children. H. Martirosian mentions that although no one supposedly knew when Easter was, her grandmother always had eggs ready for the children to play their annual game of cracking Easter eggs to see whose egg was the strongest. If someone died in the family, the eggs would be boiled but not dyed. N. Zakarian reports that on September 15, a Memorial Day, people would gather and often hang a lamb or baby goat in the *tonir* and allow the juices to drip onto a pilaf—this is an old custom adapted to a new observance. New Year's Day is the biggest annual celebration. Women start preparing food several days in advance so that on the day itself they do not have to cook but can serve an elaborate buffet for all their friends who visit on New Year's Day. Strict seniority is observed in paying these visits. The table is as lavish as possible partly to treat the guests, and partly because it is believed that the prosperity of the family in the coming year depends on the lavishness of the spread. Lamb baked with garlic cloves is often served, along with suckling pigs (a Soviet influence) and special boiled kufta made with pounded, not ground, meat. When made properly, these kufta bounce on the plate; one visiting American supposedly called them "little bombs that bounce."

I close this chapter by returning to the *tonir*, that symbol of traditional Armenian foodways. Contrary to the impression gleaned from Soviet cookbooks, the *tonir* is very much a part of contemporary Armenian life.[47] Far from dying out, it has recently become fashionable for suburban houses to be built with *tonirs* in the garden. Urban dwellers, of course, must do without, but real *lavash* is still made in the city at several communal bakeries that do have *tonirs*. These bakeries cannot keep up with the demand. The commercial *lavash* made in electric ovens is unpopular because it is too thick and often uncooked at the edges. Small modern electric *tonirs* are now sold. According to N. Baratyan, they not only make good *lavash* but are useful for cooking *shashlik* as well, thereby fulfilling two of the traditional uses of the *tonir*. So although times change, many of the older foodways endure, albeit in a modified form. The Soviets may have tried to create a new type of Soviet citizen, but behind the closed doors of their homes, the Armenians have continued to observe their time-honored patterns pretty much undisturbed by the policymakers in Moscow. No wonder nationalism erupted with such force when the empire broke up—it had never died down, just gone behind the scenes.

APPENDIX

List of Informants

Arakelian, I. Mathematics instructor with two teenage children. Lived in Armenia as a child and visited during the 1970s and 1980s.

Baratyan, N. Professor at Erevan University with grandchildren. Lived in Armenia all her life.

Chamakhian, A. Graduate student in America. Lived in Erevan 1959–1991.

Ketchian, S. University instructor in America. Lived in Erevan from 1950 until 1965.

Martirossian, H. Graduate student in America. Lived in Armenia all her life; family and young daughter still live there.

Zakarian, N. Bookkeeper with grandchildren. Lived in Erevan from 1947 to the late 1970s.

NOTES

I want to thank Cathy Frierson and Patricia Herlihy, both of whom helped me considerably in the early stages of formulating the issues discussed in this chapter. My heartfelt thanks go to N. Baratyan and to all the other informants who, collectively, demonstrated the value of oral history by discussing what lies behind the written sources.

1. Quoted in Donald E. Miller and Lorna Touryan Miller, *Survivors: An Oral History of the Armenian Genocide* (Berkeley: University of California Press, 1993), 58.

2. References to the *tonir* and the baking of *lavash* are uncommon in Soviet cookbooks. This recipe is one of the few exceptions. See V. M. Mel'nik, *Kukhnia narodov SSSR* [Cuisines of the Soviet peoples], 2d ed. (Kishinev: "Timpul," 1987), 185.

3. I am using this term to mean the set of cultural values that a society assigns to meals and individual foods, including their preparation and consumption.

4. See Eric Hobsbawm and Terence Ranger, eds., *The Invention of Tradition* (Cambridge: Cambridge University Press, 1983).

5. Ultimately, the changes need to be compared with developments in Armenian cooking in the Diaspora, but this issue will not be addressed here.

6. David Lang, *The Armenians: A People in Exile* (London: Unwin, 1988), 138–139.

7. Estimates vary of the size of the Armenian population in Turkey and of the number of Armenians who perished as a result of the genocide. According to Lang (ibid., 37), about one and a half million persons out of a total population of slightly over two million perished between 1915 and 1922. Half a million Armenians became refugees in other lands, and only a hundred thousand Armenians were left in Turkey in 1922 at the end of the massacres and deportations.

8. Emanuel Sarkisyanz, *A Modern History of Transcaucasian Armenia: Social, Cultural, and Political* (Nagpur, India: privately printed, 1975), 44.

9. Susie Hoogasian Villa and Mary Kilbourne Matossian, *Armenian Village Life before 1914* (Detroit: Wayne State University Press, 1982), 91–95.

10. Mary Kilbourne Matossian, *The Impact of Soviet Policies in Armenia* (Leiden: E. J. Brill, 1962), 6.

11. In part, the veil was used as protection against kidnapping by the Turks, a not uncommon occurrence in rural areas.

12. Hoogasian Villa and Matossian, *Armenian Village Life before 1914*, 42.

13. Ibid., 33.

14. Sarkisyanz, *A Modern History of Transcaucasian Armenia*, 47.

15. Hoogasian Villa and Matossian, *Armenian Village Life before 1914*, 34.

16. Manoog B. Dzeron, *Village of Parchanj, General History, 1600 to 1937*, trans. Arra S. Avakian (Boston: Baikar Press), 145.

17. Miller and Miller, *Survivors*, 56. This remark underscores the poverty of these people and the enormous cultural distance that separated them from life in the capital. Forks had long been used in Constantinople—silver forks from the fourth century are in the Dumbarton Oaks Collection—and, in the eleventh century, the fork was reintroduced into Venetian society by a Byzantine princess. See Bridget Ann Henish, *Fast and Feast: Food in Medieval Society* (University Park: Pennsylvania State University Press, 1976), 185–186.

18. Hoogasian Villa and Matossian, *Armenian Village Life before 1914*, 36.

19. Sarkisyanz, *A Modern History of Transcaucasian Armenia*, 40.

20. Miller and Miller, *Survivors*, 57.

21. Vahan Totovents, *Scenes from an Armenian Childhood*, trans. Mischa Kudian (London: Mashtots Press, 1980), 101.

22. Bertha Nakshian Ketchian, *In the Shadow of the Fortress: The Genocide Remembered* (Cambridge, Mass.: Zoryan Institute for Contemporary Armenian Research and Documentation, 1988), 95–96.

23. Miller and Miller, *Survivors*, 59.

24. Lang, *The Armenians*, 68.

25. Totovents, *Scenes from an Armenian Childhood*, 9.

26 . See Ohannes Sheohmelian, *Three Apples from Heaven: Armenian Folktales* (Saddle Brook, N.J.: AGBU Ararat Press, 1982), and *100 Armenian Tales*, collected and ed. Susie Hoogasian Villa (Detroit: Wayne State University Press, 1966).

27. Ronald Grigor Suny, *Looking toward Ararat: Armenia in Modern History* (Bloomington: Indiana University Press, 1993), 11.

28. Arhchbishop Maghakia Ormanian, *Azkabadium*, vol. 2, chap. 1121.

29. Hoogasian Villa and Matossian, *Armenian Village Life before 1914*, 138.

30. In some areas, this word is pronounced *gata;* note the similarity with the French *gâteau.*

31. Hoogasian Villa and Matossian, *Armenian Village Life before 1914*, 56.

32. Ibid., 87.

33. Sarkisyanz, *A Modern History of Transcaucasian Armenia*, 69.

34. Venetia Newall, *An Egg at Easter: A Folklore Study* (London: Routledge & Kegan Paul, 1984), 196.

35. Hoogasian Villa and Matossian, *Armenian Village Life before 1914*, 156.

36. The discussion in this section is based on a bibliography of Soviet cookbooks that is being complied by Halina Rothstein and Joyce Toomre. When completed, this bibliography will contain more than 3,000 items.

37. These provisional figures are based only on *Ezhegodnik knigi SSSR* and need to be checked against the more complete listing of titles in *Knizhnaia letopis'*. Although the numbers will grow, I do not expect the basic story to change substantially.

38. We probably never will be able to fully disentangle these reasons, but it should be possible, ultimately, to compare the incidence of the national cookbooks, both in Russian and in the source language, with other political data to see if there is any positive correlation between the two

39. About eight titles featuring a selection of Soviet national cuisines, most of which were reprinted several times, appeared after 1973. Examples with impressive print runs are A. I. Titiunnik's 1977 *Sovetskaia natsional'naia i zarubezhnaia kukhnia* [Soviet national and foreign cooking] (760,000 copies); T. V. Reutovich's 1981 *Kukhnia narodov SSSR* [Cooking of the Soviet peoples] (455,000); and V. M. Mel'nik's 1982 *Kukhnia narodov SSSR* [Cooking of the Soviet peoples] (about 200,000, including 50,000 in Moldavian). Titiunnik's book is a technical manual for professional cooks, and Mel'nik's is the only one of this genre also to be printed in one of the languages of the republics. The blockbuster in this group of titles is V. V. Pokhlebkin's 1978 *National'nye kukhni nashikh narodov* [The national cuisines of our peoples], which was printed in 1,600,000 Russian copies, 165,050 German copies, and an unknown number of Portuguese and Serbian copies. A second edition of one million copies was published in 1989. The only other cookbook printed with such abandon was the well-known Soviet culinary showpiece, *Kniga o vkusnoi i zdorovoi pishche* [The book of tasty and healthy food]; ten million copies were printed over the forty-year period under discussion.

40. See *Armianskaia kulinariia* [Armenian cuisine], 3d ed., ed. A. S. Piruzian (Erevan: Aiastan, 1984).

41. *Bliuda armianskoi kukhni* (Moskva: Planeta, 1973). (From a series of postcard packets, *Bliuda natsional'noi kukhni.*)

42. As yet, I have found no other reference to Amiraian-Mamikonian's work.

43. Reutovich, *Kukhnia narodov SSSR*, 216.

44. Poklebkin, *Natsional'nye kukhni nashikh narodov*, 284.

45. To identify the informants, see the Appendix.

46. Ronald Grigor Suny, "Transcaucasia," in *The Nationalities Factor in Soviet Politics and Society*, ed. Lubomyr Hajda and Mark Beissinger (Boulder: Westview Press, 1990), 236–238.

47. Little reference is made to the *tonir* in the Soviet cookbooks; Pokhlebkin, who otherwise gives many details of Armenian cuisine, omits any reference to the *tonir* or to *lavash*, the traditional bread that is baked in it.

THIRTEEN

MUSYA GLANTS

Food as Art: Painting in Late Soviet Russia

The Soviet writer Ilya Erenburg used to tell of an occasion when he was strolling in Erevan with the Armenian painter Martiros Saryan, who was famous for his landscapes and still lifes of the natural beauty of his country. They crossed a street where workers were unloading a truck of peaches. Suddenly one of the workers recognized the painter and with a smile offered him a piece of fruit, saying that everything grown in the earth of Armenia belonged to its great artist. The offering was an expression of appreciation and respect.[1]

Bread, wine, salt, and all the fruits of the earth have a powerful symbolic significance in the culture of nations. Artists have historically included food in still life and genre painting to enhance its spiritual and aesthetic appeal. Food and the process of eating often express delicate nuances of sensitivity and sensuality, while at the same time tapping into basic human experience. Within any one culture, the cultural meaning of food evolves over time along with social conditions and popular taste. Food imagery not only deepens the viewer's knowledge of historical and social cultures and the details of everyday life but also intensifies the emotional dialogue between the artist and the spectator.

This chapter examines the use of food as a symbol in the painting of one particular era—the period from the 1960s to the last years of the Soviet regime—as compared to earlier epochs. Such an investigation can be instructive from both the aesthetic and social points of view. An analysis of the changing images of food during these years will add to our understanding of the emancipation of society and its art from the shackles of Socialist Realism and totalitarianism.

Food metaphors are especially revealing in Russian art because of the powerful role food has played in Russian and Soviet history. Because of long periods not only of shortages but of actual starvation, food came to represent much more than the ability to keep body and soul together. In a land where tangerines, for instance, appeared only once a year, around New Year's, their smell was a vivid reminder of the holidays and of the gifts children might find under the Christmas tree; in a world where the first cucumbers or scallions were a harbinger of spring, bananas were considered exotic, and strawberries were only a seasonal phenomenon, food became a very powerful symbol. (When a popular Russian comedian was asked upon returning from the United States when one might buy the earliest strawberries there, he replied "Seven o'clock, when the supermarket opens!" The line became one of his most popular jokes.) People quote the lines of the prerevolutionary poet Igor Severianin, "How sweet and delicious were pineapples in champagne!" as a symbol of a glamorous and exciting world. For years, people associated pineapples, oranges, and other fruits with the white sails of their dreams crossing transparently blue seas from exotic places where life was different and wonderful. In a recently published novel *The Onyx Chalice* there is the story of a woman who, never having taken a drink herself, had a special fondness for liquor bottles with elaborate foreign labels. "From the time of her childhood, when she was always hungry and life was full of shortages, a full refrigerator and shelves of canned food were important to her, not only as symbols of prosperity as, for example, some people regarded crystal or fine china, but because food represented security and comfort."[2] Food was, and still is, a poignant and evocative device. Even today, in order to show extraordinary hospitality or respect Russians try to lavish on guests not so much a special recipe or elegance of service as top-quality food, be it expensive caviar, smoked fish, foreign cheese, or imported sausage.

Throughout the post-Stalin years, artists used food imagery in a variety of ways. In the 1960s and 1970s, when painting, along with *sam-* and *tamizdat* in literature, became an active tool in the struggle for freedom, and progressive artists used their work as a form of resistance, the food metaphors that appeared in art differed from those of the perestroika and post-Communist periods.[3] The distinction between these periods will be analyzed in this essay.

Food has been depicted in Russian painting since the time of Old Russia. One finds food metaphors already in icon paintings, for example, in the variations of the Trinity theme. From medieval times onward, food images served artists in a variety of ways. The kinds of food selected by an artist revealed a great deal about his views, his goals, and the culture in which he worked. In the eighteenth and early nineteenth centuries, with the development of secular art, painters put food on their canvases primarily for decorative effects and to create a festive mood. The spectator is struck by the translucent fruits and berries in beautiful vases in the compositions of Aleksei Belsky and Ivan Khrutskii.[4] These elegant fruits and vegetables, along with velvet draperies and lace tablecloths, were also meant to form an eye-appealing background for the portraits of languid beauties and genres scenes that were the focus of their paintings.

The depiction of common, everyday foods came later, with the growing interest in the common people and their daily existence, and was represented in the innovative work of Aleksei Venetsianov. In his *Cleaning Beets* (1820) and *The Girl with Beets* (1824), fruits and vegetables fresh from the earth represented the attractiveness of peasant life and unembellished nature. From the mid-nineteenth century onward, food in painting, as in the work of Pavel Fedotov, achieved a new significance, becoming part of the content as well as the form and intensifying the social content. In *A Poor Aristocrat's Breakfast* (1849), for instance, Fedotov shows an impoverished aristocrat trying to conceal his shamefully modest breakfast from somebody knocking at his door. The simplicity of the food contrasts with the still elegant interior of the room of this once wealthy man. The chunk of dark bread on the table plays a major role in the context of the composition and its strong social statement. Although the national realists, the Peredvizhniki (Wanderers) did not generally pay much attention to food, the few images they did use expressed social ideas vividly. In Vasili Perov's *Tea-Drinking in Mytishchi, Near Moscow* (1862), for example, the food shows not so much the diet of the fat clergymen as their indifference to the wretched and starving. The tempting viands are unavailable to the soldier, and the whole composition, in which the priest drinking tea and the blind Crimean War veteran begging for alms with his boy attendant are placed on opposite sides of the table, emphasizes the social separation of the two groups.

By the first few decades of the twentieth century, interest in food as a subject of art had increased, although it took a rather different turn and was related to the new world view developed by young avant-garde artists as revealed in the first exhibitions of the Knave of Diamonds group in 1910. This art rejected the narrative painting of the Peredvizhniki and proclaimed an entirely novel aesthetic concept. Such artists as Ilya Mashkov, Piotr Konchalovskii, and, later, Pavel Kuznetsov, a member of the Blue Rose group,

Vasili Perov, Tea-Drinking in Mytishchi, near Moscow, *1862. State Tretyakov Gallery, Moscow.*

were attracted by the plasticity and texture of material things, which they rendered on canvas in novel ways. They combined indigenous arts and crafts (icons, church architecture, the *lubok,* peasant artifacts and urban folklore)[5] with the products of Western modernism and applied to Russian art "neo-primitivism," "cubo-futurism," "rayonism," and so on.[6] For them, food became an excellent experimental object. The paintings of Mashkov, Konchalovskii, and others reflect their impetuous temperaments; they are not so much contemplative as they are ardent champions of everything earthy and carnal. Their still lifes, with fresh fruit, freshly baked bread, and gleaming glasses of wine, are hymns to the joy of existence.[7] But during the revolution and in the period shortly afterward, their work began to reflect the conflicts and hardships of the new era. The simplicity of Kuzma Petrov-Vodkin's *Still*

Food as Art

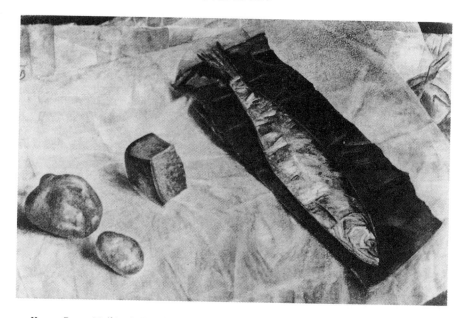

Kuzma Petrov-Vodkin, Still Life with Herring, *1918. State Russian Museum, St. Petersburg.*

Life with a Herring (1918) and David Shterenberg's *Aniska* (1918), for example, reveals more about life in the early Soviet period than almost any other painting of the time or anything in literature. A few dry herring on a newspaper, or on a dish too big for them, a slice of coarse bread, a few potatoes and sometimes a jug of milk—this was the assortment of basic objects laconically painted which emerged in place of the glowing abundance of former years.

Although Stalin's ideologues rejected the still life genre as lacking social meaning, food was widely used to glorify the beauty of Soviet life and the happiness of the people. As with everything else, it had become a stylistic device for propaganda, and the more terrifying the regime became, the more elaborate and optimistic were the paintings. Food was now an important symbol of well-being. A good example is Sergei Gerasimov's *Feast at the Collective Farm* (1937), painted in the year of the Great Terror when the peasantry was virtually destroyed. The picture, however, shows a healthy, happy group of peasants gathered around a table covered with enticing food and listening cheerfully to a man proposing a toast (probably to Stalin's health).

Food was one of the symbols used by the regime, even though party

Sergei Gerasimov, Feast at the Collective Farm, *1937. State Tretyakov Gallery, Moscow.*

ideologues condemned symbolism and restricted artists to lifelike naturalism. The mountains of apples, pears, grapes, and everything else grown in Soviet soil attested to the wealth of the country under the Bolsheviks. What, if not false symbols of a fictitiously prosperous life, were the depictions of abundance on such huge canvases as Piotr Kotov's *Michurin* (1939) and Aleksandr Gerasimov's *Stalin Visiting Gorky* (1939)? It was decreed also that food should illustrate the humanity of the party leaders and their closeness to the common people. Shown visiting friends, eating and drinking, they almost seemed like everyone else.

At the same time, it was not easy to please the authorities. Food could be shown as neither meager nor overabundant. Thus Ilya Mashkov's *Pineapples and Bananas* (1938), which meant to demonstrate the happiness of Soviet life, was condemned as lacking political significance and distorting reality by featuring the exotic fruit typical of the prerevolutionary era or of capitalism. A poem by Vladimir Mayakovsky contains these lines: "Eat your pineapple, chew your hazel-grouse! It is in any case your final day, bourgeois!"[8] On the other side, the depiction of inadequate or poor food was tolerated only if it served to show the hardship imposed by enemies, as in Arkadi Plastov's *Harvest* (1945), featuring the simple meal of an old man and two children who were harvesting because there were no young men left after the war. The loaf of black bread and

Food as Art

Arkadii Plastov, Harvest, *1945. State Tretyakov Gallery, Moscow.*

the jug of milk were condoned in this work because they illustrated the deprivations inflicted by the Nazis. Socialist Realism, the only style approved by the regime, forced art to create a nonexistent world of chimerical happiness.[9]

During Stalin's time, in art as in reality, people were deprived of as much private life as possible. Depicted in large crowds, involved in social activities, working, taking part in meetings and sport competitions, they were social types and ideological symbols, with no room for private personal emotions. People were almost never shown in domestic surroundings—at home, drinking tea, reading, playing with their children, embracing their spouses, cooking, entertaining friends. Such activities were branded self-indulgent and shameful. Even when the rules were somewhat relaxed after the war and people were permitted to be shown in more private situations, the scenes were still required to signify some social value, as in *Again a Bad Grade* (1952) by Fiodor Reshetnikov and *Moving to a New Apartment* (1952) by Aleksandr Laktionov. Even so ardent a Socialist Realist as Arkadi Plastov was criticized for choosing "meaningless and atypical" themes, by which the official critics meant, for example, the warm scene of the modest supper of the tractor

Piotr Konchalovskii, Aleksei Tolstoi Visiting the Artist, *1940–1941.*
State Russian Museum, St. Petersburg.

operator brought to him by his little daughter (*The Tractor Operator's Supper,* 1951). The social responsibilities of the people, their readiness to be good citizens and serve their country, the government's benevolence toward them — these were the accepted themes during the years of Stalin's reign. If an artist tried to do something different he was sharply criticized. A case in point is Piotr Konchalovskii's portrait of the writer Aleksei Tolstoi (1940–1941), which sought to emphasize his subject's marvelous buoyancy by seating him before an elaborate meal of meat, smoked fish, and wine, served on fine china, in order to convey a mood of *joie de vivre.* The authorities disapproved on two counts: first, the food itself was too "gourmet" and did not accord with communist notions; and second, the painting created too strong a mood of individuality and spiritual independence. Konchalovskii was accused of "fencing himself off from the turbulence of Soviet life behind countless bouquets of flowers, piles of apples, and an intimate little world of favorite things."[10]

Yuri Kugach, The Mistress of the House, *1970. State Tretiakov Gallery, Moscow.*

This "intimate little world," however, despised by the regime in every way, was precisely what most appealed to people in the post-Stalin era, both in life and in art. The atmosphere of those days and the aspirations of the people were well described in Erenburg's novel *The Thaw.* Exhausted from the war, evacuation, prisons, and camps, people found life in communal apartments enjoyable and greatly appreciated each day of peace and hope. Even the "sip of freedom" brought by the "thaw" fundamentally diversified the arts. The goal of painting after Stalin's death was to rid itself of the ever-smiling hero of Socialist Realism[11] and to return to reality. Now art confirmed the right of the people not just to work and suffer for the "welfare of the Motherland" but also to enjoy their private lives. At last it was possible to talk about ordinary things and to express personal emotions. More frequently now, people were shown at home with their families, fishing or gardening, and women were portrayed as more feminine, gentle, and fragile than the strong and masculine women in the works, for instance, of Aleksandr Deineka. These new women were shown reading, dreaming, rocking the cradle, and cooking, while men were at last permitted to relax in the cozy atmosphere of their home, enjoying life with their loved ones. Children were shown in these pictures playing, eating, and swimming instead of greeting comrade Stalin and his clique.

The simplicity of everyday life became a way for the artists to show the delicate complexity of the human spirit. Images of people baking bread, churning butter, digging potatoes, and eating together expressed the idea

Viktor Ivanov, Family, *1945, 1958–1964. State Russian Museum, St. Petersburg.*

that food and its preparation is a basic foundation of life, symbolizing the eternal chain of existence in the face of transient troubles, merciless leaders and regimes. A sense of harmony, peace, and the warmth of home pervades Yuri Kugach's *The Mistress of the House* (1970), showing an attractive young woman, modestly dressed, standing in her kitchen door holding a bowl of freshly baked *pirogi*. Now such simple food as sausage and fried eggs in an old pan—Valeri Vatenin's *Family* (1963) and *Scrambled Eggs* (1964)—replaces the mounds of juicy fruits and colorful vegetables served on decorative plates. The kitchen, previously despised as a suitable topic for art, has now replaced the huge stadiums and vast halls of party meetings. To the family depicted around the table, food has become a unifying element.

Viktor Ivanov went even further. In his painting *Family, 1945* (1958–1964), he attached a deeper social meaning to the family he showed eating together: here, home and family appear as a haven from the troubles outside. Ivanov shows a peasant family in a humble room eating a less than modest meal. Every detail gives the impression that they are in their own world, detached from the rest of the universe and linked not only by blood but by their common bitter fate. Here food serves to embody not only the wretchedness of life but also human endurance and eternal continuities.

In striving for the "not transient," there was in the 1960s and 1970s a trend among painters, writers, and filmmakers to focus on national values which had been neglected during the years of totalitarianism. The revival of national traditions was seen as a salvation for the people. In Russian literature there were the "village prose" writers—Valentin Rasputin, Vasili Belov, Vasili Shukshin, and others. Many films made at that time were based on their novels and stories, e.g., the film *Snowball Berry-red* (1967) made by Shukshin, who was both director and actor. In painting, as in literature and film, the past was idealized. Old villages and their denizens were portrayed as the custodians of traditions and morals. This message was already clear in the works of Viktor Ivanov, one of the first to express national feelings, *russkost'* (Russianness). *Russkost'* is notable in the works of Viacheslav Kalinin, Viktor Popkov, and many other Russian artists.

In the republics, where many non-Russian creative intellectuals also expressed national awareness, writers and artists of different nationalities emphasized the particulars of each culture,[12] and in painting, of course, depiction of ethnic dishes was one way of doing so. In addition to simple food, all sorts of utensils were involved, as in Vladimir Stozharov's *Bread, Salt and Bratina* (1964). The bread and salt, the homespun fabric of the embroidered towel, the smooth surface of the *bratina* (loving cup) and the old wooden walls were a metaphorical assertion of national character, of the warmth and simplicity of the Russian people and their cultural values. The beauty of simple things and closeness to nature were highlighted. One could feel in the works of these artists the softness of freshly baked bread, the plumpness of ripe fruit and the coolness of the silvery fish. Bread and salt were frequently used by the artists because they are traditional emblems of Russian culture, rich in symbolism.[13] They have always symbolized life, hard work, and prosperity. The expression *Ne khlebom edinym zhiv chelovek* (Man does not live by bread alone) and the greeting *Vstrechat' khlebom-sol'u* (To welcome with bread and salt) stress this clearly. For the most part, these paintings were done in rich and decorative color combinations which often served to accentuate national peculiarities. Thus in Stozharov's still life the golden brown and greenish tones dominate, combined with spots of white and red, the moderate colors of Russian nature, while Turgul Narimanbekov's *Lunchbreak in the Fields* (1967) employs all the vivid colors of Azerbaijan. Although most of these works were still not completely free of the past in their interpretation of life and style, they won acceptance because of their sincere and genuine appreciation of a life in which people and the objects around them, including food, complement each other.

Obviously, the art of this period was not purely of the optimistic variety. There appeared simultaneously a different tendency in painting deriving from

Vladimir Stozharov, Bread, Salt, and Bratina, *1964. State Tretyakov Gallery, Moscow.*

an increasing dissatisfaction with past and present, a loss of illusions, and a deep anxiety about the future. This was strongly developed in writings such as Aleksandr Solzhenitsin's *One Day in the Life of Ivan Denisovich* (1962); in performances at the Taganka Theater, which opened in the spring of 1964; and in "nonconformist" art—all of which have been more fully studied elsewhere. But it was present also in a new form in "official" art, a fact which has not been adequately recognized. Discontent, loneliness, and self-absorption of the alienated human being began to pervade many works of the period. Among the first paintings to reflect the new approach was *Breakfast* (1962) by Andrei Vasnetsov. The painting is striking in its combination of simplicity and emotional tension. This scene of an ordinary meal is composed in such a way as to give the impression of a philosophical generalization. The center of the composition is the motionless figure of a young man at breakfast, sitting at a table and staring bitterly ahead, against a sparsely outlined background. The meaning of his holding a cup with milk close to his cheek is unclear— whether steeling himself for what is coming or trying to defend himself. The

Food as Art

Viktor Popkov, The Bolotov Family, *1967–1968. State Tretyakov Gallery, Moscow.*

milk and bread in this picture, necessities of life and symbols of peace, seem at odds with the overanxious mood of the painting.

Among the most original interpretations of these trends are the works of Viktor Popkov. In *The Bolotov Family* (1967–1968) a mother, father, and child are shown in their kitchen at an ordinary moment in their daily life. The father is reading a newspaper; on the wall behind the standing mother is a grater and, on the table, a coffeepot and tray. The alienation between these people is reflected in the women's absent stare and her husband's absorption in his newspaper. The paper in his hands seems like a barrier between him and his wife. Popkov intensifies this psychological distance through use of ordinary household articles, placing the grater, a pan, and a single key on the wall far removed from each other so that every item seems to exist in isolation. Thus both the human figures and the articles around them contribute to a strong impression of alienation. Paintings such as this foreshadowed the typical features of the following decades, with the once-dominant role of food gradually giving way to a variety of more complex functions.

Disillusionment, frustration, and bitterness were the dominant emotions in the 1970s and 1980s, replacing the horror of Stalinism and the unrealized expectations of the "thaw" with the years of Brezhnev's semitruth and semi-freedom. Art became once more a powerful mouthpiece of social problems and human emotions. Everything not discussed openly was now expressed through art, mostly in symbolic ways. A good many of the themes already developed in the 1960s survived throughout the following decades. However, the ostensible topics were for the most part only a pretext for conveying underlying layers of meaning which the viewer had to discover. Genre scenes became more intimate, an intimacy intensified by all sorts of stylistic devices. Often the composition involved figures and objects in the foreground, giving the impression that the picture was addressed directly to the spectator. And if the nonconformists were much more direct in depicting raw reality, "official" artists had their own methods of doing the same thing more cautiously but still rendering a world with its own spirit and attractiveness.

In painting as in literature, everyday existence now became a more significant topic than ever. What the writer Yuri Trifonov did in his novel *Exchange*, Ludmila Petrushevskaya and Tatiana Tolstaya in their "women's prose," and Bulat Okudzhava and Vladimir Vysotskii in their songs was likewise achieved in painting. Ordinary life was used to examine the extent of the psychological and spiritual damage that had been done to human nature and the likelihood of salvation.

The motifs of everyday life—food in particular—became even more pronounced as an assertion of continuity and stability amid the chaos of existence. At a time when the outside world could still burst into one's home and bring disaster, people realized more and more that they were alone in the universe. The danger was perceived as spiritual rather than physical, with the intensifying destruction of *dukhovnoye* (the spiritual) looming against a background of superficial well-being. The commonplace objects around people could not protect them from this invisible invasion, and the efforts of human beings to save their spiritual values became their only hope of salvation. Artists adopted these themes as their principal mission. The poet Larisa Miller writes: "Although there is nobody left to pray and insanity prevails everywhere in the chaos, one must hold on to something, some mooring capable of surviving the torrential rains. One must cling to every second of simple routine: to the light of a lamp and the ticking of a clock; to old photographs and the hand of a child."[14] Ordinary things like dirty dishes in the sink, the steam from a

Food as Art

cup of coffee on the table, a boiling teakettle on the stove—these, as in Dulat Aliev's *The Feast of Dishes* (1985), provide the illusion of serenity and stability.

How these new approaches differ from those of the past becomes clear by comparing Valerii Vatenin's *A Mug of Beer* (1966) with Viacheslav Kalinin's *A Beer Mug* (1987). In Vatenin's work one does not see any people—only a laborer's toil-worn hands at rest on the table. The beer mug in front of the invisible man implies the relaxation he has earned. Every detail rings true in this picture; objects are shown in their direct and uncomplicated meaning. In Kalinin's painting, however, every detail seems at variance with every other. The man and woman drinking beer are painted in an expressionistic manner. They seem pretentious and ill at ease; the awkward twist of their bodies reveals a striving to seem important. Their pseudo-elegant clothes and affected postures contrast with the decadence of their images and the beer in the cheap mugs. As a final touch, Kalinin places twisted and neglected buildings in the background so that the viewer realizes with a pang of compassion that this couple is trying in its own awkward way to create artificially the vanished beauty of life. Paintings like this show how, under the pressure of overwhelming disappointment, the human spirit changes and loses hope.

The abandonment of the human being found many novel expressions in painting. Often people were shown sitting around a table sharing a meal in celebration or in mourning. Artists used food to deepen the mood of loneliness and alienation, which was the principal motif of art in the past few decades. The people celebrating together remain strangers, and their relationship will end with the last sip of wine or beer. Tatiana Nazarenko returns again and again to such hopeless feasts in *Friendly Dinner* (1982), *Summer at Bykovo* (1984), *The Big Table* (1988), and other paintings. In these works the decorative function of food is either lost or greatly minimized. The focus is on the behavior and emotions of the people gathered for the meal; the food on the table separates them rather than uniting them. This is emphasized in Aliev's *Fellow Citizens* (1983), where the drunken boon companions crawl blindly away from each other in profound self-absorption.

During this period the theme of *zastolie*—a word with no English equivalent but which may be defined as "having a party and sitting together for a long time enjoying food, drinks, and conversation"—developed various meanings and is often used by artists to show how *zastolie* is equally able to unite people and to separate them. It is particularly distinctive in the paintings of Kalinin, in almost all of whose works food is present—a bottle of vodka and a glass, a herring and a lemon, items which are part and parcel of the everyday life of the common people, Kalinin's heroes. Caviar and ripe fruit, gourmet

Tatiana Nazarenko, The Big Table, *1988. Courtesy of the artist.*

meals and expensive wines, exist only in the houses of the rich and powerful. Kalinin is not interested in their spiritual torments or those of the intellectuals, choosing instead the destruction of the souls of the masses, the people of Russia. He depicts their crude love scenes, primitive feasts and savage drunken fights, and always there is *zastolie*—vodka or beer—because drinking is the only way to relax and forget the hardships of life. But in Kalinin's works drinking has another meaning: to these people, to be drunk means to achieve power over those who are weaker and more dependent. The artist contrasts the ugliness of hard liquor and its consequences to *chaepitie* (tea-drinking), a symbol of moral values and purity. To the artist the tradition of tea-drinking is an inseparable part of the Russian national character. Kalinin takes the fate of these people painfully to heart; his frequent depiction of tea-drinking around the samovar is an expression of his national feelings, the *russkost'* previously alluded to. One of his earliest works in this vein was *Tea-Drinking*, in which he dwells on the wrinkled features of old people drinking tea while sucking lumps of sugar, smacking their wet lips, and wiping their foreheads. During the 1980s, this idyllic atmosphere gradually gave way in Kalinin's works to the bitter realization that the national past is gone forever and irretrievably, a sense that pervades *My Village* (1987) and renders it a farewell to the past: almost nothing is left of the old days except a broken teakettle, a few potatoes, and an old rooster. Even the faces of the old villagers are half gone, melted into the background of nature.

The past became a popular theme and a tool for analyzing the present individually interpreted by each artist. Natalia Nesterova refuses to give up

Food as Art

Natalia Nesterova, People with Cakes, *1982. Omsk Regional Fine Arts Museum.*

the past, however. She fights for it and revives its idealized charm in such paintings as *The Terrace, Evening* (1986) and *Broken Dishes* (1983). She uses the past as an oasis from the ugliness of reality. Soft cakes, sweet candies in elaborate dishes from the old days, even pieces of exquisite porcelain are shadows of former beauty. The combination of ornate objects, delicious food, and people in aloof poses evokes nostalgia. Even if they are only memories or dreams they nonetheless convey a sense if not of hope then at least of peacefulness.

Paintings such as Nesterova's *The Queue* (1986) and Korkodim's *They Are Waiting for Food* (1987), for example, mark a new way of representing food, not depicting it directly but only by implication, permitting the artist to show how casual are the relations between the people standing in line for food. Isolated from each other, they are linked only by the common struggle for existence. In another of Nesterova's paintings, *People with Cakes* (1982),

Ilya Kabakov, Whose Grater Is This? *1987. From Matthew Cullerne Bown,*
Contemporary Russian Art *(New York: Philosophical Library, 1989).*

the role of implied food is even more striking: men and women are walking
with cardboard cake boxes in their hands, suggesting cakes; the figures are
faceless, painted in white, approaching each other but deeply self-absorbed
and unaware of each other. This alienation contrasts with the cakes, which
by definition are supposed to bring people together in celebration, and in
this contradiction lies the power of the painting. Food is now distanced from
reality, and there is less and less effort to imitate it. The connotations of
food and its relation to reality are now based on other elements in the
painting. Food is left with only the significance which the artist gives it by
her will. It may be useful to compare this with what Andy Warhol did in
his painting *Peaches,* in which a can of fruit takes the place of real peaches.
The image loses touch with its prototype and begins a new, independent
life.[15] Ilya Kabakov, a leader of postmodern art, makes this point in *Whose
Grater Is This?* (1987), showing a grater on an empty wall with a sentence
written in each of the two corners: "Anna Petrovna Savchenko: Whose grater
is this?" and "Nikolai L'vovich Kruglenko: Dunno." Kabakov thus creates
with details from a communal apartment kitchen the entire, all-pervading
atmosphere of Soviet life. The painting is equally open, however, to other
interpretations.

The implied presence of food is used at times to create an air of mystery.

Food as Art

Natalia Nesterova, Laugh, *1989. Courtesy of the artist.*

Nazarenko does this in *Masquerade* (1989). Here a group sits around a table gazing at the viewer but with their faces masked. They seem to be together but in fact are strangers, as isolated from each other as possible. Life is a masquerade, says the artist, a mirage with everyone hidden behind his mask. Closely akin to this picture is Olga Bulgakova's *The Feast under the Moon* (1980). In the milky moonlight people seem unreal, aliens from another world. The composition consists of a combination of triangles: the triangles of dishes on the table, the cone-shaped goblets of vivid red wine, and the human figures, involving the viewer in a strange round of diverse emotions.

The juxtaposition of people and food often leads to unpredictable artistic results, and Nesterova's works are full of them. In *Red Restaurant* (1986), people and food create an entity. Neither means too much alone, but taken together the robotlike figures and the waxen fruits on trays symbolize the triumph of materialism. In *Vases* (1989) she goes even further, replacing human heads with vessels. She is saying that this substitution of the inanimate for the animate is possible, even unremarkable, because people have lost their humanity.

The leitmotif of lost humanity degenerates gradually in these decades into a depiction of outright savagery, with the idea of human ruthlessness often expressed in terms of those who devour and those who are their victims. First the devourers are shown in quite a direct way, as in Nesterova's *Laugh* (1989) or Kalinin's *People Devouring the World* (1988). Both pictures depict people with muzzles instead of faces and with gaping jaws grabbing and eating everything in sight—meat, fish, vegetables, fruit, bread, honey. These frightening creatures threaten to become masters of the world. The actual food is drawn with broad, thick brushstrokes, making it appear artificial, like food for monsters. And monsters they are. Similar creatures, with the same long sharp teeth, are found in Konstantin Zvezdochetov's series *Perdo* (1987), in which a juicy watermelon has become the apple of discord between two hostile tribes for whom the dark pink pulp of the melon symbolizes the female. The huge slice in the center of the picture is menacing and seems almost alive.

Oleg Tselkov, an artist who has received worldwide recognition, has over the decades portrayed this same image as *Homo soveticus*. Obtuse thugs with knives preparing to slice a watermelon, chasing something invisible, or coming at the viewer with open mouths glare from virtually all of Tselkov's paintings. These red, egg-shaped heads fill the entire space of the canvas and seem to overflow the borders of the painting. They are terrifying in their utter inhumanity and propensity for evil. They appear in Tselkov's *A Group Portrait with a Watermelon* (1963) and *Eaters* (1986), but one also encounters them in the novels and stories of Aleksandr Khurgin and many others.[16] In Savchenko's painting, ironically named after Pushkin's *Story of the Fisherman and the Golden Fish,* two such monsters with deformed heads and faces are drinking vodka at the seashore, and the bottle of vodka is a clear badge of their cruelty and brute power.

Many paintings from the eighties to the present have overtones of tragedy, mirroring the despair, frustration, pain, and fear prevalent in society as a whole. They convey the message that transformations in human beings can be even more threatening than changes in the circumstances of life. "A man is more frightening than his skeleton," said Nobel prizewinner Joseph Brodsky.[17] Images of cruelty are now depicted directly, a reflection in painting of the altered aesthetic principles of so-called postmodernism—it was now permissible to deal with any subject without exception. Ugliness and horror equal the beautiful in art. Baudelaire's "flowers of evil" of the past have grown into "the beautiful." Evil, degradation, and destruction are now precisely depicted. Tragedy, which is everywhere in the former Soviet Union, has compelled the artist to focus on ruthlessness and rapacity.

Kalinin anticipated the emotions of the approaching era in his works in the 1970s, and even at that early date he went further than most other artists. To many his pessimism seemed groundless, but he knew that cruelty inevitably turns into killing and that the people who devour the world kill their victims first. This is the tragedy of a society in which human life is so little valued: "everywhere, in towns and villages, people are killing each other in cold blood. . . ."[18] Although this was written by the Russian writer Yuri Nagibin in 1991, Kalinin felt it acutely much earlier and repeated it in diverse variations, always with new twists. The horror expressed in his scenes of animal slaughter rises to the level of social generalization: the killing of an animal for food turns into a parable on the triumph of evil. These paintings are a reflection of the artist upon life. Slaughtering a pig for a wedding is a necessary job which leaves a man indifferent. To him, killing an animal is only one of his duties, the knife merely one of his tools. When he tires, he drinks his vodka and smokes a cigarette, too much the dullard to think about his actions. This is Kalinin's message in *The Wedding Preparation* (1975). The same theme is treated very differently in *The Funeral Repast* (1974) and *Who is to Slay the Rooster* (1978). The former painting captures the moment when the head of the victim has just been chopped off and blood flows into the bowl. In the latter painting, the killing is just about to take place: the knife is poised to slit the rooster's throat. In both works the spectator is struck by the expression of bestial enjoyment on the faces of the people doing the killing. Long fingers delicately stroke the rooster's throat like a pianist trying the keyboard. Killing is fun. In this novel way, as a victim on the border between life and death, as a symbol of ruination—food appears in a number of works.

Fantasy and mockery, bitter humor and irony, are often present in these works, but a hint of bravado reduces the humiliation and saves what is left of people's dignity. It is a very special form of both protest and defense.

Federico Fellini, the Italian film director, wrote in the 1950s that the peculiar misfortune of modern man is alienation and the only way to overcome this is for one lonely person to communicate with another.

In this brief overview of the time from the 1960s to the fall of communism we have seen the use of food images in art drastically altered. At the start of this period food symbolized the joy of life in the simple human sense, the joy of people who have managed to survive and have emerged from the dungeon of the past into a normal world where the sky is blue and the sun is shining. In the following decades, when frustration and disappointment became the overwhelming emotions, food and eating became devices to convey horror, cruelty, and fear. Unlike film and literature, painting on the whole did not express the new hopes of the times of perestroika.

NOTES

1. See I. Erenburg, "Neistovyi Saryan" [The passionate Saryan], *Sobranie sochinenii v deviati tomakh,* vol. 6 (Moscow: Khudozhestvennaya literatura, 1965), 599.

2. Yuri Maletskii, *Oniksovaya chasha* [The onyx chalice], *Druzhba Narodov,* no. 2 (1994), 68.

3. After the first confrontation of artists with the regime at the Manezh in 1962, when Khrushchev crushed the artists at the exhibition "Thirty Years of MOSKH," there emerged an artistic movement known as "unofficial" or "nonconformist" art. See Igor' Golomshtok, "The History and Organization of Artistic Life in the Soviet Union," in Marilyn Rueschemeyer, Igor Golomshtok, and Janet Kennedy, eds., *Soviet Emigré Artists* (Armonk, N.Y.: M. E. Sharpe, 1985); Priscilla Johnson, *Khrushchev and the Arts* (Cambridge, Mass.: MIT Press, 1965); A. I. Morozov, *Pokolenie molodykh* [The generation of the young] (Moscow: Sovetskii khudozhnik, 1989).

4. I. Bolotina, *Still Life in Russian Art* (Leningrad: Aurora, 1987), 10.

5. The *lubok* is a popular woodcut in which text and illustrations were given equal importance. See Evgenia Kirichenko and Mikhail Anikst, *Russian Design and the Fine Arts, 1750-1917* (New York: Abrams, 1991), 47. See also Dmitrii V. Sarabianov, *Russian Art* (New York: Abrams, 1990), 43.

6. "Neo-primitivism," "cubo-futurism," "rayonism" were avant-garde styles in Russia in the first decades of the twentieth century. See Alan Bird, *A History of Russian Painting* (Boston: G. K. Hall, 1987), 200-205; John Bowlt, "Art and Architecture in the Age of Revolution, 1860-1917," in *Russian Art and Architecture,* ed. Robert Auty and Dmitrii Obolenskii (Cambridge: Cambridge University Press, 1980), 126-134.

7. Bolotina, 14, 17.

8. Vladimir Vladimirovich Maiakovskii. *Poemy. Stikhotvorenia* [Poems] (Moscow: Moskovskii Rabochii, 1973), 72.

9. The definition of Socialist Realism has been discussed for many years. See Bird, 257-260; Golomshtok, 20-25. Also see Lev Kopelev, "Vpered k pozavchera" [Ahead to the day before yesterday], 12-13; Vladimir Gusev, "Gde fal'sh i gde istina" [What is false and what is true], 14-19; and Hubertus Gassner and Ekhart Gillen, "Ot sozdania utopicheskogo poriadka k ideologii umirotvorenia svete esteticheskoi deistvitel'nosti" [From the creation of utopian order to the ideology of pacification . . .], 27-59, in *Agitatsia za shchastie. Sovetskoe iskusstvo stalinskoi epokhi* [Propaganda for happiness: Soviet art in Stalin's epoch] (Dusseldorf-Bremen: Interarteks-Edicion Temmen, 1994).

10. Y. Gerchuk. *Zhivye veshchi* [Living things] (Moscow: Sovetskii khudozhnik, 1977), 113.

11. Morozov. *Pokolenie molodykh,* 10.

12. D. Sarabianov. *Pod znakom iskanii. Zhivopis' Sovetskogo Zakavkazia. Stankovoye Sovetskoye Iskusstvo* [Paintings of Soviet Transcaucasia] (Moscow: Sovetskii Khudozhnik, 1974), 104.

13. Aleksandr Strakhov. *Kul't khleba u vostochnykh slavian* [The cult of bread among the eastern Slavs] (Munich: Verlag Otto Sanger, 1991).

14. Cited in N. Leiderman and M. Lipovetskii. "Zhizn' posle smerti" [Life after death], *Novii Mir*, no. 7 (1993), 242.

15. Aleksandr Genis, "Luk i kapusta" [Onions and cabbage], *Znamia,* no. 8 (1994), 192.

16. See A. Khurgin, "Strana Avstralia" [The country called Australia], *Znamia,* no. 7 (1993), and "Tri rasskaza" [Three stories], *Yunost',* no. 4 (1993), 43–46.

17. Cited in L. Goldin, "Koshmar poverkh epokh i kontinentov" [A nightmare over epochs and continents], *Kul'tura,* no. 23 (June 11, 1993), 10.

18. Y. Nagibin, "Tsvety na mostovoi" [Flowers on the pavement], in *Viacheslav Kalinin* (Moscow: Izdatel'stvo "Znanie," 1991), 35.

Contributors

MAURICIO BORRERO is Assistant Professor of History at St. John's University in New York City. He is completing a monograph entitled *Hungry Moscow: Scarcity, Survival, and Urban Society in the Russian Civil War, 1918–1921.*

PAMELA CHESTER, a Fellow at the Davis Center for Russian Studies at Harvard University and faculty member at Brandeis University, has written widely on Tolstoy and Tsvetaeva. She is co-editor, with Sibelan Forrester, of *Engendering Slavic Literatures.* She is working on a book about Tsvetaeva's autobiographical prose.

CATHY A. FRIERSON is Associate Professor of History and Director of the Center for International Education at the University of New Hampshire. Among her publications on late nineteenth-century Russia are *Peasant Icons: Representations of Rural People in Late Nineteenth-Century Russia* and her annotated translation, *Aleksandr Nikolaevich Engelgardt's Letters from the Country, 1872–1887.*

MUSYA GLANTS, an art historian who received her Ph.D. from Leningrad State University, is a Fellow at the Davis Center for Russian Studies at Harvard University. She consulted for the television series *The Hermitage: A Russian Odyssey,* which was nominated for an Emmy award. She has published widely on Russian painting and sculpture of the nineteenth and twentieth centuries and is especially interested in the role of Jewish artists in Russian art.

DARRA GOLDSTEIN is Professor of Russian at Williams College. Her publications include *Russian Houses* and *Nikolai Zabolotsky: Play for Mortal Stakes.* She has also published cookbooks on the cuisines of Russia and the

Republic of Georgia, and her *Georgian Feast* received the Julia Child Award for best cookbook of the year in 1993. She is working on a comprehensive cultural history of Russian food.

LEONID HERETZ, a Fellow at the Davis Center for Russian Studies at Harvard University and Assistant Professor of History at Bridgewater State College, is a specialist in the cultural history of late Imperial Russia. He is currently preparing a book based on his dissertation "Russian Apocalypse, 1891–1917: Popular Perceptions of Events from the Year of Famine and Cholera to the Fall of the Tsar."

RONALD D. LeBLANC, an Associate Professor of Russian at the University of New Hampshire and a Fellow at the Davis Center for Russian Studies at Harvard University, has written on the use of food imagery and eating metaphors in the works of such writers as Narezhny, Gogol, Tolstoy, and Bulgakov. He is working on a book about food, sex, and carnal appetite in the nineteenth-century Russian novel.

HORACE G. LUNT is the Samuel H. Cross Professor of Slavic Languages and Literatures emeritus at Harvard University. Among his major publications are *A Grammar of the Macedonian Literary Language, Old Church Slavonic Grammar* (7th ed.), and *Fundamentals of Russian* (2nd ed.). He is preparing an annotated translation of the *Rus' Primary Chronicle*.

GEORGE E. MUNRO is Professor of History at Virginia Commonwealth University. He specializes in eighteenth-century Russian social and economic history and has translated and edited the last volume of S. M. Soloviev's *History of Russia,* published as *The Rule of Catherine the Great: War, Diplomacy and Domestic Affairs, 1772–1774.* He is completing a book on St. Petersburg in the reign of Catherine II.

HALINA ROTHSTEIN is an independent scholar who has published in the area of Polish and Russian history and culture.

ROBERT A. ROTHSTEIN, Professor of Slavic Languages & Literatures and of Judaic Studies at the University of Massachusetts, Amherst, has published in the fields of Slavic and Yiddish linguistics, folklore, and culture.

SNEJANA TEMPEST is Assistant Professor of Russian at Middlebury College. She has written on Slavic folklore and the methodology of second-language acquisition. She specializes in developing instructional software and has produced a multimedia language placement exam for Russian. She is collecting material for a project in childlore and translating a massive anthology of Russian folklore.

JOYCE TOOMRE, Slavist and culinary historian, is a Fellow at the Davis Center for Russian Studies, Harvard University. Among her publications on food history is her annotated translation *Classic Russian Cooking: Elena Molokhovets' A Gift to Young Housewives.* Her current research, on the foods of the former Soviet republics and the foodways of ethnic Boston, focuses on foodways as markers of ethnic identity.

Index